Philosophy's Role in Counseling and Psychotherapy

Philosophy's Role in Counseling and Psychotherapy

Peter B. Raabe, PhD

JASON ARONSON
Lanham • Boulder • New York • Toronto • Plymouth, UK

Published by Jason Aronson
A wholly owned subsidiary of Rowman & Littlefield
4501 Forbes Boulevard, Suite 200, Lanham, Maryland 20706
www.rowman.com

10 Thornbury Road, Plymouth PL6 7PP, United Kingdom

Copyright © 2014 by Jason Aronson

All rights reserved. No part of this book may be reproduced in any form or by any electronic or mechanical means, including information storage and retrieval systems, without written permission from the publisher, except by a reviewer who may quote passages in a review.

British Library Cataloguing in Publication Information Available

Library of Congress Cataloging-in-Publication Data

Library of Congress Cataloging-in-Publication Data Available

ISBN 978-0-7657-0917-2 (cloth : alk. paper) -- ISBN 978-0-7657-0918-9 (electronic)
ISBN 978-1-4422-5085-7 (pbk : alk. paper)

∞™ The paper used in this publication meets the minimum requirements of American National Standard for Information Sciences Permanence of Paper for Printed Library Materials, ANSI/NISO Z39.48-1992.

Printed in the United States of America

This book is dedicated to my friend Daniel
who has been a constant source of inspiration.

Contents

Acknowledgments

Introduction
    Some Philosophical Background
    Philosophy, Science, and Medicine
    Philosophy and Metaphors for the Mind
    About This Book

I: Psychotherapy at the Start of the Twenty-first Century

1   Problematic Paradigms
    "Mind" and "Brain"
    Classification and Diagnosis of "Mind Illnesses"
    Informal Diagnoses
    Social Influences

2   Problematic Practices
    The So-called Medical Model
    Medications
    Happiness Pills
    Iatrogenesis as a Causal Explanation (Etiology)
    Causation and Free Will
    Genetics

3   Contemporary Modality
    Science, Medicine, or Talk Therapy?

II: Philosophy as Therapy

4   Past Precedence
    Philosophical Therapy in Antiquity
    Therapeutic Philosophy in More Recent History

5   The Clinic's Appropriation of Philosophy
    Therapeutic Philosophical Contents
    The Therapeutic Benefits of Philosophy in Psychotherapy

6   Psychotherapeutic Philosophy
    Wants And Needs
    What is Philosophy?
    Counseling as Philosophical Therapy
    Recognition

	Trust	189
	Emotions (Affect)	191
	Insight	196
	Antidote for Guilt, Shame, and Stigma	200
	Alternative Perspectives	205
	Meaning	208
	"Clinical Philosophy"	209
7	Preventive (Prophylactic) Philosophy	213
	Teaching (Heuristics) for Prevention	222

III: Application

8	An Education Plan	231
	The Study of Philosophy	237
	Differences Between Philosophy and Psychotherapy	240
	Finding the Philosophical Issues	249
9	Teaching "Sanity"	261
	General Course Content	266
10	Three Case Studies	295
	Case #1: "Luke" the Disgraced Monk	296
	Case #2: "Kay": Authenticity	307
	Case #3: "Harding": A Man of War	329
	Conclusion	337
11	Recovery, Cure, and Philosophy	339
	The Medication Trap	343
	The Denial of Possibility	345
	The "New" Concept of Recovery	349
	A Paradigm Shift	355
	Philosophy	366

Appendix: Oppositional Defiant Disorder (ODD)	373
Oppositional Defiant Disorder	373
Bibliography	377
Index	389
About the Author	405

Acknowledgments

Contrary to conventional beliefs, philosophy is not a solitary pursuit in which the philosopher sits and thinks in isolation from the rest of humanity and the natural world. I owe a lot to the many people with whom I have shared my thoughts. For example, the idea for chapter 7 ("Preventive (Prophylactic) Philosophy") came from my association with Dr. Susan Gardner, Director of the Vancouver Institute of Philosophy for Children, Professor of Philosophy at Capilano University, good friend, mentor, and benefactor of mine.

I would also like to thank the following:

Glen Baier of the University of the Fraser Valley (UFV) philosophy department for his constant support for, and defense of, my efforts to further philosophical counseling both within academia and in the community. Anastasia Anderson, currently head of the Philosophy department at UFV, and Paul Herman, Moira Kloster, Jeffrey Morgan, and Wayne Henry professors in the Department of Philosophy at UFV for the value they see in my work.

Dr. Young E. Rhee, Hee-Bong Choi, his wife Haesoon Park, and daughter Younjoo Choi, Sung-Jin Kim, Soo Bae Kim, An-bang Yu, his wife Hsiu-Feng Wu, Lin Ching-Hsiu, Annegret Stopczyk, José Barrientos Rastrojo, and so many other philosophers and philosophically minded individuals I met at various conferences in Korea, Taiwan, Germany, and Spain over the past few years for their keen interest in my work, for arranging to have me present papers and workshops, for their kind hospitality during my visits, and for their friendship. I apologize to all those whose names I have missed.

The various members of the SAPC, past president Sheetal Deo, and especially the 2012–2013 members Devan Christian, Marcy Howell, Dana Kreitzer, and Jaipree Mattu for motivating me during the most solitary work of research and writing. Their enthusiasm and hard work in both promoting the idea of philosophy as a legitimate alternative to drug therapy for mental illness, and putting it to work in the local community, was and still is inspiring.

Teresa Spurr and Tania Fierro for their helpful academic, professional and social discussions. Tania's partner Pedro for his warmth and willingness to assist the students of the University of the Fraser Valley (UFV) Student Association for Philosophical Counseling (SAPC).

Karli Menagh, Departmental Assistant in the UFV Philosophy Department, for her helpfulness in resolving my many computer problems, book ordering issues, and assistance in dealing with general clerical distractions. And Sarah Russell of SKR Design LLC for her work on my web site and other computer matters.

The Administrators of the University of the Fraser Valley for generously granting me the sabbatical which gave me the time and resources to immerse myself in the writing of this book.

Shlomit Schuster, from Israel, for the role model she is to me due to her fearless and steadfast defense of her vision for philosophical counseling; and for her friendship.

Amy King, Acquisitions Editor with Jason Aronson and Lexington Books for her patience and her professional advice. Thank you also to Kelly Blackburn, Assistant Editor at Lexington Books, as well as Lisa Rosinsky and Christine Fahey, Assistant Production Editors at Rowman and Littlefield Publishing, for their helpful advice and guidance.

And last but never least, my family: our son Tim and our daughter-in-law Barbara for their interest and encouragement. And, of course, my wife Anne whose perspective from outside the hypothetical discourse of the academy kept me mindful of what needs to be said about the importance of philosophy in relieving individuals from the burden of a multitude of so-called mental illnesses.

Introduction

> "The value of philosophy lies not in furnishing solutions but in defining difficulties and suggesting methods for dealing with them."
> —John Dewey (1859–1952)

> "The mind which has become accustomed to the freedom and impartiality of philosophic contemplation will preserve something of the same freedom and impartiality in the world of action and emotion."
> —Bertrand Russell (1872–1970)

In mid-July 2013, police found a baby and a two year old drowned in their bathtub at home. A few days later their mother's body was discovered at the bottom of a local river. After interviewing the woman's husband—who was the father of the children—police said they did not suspect foul play. A television news reporter told her viewers that the mother had been suffering from a "mental illness" called postpartum depression (PPD). In an interview with the reporter, the facilitator of a local young mothers support group said that postpartum depression is a terrible illness, and suggested that it could have caused the mother to do what she did. This case raises a number of questions that were left unanswered by the news report. Is PPD an illness that can cause women to do terrible things? What brings on this so-called mental illness? What is a mental illness? Could this terrible tragedy have been avoided? And what was the husband's role in all of this? These are just some of the questions that should always be raised when a story surfaces in the media in which a "mental illness" is the implied cause of a terrible tragedy. But while questions concerning the claims made about "mental illnesses" are easy to come by, finding answers for them is much more difficult.

This book discusses three areas that are often neglected, or simply ignored, in books on the topic of so-called mental illnesses: (1) the prevention of "mental illnesses"; (2) the recovery from, and cure of, "mental illnesses"; and (3) the importance of philosophy in treating "mental illnesses." But what exactly is this mysterious thing called a "mental illness" or "mental disorder" that was at one time called "lunacy" and "insanity"? Is it demon possession; is it biological malfunction; is it social disapproval of behavior outside the norm; is it a political way to control citizens; is it chemical imbalance in the brain; is it brain disease; is it irrational thinking; is it a lack of will power; or is it just bad behavior? In fact the term "mental illness" has been used to describe all of the above at some time or another, even by the most educated, intelligent, and eteemed members of society. Unfortunately, the application of scientific and medical reasoning has not resolved the confusion because contemporary scientists and medically trained individuals still can't seem to agree on what so-called mental illness is. And if there is uncertainty about what it is then there can't be any agreement about how to treat it.

At the beginning of the school term, at the University of the Fraser Valley, I ask my students to write their thoughts anonymously on a sheet of paper regarding what they believe mental illness actually is. Here are some of the responses, in no particular order, from twenty-seven third-year university students from the class of 2011:

- Mental illness is someone's mental capacity or makeup that differs from the "normal" range of most people's mental capacities or make-ups. It may involve a person holding false beliefs about the world as true.
- It has to do with chemical imbalances in the brain. I think mental illness has many aspects, and ways to treat these illnesses has not been completely figured out.
- Mental illness is the lack of well-being in one's psychological state, which can involve the absence of aspects which should be present, or the presences of aspects which should not exist.
- Mental illness is where an individual is out of homeostasis.
- I would define mental illness as some sort of shift in a patient's mind that openly differs from the average person in today's society. Mental illness is a product of difficulties found in life, biologically, physically, socially, and morally.
- Mental illness can affect any of the population and therefore has inspired fear and exaggeration within society. But as we progress with medication, imaging, and understanding, we are learning new and better ways to manage illness and regain mental control.
- It is argued that there is a lack of validity of the extent to which the word "illness" is used, as mental illness is not identical and does not share many characteristics with what we know to be medical illnesses. The idea of "normality" and its borders may be argued as well.
- Mental illness can be something chronic that is developed over time or sometimes obtained at birth.
- Mental illness is similar to physical illness in that it is normally beyond the control of the patient.
- Mental illness is a state in which someone is not mentally where they desire to be.
- Mental illness is an organic brain disease that does not discriminate. It affects young and old, wealthy and poor populations. It is not a choice.

- Mental illness is a disorder of the mind. It's not necessarily a bad thing—some mental illnesses can actually be quite beneficial. Some mental illnesses can create new unique ways of seeing things. They may simply be a different way certain minds work. It raises the question of who got to decide what "normal" brains really are and exactly how they should work.
- Mental illness has a biological origin that generally requires the administration of psychoactive medications. It's a state of imbalance.
- Mental illness is a disconnect in the brain.
- Mental illness can vary from culture to culture and what is considered as an illness can depend on the ideas and values of a society. Mental illness can be biological and it can be psychological.
- Mental illness is when a person cannot function "normally" due to interference of the brain caused by biological imbalance.
- Mental illness can involve brain chemical imbalances, thought processes, psychological disturbances, physiology, emotions, and behavior. This makes it complex.
- Mental illness is something a person lives or deals with due to chemical imbalances in the brain.
- Individuals with mental illness can usually not overcome it on their own.

This variety and dissimilarity of responses to my request to students to "explain what you think mental illness is" illustrates that it is not at all clear to young people what exactly the definition of so-called mental illness actually is. But this confusion and uncertainty is not only present in the younger generation. The professional literature, both theoretical and practical, is full of contradictory explanations and question-begging definitions. Discussion tends to diverge into two main streams: those who believe "mental illness" concerns incorrect thinking, problematic beliefs, and mistaken assumptions in the mind, and others who believe it involves the organic or chemical malfunctioning of the biological brain.

Sigmund Freud wanted the investigation of so-called mental illnesses—called psychoanalysis—to be recognized as a biomedical science. Psychiatry and clinical psychology then evolved from the empirical science of psychology. But the methods in counseling and psychotherapy that have been clinically proven to be the most effective are far removed from the sciences. They are the so-called "talk therapies," such as Rational Emotional Behavior Therapy (R.E.B.T.), Existential Therapy, Cognitive Therapy, and Logo Therapy. These are non-medical approaches that are largely fashioned after the sort of discussions held in philosophy. Unfortunately, most clinical psychologists, psychotherapists, and counselors receive little if any formal training in philosophy before they offer their techniques as a service to the public. This leaves them inadequately prepared to deal with issues such as ethical decision-making, sorting out confused reasoning, coming to terms with religious beliefs, defining reality, determining what it means to be a "normal" person within society, defining one's true self, and generally helping individuals to overcome the problems which cause emotional suffering, cognitive distress, and so on.

Unfortunately, while the heart of all talk therapies is the practice of philosophy, most students and professionals have no idea that this is the case. Students are taught the methods or techniques of the various psychotherapies without ever gaining a solid understanding of the content or practice of philosophy. For example, I've spoken with a number of students who told me they had learned the method of Existential therapy, but they were unable to tell me what existentialism is all about because they had never been taught this. They had no understanding of the substance behind their verbal techniques. This is similar to teaching someone how individual chess pieces move on the board without explaining what chess is all about. As Jerry A. Mobley, Associate Professor of Counseling Psychology at Fort Valley State University in Georgia, wrote in a letter to me, "Through ignorance of even the basics of philosophy, counselors have limited the quality of our approaches, and re-invent the stuff philosophers disposed of long ago." Without an understanding of the philosophy at the heart of the various psychotherapeutic techniques students will be like the player who knows how the chess pieces move but cannot see the dangers in one move and the advantages in another.

It's possible to differentiate therapy for emotional suffering and cognitive distress into three broad categories: biological medicine, psychological science, and therapeutic philosophy. But this requires a clear differentiation between the biological causes of brain disorders, and the existential problems that are the reasons for the suffering and distress defined as so-called "mental illnesses." The categorizing of emotional suffering and cognitive distress as "illnesses" or "disorders" has created the impression that this kind of suffering and distress have their origins in the malfunctioning substrates of the biological brain. This in turn has led the providers of mental healthcare services to adopt an overwhelmingly biological perspective of mental suffering and distress, and an overpowering medical approach to treatment for so-called psychiatric morbidity. Sadness, anger, fear, joy, confusion, and so on are all considered to be caused by chemical activities in the brain. In defining human thinking as being just the biological functions of their brains, biological psychiatry has eliminated the person: the active agent who is motivated by reasons and intentions. Emotional suffering and cognitive distress are being diagnosed as chemical imbalances in the brain, thereby discounting the many events in life that may have been the reason for the upset. While psychoanalysis holds the unconscious to be the driving force behind what a person does, biological psychiatry sees brain chemicals. The biological perspective of human thinking disallows any discussion of the beliefs, values, fears, and assumptions which are the necessary elements that make a human being a living person. With the elimination of both the patient's thoughts and life circumstances from much of psychiatry and Freudian psychoanalysis, help for emotional suffering and cognitive distress by these dominant methodologies has been largely reduced to psychopharmacology: the prescribing of brain-dulling drugs.

A better alternative to the ingestion or injection of psychotropic drugs is the attempt to alleviate mental suffering by means of the many different "talk therapies." This form of help is found in various mental health care services such as counseling, psychotherapy, and social work. This book argues that every student whose aim is to work in the field of mental healthcare ought to be taught the content and practice of philosophy as part of their mental healthcare training. A philosophically trained counselor or therapist will be a much more capable helper to individuals suffering from emotional and cognitive distress than those whose training is predominantly in the medical approach of psychiatry, or the scientific approach of psychology.

Some academic philosophers claim that philosophy can't be properly defined, and that any attempt to do so can't be clearly understood by non-philosophers. But a philosopher who says that he or she can't explain what he or she is doing with philosophy clearly doesn't know what he or she is doing. Philosophy can be very simply defined as a practice that involves examining the reasons we have for the values we hold as good, and the beliefs we hold as true, so that we can free ourselves from blindly following tradition, slavishly obeying authority figures, or acting only on our feelings. It also includes helping others to do the same. This general definition of philosophy harks back to ancient times, to the philosophers who came well before Socrates, Plato, and Aristotle. And each one claimed that the practice of philosophy can lead to living a better life.

The practice of counseling and psychotherapy with philosophy can have a profound effect, especially on the lives of distressed individuals who have been labeled "mentally ill." Take for example a metaphysical or epistemological discussion on the topic of reality. A student in class may find this to be merely a fascinating, if somewhat taxing, mental exercise. But for a confused and distressed individual who actually came to me for counseling with philosophy, finding an answer to the question of how we know what is real was much more than merely an academic exercise. His sense of being situated in, and belonging to, the world we call "real" depended on his being able to distinguish the real world from illusions. Counseling with philosophy helped this person clarify his thinking and define reality in a way that lessened his sense of estrangement, reduced his fear of losing control and thereby ending up locked in an institution against his will, and made his life much more bearable. I fact philosophy helped this person recover from what had been clinically diagnosed as a so-called mental illness.

There is no precise, universally agreed-upon definition of the term "mental illness." It is generally applied to people whose behavior, thinking, and emotions are deemed to be outside the realm of the generally accepted social norm. There is no conclusive evidence that any of the hundreds of so-called diagnosable "mental illnesses" are due to biological malfunctions or chemical imbalances, or that any of them can be cured with psychoactive drugs. These claims may seem unfounded, and even shocking, but they will all be supported with research data in the following chapters. Given that many individuals who have been diagnosed as being "mentally ill" have been helped to overcome their diagnoses with talk therapy, and since talk therapy is largely based on philosophy, it is fair to say that the practice of philosophy can actually help individuals overcome "mental illness." This is not a new idea. It goes back to ancient times when philosophy was still in its infancy.

It might be argued that if an individual is cured with philosophy then the original diagnosis of "mental illness" must have been mistaken. But due to the number of diagnosed "mentally ill" individuals who have been helped to overcome their "mental illnesses" with philosophy this conclusion is unfounded. The fact that philosophy has actually helped individuals to overcome their diagnosed "mental illnesses" throws into doubt the diagnostic assumptions used to defend the biomedical approach to both diagnosis and treatment. The following chapters aim to prove that the clinician who employs philosophy in counseling or psychotherapy has a better chance of relieving emotional suffering and cognitive distress than those who practice methods which are devoid of a knowledge of philosophy, who assume emotional suffering and cognitive distress are caused by a malfunctioning brain, or whose treatment approach is primarily reliant on medications.

SOME PHILOSOPHICAL BACKGROUND

At the time of Socrates, Plato, and Aristotle philosophy was considered to be very important for several reasons. Not only did it consist of the formal inquiry into everything that humans wondered about, but it was also the attempt to understand life in such a way that it could be lived to the fullest, and at a most enjoyable level humanly possible. In other words, philosophy served a very practical purpose: the enhancement of human life on earth.

More than two thousand years ago, Epicurus characterized philosophy as "therapy of the soul" (also translated as "mind"). He said that if a philosopher's arguments do not relieve any human suffering then they're just pointless arguments. The Stoics also made it clear that philosophy is not merely the memorization of abstract theories or the exegesis of formal texts. They held that it involves learning the art of living well. Socrates used philosophy not to teach concepts but to encourage his discussion partners to examine their thinking and attitudes about almost every issue imaginable, including such issues as the meaning of life and the existence of God. He welcomed disagreement and challenges to his own thinking, acknowledging that what he himself believed might be in error. It was because he questioned everything, including the authority of organized religion and of the state, that he was eventually charged with the crime of corrupting the young people of Athens. But again, Socrates didn't question things in order to make trouble; he questioned as an example to others, so that people would learn to think for themselves, and to make better decisions that would lead to their living a morally good and meaningful life. Besides wondering about science and mathematics, Socrates and the other early philosophers were the original counselors and therapists. They helped people to think about ordinary life problems, and come to some sort of acceptable solution that could be incorporated into the actual lives they were living. Of course these early philosophers were well aware of physical or somatic human problems that couldn't be healed or alleviated simply by means of discussion. They left the treatment of these sorts of problems to the physicians.

In ancient Greece and also other early cultures, people who were out of the ordinary or "abnormal" were not necessarily considered to be mentally ill. In fact individuals who heard voices or saw visions were often considered to be blessed by the gods, and gifted rather than cursed. They were treated accordingly. Other issues, such as the agony over a lost love, confusion over the morality of a personal decision, or distress over family conflicts (see Appendix) were not at all diagnosed and treated as any kind of organic illnesses like they are in clinics today. They were dealt with by philosophers who considered themselves "therapists of the soul."

When the dark ages came along—the age during which, in the Western world, religious reasoning was considered to be the only approach to the "Truth"—individuals who had in the past been seen as "gifted" were now considered to be "possessed by the Devil." One of the main reasons for this was because anyone claiming to be spiritually gifted or enlightened was considered to be a threat to the authority of the church. Demonic possession became the dominant diagnosis for mental suffering in medieval times, and burning at the stake was not an uncommon "treatment." This served a very useful function for the church: it got rid of many of the critics who had dared to challenge its political structure or its dogma. But almost all of the criticism during the Dark and Middle Ages was in the form of quasi-theological argument. Not surprisingly, philosophy suffered from serious stagnation during this time period. Not only was any inquiry into the functioning of the world reduced to an examination of what has been called "natural law" or nature under the control of God, but the most well-known philosophers, such as Augustine, Anselm, and Aquinas, were also all important religious figures who defended their church's most bizarre (from today's perspective) descriptions of the natural world, human events, and the functioning of the human body and mind, with supernatural explanations. The intellectual elite resided within religious orders, and the church's perspective on everything was considered to be the God-given "Truth."

This eventually evolved into the so-called Age of Reason in the late fifteenth century. Rationalist philosophers such as Spinoza and Leibniz based their arguments on logic thinking rather than religious dogma. As the demand rose that claims be supported not only by logic but also by material evidence or empirical proof, the church slowly began to lose its authority as the only source of "Truth" about both the physical world which humans inhabit and the greater universe in which they are situated. Secular individuals, for example Copernicus and Galileo, presented empirical or scientific evidence about the organization of our galaxy that could no longer be refuted with religious tenets. Eventually even reasoning was seen to be insufficient for the establishment of accurate knowledge of the "Truth." The philosopher Immanuel Kant pointed this out in the late 1700s in his book *Critique of Pure Reason*. Empiricism thus became the dominant arbiter of "Truth."

With the ascendancy of the empirical sciences, with the help of the empiricist philosophers like John Locke and David Hume, knowledge itself suffered another setback. Now instead of finding themselves in a world oppressed by religious beliefs and spiritual arguments, philosophers found themselves in a world being flooded by hard scientific facts that were coldly draining meaning and significance out of all areas of human life.

PHILOSOPHY, SCIENCE, AND MEDICINE

In the seventeenth century, the Western natural sciences and the medical sciences left their attachment to philosophy behind to become separate disciplines. Natural scientists left most of theoretical and abstract reasoning to philosophers, and focused their attention instead on the substance, the organization, and the functioning of the material world. Medical doctors also devoted their attention to suffering that was located in the physical body rather than the numinous "soul." But with all this attention on physical reality, the events which transpired in the mind were separated off as activities in a largely unfathomable realm. The mind was officially disconnected from the material world by René Descartes with his body-mind dualism thereby allowing defenders of the empirical worldview to simply ignore what goes on in the mind as being outside their scientific domain. Medical doctors, whose training was in chemistry, physiology, surgery, and so on, had no idea what to do with individuals who were suffering from emotional pain and mental distress. So with burning at the stake no longer an acceptable form of treatment, people whose thinking was deemed problematic or abnormal were instead now removed from the "normal" community and locked away—for their own good, and the safety of the community—in prisons, and later in so-called insane asylums.

During this blossoming of empirical or scientific reasoning, philosophy was slowly being crowded out of mainstream professional and academic discussions. Since philosophers were no longer needed to think about and discuss problems in areas such as biology, geometry, or medicine they found themselves being relegated to meaningless questions such as, "How many angels can dance on the head of a pin?" and "If a tree falls in the forest and there's no one there to hear it, does it make a sound?" Philosophy was a sort of catch basin for discussion about those abstract, theoretical, and even religious issues which held little interest for the majority of other professionals and scholars. In other words, philosophy was well on its way to becoming a purely conceptual academic exercise, enjoyed by those with lots of money and time on their hands, and useless to those involved in the practical affairs of the material world.

In the late nineteenth century, some educated individuals began to become concerned that one area of human suffering was being largely ignored by both the scientific and medical establishment: the mind. I use the word "mind" loosely here to include suffering that some would say is actually located in the "soul" or the heart. It was discovered that many of the people locked away in insane asylums were not the victims of some biological malfunctioning of the brain. Instead some were distracted by hunger, others were distressed by poverty, and still others were distraught by mental or physical abuse, or dispirited by the hardships of life. In fact the asylums also housed many individuals who were not at all lacking in financial wealth and material possessions who were likewise suffering from mental pain. It was to these well-off individuals that the scientific and medical establishment first began to turn its attention. Neurologist Sigmund Freud became one of the most famous medical doctors to turn his diagnostic gaze on the so-called emotional suffering and mental distress of the rich. Freud, Jung, and others attempted to treat what they called mental illnesses by transforming the ancient therapy for the "soul" into a medical science, which they called psychoanalysis. The foundation upon which psychoanalysis is built is the belief that each human being is controlled by wishes and desires stored in a dark and personally inaccessible unconscious part of the mind. Psychoanalysts believe that, in order to live a happy, "normal" life, the "dark" matter of each individual's unconscious must be removed by the surgical-like procedure of analysis which could only be accomplished by a professional. And although Freud revised many of his early theories, and had only minimal success treating his own patients, his attempts to discover and explain the scientific "truth" about what the mind is and how it works, and even the technical language of psychoanalysis itself, had a tremendous impact on how people think and speak about the human condition right up until today.

But not everyone agreed with Freud's assumption that every distressed patient was in need of deep psychoanalysis—a kind of "surgery" of the unconscious. In fact some psychoanalysts rediscovered philosophy as an effective treatment method.

PHILOSOPHY AND METAPHORS FOR THE MIND

During the 1940s and 1950s, with the rapid advancement of computer logic and language, Western philosophy fell into a kind of second Dark Ages with the invention of logical positivism. Logical positivism was the pseudo-scientific combination of hyper-rationalism and empiricism. It was an attempt to bring certainty into what was regarded as the perennial uncertainty inherent in philosophical discourse. It was also the erroneous assumption that processing information is the same activity as thinking about it. The central notion of the logical positivists was that only the material world can be said to exist, and that therefore the only reliable knowledge available to humanity is that which is based on either mathematics or empirical evidence. Abstraction in language was seen as the reason so many philosophical problems were left unresolved. So symbols were created to represent words and statements which could then be manipulated like mathematical equations to determine the ultimate truth or falsity of any proposition. These philosophers felt that "Truth" in areas such as metaphysics and moral philosophy was unverifiable, so discussion in these areas was seen as pointless. It was therefore simply abandoned. By making philosophy so obscure and unpractical that no one but specialized philosophers took the time to bother with it, these logical positivists succeeded in condemning philosophy to busy itself with the abstractions that existed only within the walls of the academies, and then only within philosophy departments.

At this same time behaviorism was the leading theory in psychology. Its proponents regarded not only animals but human beings as essentially nothing more than simple mechanistic organisms capable only of responding to the stimuli in their environment. Behavior was believed to be the only thing about a living creature that could be observed and studied with certainty. The unobservable thinking processes of sentient beings as an area of study was simply out of the question. Almost everyone is familiar with the dog used in a laboratory experiment by the psychologist

Introduction

Ivan Pavlov. He rang a bell whenever he brought food to the dog. After a while just ringing the bell would cause the dog to start salivating in anticipation of the food. Pavlov claimed this proved that dogs don't reason; their salivary glands merely respond to a stimulus like the ringing of a bell. The problem with this experiment of course, is that it is based on the assumption that dogs don't think about the food that's about to arrive; don't or can't anticipate it—an assumption which anyone who has ever had an animal as a pet knows to be utterly absurd. In fact just thinking about a favorite food can also make a human salivate. Unfortunately, psychologists were happy to apply Pavlov's mechanistic, deterministic reasoning to the human animal as well.

But this reductionist, mechanistic, cause-and-effect, stimulus-and-response description of intelligent beings, both animals and humans, fit well with psychoanalysis. Freud and others had argued that human beings were somewhat like machines, which *believed* they had will and intention but were unfortunately simply driven by desires hidden in the unreachable unconscious. In other words, a person was nothing more than an organic response mechanism whose actions were controlled by the hidden response apparatus within the brain. But when psychoanalysts were challenged, even by skeptical colleagues, to prove the existence of the id, ego, and super ego in the unconscious their response was that these terms were merely metaphors; they were never intended to describe actual ontological elements in the brain. Of course this raised the question, "Then what sort of things did these metaphors represent?" This is a question Freudian psychoanalysts have still not answered adequately to this day.

The reductionist, mechanistic, deterministic belief that human behaviour is controlled by nothing more than chemical and electrical reactions in the brain led to the gradual development of the idea that anyone suffering from emotional or cognitive distress was in all likelihood suffering from some sort of biochemical malfunctioning within the organ, brain. In other words a so-called mental illness was said to have the same sort of organic causal origins as a somatic pathology. In fact anyone wanting to study psychoanalysis had to be a medical doctor first. This in turn led to the development of a vast quantity and array of medications called psychopharmaceuticals, and the promotion of the idea that these products were the most efficient and effective forms of treatment for so called mental illnesses.

In the meantime, beginning in the 1950s, psychoanalysts such as Albert Ellis, Viktor Frankl, and others came to believe that human beings were not simply controlled either by their biological mechanisms or by their unconscious, but were capable of choosing how to act and what to believe. They maintained that humans were in fact quite capable of thinking for themselves, something which behavioral scientists had largely dismissed as irrelevant. These psychoanalysts had also studied philosophy either privately or as university undergraduates. They realized that philosophy could be very useful in treating their patients who did not require the surgery-like psychoanalytic invasion of their innermost thoughts. They also saw that the philosophers working exclusively on abstract theories in the universities were not at all interested in helping ordinary people resolve their real-life problems. So they developed therapeutic methods based on philosophy, such as Rational Emotive Behavior Therapy, Logotherapy, and Existential Therapy. But they called their practices "psychotherapy" to distinguish them from both abstract philosophy and psychoanalysis. Treatments consisted mainly of so-called talk therapy in which a therapist has a carefully reasoned philosophical discussion with the patient about his or her problems, concerns, fears, and so on. These methods were then taught to psychotherapy students in universities. In other words, students of psychotherapy were being taught treatment methods which consisted largely of philosophical discussions, but these students had not themselves been educated in philosophy. They had little if any of the understanding of philosophy which the pioneers of psychotherapy had. So while, on the one hand, many philosophers were advancing the sterile theorizing of logical positivism in their universities, on the other hand many psychotherapists were applying the more useful areas of philosophy as a central element of their practice. But they were teaching their techniques to students without first teaching them the content or practice of philosophy on which their methods were based.

This development brought to light a tremendous confusion that existed then, and still exists today, in the field of psychotherapy. It has still not been clearly determined whether psychotherapy is a kind of science concerned with a triple-layered metaphorical structure in the brain (id, ego, and super ego) which comprises the so-called unconscious, whether it is the application of medical knowledge to the biochemical malfunctions of an organic brain, or whether it is the practice of philosophy in resolving the emotional suffering and cognitive distress in a person's mind. It could be argued that in fact all three perspectives are viable. But the confusion becomes a serious problem when a decision must be made in regards to choosing the best treatment modality.

What's adding to the confusion in North America today is that professionals are basing their official definitions of "mental illness" not on medical tests but on what type of treatment and how much treatment third party medical insurance companies are willing to pay for. Medical insurance companies are typically only willing to pay for the treatment of problems that are clearly defined in medical terms. This means that, in order to get medical insurance companies to pay for psychotherapy, a great amount and variety of emotional suffering and cognitive distress, especially in the United States, are now being defined as medical problems. Things like confusion about what to do with life, grief over the loss of a loved one, talking back to parents, and even shyness are being diagnosed as "mental illnesses," not because therapists actually believe them to be biological illnesses, but because if they don't label them as such, third party medical insurance companies will refuse to pay for the therapy. This has led to the unusual phenomenon of huge numbers of suffering and distressed individuals in the United States being diagnosed with so-called mental illnesses such as clinical depression, anxiety, and schizophrenia. Ironically this makes it seem like there are far more mentally ill people in the US than anywhere else in the world. So, while the various metaphors for the functioning of a tripartite mind are unexplainable in substantive terms, the most absurd metaphor in the field of psychotherapy today is the word "mental illness" because it confuses physical illness with problematic beliefs, values, fears, assumptions, and so on.

And finally, to add even more to the confusion, Western diagnostic criteria for so-called mental illnesses are culturally specific. For example, the North American diagnosis of "dependent personality disorder" refers to a person who is uncomfortable when not engaged in a significant interpersonal relationship. Yet in other, more group-oriented cultures, it is the strongly independent person who might be seen as being abnormal. Interestingly in our own competitive society, where self-reliant individualism is admired, psychotherapists don't recognize any *"independent personality disorder."* Cultural specificity makes little sense as a contributing factor in the diagnoses of medical illnesses, yet it is an integral part of today's diagnoses of so-called mental illnesses.

While the terminology of the medical sciences is employed by psychotherapists in diagnosing and classifying their patients, many of them actually utilize philosophical discussions as treatment. This raises the question, "If mental distress can be alleviated through philosophy, why aren't counselors and psychotherapists better educated in the content, and better trained in the practice of, philosophy?"

Michaela Amering, with the Department of Psychiatry at the Medical University of Vienna, Austria, explains that she deals with the "misery, injustice, and inconsistencies of the world by forgetting about them, by not letting things get to me too much, or by looking the other way" (p. 236). This might be a relatively simple task if that misery, injustice, and inconsistency are "out there" in the world, and not at home in your own life. But surely there is a better way to deal with these life circumstances than to simply turn your back on them? Learning how to reason about them, putting life into rational perspectives, understanding what may logically be expected from yourself in terms of dealing with personal and social issues is sure to be more helpful to one's peace of mind than simply "looking the other way." But ignoring it all may be all that some suffering individuals are able to do because people are not born with well-developed faculties of reasoning, rationality, and logic. These must be learned and yet they are rarely taught to the clients of counselors and patients of therapists.

Shawn Michaud, a senior student in my Philosophy for Counselors course in the winter semester of 2012 at the University of the Fraser Valley (UFV) wrote this note as part of her final essay assignment. It is quoted with her permission:

> In my studies as a social work student, everything we were taught in sociology and psychology indicates that mental illness does exist, and what types of pharmaceuticals are used to treat it. Then I came across a Philosophy for Counselors class in my final year of my degree that seriously challenged all of this. I found myself initially irritated, and then confused. What do you mean that mental illness does not exist? What kind of a ludicrous statement is that? But I vowed to keep an open mind and discovered an alternative approach to working with future clients . . . philosophy. So what is the point of learning philosophy? From a social work perspective, our job is to help our clients restore social functioning. By incorporating philosophy into our practices, we can help those clients restore that functioning. Because philosophy introduced me to logical fallacies and much more, I can now deal better with the variety of problems that mentally ill clients present.

ABOUT THIS BOOK

Psychiatrist and psychotherapist Edwin Hersch writes that the philosophical positions we adopt are important in establishing what terms like "psychosis," "psychopathology," "delusion," and "mental illness," really mean to us (p.31). Throughout the writing of this book I have felt compelled for two reasons to write the term "mental illness" either in quotes or to refer to it as "so-called mental illness." I did this, first of all, to drive the point home that the philosophical position on mental health and "illness" in this book is unlike the traditional one found in the majority of contemporary psychoanalytic, psychiatric, and psychotherapeutic literature. And second I did this because I had to constantly remind myself that I was not working with that misleading traditional perspective. I found it necessary to remind myself of this fact because, like the majority of North Americans, my thinking is so thoroughly saturated with the dominant biomedical model that using the term mental illness without the quotation marks immediately brings a host of erroneous concepts to mind. Furthermore, I use the word "psychotherapy" as a generic term referring to all the various non-medical mental healthcare methodologies, including at times psychoanalysis, psychiatry, psychotherapy, and counseling.

This book makes two connected arguments: first that post-secondary counseling and psychotherapy university programs ought to include philosophy as one of their required courses. This is in order to fortify the so-called talk therapy component of those fields. And second, that the use of philosophy in the prevention and treatment for so-called mental illness is an important sociological and "medical" reason why post-secondary institutions ought to keep their philosophy departments active and healthy. Added to that is the corollary that philosophy ought to be taught in pre-secondary institutions in order to act as a preemptive form of "inoculation" for young students against the kind of mental suffering and emotional distress that is at the present time so readily diagnosed as "mental illness."

Philosophy is useful to the fields of psychotherapy in three main ways: first, internally as an investigation of the meaning of the empirical data that are constantly produced to defend the etiological, diagnostic, prognostic, and treatment assumptions within the various fields of practice. This will be the general approach in the first two chapters. Second, philosophy is practical; it is a tool that is already being utilized, under psychological designations, by psychotherapists in all the many schools of therapeutic practice. This aspect is discussed primarily throughout chapters 3 to 5. And third, inter-personally, as discussed in the remaining chapters, as a heuristic device that can be taught to, and used by, those troubled individuals who request the assistance of practitioners. Of course these three themes overlap and intertwine extensively.

Philosophy is often accused of being merely critical, with the added observation that it is easier to criticize than to offer alternative perspectives or solutions. But this book is not just a critique of current theories and practices in the field of mental healthcare. It also offers viable alternatives. My main argument in this volume is that human suffering is often mistakenly diagnosed as mental illness, and that the treatment for these so-called mental illnesses is then often grossly inappropriate, such as with unnecessary psychotropic medications, electro-convulsive shock treatments, and brain surgery. Even when treatment is non-biological it is often problematic in that it is unnecessarily inadequate and ineffective, such as when the practitioners of talk therapy lack even a basic level of training in the practice of philosophy.

This book examines the differences between psychotherapy and philosophy, as well as the similarities between so-called talk therapy and philosophy. The point of this book is that "talk therapy," in whatever form it may take, will always be of poor quality if the therapist is not familiar with both the theories and application of philosophy. It is my hope that, in the twenty-first century, therapy for the mind will be dramatically improved because medical experts will discard the detrimental belief that drugging the brain is therapy for the mind. I also hope that this book will motivate academic institutions to thoroughly educate their students of counseling and psychotherapy in the practice of philosophy as treatment for so-called mental illnesses.

Part I of this book deals with psychotherapy as it exists today, at the start of the twenty-first century. The first chapter clarifies the confusion surrounding the definitions of the words "mind" and "brain" to show that they are very different in kind. This clarification is a requisite first step in any discussion of what constitutes mental health. It is also necessary in the examination and critique of the current classificatory methods and diagnostic approaches to so-called mental illnesses. This includes the informal Freudian psychoanalytic labels of transference, resistance, denial, negativism, projection, and suppression. Given that the predominant contemporary treatment paradigm of "mental illness" assumes a biological origin, this chapter ends with an investigation of some of the most significant social influences on the "discovery" of so-called mental illnesses, and their classification, diagnosis, and treatment methods.

The second chapter continues the discussion of the serious problems inherent in the field of mental healthcare services. The so-called medical model that is presently considered to be the ideal treatment protocol for most "mental illnesses" is discussed in comparison to its meaning in the treatment of corporeal morbidity. While medications are often called for in combating physical diseases, their use in treating non-physical distress in the mind raises complex issues which are connected to the distinction between the mind and the brain discussed in the first chapter. The causes or etiology of "mental illnesses" are often said to be a predisposition or weakness in the very genetic makeup of the suffering individual. But research has also shown that, paradoxically, a "mental illness" can have an iatrogenic origin: having been created by the attending physician. This is, of course, a very controversial claim, especially for those who see biogenesis as the most logical explanation for the onset of "mental illnesses." But iatrogenesis is not without merit. This discussion of the origin of "mental illnesses," or the causal factors involved in their onset, raises the specter of materialist reductionism and deterministic explanations which eliminate the possibility of the suffering individual's free will in any effort at recovery.

Chapter 3 is an overview of the various contemporary approaches to counseling and therapy. There are literally hundreds of individually named, overlapping practices, with more being devised all the time. It is impossible to discuss all of them, so included in this chapter are the generally agreed-upon descriptions of only the main treatment methods: Psychodynamic Therapy, clinical and counseling psychology, Adlerian Therapy, Existential Psychotherapy, Gestalt Therapy, Person-Centered Therapy, Reality Therapy, Behavior Therapy, Cognitive-Behavior Therapy, and Eclecticism or Multi-Modal Therapy. What should become apparent in these descriptions is how extensively the originators of the various psychotherapeutic methodologies have borrowed from both the content and the practice of philosophy.

The second part focuses on philosophy as both a therapeutic method in the past, and as a major constituent of contemporary modalities. Chapter 4 begins with a brief overview of how philosophy was perceived and employed as a therapy for the "soul" or mind from the pre-Socratics onward. The two main authorities in this field, Martha Nussbaum and Pierre Hadot, are cited extensively during the discussion of the ancient philosophic schools. So-called therapeutic philosophy declined substantially during the Dark Ages, but resurfaced to a lesser degree in more recent history. The fifth chapter looks at how contemporary psychotherapists have taken over the practice of philosophy due to the indifference of modern-day academic philosophers to helping non-theoretical (real) people in non-hypothetical difficulties. There is a review of the major psychotherapies, such as psychoanalysis, Adlerian Therapy, Existential Therapy, and so on, but this time with a focus on the specific philosophical contents and practices inherent in their methods. This chapter concludes with a discussion of the therapeutic benefits of the use of philosophy in counseling and psychotherapy.

Chapter 6 discusses philosophy as a therapeutic method in mental healthcare. It begins with a general discussion of what patients or clients want and need from their sessions with a counselor or therapist. Since the argument in this book is that philosophy ought to be taught to counseling and therapy students, this chapter clearly answers the question, "What is philosophy?" It then goes into an examination of the claim that counseling can simply be described as philosophical therapy. This has been disputed in the past by both counselors and philosophers alike. Next there is a discussion of the various aspects of counseling and therapy that must be accounted for if an application of philosophy is to be of benefit in the treatment of so-called mental illnesses. These include the following: recognition of the fact that a problem exists; trust that the counselor using philosophy will be up to the task, as well as trusting that the actual practice of philosophy in counseling or therapy will be beneficial to the client; the appropriateness of philosophy in dealing with the emotions (referred to as "affect" in psychotherapy); how philosophy can help suffering individuals gain helpful insights into their difficulties; how a philosophical discussion can be an antidote for the guilt, shame, and stigma surrounding the diagnosis of a so-called mental illness; philosophy's usefulness in finding alternative perspectives on the perception and alleviation of troubling life issues; and how philosophy can be very helpful in both finding and making meaning in life. And finally there is a critique of Peter Koestenbaum's "Clinical Philosophy." He is perhaps one of the earliest contemporary advocates of philosophy as therapy. His book on clinical philosophy, titled *The New Image of the Person*, was published three years prior to the generally accepted beginning of what is often called the "Philosophical Counseling" movement by Gerd Achenbach in 1981.

The seventh chapter deals with a completely new concept: teaching philosophy to youngsters in order to prevent the kind of emotional suffering and cognitive distress that can be clinically diagnosed as "mental illness." In the area of criminology, preventive measures have been shown to be much more cost-effective, for both the community and the offender, than any program of recovery after a crime has been committed. It therefore seems reasonable to assume that a program of "preventive philosophy" would be equally as beneficial to individuals and their communities in the avoidance of the economic burden created by so-called mental illnesses. This chapter also includes discussion concerning the ideal collaborative relationship between the counselor or therapist, when he or she becomes the teacher and the client is the student, of a philosophical strategy of prevention.

The third part turns to discussion about the application of philosophy in counseling and psychotherapy. Chapter 8 offers concrete suggestions on what an education plan in philosophy for counselors and psychotherapists ought to contain, including the requisite aptitude and attitude of the teacher. There is also a detailed discussion of twenty major differences between philosophy and psychotherapy. This comparison makes plain the fact that psychotherapy is not sufficiently like philosophy to rule out the need for philosophy in psychotherapy, nor is philosophy as therapy simply an inferior version of psychotherapy. This chapter then turns to the task that students often find the most difficult: locating the philosophical issues in the complex narrative presented by the suffering patient or client. Concrete advice is offered on how to do this, and two case studies are presented to illustrate the process.

Chapter 9 investigates the process of teaching the client or patient the content and practice of philosophy in order to make them more proficient in examining their own lives. In other words, the counselor or therapist is willing to teach the client or patient the very same philosophical content and skills she herself possesses. This is not often done in standard psychology or psychotherapy classes. A fairly detailed framework is then given of what a course of philosophy for counselors and therapists might look like. There is also a simplified outline of a course of this type that I teach to upper-level students at our university. Discussion then turns to why there is no mention of non-Western philosophy in this book, and also why teaching philosophy to students and clients or patients is not always enough. Sometimes there is a need for social activism to improve one's personal circumstances or to change the larger political system. When both the students of counseling or psychotherapy and their eventual clients or patients study philosophy their collaboration over life's problems will be doubly effective.

Three actual case studies from my practice are presented in the tenth chapter. The first case, concerning a disgraced monk, is annotated with suggestions for questions that could be asked during the counseling sessions, issues for further discussion, and comments on things the counselor should notice. The second case concerns the topic of authenticity being true to oneself. Because it is a case I dealt with entirely by e-mail, my discussion with the client is presented in its entirety without any alterations. This allows the reader a unique opportunity to witness a counseling dialogue that has not first been filtered, edited, or censored. The third case is presented in standard narrative form and deals with military man's overlapping professional and personal concerns.

The last chapter covers two concepts that have been discussed to a limited extent in some of the psychotherapeutic literature, but which have only rarely made it into practice. These are the concept of recovery and the aim for a cure. Research has revealed that there is surprisingly little expectation among psychotherapists and other mental healthcare services providers for the recovery or cure of their patients. Neither considered to be a realistic goal for counseling or therapy because both recovery and cure are believed to be unattainable in almost all cases. But treatment outcomes data are presented in this chapter which shows that a significant percentage of individuals diagnosed with "mental illnesses" do in fact recover, even without any treatment whatsoever. Not surprisingly, many of those who receive treatment also recover and are even cured. There is no logical or medical reason why recovery and cure shouldn't be considered attainable treatment goals. For recovery and cure to become the "new" goals in mental healthcare, a paradigm shift is required in all areas of mental healthcare, from the definition of mental illness, to diagnostic criteria and treatment methods, to prognosis and outcome expectations, and even prevention. Thinking about mental healthcare services must also include a recognition of the appropriateness of philosophy as part of its practices.

The call for a paradigm shift in any field always means that there has been a discovery of fatal problems within the status quo. This is where the first chapter begins.

I

Psychotherapy at the Start of the Twenty-first Century

"The usual therapist imposes himself on the patient without being aware of it."
—Martin Buber (1878–1965)

ONE

Problematic Paradigms

On March 11, 2002, a middle-aged Canadian man strangled and shot a
six of his sleeping children, set the house in which he had left them o
fire, and then drove to his mother-in-law's house to force his young wi
(who had legally separated from him) into his truck. He then drove he
back to watch their house, with the children inside, burn to the groun
Next he gave a letter to his wife which said in part "You wanted to be le
alone, well now you're all alone," and finally he staged his own suicid
But when he was later arrested by police and charged with murdering h
six children he claimed he was not to blame because mental illness ha
caused him to do what he had done.

A highly regarded forensic psychiatrist hired by the defense testifie
that what had caused the man to kill his children was actually a numb
of diagnosable mental illnesses, specifically depression, adjustment di
order, and extreme narcissism. But an equally respected psychiatrist fo
the prosecution disagreed. While he assented to the criteriological dia;
nosis given by the defense psychiatrist, he testified that these three cond
tions were not so severe an obstruction to the man's brain functions "th
his ability to think, to generate choices, was significantly impaired" (Tai
ner p. A3). In other words, in the prosecution psychiatrist's profession
opinion the diagnosed mental illnesses could not be said to have *caus*
the man to do what he did. Who is right? The contradictory conclusior
of these esteemed professionals will come as no surprise to anyone fami
iar with the *Chicago Institute for Psychoanalysis Report* which found th
there is "an inability in developing consensus among a group of analys
in making independent formulations of the same case material" (Schi
1999, p. 181).

A first year university student in my informal logic, or critical thinl
ing, class argued that the man was not culpable because human emo

tions, such as a murderous rage, just occur unexpectedly, caused by powerful chemical reactions in the brain over which we have no conscious control. But a second student asked, "If that's true, how come I can control my emotions? If I want to get angry all I have to do is think about what makes me angry. If I don't want to get angry over something I just take a deep breath, maybe count to ten, and tell myself not to get angry."

This initial interchange set the stage for a lively class discussion on the topic of the relationship between the brain and the mind. Does one control the other? Are both out of our control? Are they one and the same thing? Are they different things? Is the mind a "thing" at all? These questions are not new. They have been debated for centuries by philosophers, theologians, scientists, physicians, and others. What is relatively new is the so-called treatment of problems in the mind by professionals. Furthermore, the treatment of mental problems has itself become a problem due to the often vague and ambiguous use of the words "mind" and "brain."

There are many books currently available that are critical of the more than 400 theoretical orientations in counseling and psychotherapy, especially of the so-called medical model of treatment predominant in the field of psychiatry, and specifically biological psychiatry (Ross; Ballou; Fulford; Horwitz; Maj; Radden; Ross; Schill; Simon). The authors, many of whom were trained in clinical methodologies, including psychiatry, point out that there is a vast array of problems in both the diagnosing of so-called mental illnesses, and in what is typically being offered as treatment to the sufferers. And the problems are not isolated; they are systemic. For example: Professors of psychiatry Colin Ross and Alvin Pam point out that psychiatric theory has been developed primarily from case studies of women patients, "but with definitions of symptoms and normality, interpretations of symptoms, definitions of cure, and methods of treatment created almost exclusively by men" (p. 219). In fact the thesis of their book is that the entire field of biopsychiatry is based on unreliable pseudo-scientific research based on male-biased interpretations. Paula J. Caplan, Professor of Applied Psychology and Assistant Professor of Psychiatry in Toronto, also points to two so-called mental illnesses that are gender-specific to women; in other words they are misogynistic. The first is "self-defeating personality disorder" (SDPD). It applies to what Caplan calls the "good wife syndrome" in which the woman puts the needs of others ahead of her own, and she settles for less than she could have had without complaint. "Thus, after a woman has conscientiously learned the role her culture prescribes for her, the psychiatric establishments calls her mentally disordered" (p. 158). She points out that there is no equivalent diagnosis for self-serving males, no "delusional dominating personality disorder" (DDPD). The second misogynistic "disorder" is "late luteal phase dysphoric disorder" (LLPDD) commonly known as premenstrual syndrome (PMS). Caplan says it creates serious problems for a woman who experiences physical or mood problems associated with her menstrual cycle to be diagnosed as having a "mental disorder" for which psychiatry says there is no cure (p. 160).

Imagine a person who is suffering from a headache due to the chemical changes in the body brought on by over-exposure to the sun. The headache causes the person to experience and exhibit mood changes. No one would argue that the mood changes accompanying such a headache should be given a "mental illness" label, such as "cephalalgia syndrome." And no one would then say that it was the "cephalalgia syndrome" that caused the mood changes. The mood changes in women that are labeled the "mental illness" of "late luteal phase dysphoric disorder" (LLPDD) or PMS are somewhat analogous to this. Interestingly the so-called mental disorder of PMS disappears of its own accord when menopause sets in. A similar situation exists with the so-called mental illness of postpartum depression (PPD). Hormones are cited as the cause of the woman's depression and distress, while the often difficult circumstances of her private life are ignored. Then the PPD is blamed for the woman's unacceptable moods and behaviors, and medications are prescribed as though chemicals are the solution to her problematic domestic life.

Psychiatrist and psychotherapist Edwin L. Hersch explains that biopsychiatry is "a broadly based movement that emphasizes a particular set of philosophical assumptions" namely that the biological, physical, and somatic or bodily aspects of a human being constitute the true, and even sufficient, basis of psychological life. Biological psychiatry is based on a materialist and reductionist philosophy that is considered sufficient and adequate in dealing with people's emotional and mental distress. The so-called mind/body problem common to philosophers is resolved in biopsychiatry with the position that "'the body, the brain, and the biological' is what is 'really real' and most worthy of our efforts and attention" (p. 331). This narrow focus has led to enormous problems in the diagnosing and treatment of troubled people, not only for individual patients, but also for families, communities, clinics, and national and private medical insurance providers. But before the problems inherent in the diagnosing and treatment of mental illnesses can be addressed it's necessary to first investigate how the terms "mind" and "brain" are being applied in the mental health care services, and then determine what they might actually refer to.

"MIND" AND "BRAIN"

In her book *Night Falls Fast: Understanding Suicide*, Kay Redfield Jamison, professor of psychiatry at Johns Hopkins University School of Medicine, maintains that 90 to 95 percent of people who commit suicide were suffering from diagnosable psychiatric illnesses. Jamison's assumption of mental illness raises the specter of several fallacies such as "true by definition," "hasty assumption," "begging the question," and *"a priori"* because the act of committing suicide is simply defined in retrospect as due to mental illness since no sane person would want to kill him- or herself. It is the kind of defense used in some murder cases: "Because my client killed his entire family he must be mentally ill since no sane person would commit such a terrible crime." But this is like saying that a person who wins a race must have been the winner before the race began. The habit of retrospectively assuming, or attributing mental illness after the fact, as the cause of a person's behavior has not only seriously deflated the legal profession's trust in the diagnostic and therapeutic abilities of today's mental healthcare professionals, it has also led to the general public's confusion and bewilderment regarding what actually constitutes "mental illness."

What does mental illness make people do? What does it do to people? When are someone's behaviors or actions actually caused by so-called mental illness? Are mental illnesses infectious? Can they run in families? Why are some mental illnesses at times referred to as "clinical"? Can they be prevented and cured?

In the professional and academic literature so-called mental illnesses are often described in such vague and ambiguous language that they have become quite mysterious to the general public. And yet there is in fact nothing mysterious about so-called mental illnesses. The reason it mystifies so many people is because mental distress and suffering has been medicalized. The medicalization of mental illness keeps the treatment mysterious, sustains the expert's position as the authoritative holder of esoteric knowledge, and helps maintain the clinician's position of power over both the illness and the patient. The expert's and clinician's diagnosis, prognosis, and treatment protocol will not be questioned if the patient is led to believe that the condition is complex and medical, and therefore beyond his or her lay ability to comprehend.

So-called mental illness is based on the claim that conditions like sadness, confusion, and distress are caused by neurological breakdown: misfiring synapses and malfunctioning ganglion in a defective organic brain. But by using only logic, it is a simple matter to reach the conclusion that the mind cannot be equivalent to the brain. We know what we are asked to do when someone says, "Make up your mind" because this can be done intentionally by most people. But it would be meaningless for someone to say, "Make up your brain" because this is not humanly possible. It is undeniably far easier to change your mind than to change your brain; a person can be absent-minded but not absent-brained. It makes perfect sense to ask, "What's on your mind?" It makes no sense whatsoever to ask, "What's on your brain?" Self-development literature often makes reference to "mindfulness" but not "brainfulness." A person is sometimes said to have "lost his mind" but rarely "lost his brain." Clearly the mind and the brain are commonly perceived very differently; and because these terms are understood to represent two very different things, it must be the case that they are not identical.

There are numerous books, for academics, clinicians, professionals and for a general readership, containing detailed discussions of the various theories that have been put forward on how the mind and the brain ought to be defined, and how their interaction ought to be explained. For example, the brain might be compared to a battery where the mind is like the electricity produced by that battery. This supervenient relationship, in which mental content is deemed dependent on organic brain functioning, is termed "epiphenomenalism" in philosophy of mind. But this is a faulty analogy because the electricity produced by a battery has no meaning—in a sense it is random—whereas the thoughts which make up the mind are indeed meaningful to the owner of the brain. It could also be argued that the electricity from a battery can produce movement in the armature of an electric motor in the same way that a person's thought can raise his arm. But this analogy fails again because the electricity does not act from intention, it has no intrinsic reason for moving the armature, while the person may have a very good reason for moving his arm intentionally. The question of how a person's thoughts are able to initiate movement in the material body is still under serious discussion in the academic circles of philosophy, psychology, physiology, and neurology. But this question is irrelevant to counseling and therapy because it is not the action of the mind on the body, the effects of thoughts on physical movement, that is at issue in counseling and therapy. Here the topic of mind involves the person's reasons, his meaningful thoughts, such as his values, beliefs, fears, assumptions and so on, as well as the effects of those thoughts on his own life and the lives of others.

Suffice it to say that generally, in both academic and mental healthcare literature there is great confusion as to whether the mind and the brain are two things or one, and whether they are in fact even different "things." In much of the mental healthcare literature the two terms are used as though they were synonymous. For example, throughout his book *Philosophy of Psychopharmacology* Professor of psychiatry Dan J. Stein uses the term "brain-mind" to indicate that they are not separate entities made of different sorts of things—as suggested by Cartesian substance dualism—and that these two "constructs are, in fact impossible to disentangle" (p. x). Both my *Penguin Roget's College* desk thesaurus and my computer's *Word* thesaurus offer the word "mind" as a synonym for "brain." But as pointed out above, the mind and the brain seem to be two very different entities that seem to function very differently, although within the same person. Does this mean the mind and brain are in fact opposite "things" that consist of the same kind of material?

In his book *The Concept of Mind*, Gilbert Ryle explains that the belief that mind and matter are materially identical opposite things amounts making a "category mistake" because it is based on the mistaken belief that they are "terms of the same logical type." He says that it is perfectly acceptable and correct to say that minds exist and material bodies exist. But they employ the word "exist" in two different senses, in somewhat the same way that a good *book* exists and in that book a good *argument* exists. The good book is rectangular but, while the argument can be called "good," it can't be said to have a geometric shape because it doesn't exist in the same way that the book exists (Timko & Hoff p. 69). Likewise, the brain has a definite geometric shape, the mind does not.

In his book *The Mind and its Discontents* Grant Gillett gives a very effective definition of what the mind is all about. He writes,

> A mental life is a narrative construct or product of the integrating activity of a concept-using subject as a person in relation to others. . . . Thus, acting and relating are the foundations of the psyche rather than merely receiving, assembling, and connecting representations. (p. 138)

What Gillett means is that the words "mental" or "mind" don't refer to any concrete objects, such as neurons or ganglia in the brain. Instead they refer to "a mental life" consisting of non-material "narrative" elements such as beliefs, values, fears, and assumptions that we each have as individuals, and which we share with others. These propositional mental elements define each person as a unique individual among others. They are what constitute each person, and what affect the way each person processes the input from the world and the people around them. A brain of some sort is universal to all living creatures, but each creature does its own thinking and therefore has a distinctive mind of its own. It may not be accurate to say that creatures without language have a mind consisting of propositional content, but they nonetheless share the human mental quality of intentionality: the "emotions essentially involving judgments or appraisals" (Atkinson p. 548). The mind is what makes "me" me, and makes me distinct from you and everyone else in this world. While the brain is the functional container, the mind is the personal and meaningful content. And while the brain's functioning consists of the occurrence of causal connections among neurons, the mind's functioning consists of making meaningful connections among thoughts that are chosen or discovered by the person. The scientific reductionism to which psychotherapy aspires "objectifies the person by squeezing all the meaning out of their experiences" (Slade p. 83). M. R. Bennett, Professor of Physiology and University Chair at the University of Sydney, and P. M. S. Hacker, Fellow of St. John's College, Oxford state the relationship between mind and brain very simply. "Human beings, but not their brains, can be said to be thoughtful or thoughtless . . . people but not their brains, can be said to make decisions or be indecisive." They explain that it is committing a "mereological fallacy" when neuroscientists make the mistake of ascribing attributes—such as seeing, hearing, smelling, tasting—

to the constituent parts of the human being that logically apply only to the whole person (p. 73). In other words, the person, not the brain hears sound and understands its meaning because the mind, not the brain understands what the sound is all about—that the sound is a word, and that the word is the name they have been given. This makes so-called mental illness, in part, a problem in the mind's capacity to understand meaning, not a disease or malfunction of the neurons in the brain. Whenever there is talk of a so-called mental illness what is actually being referred to is not brain malfunction, it is problems in the meaningful content that is interconnected in the mind. In other words mental disorders are problems located *in* the brain—as opposed to in the liver—without being malfunctions *of* the brain (Graham p. 24).

Philosopher John Davis pointed out that "to discover the essence of the concrete one must become more and more abstract; it cannot be discovered by concentrating one's attention on the concrete" (p. 22). This is certainly true of the brain and its relationship to the mind. While the brain is concrete and biological, the mind is non-concrete and propositional. "The mind is not a kind of thing" (Bennett & Hacker p. 105). While the brain may be described as being bicameral, it would be completely inappropriate to speak of a "bicameral mind" (as Julian Jaynes did in his book) because the mind is not a divisible corporeal organ. It is a conceptual construct that is describable only in the abstract, consisting of thoughts and emotions, or in the language of psychology, cognitions and affect. While the brain has an operative role—the physical functioning of the body—the ideas in the mind have behavioral potency for the person. Their meaning and significance are often so strong that they can override very powerful evolutionary survival urges. For example, a person will go on a hunger strike with the intention to draw attention to an injustice in the world. This self-sacrificing action is not merely an effect of brain cell activity; it is charged with meaning and significance for that individual which she wants to share with others. Meaningful intentions are no more materially determined in the brain than values, beliefs, fears, experiences, and opinions are. The reliable predictability found in material cause-and-effect relationships is clearly lacking in the meaningful psychological events that take place in the mind. We are able to predict chemical reactions far better than we can predict human thought and behavior because chemical reactions are determined by cause-and-effect mechanisms, scientifically describable as natural laws, while human thought and behavior are not. Dr. Laurence Simon puts it this way: "While there is an intimate relationship between biology and psychology, the two fields have their separate domains and methodologies, and neither field can reduce the other to it or afford to ignore the relationship between the two enterprises. . . . Psychology and the self are not reducible to the laws of other fields" (p. 176).

The mind consists of both a priori and a posteriori propositions. Mental propositions consist of both facts and attitudes such as doubts, beliefs, desires, values, fears, and assumptions, toward the propositional content. For example, a person's mind may consist of the "factual" knowledge that love and respect exist in the world, as well as attitudes toward this knowledge such as the doubt that she is worthy of love and respect, the belief that she is unworthy of love and respect, the desire to be loved and respected, and so on. These can, of course, lead to unusual or even socially unacceptable behaviors. But notice that none of this propositional content—the knowledge, doubts, beliefs, desires, values, fears, and assumptions—has any material existence. While the defining characteristic of the brain is its physical structure, the defining characteristic of the mind is its complex "intentionality" as philosopher of psychology Franz Brentano called it (Campbell p. 9). Mental content is always thoughts or attitudes *about* something. The mind necessarily always consists of two elements: consciousness and intentionality (see Graham p. 30–35).

Much of daily social life involves the person's mind thinking about things or situations which may then motivate the body to act. To illustrate, consider how brain research explains what makes us feel good. All introductory psychology texts discuss the fact that when a person recognizes someone in the street and then meets with that familiar individual whom they like, dopamine is released into the blood stream giving that person a "good feeling" about the meeting. Notice that the recognition of the familiar person ("I know that person") and the thought ("I like that person") come prior to the dopamine being released into the blood stream. The thought process then initiates a feel-good response in the body. The person would say, "I recognized and like that person, and that makes me feel good about our meeting." It would be absurd for that person to claim that the hormonal cause precedes the thought-effects: "I feel good about meeting him or her and that makes me recognize and like that person." The body does not initiate the thought process; that would be a reversal of the cause and effect relationship. The thoughts cause the pleasurable physical or bodily response.

There is another reason why propositional mental content, such as recognizing and liking, even when it is considered to be functioning abnormally, cannot be defined in reductionist neurological or biological causal terms: mental content is often both normative and tentative. These two states cannot be said to apply to biological causation. In other words mental propositions are often beliefs or assumptions about what ought to be (normative), and these beliefs can be doubted (tentative). The mental propositions of the pleasant meeting example above might go something like this: "I believe I know that person, so I *should* say hello. I assume this will be a pleasant experience because of our past encounters, but I *might be wrong*." Normative and tentative language such as this is mental content, and it makes no sense to try to explain it in terms of biological cause and effect relationships in the brain. Assumptions and doubts about meeting are not caused by neurological or chemical activity in the cerebral cortex (Thornton, 2004, p. 198). It makes no more sense to reduce the non-material thoughts in a brain to neurons and chemicals than it does to reduce the non-material information, thoughts, and arguments in this book to paper fibers and ink marks.

Thomas Nagel's thoughts on the debate between evolution and creationism apply equally well to the discussion of the relationship between the mind and the brain. He writes that there is

> a failure of psychophysical reductionism, a position in the philosophy of mind that is largely motivated by the hope of showing how the physical sciences could in principle provide a theory of everything.... Consciousness [and cognition, including reasoning] is the most conspicuous obstacle to a comprehensive naturalism that relies only on the resources of physical science. (p. 4, 35)

In other words, while the physical reductionism of the sciences can explain the neurological functioning of the material brain, it is inadequate for explaining the mental phenomenon of consciousness which includes the essential human propensity for the mental activity called reasoning. What consciousness is exactly, and how it induces brain and body functioning is a puzzle that philosophers and biological scientists have not yet solved. And it need not be solved for the purpose of this book because that "how" is irrelevant to the discussion of the enormous ontological gulf between the mind and the brain. What is of importance here is the obvious fact that what constitutes a conscious mind is clearly not brain matter, and vice versa.

Susan Kemker, Staff Psychiatrist in the North Central Bronx Hospital, writes that, in her experience, psychiatric residency training creates a bias in new doctors toward a biomedical orientation because it "tends to discourage critical appraisal of biomedical reductionism" (Ross and Pam 242). In their book *Pseudoscience in Biological Psychiatry* Colin Ross and Alvin Pam caution the mental health community that the drive of reductionist biomedical psychiatry is likely to make what's on the patient's mind completely irrelevant (p. 116). Professor of Philosophy Emeritus Gary Madison maintains that a purely biopsychiatric or neuropsychiatric approach to emotional suffering and mental distress can lead psychiatrists to overlook the fact that "their job is not to cure 'diseases' but to help specific individuals" to overcome their problems He is concerned over the fact that psychiatry seems to be in the process of abandoning talk therapy altogether in favor of psychopharmaceutical treatments for their patients, "whose greatly restricted goal is simply to 'manage' their disturbances and insure that they are not too much of a danger to themselves or others" (p. 277). This goal seems to be more focused on benefits for the clinician and society than for the patient.

At the risk of restating what should be fairly obvious by now, the mind is not a material object like the brain. It is an abstraction consisting of beliefs, values, assumptions, fears, and so on. The brain is not an abstraction; it is an organic part of the physical body. Changing one's mind is not the same as changing one's brain. There is no such thing as "mental content"; it is not something *in* the mind. The content of the brain simply *is* the mind. The mind *consists of* the content. It consists of both a priori and a posteriori propositions. The mind is propositional, not biological. Mental propositions consist of propositional attitudes—such as doubts, beliefs, desires, values, fears, and assumptions *about* something, or toward propositional content. Soviet psychologist Lev Vygotsky even went so far as to conceive of the mind as "an activity which extends beyond the skin to inter-penetrate with other minds in interpersonal exchanges" (p. 195). From this perspective minds do not operate in isolation; they are socially interconnected with others. An original insight can be the product of two minds, or many minds in a group, working together on the same problem. This is the point that was made by Matthew Lipman who promoted the idea of a "community of inquiry" where many young minds working in combination create original thoughts (1988).

An argument that is often made in defense of the biological model of so-called mental illness is that brain scans have been employed that produced evidence that mental malfunctions are in fact problems of the brain. But Judith Horstman discusses five flaws inherent in brain scans in her book *Brave New Brain*. Very briefly, they are that first, research with brain scans lacks the randomized sampling and a real-world environment required by proper scientific data collection; second, functional Magnetic Resonance Imaging (fMRI) scans don't measure the direct brain activity in a specific area nor at a specified time; third, the colors that appear on the computer screen don't accurately reflect how a single activity is in fact widely diffused throughout the entire brain; fourth, the colorful image of a brain on the computer screen that is so often shown in the media is not just one person's brain doing one activity but is rather a statistical average of various people's brains doing various activities; and fifth, there are many dissimilar activities that will make one area of the brain "light up" (p. 80–83). Clearly the claim that fMRI brain imaging somehow shows that mental illnesses are biological brain diseases has no basis in factual medical science.

So how is mental illness related to the biological brain? There is considerable equivocation in the media and in lay discourse when the term "mental illness" is used. Sometimes it refers to psychological or mental distress and suffering, while at other times to chemical or physiological problems in the biological brain. In much of the mental health literature, the words "brain" and "mind" constitute a distinction without a difference. Unfortunately this equivocation is rampant in the professional mental healthcare field as well when, for example, there is talk about a "medical model" in treating a person who has been diagnosed with an ambiguously defined illness of the mind. But discussions of the mind, as though mental states are brain states, is an act of transmuting non-material cognitive activity into a material/organic process. The term "mental illness" is the reification of a symptomatic diagnosis into a natural disease entity. An epistemic problem of the non-material, propositional "narrative" that constitutes the mind is incorrectly defined as a faulty organic matter. While realist/materialist assumptions are valid in relation to the physical brain, realism and materialism do not apply to propositional contents and attitudes—such as knowledge, beliefs, values, desires, doubts, fears, and assumptions—which constitute the dynamic and intentional elements of the immaterial mind. To put it very simply, if the container gets damaged the contents may spoil. But fixing the container is not identical to altering the contents.

In the same way that biological psychiatrists have for years mistakenly focused on various substances as the cause of substance abuse and addictions, they have mistakenly focused on the brain as the cause of so-called mental illnesses. By way of illustration, in a March 25, 2013 interview in Maclean's magazine, Dr. Allen Frances, Duke University Professor emeritus and former chair of the *DSM–IV* task force responded to the magazine's criticism that behavior such as a child talking back to its parents ("ODD"—see Appendix), caffeine use, occasional forgetfulness, grieving, and nail biting are mistakenly diagnosed as *mental* illnesses (p. 56). Dr. Frances maintains that our understanding of the human *brain* is very primitive, and that the *brain* "doesn't reveal its secrets easily." In effect he has assumed the question about the mind to be identical to the question about the brain, and thereby revealed his belief in the mind and brain's equivalency. His reply implies that human behavior, such as caffeine use, grieving, or nail biting, is brain-generated rather than that it is motivated by reasons the person has in mind.

Another problematic belief that persists in psychotherapy, despite evidence to the contrary, is that of the existence of an unconscious which surreptitiously controls and determines the actions of the patient. But the existence of the Freudian unconscious has long been disproved and thereby discredited by means of both logical argumentation and clinical trials and observation. See for example *The Challenge to Psychoanalysis and Psychotherapy* edited by psychiatrists Stefan de Schill and Serge Lebovici and philosopher John Searle's book *The Rediscovery of the Mind* especially chapter 7, "The Unconscious and Its Relation to Consciousness." Since there is no mysterious unconscious that is hidden from, and inaccessible to, the patient it is fair to say that individuals act according to consciously held beliefs, values, fears, assumptions, and so on that are at times simply relegated to the background, behind more immediate thoughts. But these are still contents of the mind and constituents of the individual's personality which can be made available for close self-examination or revealed for discussion with family members, friends, counselors, or therapists.

The constituents of so-called mental illnesses are described in many different ways in the psychotherapeutic and psychiatric literature such as emotional suffering from psychological and physical abuse, trauma from natural disasters, violence, or war, loss of hope, an uncertain or problematic identity, a lack of meaning in life, low self-esteem, a lack of a sense of power and personal responsibility for the vicissitudes of life, an underdeveloped ability at metacognition, and so on. But this list raises the obvious question: are these in fact "illnesses" or "disorders"?

The words "mental" and "illness" make a peculiar combination. It's odd to speak of "mental illness" as some sort of existing entity because the term "mental illness" refers simply to emotional suffering and/or distressing thoughts. No one would think to use the term "emotion illness" or "thought illness," or, more technically, "affect illness" or "cognitive illness." The word "illness" is totally inappropriate when it's associated with emotions or thoughts. And yet that's exactly what "mental illness" refers to: problematic (in some way) emotions or thoughts. It would be more correct to claim that a patient's thoughts or attitudes *about* something are in fact "ill." For example, we speak of a plan or idea being "ill conceived." When a plan is "ill conceived" perhaps this could be diagnosed as "plan illness." Of course this is just facetiousness to illustrate how inappropriate the term "mental illness" actually is. The inappropriateness of the term "mental illness" becomes even more evident when it is relabeled as "mind illness."

CLASSIFICATION AND DIAGNOSIS OF "MIND ILLNESSES"

The nosology or classification, and diagnosing of mental illness began in the late nineteenth century with Freud. Psychiatrist and psychotherapist Edwin L. Hersch describes Freud as a man of his times whose work reflects the nineteenth-century model of an objectivist and mechanistic science. He points out that in his writings there is ample evidence of Freud's realism, his objectivism, and his empiricism. Early in his career Freud wrote that he hoped the "psychical processes" could one day be represented as "quantifiably determinate states of specifiable material particles." Yet his theorizing, and the terminology he introduced with it, such as "transference," "projection," and "conversion," reveal that Freud embraced Cartesian dualism which holds that the mind and the body are two separate and distinct entities. Freud attempted to remove all subjective elements from the patient-therapist discourse in order to locate the obscured "objective truth" that he felt lay hidden in his patients' minds. He viewed "mental apparatus" as "an independent thing that can be objectively investigated much like other natural objects" (p. 303–4). He wrote,

> The Oedipus complex is an example of an "internal" concept that has been accepted as an "objective fact" in orthodox Freudian theory. From this perspective we can say that classical Freudian psychoanalysis "discovered" the Oedipus complex *out there in the world*; it did not just create is as a concept. . . . It is a universally valid "feature of the human mind" and an essential product of both normal and abnormal development. (Ibid)

His therapeutic approach involved detecting and investigating *intra*psychic phenomena and the psycho*dynamics* or interplay between competing and conflicting drives and internal "structures."

Hersch maintains that classical Freudian theory seemed to "overstructure, overselect, and sometimes even overshadow the data presented by the patient. Especially with regard to the *experiential* data." Freud faced a dilemma because "his sympathies were with the objectivist side of the epistemological debate, yet his subject matter was subjective in all its richness." But the philosophical paradigm of science that Freud adopted "never quite fit his subject matter. Perhaps the apparent contempt for philosophy evident in his *New Introductory Lectures* hampered Freud's efforts to see this" (Hersch ibid).

The criteria that have guided the classification of mental disorders since the days of Freud are not scientific knowledge or empirical research. Craig R. Lareau, forensic psychologist and Director of Forensic Psychology at Patton State Hospital, and author of the essay "The *DSM–IV* System of Psychiatric Classification" maintains that research has shown shortcomings in scientific foundations to be the "primary reason for the inadequacy of psychiatric classification embodied in the *DSM*" (p. 209). Derek Bolton, professor of philosophy and psychopathology at the Institute of Psychiatry, Kings' College London, and Jonathan Hill, professor of child and adolescent psychiatry in Manchester, explain that

> The definition of psychiatric syndromes are in many respects arbitrary. For instance definitions of depression differ over the symptoms that are required, their duration, and whether they have to be associated with impaired functioning before a diagnosis is made. (p. 255)

The process of classification has also been characterized as "the need to achieve professional consensus . . . without regard to etiology" (Horwitz 108, 73). In effect, the classification of mental disorders is the establishment of what the philosopher René Descartes called a "belief community" because it deals with so-called realities that cannot be empirically measured or verified (Schrank p. 135). The assumption in much of the mental healthcare services is that the cause of non-empirical "disorders" doesn't need to be known if their treatment is effective. The problem is that while pharmaceutical treatments of so-called mental disorders may serve to reduce some symptoms in the patient, they do not address either the exogenous (external) causal factors nor the underlying internal reasons. Even the avoidance of medications by means of psychotherapeutic "talk therapy" is often merely a means by which to "discover" diagnosable symptoms in what the patient says.

But diagnosing in the field of mental illness is not at all an exact science based exclusively on the identification of psycho-pathological symptoms. It often depends on the beliefs and values of the attending clinician. Psychoanalytic psychotherapist Charlotte Prozan maintains that "defining a piece of behavior as a symptom is an expression of a value held by the therapist" (p. 312). Psychiatrists Michaela Amering and Margit Schmolke give the example of a woman who had been diagnosed with bipolar disorder, who valued her energy and stamina as a positive attribute in her role as the single mother of three young children. But her psychiatrist considered her energy as evidence of hypomania and prescribed a neuroleptic drug for her. Not surprisingly, the woman did not take the medication (p. 217). This is just one example of a person seeking professional help with a difficult life situation who finds herself diagnosed with a mental illness. "Mental illness" is sometimes defined as behavior that causes significant harm to the individual, and perhaps others as well. This raises the question of whether this woman's energy was in fact causing her, or anyone else, any harm. It also points to a paradox: there are many common behaviors that are in fact considered to be "normal" which also cause harm to both the individual and others, such as dropping out of school, criminality, smoking, driving while under the influence of alcohol, not seeking inoculations against common diseases, taking on too much debt, overeating, participating in dangerous sports, and so on (Bolton 2008 p. 171). None of these are formally diagnosed as mental illnesses and treated with medications. In his essay "Implications of Comorbidity for the Classification of Mental Disorders: The Need for a Psychobiology of Coherence," C. Robert Cloninger, with the Department of Psychiatry at the Washington State University School of Medicine, explains that in clinical practices the primary diagnosis of patients is not consistent because it is not entirely objective or value-free. It depends on "the interests and skills of the clinician, the chief complaint at the time of presentations, the treatment facilities available, and reimbursement policies of available insurance" (Maj et al. p. 84).

A mental illness is entered into nosological and diagnostic manuals and into professional practice, not by empirical biomedical research, but by a majority vote of an editorial committee (see Maj et al). Craig R. Lareau cites numerous problems with how so-called mental illnesses are classified and the way diagnostic criteria make it into the *DSM*. For example he begins by saying that "the psychiatric disorders listed in the *DSM-IV* are not based on any theory of psychopathology" (p. 209), and that "scientific underpinnings do not even support the more limited uses suggested for the *DSM* in clinical settings" (p. 214). He goes on to say that due to the overlap of numerous common symptoms among multiple disorders "diagnostic reliability suffers, and it is difficult to determine many issues of validity" (p. 211). On the other hand, for the *DSM-I* diagnosis of obsessive-compulsive disorder, "it is possible for two different people to meet the diagnostic criteria for the disorder *and not share even one symptom in common!*" (p. 220. Italics in the original). The clinical occurrence of comorbidity as the rule rather than the exception, and the variability of symptomatic criteria, "places many of the *DSM* diagnoses in doubt" (p. 221). And yet the type of language used by psychotherapists—such as medication, comorbidity, patient, prognosis, and relapse—makes all forms of counseling and psychotherapy sound as though they are medical practices. And this medical-sounding language reifies words like schizophrenia and depression to make them sound as though they were somatic pathologies. But this is completely misleading. So-called relapse into depression is not the reoccurrence of an illness. It is some sort of troubling *life situation* that leads to emotional distress which needs to be taken care of. The suffering that has been clinically diagnosed as the "mental illness" of depression is sometimes actually a broken heart. Depression has been compared to the pain felt after an injury (Amering and Schmolke p. 42). The therapeutic medical focus is misplaced when it is aimed at preventing the "recurrence" of the "depression" (the pain) rather than on the recurrence of the life situation (the cause of the pain) that has led to that person's emotional suffering and mental distress. The so-called medical model of treatment for "mental illness" will be discussed in greater detail in the next chapter.

In a 2011 article titled "Mind Games" in the University of Toronto Magazine, Edward Shorter, the Hannah Professor of the History of Medicine at the University of Toronto says the *DSM* is "profoundly unscientific" because many of the disorders described in the *DSM* are not actual disease entities discovered through scientific method:

> Instead they result from political deal-making among different factions in the professional community, each with conflicting ideas about causes and treatments of psychological problems.

The result, he says, is a description of mental disorders with too little relation to real diseases. Shorter goes on to say that some of the disorders overlap so much that they are almost impossible to distinguish from each other. He calls them "distinctions without a difference."

On the other hand, Dr. David S. Goldbloom, a University of Toronto professor of psychiatry says that *DSM* labels are simply a common language used by professionals to communicate easily with each other. He argues that other medical diagnoses, such as high blood pressure, also exist along a continuum, and that a diagnosis of high blood pressure is based on a consensus among physicians as to what constitutes a problem matic blood pressure (Kleiner p. 33–36). But the dispute with the diagnosis of mental illnesses does not hinge on doubt over a continuum of severity; it is doubt over their very existence. Goldbloom's argument simply ignores the fact that blood pressure can be objectively measured with an instrument whose numbers will look the same to all who view them. While the subjective evaluation of the numbers on the blood pressure gauge may vary among consulting physicians, the numbers on the gauge remain the same. This cannot be said of so-called mental illnesses because there are no reliable medical instruments or biological tests that can be used to consistently measure mental states. There are no objective numbers that correspond to mental functioning that can be subjectively evaluated. A patient's distress can be assessed and then diagnosed completely differently by different mental healthcare experts. As William Fulford, Professor of Philosophy and Mental Health at the University of Warwick, points out, "All [clinical] decisions stand on two feet, on values as well as on facts, including decisions about diagnosis (2004, p. 208). The values are the subjective evaluations of the attending therapist.

In their book *Philosophical Issues in Psychiatry* Professors of Psychiatry Kenneth Kendler and Josef Parnas point out that the official psychiatric nosology as published in the 1968 version of the *Diagnostic and Statistical Manual of Mental Disorders (DSM–II)* was an etiologically based system. It differentiated between organic and psychological disorders. It understood organic disorders as emerging from distinct pathological processes in the organic brain, and "functional" conditions as arising from intrapsychic conflicts. But the third edition, the *DSM–III* published twelve years later in 1980, presented a new "atheoretical" and "descriptive" nosology which did not differentiate brain problems from mind problems, thereby conflating the brain and the mind. He points out that this "diverges from nearly all diagnostic systems in the rest of the field of medicine," and yet it is the basis on which psychotherapy proceeds to initiate treatment (p. 7). This makes it seem as though the authors of the *DSM-III* believed that it makes no difference whether biological treatment is applied to a psychological problem, or psychological treatment is applied to a biological problem.

In the 1970s and 1980s, books were written and movies were made about people who were inhabited by as many as two hundred different personalities. After mental health authorities voted to call this mental illness "Multiple Personality Disorder" (MPD) hundreds more cases were diagnosed. But when critics intensified their research it was discovered that MPD never really existed; it had been fabricated by over-zealous but well-meaning mental healthcare professionals. To hide their embarrassment the authors of the *DSM* voted MPD out of existence and created a new mental illness to replace it called "Dissociative Identity Disorder" (DID) which is rarely diagnosed. Since then a number of other mental illnesses have been voted into, or out of, existence. What is a mental illness if it can simply be voted into and then out of existence?

Biological psychiatry makes two critical errors in defining mental illness. First, it adopts a realist epistemology. It assumes that the knowledge and mental activity that comprise the mind and mental function are reducible to the chemical or electrical operations of the organic brain. This reductionist model of the mind is an essential aspect of biological psychotherapy. The biological model reduces the operation of complex human beings—the possessors and creators of meanings and values—to the properties of their individual parts: organs, bones, muscles, neuron ganglia, chemicals, and so on. The logic of this realist model reduces mental illnesses to disordered molecular or cellular structures and activities in the brain. Realist biological models of mental function and mental illness claim that the primary causes of mental "diseases" are in genetic and biochemical factors. They locate the pathological qualities of psychological conditions in the material properties of brains, not in the symbol systems or propositional content which constitutes the mind (Horwitz 3, 143).

The second mistake is that biological psychiatry reifies mental illness by defining symptom-based diagnostic categories as quasi-disease entities "despite the lack of scientific support for the disorders" (Lareau 222). The reification of criteriological categories is in fact committing a "category mistake": emotional distress and cognitive confusion are defined as organic pathology. Although fetal alcohol syndrome, Alzheimer's, Tourette's, and other biological disorders affect thinking, they are not mental illnesses. Of course, they all interfere with the proper functioning of the mechanisms of the brain and prevent what is considered "normal" thinking. These biological disorders affect the person's ability to effectively deal with beliefs, values, fears, assumptions, and so on but they are not problems *caused by* the individual's beliefs, values, fears, and assumptions. This is what differentiates brain diseases from so-called mental illnesses. Mental illnesses simply are problematic beliefs, values, fears, assumptions, and so on; they have no physical existence. As soon as mental problems are found to have an organic cause they are no longer mental problems; they are organic brain problems. This is the point Thomas Szasz and other mental healthcare professionals have been making since the 1950s in response to the drive by psychiatrists to have the so-called medical model of biological psychiatry be the exclusive treatment paradigm in mental healthcare.

The ontology of mental illnesses then is founded on two misconceptions: that the mind is the same as the brain, and that the symptomatic diagnosis of a mental illness is identical to the discovery of an organic disease. Neither of these perspectives is justified. In North America mental illness is entered into diagnostic manuals and into professional practice, not by empirical biomedical research, but by a majority vote of the editorial committee which compiles and publishes the American Psychiatric Association's *Diagnostic and Statistical Manual of Mental Disorders (DSM)* (see Maj).

What is the ontological status of a mental illness such as depression when that mental illness is simply a label applied to an aggregate of symptoms? The answer is, it has no material existence in reality at all, no ontological status whatsoever. The classification of mental illnesses is the result of what has been called "insidious reification" which refers to the conceptual creation of disease entities and treating them as though they actually have a substantive existence (Thornton, 2007 p. 180). The various symptoms in combination—sadness, hopelessness, and low self-esteem—are reified and discussed as if this distress were a unified illness or disease known as "depression."

The North American mental healthcare system is suffering from a case of what I have elsewhere labeled "hyper-diagnosia," the over-diagnosing of healthy individuals. Similar to the infamous "medical student syndrome" where medical students come to believe they're suffering from every disease they study, healthy individuals have come to believe they're suffering from various mental illnesses due to the misleading claims of psychiatrists, psychotherapists, medical professionals, and the pharmaceutical industry. Even the most normal of human conditions are now being diagnosed as pathological brain disorders. For example, grieving for a loved one, finding it difficult to speak in front of an audience, a child talking back to his parents or having a tantrum, occasionally forgetting where the car keys were left, nail biting, not enjoying sex as much as in the past, and being too full of energy or not energetic enough are all formally defined as psychiatric disorders of the brain. These have all been officially catalogued as diagnosable mental illnesses. Between 1980 and 1990 the diagnosis of "Attention Deficit Hyperactivity Disorder" (ADHD) jumped from 400,000 to 900,000 cases in the United States alone, and the frequency of treatment with drugs has gone from 28 percent to 86 percent (J. Bakan p. 73). It's interesting to note that about 80 percent of patients diagnosed as suffering from ADHD are energetic little boys. It is also interesting to note that the two basic principles guiding the *DSM-IV* definition for "mental disorder" is that, first, the condition must have "negative consequences of the person, some sort of pain, distress, discomfort, or disability"; and second, "the disorder is a dysfunction of some internal process within the person" (Bartol and Bartol p. 210). But ADHD clearly does not meet the first criterion because kids diagnosed with ADHD typically don't see themselves as being in pain, distress, discomfort, or disability; and it doesn't meet the second criterion because there is no clinical evidence that a child with this so-called disorder is in fact suffering from a dysfunction of some internal process.

The criteria for the relatively new diagnostic category of "Pediatric Bipolar Disorder" (PBD) are childhood aggression, irritability, nightmares, oppositionality, and emotional lability. Since the year 2000 the diagnosis of PBD in children and infants in the United States has increased 44 times from the previous decade. According to a report published in the *Journal of the American Medical Association* and discussed in a July 7, 2004 article on the MSNBC web site (at http://www.msnbc.ms com/id/5111202/), an estimated 26.2 percent of Americans ages 18 and older—about one in four adults—suffer from a diagnosable mental disorder in any given year. This amounts to almost 60 million Americans suffering from a diagnosable mental disorder in any given year! In 201 CBC television reported that, according to the Canadian Mental Health Association, more than 50 percent of the Canadian workforce are suffering from a diagnosable mental illness. In March 2013 they reported that in 5 Canadian students suffers from mental illness. An estimated 1 in 2 Americans, or almost 14 million people, is said to suffer from the new mental illness: "compulsive hoarding syndrome." In their book on criminal behavior, psychologists Curt and Anne Bartol write that "approximately half of the people in the United States will qualify for a DSM diagnosis at some point in their lifetime" (p. 210). Are these accurate numbers? Are they even reasonable estimates?

Yes, they are, given the fact that it's possible to diagnose 100 percent of the population with at least one mental illness when applying the broad diagnostic criteria listed in the *Diagnostic and Statistical Manual Mental Disorders (DSM)*, the so-called Bible of North American clinicians. The diagnosing of "mental illnesses" has become so rampant and widespread that even in cases of serious crimes, such as multiple shooting the media routinely report their automatic assumption that the perpetrator was likely suffering from some type of mental illness (Shamir p. 47 Psychologists Curt and Anne Bartol report that one study revealed that mental illness is presented as the basic motivation for crimes in the vast majority of shows on television and other entertainment media. "On prime-time American television, 73% of all individuals characterized as mentally disordered also display some violent behavior" (p. 208).

What all these shocking statistics indicate is that both ordinary individuals and clinicians in North America, and increasingly in other nations, have come to believe that so-called mental illness is an out-of-control epidemic. Health authorities are going so far as to call so-called "mental morbidity ... the twenty-first century plague" (Shamir p.45). But what these numbers actually indicate is simply that we are all the subject of out-of-control diagnosing—we're victims of "hyper-diagnosia."

Nosological categories were originally created by psychiatrists in order to raise the prestige of their field by making their methods appear to be objective, scientific, and medical. Diagnosing also helped "to guarantee reimbursement from third party health insurance companies, to allow medication to be marketed, and to protect the interests of mental health researchers and professionals" whose income depended on a steady flow of patients for treatment (Schill & Lebovici p. 77). Much of what intensive individual psychotherapy treats people for, such as "gross dissatisfaction with the course of their lives, difficulties in the areas of interpersonal relationships or work adjustment, school or work inhibitions, etc." were not at first considered formal diseases by the health care insurance providers. So to gain approval for imbursements from insurance companies many human existential difficulties were labeled as disease entities with medical sounding names (Ibid). This guaranteed that health care service providers would get paid and also have lots to do. As philosopher, existential psychotherapist, counseling psychologist, and professor Emmy van Deurzen-Smith puts it:

> The ubiquity of "pathology" and "trauma" in psychotherapeutic systems is not unlike the omnipresence of sin in religious systems. The more trauma there is, the greater the need for therapists, in the same way that "sin" guarantees the need for clergy. (p. 2)

Nosological models handicap rather than help in understanding both the distress that can emerge from the difficulties of everyday life, as well as the so-called deviant behavior that is not the result of biological brain dysfunction (Horwitz p. 109, 81, 15). Diagnosing a patient entails creating a list of subjective observations about the patient, and then applying a label to that list which the diagnostic literature deems appropriate for those observations. But labeling the patient then creates in the clinician a *biased perception* of the patient that is actually induced by the very label the clinician has just applied. The reason for this is because the label adds diagnostic criteria from the literature which were never part of the clinician's original observations. Diagnosing creates a vicious circle in which observations lead to a label, labeling adds unobserved diagnostic criteria, the unobserved diagnostic criteria induce a biased perception in the clinician, which then leads him to assume the presence in the patient of the unobserved criteria. The very act of diagnosing adds unverified assumptions about what the patient "must be" experiencing based on the diagnosis. Treatment is then justified by those self-referential assumptions. For example, Pat was diagnosed as having schizophrenia. During one of her required monthly visits, her psychiatrist said he was going to prescribe an anti-hallucinogenic drug for her to take in order to stop the voices in her head. But Pat told him that she wasn't hearing voices in her head. The psychiatrist replied, "You have schizophrenia, and schizophrenics hear voices. So I want you to take these pills." This is a true story.

Of course diagnosing in the field of medicine also creates in the mind of the physician a particular perception of the individual. The difference between the physician and the psychotherapist is the fact that the physician always treats the symptoms with the goal of a cure while psychotherapy in general has no such goal in mind. The implicit and pervasive assumption in psychotherapy is that all mental illnesses are chronic and incurable (see Amering and Schmolke). The adage in alcohol recovery programs is "once an alcoholic, always an alcoholic." This erroneous mantra has been covertly adopted by psychotherapy for both addiction recovery and recovery from so-called mental illnesses despite empirical evidence to the contrary. This topic will be revisited in chapter 11.

Newsweek health writers Barbara Kantrowitz and Pat Wingert, authors of *The Menopause Book*, write that the American Psychiatric Association first considered adding "Premenstrual Dysphoric Disorder" (PMDD) to the edition of the *DSM* published twenty years earlier, but didn't because women's health advocates protested. The women's health advocates claimed that making PMDD an official disorder would pathologize female biology and incorrectly label women as mentally ill. But Kantrowitz and Wingert point out that, as with so many other disorders, the PMDD diagnostic label might actually help to convince insurance companies to pay for treatment, which would be a good thing. And for some women, medical recognition of their premenstrual problems might also be comforting. In effect Kantrowitz and Wingert are advocating for pragmatic criteria for diagnostic labels, rather than that of medical science.

The practice of conceptualizing mental distress as disease or illness and diagnosing it as mental disorder has raised a number of serious problems in society. For one thing, the rampant diagnosing ("hyper-diagnosia") of so-called mental illness currently in vogue in the psychotherapeutic community diffuses the concept of illness, distracting research and treatment away from legitimate brain pathology. And furthermore, pathologizes and then medicalizes ordinary human experiences. According to Allan Horwitz, professor of sociology at Rutgers University this means that for the members of the board who determine which mental disorders to add or remove from the book,

> problems of ordinary life such as dealing with troublesome children and spouses, poor marriages, frustrations in careers, personal identity crises, and general unhappiness had to be reconceptualized as discrete forms of individual pathology. . . . Chronic dissatisfaction with life could be renamed "dysthymia"; the distress arising from problems with spouses or lovers could be called "major depression"; the disturbances of troublesome children could be renamed as conduct, personality, or attention deficit disorders. . . . In the absence of a valid definition of mental disorder, there is no limit to the number of discrete conditions researchers and clinicians can develop. (p. 72–74)

The four psychiatrists who edited the book of collected papers that were delivered at the 11th World Congress of Psychiatry in Hamburg, Germany in 1999 wrote in their introduction,

> That current diagnostic categories really correspond to discrete natural disease entities is appearing now more and more questionable. . . .

> Thirty years of biological research have not been able to identify a specific marker for any of the current diagnostic categories. (Maj p. ix)

In 1997 a formal dialogue between seven New York psychiatrists and nine "consumer-practitioners" criticized the medical model and the current quasi-biological diagnostic system as "disempowering and detrimental when used to the exclusion of other explanatory frameworks" (Blanch p. 69, 71).

Psychotherapists may claim that they don't subscribe to the practice of diagnosing their patients according to the criteria set out in *The Diagnostic and Statistical Manual of Mental Disorders* (*DSM*) or the *International Classification of Diseases* (*ICD*). But this raises the question, "Why are these manuals printed and sold by the thousands every year?" Total sales of the *DSM* by 1993 was US $23 million; by 2005 it had reached around US $80 million; today total sales are well over US $100 million. Doesn't this mean someone is buying them? It would be safe to assume that psychotherapists are buying them and using them to diagnose their patients. It's unlikely that they're being read for entertainment purposes only.

While some psychotherapists have assured me they don't label their patients, their former patients who come to see me tell me a very different story. Most of my clients are willing and able to tell me in detail what labels their former therapists have attached to their files. The formal diagnoses they have been given by these therapists, such as depression, anxiety, and schizophrenia, are straight out of the "official" North American diagnostic manual, the *DSM*. And included with those are often several informal diagnoses as well.

INFORMAL DIAGNOSES

Students in undergraduate psychology classes are still taught "informal" diagnostic terms such as "transference," "denial," "repression," and so on. If it's true that the field of psychotherapy has abandoned diagnosing and labeling, then why are the students of counseling and therapy still being taught this specialized professional language of clinical judgments?

Psychotherapists may claim that those who criticize the diagnostic terms used in psychotherapy are simply misinterpreting Freud. But this is a poor argument. Freud's work has been around for a long time, long enough for analysts and their publishers to furnish extremely meticulous interpretations to their readers, and for clinicians to develop a very thorough understanding of what he seemed to be talking about. Many of the criticisms of psychotherapy don't at all originate in a misinterpretation of Freud. They are accurate commentary on the endogenous confusions and contradictions at the very heart of contemporary psychotherapy itself.

Sometimes psychotherapists argue that Freudian diagnostic terminology is not to be taken literally because we should now understand these terms to be only metaphorical. But this raises the questions, "For what are these terms a metaphor? What do these metaphors represent?" And, "How are we to determine which terms are to be taken as mere metaphor and which are to be taken as literal?" It seems that when the metaphoric language is penetrated there is nothing concrete left to work with. Stefan de Schill, Vice President of the International Institute for Mental Health Research in Geneva, writes that no field accepted as science uses metaphor and analogy as profusely, nor "has such disagreement among peers about so many key words" as is found in psychoanalysis today. He goes on to say that the way the vocabulary of psychoanalysis has developed has led us to "mythology disguised as reporting" (p. 62–3).

In discussing the diagnostic terminology devised by Freud and his followers it's important to keep in mind the historical time period in which Freud was working and developing his theories: a time when men were understood to be the bread winners and the head of the household, when it was believed to be in women's essential nature (i.e., they are believed to be biologically programmed) to become mothers and housewives, and when the authority of experts was never questioned, especially when that authority was either the famous neurologist named Freud or someone trained in his method. These were some of the myths accepted as fact in Freud's day. Unfortunately much of the terminology devised by Freud persists, and is still perpetuated, today.

The problematic terminology that still permeates psychotherapy today is not only the formal diagnoses of the so-called mental illnesses, but also the informal judgments made by psychotherapists in regard to the results of their therapeutic methods. I will therefore call them informal diagnoses. These diagnoses include transference, repression, resistance, denial, negativism, projection, and suppression. Again, these are not the names of any formal mental illnesses found in the North American or international nosological manuals meant to assist in diagnosing, because they're not precisely the symptoms of any psychopathology. And yet they are an integral part of the language which psychotherapists use to describe and label what they see as problems in their patients. They are reductionist naturalistic labels which suggest that the diagnosed affliction *causes* certain types of undesirable behavior—the undesirability of which is defined by the therapist. This labeling is a case of confusing naming with explaining: it is the assumption that giving suffering or distress a clinical-sounding name "explains and offers intervention leverage" (Gambrill p. 412). But nosological labeling is never explanatory. A symptomatic diagnosis is only the labeling of an effect, and "appeals to effects are typically not explanatory. Instead, they serve to describe phenomenon that in turn require explanation and elucidation" (Bechtel and Wright p. 118).

When a person is observed or diagnosed by a psychotherapist as exhibiting one of these supposedly problematic traits the therapist has in fact misinterpreted what is going on. Take, for example, when a psychotherapist sees in his patient the symptom of so-called transference. In reality the characteristic of transference is in fact not something carried out by the patient. Instead it's a dynamic, one which is sometimes positive and sometimes negative, within the therapeutic relationship between the patient and the clinician. Most therapists would agree. But they would not agree that the problems that arise, which the therapist will label either negative or positive transference, are most often the therapist's fault. So-called transference is not something the patient is exhibiting or suffering from. It is nothing more sinister than a natural response by the patient to the therapist's behavior. That which the therapist calls "transference" is usually a response by the patient to the therapist that is understandable and totally justified by the patient's experience of the way the therapist is relating to her.

It's a teacher's job and responsibility to help the student understand what is being taught. When the student doesn't understand the teacher, the onus is, and always should be, on the teacher to try again. But what often happens when a student doesn't understand? The teacher blames the student for not paying attention, for not thinking hard enough, and even for not being smart enough. But, in fact, when a student doesn't understand what is being taught it always means the teacher is not teaching well enough, because it is the teacher's job to help the student understand according to that student's learning ability. Locating the responsibility in the student who doesn't understand what the teacher is saying is the same as locating the responsibility in the patient who doesn't understand what the therapist is saying. Lack of understanding in either the classroom or the therapist's office are very similar in that they're both the result of a problem in the *interaction* between two individuals: the teacher and student or the therapist and patient. One is trained, one is not; and more importantly, one is an authority figure, the other is not. So when the therapist claims that when his patient doesn't understand him this is due to the patient's so-called denial or resistance, the therapist is in fact displacing responsibility away from himself, and holding the patient responsible for the shortcomings of his own practice within that therapeutic relationship. The same applies to a situation in which the patient disagrees with the diagnosis of his symptoms. Typically the therapist will label this as the patient's denial rather than admit that perhaps the diagnosis is misguided.

Second, the therapist's external perspective of the therapeutic relationship can be significantly different from the internal perspective experienced by the patient, and this difference can lead the therapist to unfairly label the patient.

A patient will sometimes disagree with her therapist; at other times the patient will express a lack of understanding about why the therapist is saying what he is about her so-called mental illness. For example the patient may disagree with the therapist who says she is being difficult, or the patient may not understand why the therapist is claiming that her thinking is irrational. This disagreement or lack of understanding is then informally diagnosed by the therapist as "resistance' or "denial." But the diagnosis of either resistance or denial is an external evaluation by therapist from *outside* that two-person relationship. It is a phenomenological perspective of the patient's so-called illness by an authority figure who intentionally steps back and excludes himself from that dyadic relationship, thereby denying his own influence on what is taking place. The psychotherapist locates the problem within the patient, as part of her symptomatology, rather than acknowledging that a problem might exist within the therapeutic relationship. But it's really no surprise that a therapist might do this, because for a therapist to take an internal perspective, to look at the therapeutic relationship itself, is a dangerous undertaking, since it has the potential of illuminating the shortcomings of both the quality of his therapeutic method and the character of the therapist himself. So by taking only the external perspective the therapist is able to avoid criticism of his professional work and himself, and to attribute to the patient yet another symptom of mental illness that the therapist can then label and offer to treat.

These two aspects of psychotherapy—the therapist's desire to avoid responsibility for the defects in his practice or personality, and the therapist's refusal to shift perspective from external to internal—are crucial to an understanding of the informal psychotherapeutic diagnostic labels.

An examination of each one of the seven informal diagnoses will reveal, first of all, how they are defined and explained by psychotherapy, and then what alternative explanations are available. These definitions are adapted from *Glossary: Terms in the Field of Psychiatry and Neurology* by John F. Abess online at http://www.abess.com/glossary.html.

> *Transference:* The unconscious assignment to others of feelings and attitudes that were originally associated with important figures such as parents, siblings, etc. in one's early life. The transference relationship follows the pattern of its childhood prototype. In the patient-physician relationship, the transference may be negative and hostile or positive and affectionate.

In other words, whether the patient feels hostile or affectionate toward the psychotherapist, the therapist is trained to assume that the patient's feelings are created by something outside the therapeutic relationship and not by the therapist himself. Freud explains that a very strong unconscious idea that needs expression can enter into the preconscious and "exert an influence there only by establishing touch with a harmless idea already belonging to the preconscious, to which it transfers its intensity, and by which it allows itself to be screened" (1995 p. 475).

Now imagine this: the patient feels the therapist's professional manner as uncaring and aloof, or condescending and paternalistic. The patient therefore develops a dislike for the therapist's attitude. If the therapist notices the patient's dislike for him, the therapist then diagnoses the patient's negative feelings as "transference." The therapist avoids responsibility for the patient's negative feelings toward him by simply diagnosing those feelings as the patient's unconscious or residual childhood animosity toward her parents. If the patient says something like, "You don't seem to care about me as a person," the therapists thinks, "Aha, this patient unconsciously believes that her parents don't care about her." Therefore, no matter how cold, clinical, and uncaring the therapist is, the patient can't win because the therapist never considers himself part of the patient's problems. This is a convenient way for a therapist to avoid responsibility for his own inability to feel an empathetic response to the patient. To put it another way, the diagnosis of "transference' can be seen as a therapist's avoidance of his own incompetence.

In their 1950 essay titled "Techniques of Therapeutic Intervention" doctors Dollard and Miller confirm this perspective by explaining that "transference" is an incomplete description of a patient's reactions to the therapist. "The patient reacts to the therapist as to a concrete person—including his idiosyncratic attitudes, values, intentions, and reactions—and not only as a representative of a parental figure" (p. 73).

It is quite easy to see that a patient may become annoyed or even angry if the psychotherapist refuses to appreciate her point of view. But this annoyance or anger is not some sort of eruption of emotion from the unconscious actually meant for the patient's parents. I've had many clients who have told me that their psychotherapist simply refused to acknowledge when he was wrong, such as, for example, when he disagreed with what they were saying about the source of their feelings. When they pointed this out to their therapist he would then simply label their frustrations with him as "transference." As one client put it, "I wasn't frustrated with my parents. I was frustrated with my therapist's condescending attitude. But he didn't want to accept that."

> *Repression:* A defense mechanism, operating unconsciously, that banishes unacceptable ideas, fantasies, affects, or impulses from consciousness or that keeps out of consciousness what has never been conscious. Although not subject to voluntary recall, the repressed material may emerge in disguised form.

Freud believed that "the theory of repression is the pillar upon which the edifice of psychoanalysis rests" (1995, p. 907). He gives a concise definition of repression in neurotic patients in his essay "The Psychology of the

Dream-Processes." He explains that among the wish-impulses originating in an infant's life

> indestructible and incapable of inhibition, there are some the fulfillments of which have come to be in contradiction with the purposive ideas of our secondary thinking. The fulfillment of these wishes would no longer produce an affect of pleasure, but one of pain; *and it is just this conversion of affect that constitutes the essence of what we call "repression."* (Ibid p. 505; italics in original)

This informal diagnosis of repression first of all raises the question, "Why would a patient who is turning to a psychotherapist for help raise her defenses against the very help she is asking for?"

The diagnosis of repression is nothing more than the therapist's accusation against his patient for hiding what he believes to be "the Truth" as he sees it. One of my clients told me that after our many philosophical counseling sessions she finally came to the realization that her mother was a psychopath because of the way her mother had treated her as a child and young adult. This client explained that, if she had told her former psychotherapist this, the therapist would no doubt have said she had been repressing this realization in her unconscious. So I asked her why she thought she had not been repressing it. She responded by saying, "It was only after our examination of the way my mother related to me, that I eventually came to this conclusion. My belief that my mother was a psychopath didn't just jump out of my unconscious; it was a gradual realization, based on the information that came out of the many discussions we've had, and then the research I did on my own in trying to figure her out."

An observant psychotherapist will note that while some painful thoughts may be repressed because they are not consciously tolerable, this repression is not an unconscious avoidance of those thoughts. What is labeled as the symptom of an unconscious defense mechanism may simply be that person's acceptance that she is unable to make sense of a painful issue, and that it is therefore best removed from everyday thinking. With a therapist's help such so-called repressed thoughts can be recalled from memory, brought to active attention, and worked through with great success. This conscious act of self-defense by which an individual chooses to temporarily remove a painful event from immediate thought is a far cry from the theoretical unconscious "defense mechanism" which is said to somehow automatically banish unacceptable thoughts from consciousness.

Incidentally, research has shown that the claim made by psychoanalysts—that dreams and free association give access to the unconscious—is simply not true. There is no empirical evidence that there are any so-called repressed memories in an unconscious which continue to act on a person's conscious thinking and behavior (Erwin 2012, p. 69). In fact there is no convincing evidence that an unconscious part of the mind even exists (Schill 1999; Searle p. 151–73). For a detailed critique of the concept of an unconscious see my book *Philosophical Counselling and the Unconscious* (Raabe 2006).

> *Resistance:* One's conscious or unconscious psychological defense against bringing repressed, unconscious thoughts into conscious awareness.

Freud believed that whatever disturbed the progress of the work in psychoanalysis is a resistance (1995, p. 442). For him resistance "opposes and blocks the analytic work by causing failures of memory" (p. 907). It seems that the therapist who informally diagnoses his patient as being resistant is saying something like this, "Because my patient doesn't want to discuss what I want to discuss, this patient therefore has a problem." This diagnosis is based on a belief in the primacy of the therapist's point of view, and the inerrancy of his expertise and authority. In other words, whenever a patient expresses the feeling that a particular area of discussion isn't helpful to her, the therapist feels free to informally diagnose this as resistance. Again, this diagnosis relies on the existence of an inaccessible unconscious which is said to determine the patient's behavior. It is the claim that when the patient disagrees with the therapist's observations about her behavior or thinking, this is the patient's unconscious resisting on its own accord.

One of my clients told me how her therapist diagnosed and accused her of resistance when she refused to accept the therapist's claim that her suicidal tendencies originate from the fact that she was abused as a child. This client told me she had carefully explored the possibility of childhood sexual abuse in numerous intimate discussions with family members, and there was absolutely no basis to the therapist's theory that she had any sort of concealed memories of sexual abuse in her unconscious. But she was unable to convince her therapist of this, and the therapist continued to see her as exhibiting resistance. She said, "What can you do when your therapist says you're showing resistance? You either agree to accept your therapist's fabricated theory about your childhood, or she adds the diagnosis of resistance to your symptoms." I've always found my clients to be very open and truthful in what they offer for discussion. It therefore seems reasonable to assume that any therapist who believes her patient to be exhibiting unconscious resistance is looking for a problem in the patient which is in fact a problem in the therapist's own professional relationship with that person.

> *Denial:* A defense mechanism where certain information is not accessed by the conscious mind. Denial is related to repression, a similar defense mechanism, but denial is more pronounced or intense. Denial involves some impairment of reality. Pathological denial is irrational denial in the face of conclusive evidence.

Freud saw denial as a hysteria-type symptom, a "striving against idea which can awaken painful feelings, a striving which can be put side by side only with the flight-reflex in painful stimuli" (1995, p. 71). But imagine a patient—like the one who came to see me—who is diagnosed with "demon possession" by her psychotherapist. She disagrees with her psychotherapist who then diagnoses her as exhibiting denial. Or the patient who is told by her therapist that it is her own fault she was raped by her boyfriend. When the patient refuses to accept this blame, the therapist diagnoses her as being in denial. The key to recognizing the problem with the informal diagnosis of denial is to notice that when a therapist claims his patient is in denial he is in fact taking her denial personally. That is, the therapist sees his patient's disagreement with his theories as a denial of his competence, his professionalism, and ultimately his authority.

Notice that so-called pathological denial is defined as "irrational . . . in the face of conclusive evidence." But what does "irrational" mean? And what is "conclusive evidence"? The psychotherapeutic diagnosis of denial is not an empirical statement about a person's somatic or biological state; it is merely the therapist's subjective evaluations of his patient's disagreement with him. When a therapist considers his patient to be irrational in the face of conclusive evidence he is making two subjective judgments: first, that because his patient's perspective differs from his own, therefore his patient's perspective is the irrational one; and second, that what the therapist believes to be true should be accepted as conclusive evidence by anyone he would call rational. In other words, the therapist has set himself up to be the judge of his own judgments. How credible is this?

Some therapists and counselors do acknowledge that they are not infallible; they don't consider themselves the direct link to the "Truth" about their patients or the contents of their so-called unconscious. When there is a disagreement, this type of therapist is always willing to consider the fact that he might be wrong and the patient may be right.

> *Negativism:* Opposition or resistance, either covert or overt, to outside suggestions or advice. May be seen in schizophrenia.

Freud actually defines negativism differently from its modern usage. He equates it with irony, that is, the use of irony—which he describes as a negative statement that is opposite from its intended meaning—as a form of humor and avoidance of a painful issue raised by the therapist (1995, p. 724). But this section will discuss the modern understanding of negativism as outlined above. The issue of advice-giving is an important and controversial one in psychotherapy. Advice is something like saying, "This is what you should do." There's a certainty to advice because it is the claim that *this* is the correct thing to do. And there's an expectation, especially among psychotherapists, that when they give advice it won't be questioned or disputed by their patients. The patient who questions or disputes such advice is considered to be exhibiting negativism.

What some therapists will do instead of giving advice is to offer the patient a variety of perspectives for thought and a number of possibilities for behavior. What sets a good therapist apart from an advice-giver is that she has a fertile imagination, a very sharp mind's eye with terrific peripheral vision. This allows her to offer her patients a great variety of alternative points of view from which the patient can then choose a course of action that is in line with the patient's own values and beliefs. Rather than telling the patient, "This is what you should do," the therapist might ask, "What do you think about this approach . . . ?" Expressing a possible course of thought or action in the form of a question leaves the discussion open-ended, and allows the patient to demur, and consider other alternatives without being accused of exhibiting negativism.

A very different problem with the definition of negativism is the claim that it may be seen in schizophrenia. Freud was writing and practicing late in the nineteenth century, and therefore can't be blamed for his outdated perspective on schizophrenia. But the clinical understanding of this "condition" has not advanced much over the century since then. The diagnostic criteria employed in clinical settings today come from psychotherapeutic literature whose definitions of schizophrenia are not only inconsistent, ambiguous, and vague, but also blatantly contradictory. It is even described by some researchers as "a scientific delusion" (Boevink p. 26). The book *Cognitive Therapy of Schizophrenia* points out that the validity of the diagnosis is far from firmly established. The authors note that "Schizophrenia has been problematic in terms of causation and classification since it was first described over a century ago, initially as dementia Praecox . . . The validity of the diagnosis remains in question" (Kingdon and Turkington p. 3). According to psychologists Curt and Anne Bartol schizophrenia "continues to be extremely complex and poorly understood" (p. 211). Therefore the claim that negativism may be seen in the illness called "schizophrenia" is rather meaningless.

> *Projection:* A defense mechanism, operating unconsciously, in which what is emotionally unacceptable in the self is unconsciously rejected and attributed or projected to others.

Freud describes projection as a mechanism in which an unknown hostility in the unconscious, "of which we are ignorant and of which we do not wish to know, is projected from our inner perception into the outer world, and is thereby detached from our own person and attributed to the other" (1995, p. 823). This definition is somewhat misleading. Keep in mind that this informal diagnosis is merely what the therapist claims to be seeing in his patient; it is a diagnosis that is true by definition only. In other words, the therapist defines his patient as projecting when, for example the patient accuses the therapist of making inappropriate sexual advances toward her. He might say something like, "You're just projecing your sexual desires for me on to me, as though I were having sexual desires for you." I actually had a client who told me she had been in precisely this situation with her therapist. She provided me with convincing evidence of his unethical behavior toward her, but he avoided all responsibility simply by accusing her of projection. The problem with this non-formal diagnosis of projection is that the patient is always at a disadvantage, because it is the therapist who is in the position of authority and who has the power to "clinically" judge the situation. This allows him to protect his own self-interest no matter what the outcome of his sexual advances may be. He knows he can openly exhibit his unethical intentions toward his patient and later simply accuse her of projection. It will then be the 'sick" patient's words against the professional opinion of her therapist.

Psychotherapists are able to take advantage of their patients in many different ways. The term "projection" is one way because it is nothing but a clumsy subterfuge to put the patient on the defensive. There is no doubt that patients sometimes become defensive when they're required to examine their own beliefs and values, but this is a long way from the so-called unconscious defense mechanism in patients which psychotherapists call "projection."

Suppression: The conscious effort to control and conceal unacceptable impulses, thoughts, feelings, or acts.

I was raised in a strict fundamentalist Christian home. One of my most vivid childhood memories is that of having thoughts about religion and asking questions about God that were deemed unacceptable by church elders. But what does it mean to have unacceptable impulses, thoughts, feelings, or acts in a therapeutic or counseling relationship? Freud talks about the suppression of ideas in the unconscious to stifle ideas which could cause painful unwanted emotions to erupt (1995, p. 489). His explanation of the process of suppression is vague and admittedly incomplete, but he is convinced of its functional existence.

I have a client who has been diagnosed with schizophrenia. In discussions with him it has become clear to me, and to him as well, that his psychotherapist has made him very aware of what she considers to be his unacceptable impulses, thoughts, feelings, and acts. For example, she has clearly let him know that it's unacceptable for him to tell her that some of the many medications she requires him to take are not actually helping him; it is unacceptable for him to tell her that he doesn't have some of the symptoms of schizophrenia which the textbooks say schizophrenics have, such as auditory hallucinations and paranoia; it is unacceptable for him to ask his therapist questions about what he might do to satisfy his desire for female companionship; it is unacceptable for him to let his apartment become messy if he wants to be considered "normal"; and it is even unacceptable for him to expect to fully recover some day. This man was clearly trained by his therapist to suppress any number of impulses, thoughts, feelings, and acts she considers to be unacceptable for a person in her care whom she has professionally diagnosed as having schizophrenia. Suppression is indeed something a patient may practice in the company of a therapist. But the symptom of suppression originates not in the patient but in the therapist, and in the sort of suppressive therapeutic relationship the therapist has fostered.

Allan Horwitz is a professor in the Department of Sociology and Institute for Health, Health Care Policy, and Aging Research at Rutgers University. In his book *Creating Mental Illness* he cites a number of sociological studies that emphasize a variety of negative and uncontrollable life circumstances which are the source of the type of psychological distress that can be diagnosed as "mental illnesses." Among these causes are divorce, unemployment, physical illness, death of a close relation, combat experiences, serious criminal victimization, untimely bereavement, severe abuse as a child, poverty, poor housing, and a broken family (p. 159). Ironically other research has shown that the suffering brought on by these sort of life struggles often "causes" professionals to assume a brain disorder and make a diagnosis of mental illness (Szasz). This irony extends to the medical committees that decide which new symptom groups to include as newly "discovered" mental disorders in their nosological manuals. What "causes" symptom groups to be announced as new mental illnesses is not only a political decision—political negotiations and a committee's consensus vote "on the level we would use to choose a restaurant" (Lareau p. 223–24). It is also driven by the number of times a previously unknown "mental disorder" has been "observed" and diagnosed by practitioners in the field. And the frequency of diagnosis depends in large part on how often a newly "discovered" illness has been discussed in journals and books, and how much publicity these publications, and this new disorder, have received in both academic circles, on the Internet, and in the public media.

A good counselor or therapist avoids the judgmental, so-called objective diagnostic gaze that makes the patient into an object of inquiry, a "case," an embodiment of illness which is the practice in much of psychotherapy (Slade p. 81). She is careful not to treat her patient in such a way that the patient feels some of his impulses, thoughts, feelings, or acts are unacceptable within the counseling relationship. And such counselors and therapists avoid any concept of a symptomatic "norm" of behavior for any particular mental illness which the patient is expected to exhibit. This absence of expectation is very liberating for the patient. It allows the patient to experience or express a great variety of impulses, thoughts, feelings, and acts without having to consider herself abnormal, or suffering from a "mental illness."

All the examples presented above are factual; they are instances of psychotherapists refusing to accept the reality that they are not always right. And this comes from every therapist's desire to defend and maintain his position as the expert and authority, the one who knows the patient, and the patient's mental "illness," better than the patient knows herself. The diagnoses of transference, repression, resistance, denial, negativism, projection, and suppression are actually a transference of responsibility for problems from the therapist to the patient; they are a repression of the truth about a troublesome therapeutic relationship; they are a resistance by the therapist to acknowledge his own imperfections as a human being; they are a denial that sometimes the patient knows herself better than the therapist knows her; they are a negativism brought into therapy by the therapist's claim to inerrant authority; they are a projection by the therapist of his own deficiencies onto the person he claims to be helping; and they are a suppression—a conscious effort by the therapist—to control and conceal the fact that his patient is aware not only of the therapist's limitations but even of his blatant incompetence. In the final analysis, they are an attempt by the therapist to blame the victim.

Furthermore, these "informal" diagnoses of transference, repression, resistance, denial, negativism, projection, and suppression raise the question, "How accurate and meaningful are the many other diagnoses made by psychotherapists?" Making a diagnosis in psychotherapy is not an exact, empirical science like it is in medicine. It does not employ blood tests, x-rays, or urine samples. It is always only an observation of the "surface complexity" that lacks the depth of scientific and medical investigation into underlying structures (Thornton p. 202). In his essay "Mental Health and Its Limits," professor of philosophy and bioethics Carl Elliott writes,

> Not only are the pathological mechanisms behind most mental disorders unknown, but also most disorders are not characterized by any objective findings on physical examination, medical imaging devices, or laboratory tests. (p. 428)

The diagnosis of a so-called mental illness consists of a subjective evaluation, in essence a "reading into" the patient by the therapist, a judgment call based on what the therapist believes to be "normal," and how far he believes his patient has deviated from his society's conception of normal. Due to the structure of today's mental healthcare system, it is much easier to label a person as being "abnormal" than it is to prove that he is "normal."

With his book *The Myth of Mental Illness* Thomas Szasz may not have been the first, but he is one of the earliest, and perhaps best known, professionals in the field of mental healthcare who said that the public has been duped, that we have been manipulated into believing that mental illnesses are scientifically validated biomedical diseases when in fact they are nothing of the sort. Szasz was derided by many of his colleagues as a disgruntled psychiatrist who probably had some sort of grudge to settle. But in the last half of the twentieth century more and more practitioners have come forward to agree with Szasz and support his claim that mental illnesses are not biological illnesses, and that they do not and should not have any ontological status in the medical world because they are not caused by brain diseases or malfunctions. In fact the diagnostic criteria for so-called mental illnesses are so vague and general that their classification as discrete "entities" is simply vacuous. Mental illness can be made to magically disappear in an instant when reference to it in the nosological manuals is eliminated. This is what happened not long ago to homosexuality, masturbation, hysteria, multiple personality disorder, and other so-called mental illnesses. This magic is of course not possible when dealing with a physical illness. Furthermore, a mental illness can be made to disappear when it is discovered to be a physical or biological brain problem, such as Alzheimer's and Huntington's disease, Korsakoff's syndrome, syphilitic dementia, and epilepsy. Once a physical or biological cause has been recognized, the condition is moved to somatic medicine and is no longer classified as a mental illness (Slade 80). Mental illnesses are, as Szasz maintained, "created" or invented by the very act of diagnosing and classifying.

SOCIAL INFLUENCES

Despite the efforts of psychiatrists and psychotherapists to deny it, the diagnosing of mental illness is highly influenced by Western preconceptions, expectations, and norms. Research in psychiatry has been overwhelmingly based on the study and observation of Western white male subjects, while treatment has been universalized according to the so-called Western medical model.

There are many strange social aspects about "mental illnesses" that make them very different from physical illnesses. First, a person can stop being mentally ill "simply by moving from one society to another" (Gert and Culver p. 421). In other words, a problematic mental illness, such as anxiety, in one geographical location may not be considered a mental illness at all in a different location, so a diagnosis can be avoided simply by resettling (Ustun). Normality is largely culturally dependent and "what is deemed abnormal in one culture might be considered normal in another" (Lareau p. 216). There is no biological "gold standard" or universal measure when it comes to diagnosing so-called mental illnesses. Diagnostic criteria are affected by any number of social factors beyond culture. The *DSM* clearly states,

> Beliefs or experiences of members of religious or other cultural groups may be difficult to distinguish from delusions or hallucinations. When

such experiences are shared and accepted by a cultural group, they should not be considered evidence of psychosis. (Ibid 93)

Imagine the medical community saying something like this:

Physical symptoms may be difficult to distinguish from delusions or hallucinations. When physical symptoms are shared and accepted by a cultural group, they should not be considered evidence of an illness.

This kind of diagnostic contingency does not occur with the medic[al] diagnosing of organic diseases. The irony in all of this is that the psychotherapeutic community insists that mental illness is analogous to, an[d] often identical to, biological illness, and that treatment for mental illne[ss] ought to be carried out as medical practice.

In their chapter titled "Evaluation of Culturally Diverse Populations" authors Selma R. De Jesus-Zayas, Rudolfo Buigas, and Robert L. Denn[y] explain that "individuals raised in a culture that values 'seeing' an[d] 'communicating' with those who are deceased might not understan[d] why in another cultural context this behavior might be labeled as psychotic" (p. 248). Personality disorders, so-called eating disorders, an[d] agoraphobia are not universal. They are found mainly in Western societies. And the diagnosed symptoms of depression and anxiety are high[ly] varied from one culture to another. The recently "discovered" ment[al] illness of sexual addiction seems to be located exclusively within th[e] North American culture, while *"hwa-byung"* (a mental or emotional diorder as a result of repressed anger or stress) and "reset syndrome" (frequently cited as the cause of homicide and suicide in the media) ar[e] currently diagnosed only in Korea (Yi p. 195). The syndrome called *"she[n]-kui"* is found only in China, *"zār"* in North Africa, *"sangue dormido"* i[n] Cape Verde, *"latah"* in Malaysia, and *"dhat syndrome"* is in India. Why is [it] that medical problems of the biological brain can be universally diagnosed as abnormalities, but mental illnesses are often only "cultur[e]-bound" syndromes? Biological psychiatry defends its claim to the statu[s] of a medical science by simply ignoring cultural differences in its form[al] diagnostic criteria. It also isolates behaviors and experiences from the social context when claiming that so-called mental illnesses are brai[n] disorders (Horwitz p. 136, 108).

The splitting of psychological problems into illness categories is a social, not a scientific, endeavor (Horwitz p. 80). When common professio[n]al consent declines or a particular diagnosis becomes the target of to[o] much public opposition, that mental illness is declassified by the board of professionals which produces the classificatory and diagnostic manual. It thereby simply vanishes into thin air. Homosexuality—at one tim[e] listed as "sociopathic personality disturbance" before it became "soci[al] deviance"—was voted out of the *DSM* in 1973 by the American Psychiaric Association after political mobilization and public protests (Baye[r]. Multiple personality disorder, masturbation, anxious depression, hype[r]-

sexual disorder, and parental alienation syndrome, all at one time considered to be serious mental illnesses requiring extensive treatment, have also been voted out of the official nosological manuals. General anxiety disorder and dysthymia are currently under consideration for possible removal, while a variety of behaviors, such as hoarding, Internet use, caffeine drinking, and cross-dressing are being considered for inclusion. Their fate—the professional assessment of whether they are to be clinically diagnosed as mental illnesses—will be determined by yet another vote.

Given that the classification of mental illness is dependent on a majority vote of board members, and given that both public and political lobbying, and both pressure and "gifts" from pharmaceutical corporations, can influence inclusion or removal of a mental illness from the nosological manuals, and given that social customs influence what may and may not be described as a mental illness, it seems that the definition of mental illness is far from the medical/scientific activity it is made out to be.

Professor of Psychiatry Dan Stein points out that "there are no fixed boundaries between normal variations [in human emotions] and psychiatric disorder—rather the latter category reflects cultural and historical theories and values" (p. 53). With the recognition of the importance of cultural context and social influences in the definition and classification of mental illnesses it becomes clear that these illnesses are aspects of social movements. Societies "discover" and allow certain behaviors and experiences to be officially classified as mental illness, and then sustain and reinforce them by both professional endorsement and public consent. Interestingly patients formulate their symptoms to correspond to it in what is referred to as "doctrinal compliance"—patients alter their beliefs about themselves and their "conditions" in ways that "conform to the theoretical orientations of their psychotherapists" (Jopling p. 153). Furthermore, parents demand that their children be diagnosed as having medical problems, and be labeled with a "mental illness," in order to hide their own parenting inadequacies and failures. And clinicians seem happy to oblige, defending the so-called medical model of "mental illnesses" in support of their professions. But does the current treatment of so-called mental illnesses actually resemble the medical model of treatment for somatic or physical ailments?

TWO
Problematic Practices

Millie had been "in the system" for about twenty-five years. That is, not only her body but her very life had been medicalized and managed by the mental healthcare system for almost as long as she could remember. After attending one of my public presentations on a new way to perceive so-called mental illness—a new paradigm for its definition, diagnosis, and treatment—Millie came to see me privately. She told me she had come to realize that she was not a victim of an organic brain disorder and that she could now see that she did not have to believe the disease model of mental illness any more. It reaffirmed her previously long-abandoned belief that she was, in fact, not the victim of disease but instead suffering from what was done to her by several heartless human beings in her life. This freed her from the belief that the mental anguish she had endured for so many years was the effect of biological causes. It also freed her from the tyranny of the criteriological diagnosis that had been clinically attached to her, and from a reliance on the regime of drug therapy that had been prescribed for her. Most importantly, when she understood her suffering to be the result of the malicious and brutal treatment received at the hands of significant others she felt relieved of the burden of guilt and shame resulting from her belief that her brain was defective, and that this made her somehow deserving of her suffering. It was only after these insights that Millie found the strength to question the need for medications and the cogency of the medical model by means of which she had been defined.

THE SO-CALLED MEDICAL MODEL

In 1980, Dr. Robert Spitzer, psychiatrist at the New York State Psychiatric Institute, moved the revision of the *DSM* away from the psychoanalytic perspective of mental illness, and more in line with the biomedical, psychiatric model (Kleiner p. 34). The term "psychiatry" is often used as an umbrella term to denote both Freudian psychoanalysis and biopsychiatry. Although both Freudian psychoanalysis and biological psychiatrists are qualified medical doctors, Dan Stein, Professor and Chair of the Department of Psychiatry at the University of Cape Town, explains that psychiatry is now primarily "biological" in its approach to therapy for mental distress, confusion, and suffering (p. 5). This is why the term "biopsychiatry" is often used to denote the contemporary psychiatric paradigm. Freud's intention was to have the study of mental problems and their treatments become a legitimate medical science by adhering to scientific principles and procedures in all aspects of patient services. Modern biopsychiatry is indeed acting as though it were a branch of medicine, not only by using medical-sounding language—such as "patient," "diagnosis," "comorbidity," and "psychopathology"—but also by publicly promoting its practices as though they were in the domain of medical science. But Dr. Stephan de Schill writes that when psychiatrists and psychoanalysts "imitate and paraphrase the language of science, they can sound important without really saying anything of substance" (2000, p. 319).

Like Freud himself, biopsychiatrists are physicians whose training leads them to take a materialist and reductionist view when assessing, diagnosing, and treating their so-called mentally ill patients. But unlike Freudians, biopsychiatrists take a highly pragmatic clinical approach, believing that mental states are not only exclusively dependent on, but also caused by, physical or biological states of the material brain. Biopsychiatry is closely connected to, and often relies on, the fields within neuroscience such as neuroendocrinology, neuroimaging, and psychopharmacology. There is an understanding in biopsychiatry that psychological problems are psychopathologies, and diagnoses require an investigation of brain states, including neuroanatomy and neurophysiology. Approved and recommended treatment protocols include electrical, surgical, and/or psychopharmaceutical intervention. The subjective mental states of the patient—the personal reasons for the experience of, for example, depression or anxiety—are irrelevant in the consideration of treatment options. And yet the psychotherapeutic literature reports that "a history of sexual abuse in childhood appears to be strongly associated with risk for depression in adult life" (Bolton & Hill p. 258). Biopsychiatry concerns itself with the attempt to relieve the immediate physiological and psychological symptoms of distress, and is not at all concerned with addressing a history of sexual abuse in childhood.

A college basketball player, who suffered bouts of depression after a serious shoulder injury kept him from playing on his team, addressed the problem of stigma associated with a diagnosis of mental illness in a student newspaper. He is quoted in the article as saying that the stigma surrounding mental illness is a result of its not being regarded as a tangible and "real" sickness (UFV *Cascade* April 3, 2012, p. 10, 11). But in reality the exact opposite is true in both the psychotherapeutic and medical professions, and their literature. While it may be true that the general public often sees so-called mentally ill individuals as not having a "real" sickness, and as simply not putting enough effort into sorting out their own problems, many psychotherapists and physicians in fact hold the erroneous and harmful perspective that all mental distress and suffering is organic disease beyond the control of the suffering individual. Within the so-called medical model psychopathology is described as "the physical or chemical lesions interfering with the information processing function of biological systems" (Fulford et al., 2006, p. 120). The so-called medical model of mental illnesses defines emotional suffering and mental distress as organic conditions in which meaning or any other form of normal human functioning is absent (Bolton p. 270). Freud believed that the experience of being human would eventually be defined in the language of chemistry, physiology, and medical science, and "all our provisional ideas in psychology will presumably someday be based on an organic substructure" (Szasz 1978, p. 179–80).

Both the mainstream and social media are continually reiterating the belief, which is also widely held in clinical circles, that mental illness is virtually the same as physical illness. Take for example this statement: "The term 'mental illness' can still be stigmatizing, but it shouldn't be—at least in part because there's often no real distinction between a mental illness and a physical one." This is from the public website at http://jezebel.com/5472291/will-pms-be-in-the-dsm: The "Consensus Statement of the National Depressive and Manic-Depressive Association," coauthored by twenty prominent psychiatrists, government officials, and mental health advocates and published in *The Journal of the American Medical Association*, advances the idea that

> people who have depressive symptoms have a disease condition that, like untreated physical disorders, requires professional treatment. Untreated cases of depression, no less than untreated cancer, pneumonia, or diabetes cases, are serious public health problems that must be treated with high doses of medication. (Horwitz p. 99)

Notice the so-called mental illness of depression is compared to the biological diseases of cancer, pneumonia, and diabetes. Similarly, the host of a television program on how to overcome mental illness off-handedly described depression and anxiety as signs of "a broken brain." But in the essay titled "How it is not 'just like diabetes': mental disorders and the moral psychologist," Nomy Arpalay explains that, just like one can meaningfully distinguish computer hardware problems from software problems, one can also distinguish mental states and problems from non-mental, biomedical problems of the brain (p. 283). Unfortunately, many professionals and professional journals in the field of mental healthcare make the erroneous assumptions that mental problems are just brain problems. In an essay in a 2001 edition of the *British Journal of Psychiatry* Robert Kendell writes that the view that mental disorders are fundamentally different from other illnesses "has been abandoned by all thinking physicians." His view is that there is no more of a difference between mental and physical disorders than there is between circulatory and digestive system disorders (p. 491).

But a symptom of mental illness, or even a cluster of symptoms, is not like the symptom of a physical illness. It cannot be verified with objectively measured laboratory results. The mental consists of beliefs, values, desires, doubts, fears, assumptions and so on, and to say that mental illness is just like organic disease would be like saying that a belief is just like an organic disease, or that values, desires, doubts, fears, and assumptions are some sort of biological substances. As professor of psychology and psychotherapy Sohan Sharma puts it, "To equate mental illness with physical illness is to ascribe an observable physical condition to mental illness, which, per se, does not exist" (p. 49). In the essay titled "What's so Special About Mental Health and Disorder?" Rachel Cooper points out that disorders that are considered mental are not based on physical/medical evidence, they "have come to be so considered for a mish-mash of frequently contingent historical reasons" that include economic considerations and political pressure (p. 497).

Realist assumptions are valid in relation to the physical brain but not when it comes to propositional attitudes and propositional content, such as beliefs, values, desires, doubts, fears, and assumptions, which constitute the dynamic intentional subject matter of the mind. The biological model of mental illness that is common in Western societies, which holds that "mental illnesses are brain diseases," is a fiction that is due far more to the cultural and religious beliefs, political climate, and economic considerations, than to any empirical findings in medical science.

The five characteristics of rigorous science are as follows: clearly defined terminology, quantifiability, highly controlled experimental conditions, reproducibility, and predictability/testability. So called mental illnesses are not clearly defined, they are not discovered and evaluated by means of highly controlled experimental conditions, diagnoses of signs and symptoms are not consistent from one therapist to the next (i.e., they are not "reproducible") and nosological categories do not reflect illnesses whose course is predictable nor whose "pathogens" are testable in a lab. In other words, the invention of "mental illnesses" does not fit the criteria of a rigorous science. Stephan de Schill, Director of Research at the American Mental Health Foundation in New York, and Vice President of the International Institute for Mental Health Research in Geneva writes that psychoanalytic diagnosis seems to have failed to adhere to such time-honored yardsticks of science as precise definitions of terminology, clear correlation between theoretical concepts and observable, reliable predictions, criteria for confirmation of hypotheses, use of independent observers, statistical studies, etc. (2000, p. 318)

Along with their medical degree (MD) psychiatrists must complete an additional four years of residency training in mental health. A physician trained in the specialty of biopsychiatry can specialize even further in fields such as geriatric psychiatry, child and adolescent psychiatry, addictions, and so on. Assessment is based on observation of the patient behavior and formal testing of the patient by means of questionnaire and verbal exchange. But the biopsychiatrist is focused on discovering psychopathologies in the patient's responses rather than on the patient subjective thoughts and feelings about events in his life. Diagnosing consists of matching sign and symptom assessment outcomes with the criteria listed in clinical diagnostic and treatment manuals such as the World Health Organization's *International Classification of Diseases (ICD)* and the American Psychiatric Association's *Diagnostic and Statistical Manual of Mental Disorders (DSM)*. While early psychiatrists offered some psychotherapeutic discussion time to their patients, contemporary biopsychiatry does not make the time to offer any therapeutic discussions. It is primarily concerned with the medical approach to mental health problems, that is with diagnosing specific syndromes or nosological categories and the biological correlates in the brain. In fact psychiatry is working to remove all distinctions between mind and body, thereby eliminating the need for any discussions about life problems (Fulford et al. p. 16). A person emotional suffering and mental distress are treated by the biopsychiatrist as having entirely organic or neurological etiologies or causes (Hersch 330-36).

Since biopsychiatrists all possess medical degrees they are qualified and permitted to write prescriptions for medications as treatment for so-called mental illnesses. It is fair to say that medications are the primary treatment protocol in contemporary North American psychiatry. "A strongly biological version of the traditional medical model remains dominant" (Fulford et al. p. 18). This makes biopsychiatric therapy unique in the field of psychotherapy because the life-world of the person/patient is typically irrelevant when diagnosis and treatment are believed to be in accord with the so-called medical model. In fact, Joel Paris, Professor of Psychiatry at McGill University in Montreal, writes that "clinical psychology has come to rely almost exclusively on pharmacological treatment, to the exclusion of all other options" (p. xiii). Interestingly, Aristotle (384–322 BCE) maintained that the administering of drugs as a corrective measure to control a person's undesirable behavior is a chastisement that is similar to giving him a whipping (1214b, 30).

When the biomedical model of psychiatry is accepted as being the most efficacious treatment for mental distress, other forms of counseling and therapy are often simply dismissed as irrelevant. For example, in her essay titled "Being Ill and Getting Better: Recovery and Accounts Of Disorder" Rachel Cooper, a Senior Lecturer in Philosophy at Lancaster University, UK, writes the following:

> If after 6 weeks of antidepressant treatment my quality-of-life score increases, this could be for any number of reasons. If my score on symptom-based rating scale decreases, this might also be for a variety of reasons, but the likelihood of the improvement being a drug-induced effect is increased. (p. 233)

But Dr. Copper's assumption that it was likely drugs which produced symptomatic improvement seems unfounded for two reasons. First, quality of life and level of symptoms are interrelated, so it seems very problematic to claim that they can be accurately measured independently of each other. And second, the assumption that drugs produce a higher likelihood of symptom reduction than "a variety of reasons" begs the question. For example, is it true that talk therapy, which could be one of those "variety of reasons," is less likely to reduce symptoms? An assertion of the *likely* superior efficacy of psychotropic drugs, especially antidepressants, needs to be supported with evidence and not simply stated as a likelihood. In fact, all the major anti-depressant medications have been found to be no more effective than placebos in providing symptomatic relief (Kirsch, et al.). With all due respect to Dr. Cooper, it is these kinds of casual assertions of the efficacy of psychotropic drugs that continue to sustain the problematic biomedical model of mental healthcare as the dominant treatment paradigm.

Freudian analysis also began with a strong emphasis on the biomedical model, but as neo-Freudianism grows contemporary analysts have begun to shift their perspective and become much more tuned to the subjective elements of their patients' personal and interpersonal lives. Biopsychiatry rejects this approach and it is, unfortunately, becoming the dominant paradigm for the treatment of "mental illnesses" in North America.

In a paper titled "Doing Their Jobs: Mothering with Ritalin in a Culture of Mother-Blame" Ilina Singh, with the Centre for Family Research at the University of Cambridge, UK, argues that the medical diagnosis of ADHD is a form of absolution for mothers who attempt to forcibly raise "ideal and overachieving children." She writes that

> American mothers now increasingly turn to a pill [such as Ritalin] to improve their sons' behavior and performance. In that process they adopt a brain-blame narrative of their sons' behaviors that ostensibly absolves them of personal blame for these behaviors. (p. 1204)

It is emotionally easier to blame a malfunctioning brain than to find fault in one's own parenting skills. On the one hand, biopsychiatry tells us that depression is a symptom of a malfunctioning organ: the brain. But, on the other hand, psychiatrists also report that "the incidence of depressive disorders is very low in the absence of environmental stressors," and that in more than 75 percent of cases of depression there has been discovered "a precipitating life event" (Young et al. p. 3). This makes depression predominantly the effect of external or exogenous causes. So why, if emotional distress is mainly caused by external factors, is depression discussed as though it were an endogenous organic brain disorder? Does this question point to an epistemic confusion or a metaphysical conundrum?

After half a century of medical research, there is still an embarrassing lack of evidence in the form of disease-specific markers for any of the currently listed mental disorders in either men, women, or children. As professors of psychiatry Colin Ross and Alvin Pam put it, "Biologic psychiatry has not made a single discovery of clinical relevance in the past ten years, despite hundreds of millions of dollars of research funding" (p. 116). This is not at all surprising because the classification of mental disorders has no basis in medical science; it is based on the subjective observation and evaluation of people's behaviors, experiences, and actions. Psychiatry is the only branch of medicine in which "illnesses are primarily diagnosed and treated on the basis of the patient's self-report. There is no test which demonstrates that mental illness exists" (Slade p. 80). But a person's behaviors, experiences, and actions cannot be characterized or scrutinized independent of an understanding of the beliefs, values, assumptions, and intentions of the person that underpin them, or of the social settings in which they occur (Barham p. 87).

Psychotherapist and professor of psychology Sohan Lal Sharma sees the medical model of mental illness as creating a number of contradictions. For example, a physical illness is described as something that "happens to" the patient, while a mental illness involves the active participation of the individual because it is precipitated by that person's mind which consists of beliefs, values, fears, assumptions, and so on. And yet, according to the medical model, mental illness must be treated as if it simply "happens to" the patient. Also, if the therapist diagnoses a mental illness in his patient it requires a clear definition of the opposite—mental health—which does not exist. Furthermore, patients present emotional, interpersonal, ethical, and even spiritual issues, problems, and dilemmas to their therapists. According to the medical model these would then all have to be treated with drugs, electrocution therapy, surgery, and so on, or else simply be ignored (Sharma p. 52). This would clearly be considered malpractice by the medical establishment. In the end there is in fact no "medical model" of mental illness, nor of its treatment.

The actual medical model involves objective medical tests or biometrics—such as blood, glucose, and urine analysis—which identify distinct physiological dysfunction, invading pathogens, or other organic causes, leading to a diagnosis of signs and symptoms that is fairly consistent across most cultures, and finally to an established standard treatment protocol. With mental illness a diagnosis is given without any medical testing because there are no biometrics which will indicate mental illness. Signs and symptoms in the patient can be, and often are, variously interpreted by attending clinicians. Then a treatment protocol is followed which may be completely different not only from one culture to the next but from one psychiatrist or psychotherapist to the next.

The so-called scientific instruments used to diagnose mental illnesses mentioned in the psychiatric literature in defense of the medical model are simply questionnaires which require the therapist's subjective interpretation and evaluation of the patient's responses. This is not at all like a transparent medical test whose results offer definitive evidence that is generally agreed upon by clinicians. Clinical Psychologist Jay Ziskin compares the problematic diagnostic subjectivity and cultural variability in psychotherapy to a case of a person's leg being X-rayed, and then being diagnosed as a clean break by a physician in France and deemed perfectly normal by a physician in Germany (1995a p. 141). Some of the most difficult problems in psychotherapy arise not so much from the "facts" collected about the differential diagnosis of the patent's symptoms, the etiology or causal factors, or the treatment methodology as "from disagreements about how the facts should be understood or interpreted" (Fulford et al. p. 5). In his critique of the concept that the psychoanalyst is a "neutral scientific observer and instrument" in a textbook on psychoanalysis titled *The Challenge to Psychoanalysis and Psychotherapy*, which lists over 50 professional names among the contributors, Dr. Stephan de Schill points out that in looking at the human psyche a "neutral scientific instrument" "could not possibly present us with such vastly different results as these neutral scientific observers do." He adds that in psychotherapeutic diagnosis "we are dealing with individual observations, judgments, and misjudgments, the furthest thing from an objective instrument" (de Schill 2000, p. 364). Psychoanalytic psychotherapist Charlotte Prozan points out that in a 1986 article on autonomy and gender, Rachel Hare-Mustin and Jeanne Marecek also raised the issue of values in psychotherapy and concluded that "value-free psychotherapy is a myth and that neutrality itself is a value." Psychotherapy "may do little more than teach the client the belief and norms for behavior held by the psychotherapist and by society" (Prozan p. 318). The extensive subjectivity in mental healthcare diagnosis, prognosis, and treatment commonly leads to significant professional disagreements both in the clinic and in the literature.

In a famous experiment in the early 1970s, eight "sane" volunteers were admitted to a mental hospital where they told hospital staff they were hearing voices (see Rosenhan). Although all behaved normally while in hospital, each pseudo-patient was detained for treatment for between seven and fifty-two days. All of them were assigned a diagnosis of "schizophrenia—in remission" even after their release. The hospital staff did not recognize the difference between these normal volunteers and what schizophrenia is supposed to look like. In discussing this case in her book *Psychiatry and Philosophy of Science* Rachel Cooper, Senior Lecturer in Philosophy at the University of Lancaster, defends the hospital's professional staff by suggesting that this experiment shows nothing more than "that psychiatrists can be tricked," and adds, "but then who cannot?" (p. 13). But, given that psychiatrists are medically trained physicians, and given that mental illnesses are compared to physical ailments such as cancer, diabetes, and heart disease, it raises the question, "Can medical doctors be tricked by their patients in the same way these psychiatrists were? Can physicians be tricked into believing their patients are suffering from physical ailments such as cancer, diabetes, or heart disease?" The answer is a definite "no" because there are medical tests that can be used by physicians to determine the veracity of such claims. Psychiatrists can be tricked—and they can mistake "sane" for "insane"—because there are no objective medical tests that will verify their belief in the existence of schizophrenia or any other mental illnesses. This is why it is a mistake to assume that mental healthcare is practiced according to the medical model.

The persistence of the fallacious "medical model" of mental illness is due to at least nine main factors: (1) it is driven by the pharmaceutical corporations who profit from its continuance; (2) the pharmaceutical industry's misleading claims about the efficacy of medication as treatment; (3) the industry's misinformation to the public that conflates the abstract mind with the biological brain; (4) the industry's denials of the efficacy of talk as therapy; (5) the media's whole hearted acceptance of the pharmaceutical industry's misleading news releases, advertisements, and interviews; (6) "consumer" preference for a quick-fix pill over psychotherapy; (7) the belief held by both "consumers" and clinicians that medications are the least expensive treatment option; (8) the acquiescence of health care providers to their patient's demands for medication; and (9) the belief held by both "consumers" and clinicians that "mental illnesses" are somehow connected with a faulty genetic makeup..

The current force of the biological and medical models of mental disorders is a formidable and enduring barrier to research into their cultural, social, and emotional origins. Psychiatrists have drifted away from beneficial discussions about problematic life situations with their patients and are spending their time instead writing ever more prescriptions for powerful brain-altering medications.

THE MEDICAL MODEL:

Biological Tests
↓
Diagnosis ──────────→ infection
↓
Treatment protocol ──────→ antibiotic medications

PSYCHOTHERAPY:

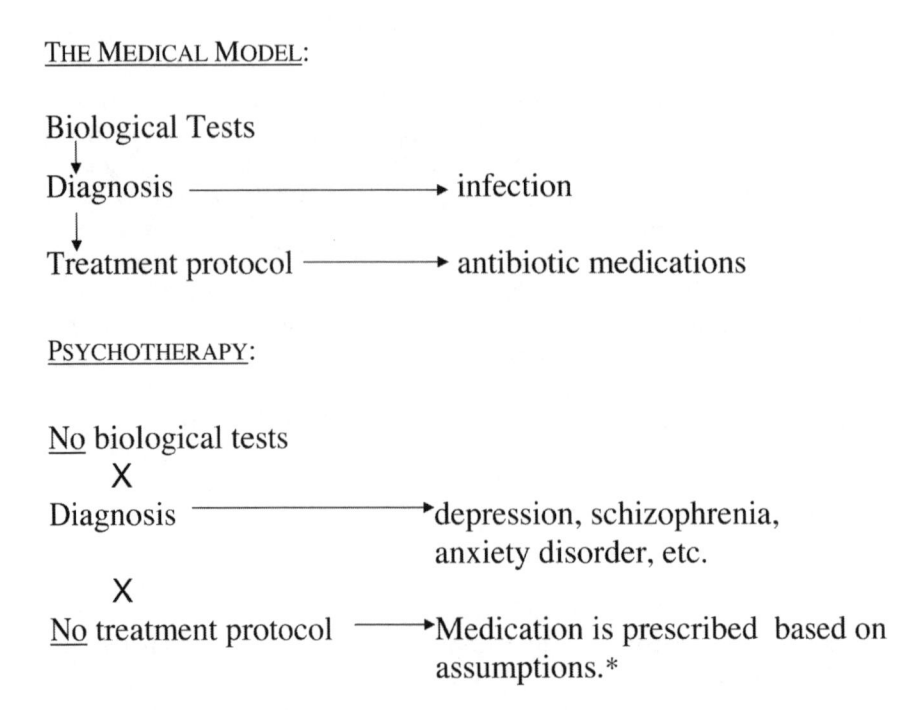

No biological tests
　　X
Diagnosis ──────────→ depression, schizophrenia,
　　　　　　　　　　　　anxiety disorder, etc.
　　X
No treatment protocol ──────→ Medication is prescribed based on
　　　　　　　　　　　　　　　assumptions.*

Figure 2.1. The Medical Model Myth in psychotherapy.

MEDICATIONS

For many of my clients who have had the personal experience of being patients within the mental healthcare system, psychotropic medications are considered "the dark side" of care for the mind. Jane phoned me to tell me that she had been admitted to the St. Paul hospital psychiatric ward. She was sent to the hospital because of serious physical problems, but they decided to put her in the psych ward because of her past history with "mental disorder." In the past the psychotropic medications she was taking caused hyperthyroidism which led to her diabetes. Recently the doctors discovered that her kidneys have finally shut down from the high doses of lithium and other medications she's been given over the years. By the time she called me she had been vomiting for two weeks, so she went to hospital because she also felt very confused. They discovered that her diabetes had gotten worse, and she also had an infection. Both of these problems, as well as dehydration from vomiting, can cause confusion. When they checked her blood they were shocked to find that her levels of psychotropic medications were significantly decreased from the usual levels in her system. This was no surprise to Jane because she had been vomiting most of her medications out. So the doctors wanted to increase her doses, but they were worried about both her diabetes and her non-functioning kidneys. She said they tried to convince her that she's not on psychotropic medications she's likely to hurt herself or others. I asked her, since the medications are currently very low in her blood due to her vomiting, does she feel like she's ready to hurt either herself or others? She said, "Not at all. In fact I've never felt mentally and emotionally better." So I asked her rhetorically what logic there is in insisting she needs more psychotropic medications—given that she feels OK and the psychotropic drugs were seriously damaging some of her internal organs? She said she feels the behavior of the doctors is absolutely contrary to both logic and common sense. She said her condition is considered chronic, and has been for some twenty-five years. Yes, she's been admitted to the psych ward when her emotions were in a shambles a number of times, but they won't accept the fact that she might actually have recovered from that ancient diagnosis of schizophrenia. She said her psychiatrist has never mentioned to her that many individuals diagnosed with schizophrenia actually recover from it, often even without any medications whatsoever (see Schrank et al. p. 133). In fact the doctor has never had a conversation with her about how she feels, or anything else other than telling her how her medications will be adjusted. The psychiatrist knows nothing about her difficult personal past of physical, emotional, and sexual abuse at the hands of family members; his focus is exclusively on her psychiatric diagnosis and the record of her psychiatric treatment. I told her I was appalled by these developments, and that she should ask her doctor about the logic of giving her more psychotropic drugs when she's feeling no ill effect from being off them, and they have been the cause of so many of her physical problems. As shocking as it may seem, the kind of treatment Jane is receiving is not unusual. In fact it's in line with the standard treatment protocol in biopsychiatry.

The problem begins with the fact that the term "mental illness" or "mental disorder" is used to denote a very wide spectrum of human conditions. On the one end are emotions and cognitions that are considered to be only mildly out of step with the accepted social norm, requiring only mild intervention. On the other end are emotions and cognitions that are disturbed by severe brain malfunctions, neuroanatomical abnormalities, diseases, and brain damage requiring extensive medical, pharmaceutical, and even surgical intervention. The problem in mental healthcare is that there is often no distinction made in cases which range over this entire spectrum. The terms "mental illness" and "mental disorder" are applied as readily to mild emotional distress as they are to serious brain trauma. What's worse is that serious pharmaceutical interventions are being utilized in cases increasingly further into the "mild" end of the spectrum.

Biological psychiatry is based almost exclusively on unsupported theories about the organic origins of mental disorder. There is an implicit bias in the mental healthcare field toward an epiphenomenal philosophy of mind which holds that physical properties of the brain cause non-physical properties of the brain (referred to as "the mind"), but not vice versa; that mental states are causally inert; and that a thought has no causal efficacy. They believe this justifies their treatment of the non-physical contents of the brain (thoughts) with physical tonics—that is, the treatment of immaterial mental states with psychotropic chemicals that operate on organic brain matter.

The fact that psychopharmaceuticals help lessen the distress of individuals who have been diagnosed with a mental illness is no proof that mental disorders are actually the result of biological causes. Dan Stein, Professor and Chair of the Department of Psychiatry at the University of Cape Town, South Africa, explains it this way:

> Although we understand a good deal about the receptors at which most psychotropics act, we understand much less about how changes at these receptors translate into further changes "downstream." . . . We do not have a complete understanding of how these changes in turn alter systems that underpin cognition and affect. . . . When a medication is effective, we cannot necessarily deduce a great deal about the mechanism involved in the relevant disorder. (p. 7, 8)

Furthermore, a psychotropic medication that flattens the feeling of anxiousness does not alter the life circumstances which caused those anxious feeling in the first place. Psychotropic medications work in general, not specific, ways. They are not at all illness-specific but work across different conditions (Horwitz p. 113). In his book *The Use and Misuse of Psychiatric Drugs*, Joel Paris, Professor of Psychiatry at McGill University in Montreal points out that psychiatrists like to believe the drugs they prescribe have "precise, scientifically-proven effects on the brain." But the fact is, while medical science understands what the drugs can do, "we do not know how they work . . . their mechanism of action is still largely a mystery" (p. 11). Anti-anxiety and other psychotropic drugs don't target any specific areas in the brain. They work in the same general way to depress the turbulence in the patient's mind as alcohol does. Paris explains that most neuroleptic drugs are "profoundly sedating" (p. 58). In fact, alcohol is a psychoactive substance, also known as a psychotropic, that has been used since antiquity (see Stein p. vii). Professor of Psychiatry Dan Stein maintains that

> currently available psychotropics almost all work by changing monoaminergic neurotransmitter systems; despite the introduction of new and useful drugs in recent decades, these continue to work on similar pathways as did the earliest agent. . . . The lack of truly innovative new interventions in psychopharmacology is worrisome to many. . . . Psychopharmacologists have warned against exaggerating what has been achieved. (p. 7)

Furthermore anti-anxiety, anti-depressives, and other psychotropics only alleviate some symptoms in some patients. At the same time, they can cause a long list of problematic side effects in all patients, such as swelling of the eyes, face, lips, tongue, throat, hands, feet, ankles, or lower legs, flat emotions, blurred vision, sensitivity to the sun, skin rashes, muscle spasms and tremors, diarrhea, insomnia, nightmares, lack of appetite, vomiting, stomach pains, anorexia, sexual dysfunction, menstrual problems, hair loss, heart arrhythmia, disrupted brain functioning, hallucinations, kidney failure, liver disease, blackouts, seizures, and at worst even death, just to name a few. Psychiatrists and medical doctors commonly prescribe a second medication to counteract the side effects of the first one they have prescribed. In their essay "An Introduction to Pharmacotherapy for Mental Disorders," John Hughes, professor of psychiatry, psychology and family practice, and Robert Pierattini, clinical assistant professor of psychology, both at the University of Vermont, explain that side effects occur because "few medications are so specific that they do not affect several biological systems." And even supposedly site-specific drugs "have diverse effects because specific neurochemical systems influence many forms of behavior" (p. 349). The effects of psychoactive medications can be compared to morphine administered for a broken bone: the morphine only offers relief from pain, and it does so for all areas of the body. It doesn't repair the broken bone, nor does it address the initial cause of the injury. Another problem is that medications are often administered as the *only* treatment, leaving the cause of the suffering unexamined and unattended. This is like claiming the morphine used to ease the pain when treating a broken leg is all that is required to treat it, without taking the next step of setting the broken bones, bracing the leg, and then helping the victim avoid the tangled branches which caused the injury.

It could be argued that psychotropic medications are indeed beneficial precisely because they relieve the patient's suffering. But this is only true to a limited extent because, while some of the initial suffering is reduced, the patient is required to endure the additional suffering caused by the psychotropic medications' many side effects mentioned above. The patient will also have to endure his or her troubling life situation, which has not been altered by the medications taken. When physicians talk about attempting to find a psychotropic drug their patients can tolerate, they don't mean a drug whose medicinal properties will act effectively on their patients. They mean a drug whose many side effects their patient are willing to endure.

Furthermore, some conditions that are common in many individuals who have been diagnosed with "mental illnesses" simply can't be improved with medications. For example, low self-esteem which is frequently diagnosed as depression often results when troubling life issues remain unresolved. But medications will not restore self-esteem because self-esteem is based on elements of the mind such as beliefs, values, a sumptions, and fears. Psychotropic medications serve a very limited role in controlling the symptoms of mental suffering, yet clinicians, drug companies, and the media have all led the public to assume incorrectly that these drugs actually address the very causes of "mental illnesses." Ultimately, treating emotional suffering and mental distress with medications aimed at the biological mechanisms of the brain is a "category mistake" (Ryle) comparable to attempting to correct a bad move in a game of chess by painting the chess piece purple. The bad move cannot be corrected by applying a material solution to the pieces because the "treatment" does not address the faulty calculations which are the non-material cause of the bad move.

The belief that great strides have been made in the effectiveness of psychotropic medications is misplaced. For example, in their essay "Psychoactive Medication and Prevention," published in 1995, psychiatrists Norman and Burrows write that pharmacotherapy for schizophrenia "has not changed a great deal in the past 30 years" (p. 645). An analysis of more than 100 follow-up studies of individuals diagnosed with schizophrenia has shown that

> the recovery rates of patients who were hospitalized after the introduction of anti-psychotics are no better than for those who were admitted around the time of the Second World War or during the first decades of the 20th century. This suggests that the course and outcome at the end of the 20th century was no better than at its beginning. Antipsychotic drugs have been used widely since 1955, but their introduction has had little effect on the longitudinal course of these conditions, nor on the rates of full recovery. (Amering and Schmolke p. 107)

A psychotropic medication, just like a quantity of scotch, will simply dull the brain of the sufferer to the point where the existential reason for the mental distress is temporarily dismissed or forgotten. Psychiatrist Joel Paris explains that most antipsychotic drugs are "profoundly sedating" (p. 57). Sedating the patient doesn't eliminate the cause of the suffering or distress. That's why going off medication, just like sobering up, returns the suffering. And just like continued use of alcohol to dull the brain can lead to alcoholism, continued use of medication to treat mental disorder can lead to a chemical dependency and addiction. And just like using alcohol can lead to harmful side effects such as cirrhosis of the liver and high blood pressure, using psychotropic medications can lead to side effects such as kidney failure and suicidal ideation. And, just like sobering up includes the suffering of a hangover, going off medications includes the suffering of withdrawal symptoms. Psychiatrists are known to warn their patients that quitting their meds "cold turkey" can have dire consequences. This is in an effort to convince their patients to continue taking them.

And worse than the fact that medications simply cause patients to forget problematic life issues, they can also cause patients to simply not care about them. This raises a completely different, and very serious matter since not caring about life problems can be diagnosed as the patient being apathetic, or in psychotherapeutic language suffering from "flat affect." The reason this is worse than forgetting is that "flat affect" can be professionally diagnosed as yet one more symptom indicative of mental illness such as depression. So treatment with medications can lead to an effect in the patient that can in turn be diagnosed as a symptom of another mental illness, or what psychiatrists call "comorbidity." This domino effect is fairly common in the pharmaceutical approach to treatment for mental suffering and distress. Research has also shown that for individuals with a favorable prognosis "medication seems to have a deleterious rather than helpful effect" in that it might actually interfere with the spontaneous recovery process (Amering and Schmolke p. 108).

During the 1980s there was strong lobbying by both parent groups, mental health support groups, and clinicians to apply various medical sounding labels to mental distress and suffering such as Depression, Bipolar Disorder, Attention Deficit Hyperactivity Disorder (ADHD), Schizophrenia, and so on. It was declared that these are endogenous, biological diseases generated within the suffering individual. This effectively cut the link that experts had previously discovered between diagnosed "mental illnesses," in both children and adults, and inferior parenting methods and other traumatic childhood experiences. When the source of mental distress was defined as endogenous there was no more need to focus on improving parenting skills or creating more child friendly social environments. While parent groups and mental health services user groups have fought hard to maintain this biomedical model of distress, advances in the research on the functioning of the brain have not led to any significant discoveries of *organic* causes of mental disorder (Fulford 2006, 252). Furthermore, psychiatrist Susan Kemker points out that in contemporary psychiatry the environmental factors contributing to so-called mental illnesses, such as schizophrenia, are relatively neglected. For example she mentions the "environmental pressure" that led to a symptomatic diagnosis of schizophrenia in a girl whose mother believed her to be the devil (p. 246). Other writers talk about biographic factors, such as physical, mental, and sexual abuse at a young age, that have led to some individuals being diagnosed as suffering from schizophrenia and other "mental illnesses" (see, for example Adeponle 120–21; Amering and Schmolke p. 62, 65, 90; Boevink p. 21; Bolton & Hill p. 258; K. Gill p. 98; Johnson et al.).

In his book *Creating Mental Illness* Allan Horowitz points out that many symptoms that are called "mental disorders" in community surveys that form the basis for implausibly high rates of mental disorders are not disorders at all but expectable results of stressful social situations.

People who are distressed because of stressful social conditions are reacting normally; they do not have mental disorders. (p. 172)

Schizophrenia is a prime example of a mental illness that is typically considered to have biological and genetic causal factors, despite the fact that research has shown there is a strong correlation between problematic family environments and the onset of suffering, which is then diagnosed as the "mental illness" of schizophrenia (see Stone p. 573–76). Schizophrenia is not at all a well-defined brain disease; instead it is an ill-defined "personal problem under the sway of the human environment" (Weiner p. 194). It has even been called "a scientific delusion" (Boevink p. 26). This raises a serious question: is it appropriate to prescribe powerful psychotropic medications which alter the brain's delicate chemical balance in order to "treat" so-called mental illnesses that are always only emotional suffering and mental distress?

HAPPINESS PILLS

The relief from mental distress that is attainable through drugs amounts to nothing more than the dulling of brain functions. What most unhappy people want is for their life situation to improve and bring happiness again. People don't want happiness to simply be a chemically produced organic brain state; they want to be happy *about* something, they want to be able to express a *reason* for their happiness; they want their happiness to be *meaningful*.

The quest for a happiness pill is as futile as the hunt for a unicorn because meaningful happiness is not an emotion that is separate from life's circumstances (Stein 2008, 45). Anti-depressants have been shown to be no more effective than placebos (Kirsch 2008); other psychoactive medications work in broad spectrums (Simon 2003, 101); they are not "illness-specific" (Horwitz 2002, 113). They interfere with brain functions just as alcohol does. This interference brings symptomatic relief, but does not resolve the cause of the person's emotional suffering and mental distress. And while the consumption of alcohol often brings a miserable hangover, psychotropic medications bring disturbing and often debilitating side effects. There is very little, if any, justification for psychiatrists and psychotherapists to prescribe psychoactive drugs to their unhappy patients in order to "stabilize" them, to facilitate the counseling or therapy process, or to bring them happiness.

The emotion called "happiness" is typically a comparative one. It consists of two related types: (a) a comparison of our situation with those of others; (b) a comparison of the current situation with its real or imagined alternative (Ben-Ze'ev 1996, 240–41). When psychotropic medication is administered it does not create the sought-after alternative. The distressing life situation persists in reality. The individual may feel better emotionally, but there is still the fact that life has not been altered the way the brain has. This can become a serious problem when the person becomes reliant on—or worse, addicted to—the medication in order to keep depressive feelings at bay. There is still the reality that it is all only a facade, since the cause of the negative feelings persists despite the fact that the feelings themselves have been temporarily suppressed with a short-term psychotropic solution. But Professor of Psychiatry, Joel Paris, points out that, unfortunately "antidepressants do not *consistently* lead to remission of depression" (p. 14; italics added). This lack of consistency has puzzled researchers and clinicians for decades, at the same time that pharmaceutical companies continued to market an increasing number of similar medications as antidepressants under various corporate labels.

Dr. Irving Kirsch and his team of British researchers in the department of psychology at the University of Hull in the UK conducted a meta-analysis of all clinical trials, published and unpublished, of four of the most commonly prescribed new generation anti-depressants, Selective Serotonin Re-uptake Inhibitors (SSRIs), submitted to the U.S. Food and Drug Administration for licensing approval, including Prozac, Effexor, Serzone, and Paxil/Seroxat. They found that, for the most part, the difference in improvement between patients taking placebos and patients taking anti-depressants is nonexistent. In other words, sugar pills are as effective in treating depression as anti-depressant medications, or to put it another way, anti-depressant medications are no more effective than sugar pills. "This means," Kirsch writes, "that depressed people can improve without chemical treatments." The February 26, 2008 press release from the University of Hull is titled "Antidepressants are ineffective for most patients, study finds." The research found that there is little reason to prescribe antidepressants to the majority of depressed patients. It was one of the most thorough investigations into the efficacy of new generation antidepressants, (SSRI) (including Prozac, Effexor, Serzone, and Paxil/Seroxat).

> The researchers obtained data on all the clinical trials submitted to the FDA for the licensing of fluoxetine, venlafaxine, nefazodone, and paroxetine. They then used meta-analytic techniques to investigate whether the initial severity of depression affected the HRSD improvement scores for the drug and placebo groups in these trials. They confirmed first that the overall effect of these new generation of antidepressants was below the recommended criteria for clinical significance. Then they showed that there was virtually no difference in the improvement scores for drug and placebo in patients with moderate depression and only a small and clinically insignificant difference among patients with very severe depression.
>
> These findings suggest that, compared with placebo, the new-generation antidepressants do not produce clinically significant improvements in depression in patients who initially have moderate or even

very severe depression, but show significant effects only in the most severely depressed patients. The findings also show that the effect for these patients seems to be due to decreased responsiveness to placebo, rather than increased responsiveness to medication.

The entire original research paper is located at the following link: http://medicine.plosjournals.org/perlserv/?request=getdocument&doi=10.1371/journal.pmed.0050045.

The fact that anti-depressants have been found to be no more effective in treating depression than placebos suggests a possible explanation for a puzzling aspect of those medications that has been perplexing physicians for some time: why the same anti-depressant pill can have very different effects on various patients, or sometimes no effect at all. It is common knowledge in medical circles that the various patients to whom a placebo is administered will report that the same placebo has had a good effect, a bad effect, and no effect at all (Stein p. 13). The same variance in the patient reports on the effects of anti-depressant medications seems to corroborate the meta-analytic findings revealed by Dr. Kirsch and his colleagues that these drugs act no differently on patients than placebos.

Still, it may be argued that while mental illnesses may not be caused by hostile organisms they are in fact produced by chemical imbalances in the brain. But professor of psychology Laurence Simon points out that the drugs used by psychiatrists and medical doctors to treat patients they have diagnosed as suffering from mental illnesses "correct no chemical imbalances in anyone's brain and cure or ameliorate no known problems in brain functioning. Rather they work in general ways affecting the mentally ill and the mentally healthy in highly similar ways" (Simon p. 101). In other words, so-called psychoactive medications do not target any specific biological causal factors because no organic pathogenic agents or chemical imbalances have been found as causing so-called mental illnesses. On the other hand, Rick Ingram, Professor of Psychology at San Diego State University, Jeanne Miranda, Associate Professor in the Department of Psychiatry at Georgetown University, and Zindel Segal, Head of the Cognitive Behavior Therapy Unit, and Associate Professor in the Department of Psychiatry and Psychology at the University of Toronto cite research which shows that "the impact of negative life events, such as loss of a loved one or loss of a job, on the onset and course of depression has been well established" (p. 41).

Unfortunately, biopsychiatry and the pharmaceutical corporations have engineered a "cognitive capture" of the common understanding of mental illness. They have advanced the technocratic medical narrative to the point where they have appropriated much of the discourse in the area of treatment modalities. In their book on recovery, psychiatrists Michaela Amering and Margit Schmolke maintain that "the overemphasis on medication in the treatment of acute symptoms has led to a neglect of the necessary psychosocial interventions and rehabilitation in community settings" (p. 108). The use of pharmaceuticals in treating mental illness is now the dominant paradigm. The drug manufacturers have disseminated the implicit threat that the treatment of mental illness without drugs can result in harm to both society and the individual sufferer. This claim has been promoted so vigorously that it has become the predominant belief among contemporary theorists, practitioners, the media, and mental healthcare services users alike. The belief that medications are essential in treating all so-called mental illnesses is now a systemic problem that has infected the thinking of mental healthcare workers and the families of those who have been diagnosed with a so-called mental illness. It has also caused those in treatment to become trapped within the medical healthcare system. Margaret Swarbrick, Assistant Clinical Professor in the Department of Psychiatric Rehabilitation at the University of Medicine and Dentistry in New Jersey, explains that "mental healthcare service users" — those who are still often called "consumers" — often avoid employment. This is, paradoxically, because they have become dependent on the expensive medications prescribed for them. The financial burden of purchasing their prescriptions makes them "not want to risk losing public benefits by becoming employed, so they avoid employment and live on subsistence-level incomes, while the medical effects of the medications increase their need for medical treatment" (p. 34). Psychotropic medications can create a vicious circle of dependency and poverty from which the patient is unlikely to escape.

IATROGENESIS AS A CAUSAL EXPLANATION (ETIOLOGY)

The news report said a man drove his truck through the wall of an elementary school and into a classroom, seriously injuring a number of children. Authorities conducting the investigation say the incident may have been caused by mental illness. Could mental illness actually have caused the driver to drive his truck through the wall of an elementary school?

Through its web site, the Royal Ottawa Healthcare Group informs visitors that depression is an illness which "causes prolonged feelings of sadness, anxiety, hopelessness, helplessness, loss of interest and motivation in previously enjoyed activities . . . low self-esteem or worthlessness" and more. The entire list can be found at the following link:
http://www.theroyal.ca/mental-health-at-the-royal/depression-and-bipolar-disorder/

Notice that they say that depression *causes* these symptoms. Nothing could be further from the truth. Depression doesn't and can't cause anything at all. It is a false causal claim. The word "depression" is a diagnostic category that always only refers to an aggregate of symptoms, never cause. Below are two diagrams to illustrate the difference between a cause and a collection of symptoms which lead to a diagnosis. The first one shows how the effect—influenza—is often mistakenly cited as being the cause of the various symptoms.

Influenza does not cause a headache, fever, and coughing. A virus causes those symptoms. The symptoms in combination are labeled "influenza" or "the flu." Medication can be given to alleviate the symptoms, the headache, fever, and coughing. But in order to heal the body when a pathogen attacks, medication must be given which fights the pathogen itself and not just the symptoms. The second illustration shows how the effect—depression—is often mistakenly cited as being the cause of the various symptoms.

Depression does not cause sadness, hopelessness, or low self-esteem. It is a misattribution to say, "She's suffering from depression." People don't suffer *from* depression. People are depressed *about* something. They suffer from various distressing life circumstances such as, for example, a wife discovering that her husband is cheating on her, and the husband then abandoning his wife leaving her to care for three young children on her own. The wife may be professionally diagnosed as "suffering *from* depression," but she is not at all suffering from depression. She is suffering from the pain of betrayal and the anguish of abandonment. Depression isn't the cause of her suffering; betrayal and abandonment are the causes of her suffering. Research has shown that criticism, aversive interchanges between married partners, and low marital satisfaction are "very strong predictors of relapse following treatment for depression." They were also found to be correlated with relapse "in a number of serious psychiatric disorders such as bipolar disorder and schizophrenia" (Half-

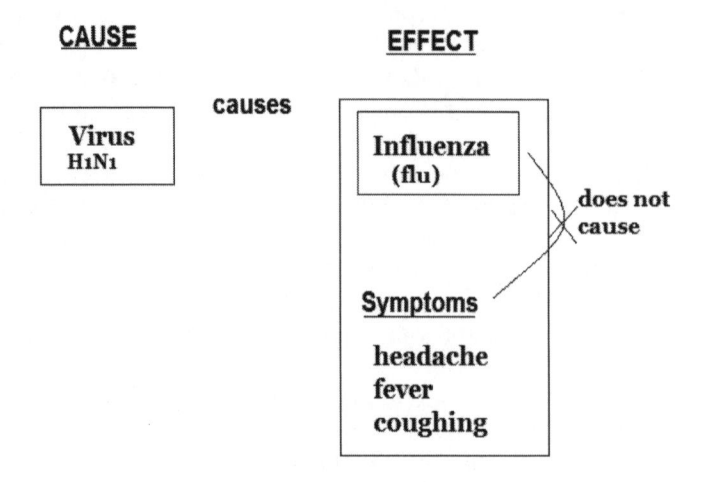

Figure 2.2. The "flu" does not cause symptoms.

```
   CAUSE                    EFFECT
              causes
   ┌────────┐          ┌──────────────────┐
   │  Life  │─────────▶│   Depression     │
   │problems│          │              ╲ does not
   └────────┘          │               ╳ cause
                       │              ╱
                       │  Symptoms   ╱
                       │
                       │  sadness
                       │  hopelessness
                       │  low self-esteem
                       └──────────────────┘
```

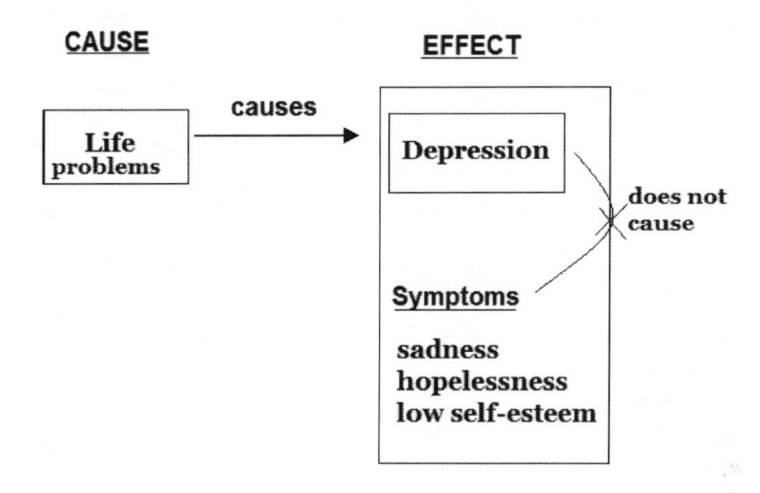

Figure 2.3. Depression does not cause symptoms.

ord p. 126). Criticism, aversive interchanges, and low marital satisfaction are the reasons behind the emotional distress. The so-called mental illnesses of depression, bipolar disorder, and schizophrenia are not the causes of the suffering. In fact marital quality "is a major risk variable for psychiatric disorder" (Ibid p. 132).

Unhappiness and distress are often labeled by psychotherapists as the "mental illness" of "depression." What the unhappiness and depression are actually *about* isn't often taken into account. When a psychotherapist uses this method to professionally diagnose the existence of a so-called "mental illness" he or she is in fact creating iatrogenic psychopathology: the very act of diagnosing invents the "existence" of an illness within the patient, which is then given a medical-sounding label.

There is a commercial on Canadian national television which tells viewers, "Depression hurts." But this is completely false. Depression doesn't cause pain, and it doesn't cause unhappiness, insomnia, lack of appetite, and so on. Depression doesn't *cause* anything at all. Depression is only the label that is applied to a number of symptoms such as persistent sadness, tearfulness, loss of interest, lack of energy, irritability, sleeplessness, and, at school, falling grades (Kosky and Goldney p. 448). To really grasp this requires a different way of thinking about mental illness from what is commonly believed. It requires a paradigm shift. And it requires a shift in language from "He's suffering from depression" to "He's depressed." This may seem like trivial word play, but the difference between believing oneself to be a victim of an attack by the "mental illness" called depression, and simply "being depressed" has enormous consequences in people's lives.

Depression *is*, in part, unhappiness; unhappiness *is not caused by* depression; it is caused by life circumstances. For example, the media reported that a young woman drove her powerful car off a steep section of a coastal highway and into the icy Pacific Ocean to her death. It was reported that the police concluded she had done so deliberately, and that a mental illness had caused her to do so. When more details of the incident emerged it was reported that she had recently been abandoned by her husband, and left to care for her newborn all by herself. Friends said she had been feeling depressed about her husband's desertion and anxious about being able to care for the newborn. So, are feeling depressed about abandonment and anxiety about the ability to care for a newborn baby, mental illnesses?

Depression and anxiety don't just strike randomly; they are always *about* something. "There is a consistent body of data implicating psychological stress in the onset of depressive episodes" (Scott and Paykel p. 516). Psychiatrist George Brown observed that clinical depression appears to be reactive rather than endogenous, and is always dependent on the person's appraisal of the occurrence of a significant event (p. 75). Authors McLoughlin, Blanes, and Darnley also cite "life events and their interpretation" as precipitating factors of anxiety (p. 563). In his essay on personality disorders, Michael H. Stone, Professor of Clinical Psychiatry at the Columbia College of Physicians and Surgeons, includes a table which correlates common parental behavior patterns with personality disorders in their offspring. For example, schizophrenia is found in individuals whose parents sent them confusing and mixed or "zany" messages; obsessive-compulsive behavior is correlated with parents who were perfectionistic, rigid, demanding, authoritarian, and overly strict; paranoia is brought on by parents who are jealous, mistrustful, cruel, and humiliating; and depression is seen as the result of parents who were hypercritical, inadequate, and neglectful (p. 574). This is in stark contrast to an essay on youth suicide in which authors Kosky and Goldney state that there are two consistent findings among suicidal youth: that they "nearly always have symptoms of depression and that they commonly experience chronic family discord and stress." They explain that chronic family discord includes

> hostile argumentative interactions between family members, to the extent that they may escalate into physical violence both between parents, with the children as witnesses, or between parents and children themselves. The discord leads to a persistent atmosphere of tension and hostility in the home environment in which the child may be unsupported or even persecuted. (p. 448)

When they go on to make treatment recommendations they discuss both the depression and the family discord as though they are two distinct stressors that contribute to youth suicides. Notice that they make the extraordinary claim that depression is a *cause* of youth suicide, rather than that depression is the *result* of the hostility, violence, and persecution experienced by the youth within a family steeped in chronic discord and stress. The depression experienced by these unfortunate youths is obviously not the cause of their suffering; it is an effect, a symptom of their dysfunctional environment. This claim—that depression, and other so-called mental illnesses, cause suffering—is pervasive in psychiatric literature.

The American Psychiatric Association's *Diagnostic and Statistical Manual of Mental Disorders (DSM)* offers a list of symptoms as the defining feature of what a particular "mental disorder" is. In effect it is saying, "These symptoms are the disorder. When you see these symptoms label them as mental illness X." This is a very important point that most professionals working within the mental healthcare system seem to be confused about: so-called mental illnesses are not causal entities; they are merely labels for a list of symptoms; they are always the *effect* of some other life events. It is the life events that are in fact the actual causes of the suffering that is then diagnosed as "mental illness."

What continues to hinder the discovery of causal factors for mental disorders is the fact that one set of symptoms can be variously identified and classified as a number of different disorders. It all depends on the clinician's interpretation of observed behavior. In fact there is continual disagreement among professionals about which symptoms ought to be listed under which mental disorder in the diagnostic manuals. This is why there are virtually no specific etiological or causal factors currently listed in professional diagnostic manuals for any of the disorders. With this level of vagueness and ambiguity in the definition of specific mental disorders, with such ontological relativism, causal claims would simply be meaningless, if not absurd.

On the one hand, biopsychiatry tells us that depression is a symptom of a malfunctioning organ: the brain. But on the other hand psychiatrists also report that "the incidence of depressive disorders is very low in the absence of environmental stressors," and that in more than 75% of cases of depression there has been discovered "a precipitating life event"(Young p. 3). For example, it has been found that 85 percent of inpatient depressives had serious instances of family trauma (Ivey et al. p.216).

The claim by some professionals and medical experts in the mental healthcare community that "we don't know what causes depression" is a misleading half-truth. A more accurate assessment is that we don't know of any *biological* causes of the so-called mental illness of depression. This is true, since none have been found. But most people, including non-professionals, can name a number of non-biological causes of depression such as a failed marriage, a death in the family, the loss of a job, low self esteem, and so on. The deliberate disregard of non-biological causes of depression is based on the forced assumption that depression must have a biological cause. It thereby perpetuates the impression that only biological explanations are valid causal explanations in the realm of so-called mental illnesses.

Practitioners often defend this mistaken claim—that the cause of depression is unknown—by maintaining that they mean the cause of "clinical" depression is unknown. The difference between "clinical" depression and ordinary depression, they say, is that the "clinical" variety is more severe and of longer duration. But how much more severe a case of depression must be, and how long depression must last before it is labeled "clinical" is a matter of subjective evaluation by clinicians. In other words, since the diagnostic criteria for "clinical" depression is very vague, ordinary depression can be labeled "clinical" whenever the clinician deems it advantageous to call it that. And conversely, clinical depression can be defined as ordinary if the clinician chooses to do so. Therefore the claim that the cause of "clinical" depression is unknown is misleading because there is no objectively measurable difference between the clinical and the ordinary.

When it comes to more severe "mental illnesses" such as schizophrenia, finding a cause is even more complicated by the fact that there is no clear definition of schizophrenia. The "illness" is completely obscured by multiple characterizations. Research for this mental illness is almost exclusively focused on finding its biological cause. But how is it even possible to find the biological cause of an illness when there are various differing accounts of its etiology, ontology, and symptomatology?

The claim that "we don't know what causes mental illness" is simply dishonest. We do in fact know what causes so-called mental illnesses: distressing life circumstances. But this knowledge is incompatible with the currently favored biomedical paradigm of "mental illness" which insists that individuals are simply suffering from eruptions of endogenous organic brain pathologies, or chemical imbalances in the brain.

Contrary to popular belief, there is no convincing laboratory evidence that any of the many diagnosed mental disorders has a clearly established biological or organic origin. In their chapter titled "Biological Vulnerabilities to the Development of Psychopathology," Robert O. Pihl, Professor of Psychology and Psychiatry at McGill University in Montreal and Amélie Nantel-Vivier, PhD candidate at the same university write that few biological findings have been specific to a single disorder, and that those that have been found "have been inconsistent and of small magnitude," and that there is "a great overlap in distributions observed between patients and controls" (p. 95).

Even those professionals who are *opposed* to the biomedical paradigm as the cause of mental disorders fall into the trap of using inaccurate causal language. For example, in his book *Creating Mental Illness*, which is actually critical of the biomedical view of mental disorder, sociology professor Allan Horwitz writes "Depression is perhaps the most widespread mental disorder and the cause of an immense amount of human suffering" (Fulford, 2006 p.96). Notice he says that depression is the *cause* of human suffering. But this is not the case at all. Depression simply *is* human suffering; the word "depression" is descriptive or definitional not causal. In effect the symptoms cause the diagnosis of depression.

The same thing is done with the word "schizophrenia." Any number of books have been written about how people *suffer from* schizophrenia and how it *causes* confused thinking, delusions, flat emotions, inappropriate laughter, rambling, unfocused speech, and so on. It is defined as a disease that strikes profoundly at one's ability to think, formulate ideas, reason, remember, or concentrate. It supposedly causes delusions, hallucinations, disorganized speech or behavior, and a whole realm of negative symptoms. Note that it says schizophrenia *strikes at* one's ability to think and so on, and it *causes* delusions and all sorts of other problems. But in fact the disruption of one's ability to think, and the experience of delusions and other negative symptoms are not *caused* by schizophrenia; they are *symptoms* labeled as schizophrenia—the symptoms lead to the diagnosis of it. Schizophrenia does not cause anything; other things, such as childhood trauma, neglect, and abuse, cause schizophrenia (see for example Boevink). The cause of schizophrenia is never explained by listing its symptoms. Social scientist Gregory Bateson has explained in detail how people don't suffer from schizophrenia; they suffer from distressingly ambiguous family circumstances. Their suffering is then labeled as an illness called schizophrenia (Bateson). To claim that the so-called mental illness of schizophrenia is caused by a chemical imbalance in the brain is a simplistic reductionist error. Research on the families of individuals diagnosed with schizophrenia shows that this disorder is clearly not endogenous to the patient. Its cause is external to the individual, and the result of a stressful familial and social situations, primarily troubling and often disturbingly ambiguous family dynamics such as when the child is told, "I love you, but you're evil, so don't touch me" (see Kingdon and Turkington). The same applies to anxiety: people don't suffer from anxiety. Anxiety doesn't *cause* fearfulness; fearfulness is diagnosed and labeled as the mental illness "anxiety." The diagnosing of mental illnesses consists of the suffering caused by life circumstances being misattributed to an internal illness. Mental distress and suffering are not causal; they are always the *effect* of some other cause. Mental illness does not cause misery; misery causes so-called "mental illness." This bears repeating: Mental illness does not cause misery; misery causes so-called "mental illness."

Brain chemistry does affect the human emotions, but human thoughts and emotions also alter the chemistry of the brain in a reciprocal relationship. Professor of Psychiatry, Joel Paris, cites research published in 2006 "that shows that changes in brain chemistry, structure, and circuitry can be the result of psychosocial influences, rather than their cause" (p. 140).

Because the brain is a material organ and part of the physical world it is seen as subject to the laws of cause and effect rather than the social frameworks of motives, actions, meanings, values, beliefs, fears, and responsibilities (Horwitz p. 5). Empirical evidence of abnormal brain structures or chemical imbalances should always be considered within the context of that individual's life. Stress, strong emotions, and the long-term ingestion of psychotropic medications to treat mental disorders have all been shown to cause alterations in both the chemistry of the brain and in the actual structures of the brain. Although many current psychology and psychiatry texts assure their readers that the predominant causes of mental disorders are structural brain abnormalities and chemical imbalances in the brain, there is simply no conclusive biomedical evidence that abnormal brain structures and altered brain chemistry are the *causes* of the human distress that is labeled "mental illness." In fact a quick search on the Internet results in many images of significantly distorted and abnormally small brains belonging to individuals who have lived completely normal lives. Diagnostic psychiatry is officially agnostic about the variety of factors that lead people to develop mental disorders. The medicalized system of classification it uses largely ignores life stressors in favor of the unsupported assumption that there are underlying organic pathologies of the brain (Horwitz p. 3).

In the chapter on psychological disorders in a university-level psychology textbook the authors list a number of factors that possibly contribute to a *fictional* character's panic attacks. They suggest that this psychopathology may have an organic cause and they list the following as possible causes: a brain tumor, endocrine dysfunction, genetic tendency, and neurotransmitter imbalance (Bernstein et al. p. 560). Notice that two of these possible organic causes—brain tumor and endocrine dysfunction—can be discovered by means of readily available medical tests, while the other two—genetic tendency and neurotransmitter imbalance—cannot. These last two possible "causes" are merely theoretical speculations, but they have gained enormous currency in the field of mental healthcare. As the authors of the *Oxford Textbook of Philosophy and Psychiatry* put it, "For all the advances in brain sciences since 1969, biochemically based causal theories remain [merely] promissory" (Fulford et al. 2006, p. 252). The neurobiological medical model of the cause of mental illness, although completely theoretical, is now the predominant justification for the employment of psychoactive medications as treatment, not for brain disorders but for problems in the beliefs, values, assumptions, and so on which constitute the mind.

Those who support the biological model of treatment argue that they don't need to know the cause or nature of a mental illness if the treatment works. This raises the question, if the cause is not known how is the best pharmaceutical treatment determined? Consider the true story of the man who, while vacationing with his wife in a tropical country, developed a painful wound on his foot. He was treated with medications for fire ant bites and released from hospital, but his condition rapidly deteriorated. Various other treatments were tried but didn't help because the cause of the lesion was still thought to be fire ants. The man's condition was becoming life-threatening. Finally one of the doctors noticed that the swelling on his foot contained puncture marks which he recognized as those made by the teeth of a venomous local snake. Anti-venom serum was quickly located and administered, and the man's condition improved immediately. Knowing the cause of the lesion in this case was critical in determining the correct treatment. But drug treatments for so-called mental illnesses is not based on a knowledge of the causes of any of the so-called mental illnesses; it is determined largely by trial and error on the patient. Obviously this offers little comfort to those who have been treated in error.

The three main projects in the psychiatric diagnostic manuals are the description of mental states and behaviors regarded as symptoms, classificatory grouping of those symptoms into syndromes, and the diagnosis of mental disorder according to those syndromes. Note the difference between diagnostic manuals in the mental healthcare field as compared to those in the field of somatic medicine: there is no attempt in the diagnostic manuals referred to by mental healthcare practitioners to list clinically observable signs of mental illness, nor do they specify a cause for any of the syndromes listed (Bolton, 2003 p. 34). Furthermore, there is no attempt to portray mental disorder in a naturalistic framework. But while this is true on the formal level of sanctioned diagnostic manuals, the specialty literature of psychotherapy, psychoanalysis, psychology, and counseling is replete with naturalistic causal claims. It is currently fashionable to assume biological causal factors for all so-called mental illnesses.

Both the professional and social media are in part responsible for promoting the belief that mental illnesses are endogenous brain diseases and/or present from birth. They present tales about troubled young people who have committed crimes that "must have been caused" by mental illness, and then argue that the parents are normal individuals, nice neighbors, and good to their children. This promotes the idea that mental illness must be endogenous to the child, it must have sprung up as if by magic, rather than having been created by bad parenting and/or other external stressors.

The host of a television morning talk show told her audience, "Youth violence is caused by poverty, unemployment, lack of housing, poor education, lack of family support, and mental illness." Notice she said that mental illness is one of the *causes* of youth violence. The truth is the exact opposite: violence against youths is in fact one of the causes of so-called mental illnesses such as depression and anxiety. All those other things - poverty, unemployment, lack of housing, poor education, and lack of family support—can cause serious emotional distress that can lead to a symptomatic diagnosis of mental illness. Mental illness is not a cause, it is an effect or result of other causes. For example, in their book on criminal behavior, psychologists Curt and Anne Bartol point out that "offenders as a group are not mentally disordered, although some become so as a result of the prison experience" (p. xxi). Mental illness does not cause individuals to commit crimes, but incarceration for crimes committed can be the cause of mental illnesses. When a girl believes she is too fat and starves herself this is not caused by anorexia. The girl's beliefs and actions are labeled with the term "anorexia." The young person who is suffering from a so-called mental illness is not the incubator and carrier of some pathogen; he or she is a victim of life's circumstances. This is not a new or radical perspective. See for example the 2002 essay "Toward a Feminist Ecological Theory of Human Nature" by Mary Ballou, Atsushi Matsumoto, and Michael Wagner (p. 103).

CAUSATION AND FREE WILL

On December 9, 2010 there was a newspaper story out of Halifax, Nova Scotia, Canada about a medical examiner who claimed that a mental illness he labeled "excited delirium" actually *caused* a twenty-year-old man's death while in the custody of police. A sensible judge later overruled this professional's diagnosis, pointing out that the man's death was much more likely due to the brutality of the three police officers who had beaten him senseless during his arrest. This is just one more unfortunate incident that brings to public attention the fact that at the beginning of the twenty-first century almost any human suffering can be diagnosed as a mental illness, and any human behavior can be excused by some mental health professional as the result of a so-called mental illness.

Recall the middle-aged Canadian man in the first chapter who strangled and shot all six of his children, set the house on fire, then forced his young wife to watch the house burn to the ground with their children in it. The battle between two highly respected experts, as the newspaper called it, both of whom are among the province's top forensic psychiatrists, is illustrative of the current state of disagreement, confusion, and ambiguity surrounding the issues of mental illness and causality in the field of psychiatry and the broader domain of psychotherapy. This particular case raised a number of important questions: Is there such a thing as a mental illness which can "cause" a person to behave in a certain way, especially in a very evil way? Is our behavior causally determined; or to put it another way, are we determined to act in a specific way by our biology, our genes, our neurons, and so on? And can a biological organ—the brain—cause irresistible thoughts and unavoidable behavior? To begin to answer these questions it is important to first recognize the two very different meanings associated with the word "cause" in psychology.

The symptoms of somatic illnesses are caused by organic factors such as, for example, fever due to an invasion of the body by foreign organisms such as viruses, bacteria, and parasites, self-induced illness such as liver disease from alcoholism, or an illness from an inherent malfunction such as kidney failure, heart arrhythmia, or glandular irregularities. But can we call mental distress or confusion, for which there is no physical cause, an "illness"? Psychotherapist and professor of psychology, Dr. Barbara Held writes that theories of problem causation in individuals diagnosed with "mental illness" include biological factors (e.g., neurotransmitter imbalances), unconscious intrapsychic factors (e.g., unconscious mental conflicts), conscious intrapsychic factors (e.g., irrational thoughts), current interpersonal factors (e.g., problematic peer or family relationships), past experiences (e.g., abuse or neglect), and sociopolitical factors (e.g., poverty, unemployment, or discrimination) (p. 59). Notice Held says that psychotherapy sees "mental illness" as caused by *either* biological factors or non-biological factors. But if an individual's suffering is due to a biological factor how can it be called a *mental* illness? Doesn't a biological factor make such suffering a biological or physical illness? North American psychotherapists routinely confuse physical malfunctions in the biological brain (neurotransmitter imbalances) with mental and emotional suffering (value conflicts, irrational thoughts, problematic peer or family relationships, abuse or neglect, poverty, unemployment, or discrimination). In other words, psychotherapists seem to ignore the difference between the biological depression, such as brought on by hypoglycemia (low blood-sugar levels), and the depression brought on by a death in the family. This is why professionals are unable to come to an agreement as to whether an act of multiple child murder was the result of a biological cause, that is a neurological malfunction in the brain, or the result of the angry and violent thoughts in the mind of the perpetrator.

When the word "illness" is used in somatic medicine it means a biological or physiological disorder. But when the word "illness" is used in the mental health field it refers to something completely different. This difference has enormous implications in regard to what is assumed about the functioning of human beings, and the treatment of individuals who suffer from one or the other kind of these "illnesses." The issue at hand, which is the cause of so much confusion in psychotherapy, is the substantive difference between a material cause-and-effect relationship in the neurological functioning and malfunctioning of the biological brain, and the non-material mental process of human thought and decision-making. Material cause-and-effect is the law-like functioning of the entire human organism including the brain, and is therefore very predictable from the perspective of biological reductionism. The material malfunctioning of the brain, such as in the case of Alzheimer's disease or Tourette syndrome (which were both considered to be mental illnesses at one time), can indeed be called a biological or medical illness. Human thought and decision-making, on the other hand, are not at all caused by the material functioning of the brain. Thought and decision-making are primarily indirectly influenced by reasons which have no material existence. Reasons are also often called causes, but they are not *material* causes. And while thoughts and reasons are contained in the brain (as opposed to the liver) this does not mean they are made of the same organic matter as the brain. Thoughts and decisions are the result of personal experiences, values, beliefs, fears, and so on, and are not simply the effect of neuronal brain activity. The development of a person's thinking is therefore rarely as easy to predict as his somatic development. Clearly, a person's problematic reasoning cannot be equated with an illness of the material brain — it would be like confusing the content with the container. Consciousness and awareness doesn't lend itself to impersonal biomedical, neurological, or brain-science descriptions (Graham p. 78). "Lesions and imaging studies cannot reduce selves to brain circuits" (Stein p. 64). Yet this is exactly what scores of clinicians and theoreticians in the mental health field have been attempting to do for the past century.

In biological reductionism the relationship between the cause and the effect (the pathogenic agent and the symptoms) of a physical illness is in most cases fairly obvious to the trained medical diagnostician. In the 1950s the American psychologist B. F. Skinner developed the theory that individual human behavior could be explained in a similar manner, without reference to the thinking behind the behavior, as a simple material cause-and-effect relationship. His "behaviorism," as it came to be called, attempted to define a "technology of behavior" which viewed human beings as sophisticated mechanisms determined to act as they do by both internal and external "antecedent physical events" (p. 22, 121). But this sort of deterministic description of human motivation results in an infinite regress. For example, a man's violent behavior could be said to be caused by the behavioral conditioning with which his parents raised him, which in turn was caused by the way their parents conditioned or raised them, which was caused by the way the grandparents conditioned or raised them, and so on back into infinity. In Skinner's behaviorism the cause of a particular effect or behavior may be due to the behavioral conditioning carried out in the distant past and passed down through the generations, leaving the behavior of the individual in the present empty of all personal meaning and significance.

Furthermore behaviorism sees reacting to stimulus as eliminating the need for any talk of reasoning; the programmed functioning of the organic brain is seen as superseding a thinking or propositional mind. While reductionism supports the deterministic model of material cause-and-effect it seems grossly out of place to use material determinism to explain the reasons for human behavior which is almost always based on personal meaning and significance. The same can be said of mental illness: it seems grossly inaccurate to use material determinism as an explanation for both the cause of human mental suffering and the behavior that results. In fact research during the past forty years has not found any biological causes for any of the many diagnostic categories of clinical mental illness (Maj p. ix).

Some philosophers consider the issue of free will to be the last unresolved problem in philosophy. The mention of free will brings philosophers to question the ontological status of the mind: is it a material thing? And talk of the mind raises the issue of the ontological status of intentions: are intentions materially determined states? The answer to both these questions seems fairly obvious: the brain is a material thing but what we call the mind is the interaction of personal experiences, values, beliefs, fears, opinions, and so on. The ideas in the mind have behavioral potency. Their meanings and significances are often so strong that they can override instinctive survival urges. For example, a person will go on a hunger strike with the intention to correct an injustice in the world. This self-sacrifice is not merely the behavioral effect of a material cause; it is a human action that is charged with meaning and significance to that individual and to other observers. Meaningful intentions are therefore no more materially determined than experiences, values, beliefs, fears, and opinions are. The reliable predictability found in material cause-and-effect relationships is clearly lacking in the meaningful psychological events that take place in the mind. We are able to predict chemical reactions far better than we can predict the course of human thoughts and behavior because chemical reactions are determined by physical cause-and-effect mechanisms, while human thoughts and behavior are motivated by reason and meaning.

The events of everyday life and interactions with significant others, such as family, friends, and society, all influence the will of the individual person and the sort of moral judgments he or she will make. But the effects of everyday life events are not the same as material causes. Of course, the thoughts a person has are not always freely chosen. Much of what a person has to deal with on a day to day basis is concerned with external, and sometimes unwelcome, factors that intrude themselves into routine thinking, such as unexpected life decisions, inter-personal relationship changes, natural events, and so on. Human beings are never in complete control of everything they think about because they cannot control everything that happens in life. Much of what happens is a function of what is commonly referred to as "luck." But people are not simply the products of luck, or their environment, or their biology. Everyone has a significant effect on the shaping of their own life by means of the decisions they make about themselves and their behavior. For example, the decision an individual makes to improve himself—perhaps after he has suffered long enough with alcoholism or drug abuse—doesn't have to be defined as being determined or "caused" by anything other than his awareness of his own pain. His decision is not materially caused; it is a decision arising from his thoughts and feelings. This is a description of this individual acting from free will.

The so-called causality found in human interactions is never directly causal at all but only influential. In other words, family, friends, and society can influence a person's thinking and behavior, but influence is not the same as a physical cause-and-effect mechanism. British existential psychotherapist Emmy van Deurzen-Smith writes,

> Every move we make, everything we decide, is more plausibly regarded as the outcome of a multitude of influences, which include elements of past, present and future expectations. There are determining factors of class and country and culture and intelligence. There are hormonal factors and genetic factors and characterological factors. There are situational, contextual and interpersonal elements to every move forward. None of these factors alone determine what will happen. (p. 96)

There is in each human being a huge gap between a meaningful thought and an action that must be bridged by a decision to either act or not to act that must also be freely made. What psychotherapy has done by claiming that a person is not responsible for a crime due to mental illness is confuse material causality with human behavior that is the result of choices and decisions. It is the claim that mental illness is both materially caused and the material cause behind behavior, leaving the criminal physically unable to think or behave differently. This reduces the human being down to the level of a machine; it removes both personal meaning and significance as well as moral responsibility from human actions; and it amounts to psychotherapy being an accessory to crime, in that it offers an avenue of escape for the criminal from responsibility for his own decisions and behavior.

In the case of the man who killed his six children, if biological reductionism and his claim of biological mental illness is accepted then it would have to be the case that he did not see any meaning or significance in his actions. This was not at all the case because the letter he wrote to his wife, and the fact that he surrendered to the police shows that he understood what he had done and why he had done it. Furthermore, "mental illness" would leave him no more responsible for the murders than he would be responsible for having a brain disease such as Alzheimer's disease or Tourette syndrome. But, as noted above, behavior is never directly caused by thoughts or emotions. In other words, the thought of murdering someone does not automatically lead to the act of murder; that would be material determinism. Determinism only exists in the interaction of material substances. Human motivation is not a material substance and is therefore not governed by the cause-and-effect law of material determinism. There is always a meaningful decision which has personal significance that must come between the thought and the action. And that decision eliminates material determinism and makes every human behavior, including that of murder, an act of free will.

The man who killed his six children also argued that he was very upset with his wife, he was feeling depressed, and this is what had caused him to do what he did. But for him to say that he was *caused* to do what he did simply because he was *influenced* by a number of different factors is an erroneous claim of material causality in his motivation. It is like saying if you ask for advice, receive three pieces of advice, and then choose to act on the second piece of advice, you haven't acted from free will because that piece of advice "caused" your decision. Both defenses used by the man who killed his children—that his mental illness caused him to kill, and that the influences of his wife caused him to kill—are invalid causal claims. Dr. Laurence Simon puts it this way:

> Thinking, decision-making, and behavior based on influences are not reducible to or describable in biological cause-and-effect terms. Unfortunately, from the early days of Freud, psychoanalysts and psychotherapists have been doing just that: claiming that the psychological activity of human reasoning is reducible to the neurochemical functioning of the biological brain. The claim is made repeatedly that confusion and distress is always symptomatic of a pathological brain. It is a mystery why this claim has survived in the mental health care profession for so long. In fact medical science has recently even refuted the claim that a "normal" biological brain is necessary for normal thinking. It has coincidentally discovered that there are a number of individuals in the world living very normal lives with only partial brains. (p.176)

Where does this leave the man who killed his six children? Clearly he was upset about a number of things: that his wife had left him, that he could not convince her to come back to him, and so on. But these life events, while they had an *influence* on his thinking, did not affect his brain to the extent that they *caused* his behavior beyond his control. His behavior was not the *unavoidable* effect of a preceding cause as it would have been if life were in fact simply a cause-and-effect mechanism, or if he had been suffering from a biological illness. His decision to kill his children not only makes him materially responsible for their deaths (we can point and say, "He is the person who did it."), it also makes him morally responsible because his decision was not caused by any pathogenic biological agent in his brain. In a physically healthy human being, decision-making always has inherent in it an element of psychological freedom because human action is always personally meaningful and significant to that individual. The problem was that this man mistakenly believed murdering his six children to be his best option in both altering the events in his life and in making a meaningful and significant state ment to his estranged wife. Stated more simply, while he knew murder is wrong, he felt that in his case it was worth it. Philosophers understand that, while human beings are not biologically determined by their brains to act directly according to their thoughts, thinking does have behavioral potency.

After a number of student suicides in a fourteen-month period, Queen's University in Ontario established a commission on mental health to find out why those students might have resorted to such drastic measures. The September 5, 2012 issue of Maclean's Magazine reported

> a range of reasons students are grappling with mental health problems: everything from the stress of moving away from home, to academic demands, social pressures, parents" expectations, and looming recognition of the tough job market awaiting them.

Notice that this list consists of exogenous "reasons" not endogenous "causes" for the students' mental health problems. And yet both clinicians and theorists continue to defend the medical model with its focus on biological causality. Most recently they have employed a new strategy: blaming genetics.

GENETICS

Recently there was much excitement about the use of genetics in causal explanations. Genetics was seen as a vindication of the medical model. The specificity of genetic claims was believed to be the "missing link" that would finalize the universal adoption of biological causal claims for mental disorders (see Ingram et al., also Hankin and Abela). But a careful study of genetics over the past 20 years has revealed that genes are never a simple causal factor. Allan Horwitz explains it way:

> In contrast to straightforward genetic diseases, the genetics of psychiatric disorders are very complicated. They probably stem from several genes, . . . they may be expressed through many different symptoms, they overlap significantly with other disorders, and they are profoundly affected by environmental forces. In addition, the symptoms relatives display are often different from those of the focal individual. (p. 140)

Notice the author uses the words "the genetics of psychiatric disorders," and says that they probably "stem from several genes," clearly indicating that the term "psychiatric disorders" is meant to refer to biological conditions. First of all, this begs the question, are so-called psychiatric disorders organic diseases or are they mental disorders? Second, if the latter then are we to assume problems in beliefs, values, assumptions, and fears are genetically inherited? It is extremely doubtful that any genetic scientist would maintain that beliefs, values, assumptions, and fears are genetically inherited. And third, if mental disorders were indeed genetically inherited then why is it that the so-called mental disorders of depression and anxiety are highly variable across cultures even where genes have crossed national boundaries?

University textbooks still perpetuate the unverifiable probabilist Freudian notion that every individual carries within them the potential for any of the many psychiatric conditions. Today their authors add genetics to this claim, and write about "genetic contributions to such conditions as obsessive compulsive disorder, schizophrenia, depression, and anxiety" as though this were a fact, without any empirical evidence (Da p. 142). But claims of so-called genetic weakness as a causal factor have actually been scientifically disproved as completely unsubstantiated. For example, a meta-analysis of research data has shown that there is no laboratory evidence that the serotonin transporter genotype has anything to do with a genetic weakness that increases the risk of depression in either men or women (Risch et al.). In fact, after some 80 years of medical research not one gene has been shown to be causally related, or even correlated, with any of the many diagnosed mental illnesses (Maj Preface). Rachel Cooper, Senior Lecturer in Philosophy at Lancaster University, UK, and author of the essay "What's So Special About Mental Health and Disorder?" writes that evolutionary psychologists have been struck by the fact that, while many mental disorders appear to have a genetic basis, they "occur at rates that are too high to merely be the result of random [genetic] mutations." She offers for examples the so-called mental illnesses of manic depression, sociopathy, obsessive-compulsivity, anxiety, drug abuse, and some personality disorders as being too widespread to be attributable to the functions of gene replication (Downes and Machcry p. 489).

Even the well-known twin studies that are still presented in both academic texts and in the popular media to illustrate how genetic transference operates, especially in the case of schizophrenia, have been shown to be completely unreliable because of various methodological flaws that corrupted the data (Ingram et al. p. 36). Twin studies, for example, are in reality "far from the ideal portrayed in the scientific literature" due to a number of factors such as the lack of representativeness of twins compared to non-twins, the age of mothers at the birth of their twins compared to those of non-twins, and the birth weight of each twin (Horwit p. 138–39). Twin studies also contain various ambiguous, and sometimes very problematic, definitions of terms such as "reared apart," "same environment," and even "schizophrenia." They have also contained biases in patient selection, and in the way that interviews were conducted. Results have been overstated, and have contained a confusion between correlation and causal claims (Ross and Pam p. 242). Contemporary twin studies fail to be compelling premises in the genetic argument for the cause of so-called mental illness.

Psychiatrists David Kingdon and Douglas Turkington write that 89 percent of people diagnosed as having schizophrenia have parents who don't have it, 81 percent have no affected first-degree relative, and 63 percent will have no family history of any kind for schizophrenia. In fact "many individuals with schizophrenia appear to have no obvious biological or genetic predisposition" to this so-called disease. Since only just over a third of genetically identical siblings develop schizophrenia, "there must also be an important environmental component to etiology" (p. 5, 6). In their book *Genetics of Mental Disorders*, Associate Professor of Psychology in the Harvard Department of Psychiatry Stephen Faraone and his colleagues corroborate this information, but increase the ratio. They write that the studies of monozygotic or identical twins show that nearly half of all individuals who have a schizophrenic co-twin do not become schizophrenic themselves. They argue that this must be because "some environmental feature must have triggered schizophrenia in the ill co-twin." Twins are no more likely to develop so-called mental illnesses such as schizophrenia, manic-depressive disorder, or reactive psychosis than the general public (p. 30, 38). They go on to point out that "twin studies provide the most solid evidence for what clinicians have known for years: the environment plays a substantial role in causing most types of mental illness." And they refer to studies which have shown that twins are neither more nor less likely to develop schizophrenia, manic-depressive disorder, or reactive psychosis than people from the general population (p. 33, 38). Psychiatrists Bolton and Hill point out that "a considerable body of research has demonstrated the effects of childhood experiences on adult psychiatric functioning," that a risk for depression in adult life appears to be strongly associated with a history of sexual abuse in childhood, and that "genetic influences do not account for this association" (p. 258, 273).

But what exactly is this new causal hypothesis of "genetic vulnerability" all about? Does it make sense to say that if Chris has the sort of gentle and empathetic personality that leads her to tears during the sad scenes in a movie, she must have a genetic vulnerability to depression? Depression is described as, in part, the emotion of sadness. And since depression is simply another word for emotional reactions such as sadness, it sounds absurd to claim that the person who feels sad must have a genetic predisposition to the development of an internally generated or endogenous disorder of the brain—that is, the mental illness called depression.

The claim that any mental illness is in part due to a genetic vulnerability or predisposition is not a scientific causal claim. It's a retrospective claim that has no predictive power. It relies on the subjective symptomatic diagnosis of a so-called mental illness to justify the retrospective conjecture of a likely genetic weakness. It is a clear example of the *post hoc* fallacy since only *after* a mental illness such as depression is diagnosed as existing in a patient is it concluded by the clinician that there is probably some sort of a genetic vulnerability present in that patient. This conclusion is not based on any empirical genetic evidence, it is merely an assumption supported by the symptomatic diagnosis. A psychological state is offered as evidence of a pre-existing biological weakness. Amazingly, professionals in various fields such as psychiatry, medicine, and even philosophy now routinely write that an emotion such as ordinary depression is probably endogenously produced by faulty genes despite the complete absence of any corroborating biological evidence other than that it seems to run in families (Radden p. 417). But this claim—that depression has some basis in the individual's genetic makeup because depression often runs in families—makes no more sense than the claim that child abuse has some basis in genetics because child abuse often runs in families, or that there is a "God" gene because belief in God also often runs in families.

Notice that when you ask, "What caused Jorg's depression?" the answer is, "It was his genetic vulnerability or predisposition to depression." How do we know Jorg has a genetic vulnerability or predisposition to depression? Because he has been diagnosed as being depressed. A perfectly vicious logic circle: his genetic predisposition caused his depression and his depression is proof of his genetic predisposition. Where is the empirical medical evidence to back up these assertions and break the fallacious circle? There isn't any. After some 80 years of research scientists have failed to find any genetic evidence of mental illness in part because they're simply not able to clearly separate genetic from environmental influences (Horwitz p.138). And they never will because the elements of so-called mental illnesses are not organic substances that can be separated in a centrifuge and studied in a Petri dish. Since the mind consists of beliefs, values, fears, and assumptions, mental illnesses are no more genetically heritable than are beliefs and assumptions about the value of the Mona Lisa.

The terms "genetic vulnerability" and "genetic predisposition" are used as a magical explanation to cover a host of paradoxical issues surrounding the highly problematic biological model of "mental illness." While this allows the diagnosed condition to remain within the realm of scientific taxonomy, it also, and more importantly, places its origin firmly within the individual sufferer. But genetics fails to explain some very important social factors which have been found to cause the onset of so-called mental illnesses. For example research data show that "when unemployment goes up, so do psychiatric hospital admissions and suicide rates" (McLoughlin et al. p. 559).

When examining cases where genetic vulnerability has been used as an explanatory device, it quickly becomes obvious that what the person with the so-called genetic vulnerability is in fact suffering from is a level of sensitivity which is unfortunately ill-suited for the familial or communal environment in which that person is situated. None of us choose the families we're born into. Some children are forced to deal with negligent, abusive, or incompetent parents, even when their parents have the best intentions. Some of these children are fortunate to be so strong and resilient that they are able to survive well enough to become normally functioning adults. But other children are born with a higher level of intellectual insight or emotional sensitivity which gives them the capacity to understand their plight and to feel its negative effects to a greater than average degree. This in turn can, understandably, lead to depression, anxiety, and so on. When doctors can find no biological cause of the emotional suffering they now have the option of simply categorizing this child's suffering with that magical label: "genetic vulnerability."

But saying that someone has a "genetic vulnerability" is nothing more than saying this person is sensitive to . . . whatever. The question is, "Sensitive to what? Sensitive to a mental illness that is an internally generated (endogenous) biological malfunction? Or sensitive to mistreatment, abuse, poverty, neglect, and incompetence?" If the latter is what the patient as a child is sensitive to then it hardly constitutes some sort of inherent flaw in his or her genetic make-up.

When it comes to mental illness, the question "What does it mean for a person to have a genetic vulnerability to it?" has only one answer: this person is more likely to suffer from external stressors than others. But this is not a biomedical answer as to the actual cause of the mental illness. It amounts to nothing more than blaming the victim, and harks back to the nineteenth century allegation of "constitutional weakness" in those who were labeled "insane." When the "genetically vulnerable" patient is diagnosed with "mental illness" under our current treatment paradigm it is analogous to treating the victim of child abuse as though that child's suffering from the abuse were some sort of weakness within the child. In reality, neither the unfortunate child, nor the child's genes, are to blame for the depth of the child's suffering!

Because the term "genetic vulnerability" contains the word "genetic" it not only presupposes, it suggests an internal or endogenous biological causality. And that's precisely what it's meant to do for two reasons: First, because it presents the symptomatic diagnosis of a "mental illness," especially one as vague as depression, as if it were an empirical fact in biology or chemistry: a proclamation of scientific truth discovered in a laboratory. It shifts discussion away from indistinct family dynamics and sociocultural stressors and plants it firmly in the "exciting" new medical field of genetics.

Second, advertisements for psychopharmaceuticals, and essays written under the auspices or sponsorship of pharmaceutical corporations, will use the term "genetic vulnerability," or "genetic predisposition," or "genetic weakness" to intentionally reify the symptomatic diagnosis of a "mental illness" so as to legitimize the belief in the endogenous biogenesis of mental suffering and confusion. This justifies the prescription and consumption of the industry's powerful and costly medications to treat symptoms as though they were biological pathogens or chemical imbalances in the brain. But Professor of Psychiatry Dan Stein points out that just as the earlier "clinical gaze" discussed by Foucault, so the more recent "molecular gaze" has its limitations. "Indeed, despite much back slapping about the value of current psychopharmacology, there has also been a great deal of exaggeration" (p. 128). Psychopharmaceuticals simply aren't delivering the amazing results at the genetic, or any other, level that the public has been led to believe they do.

Medical science will never discover a gene that causes a "mental illness" because "mental illness" is not brain malfunction, and it is not one thing. "Mental illness" is an umbrella term that includes hundreds of symptomatic diagnoses grouped under various medical-sounding labels which are then held up to be specific illnesses. No "mental illness" will ever be found to have a causal gene because, first, the descriptive definitions of "mental illnesses" overlap one another; second, the descriptive language in the literature is so vague and ambiguous that it allows a wide range of interpretations; and third because beliefs, values, fears, and so on are not genetically controlled. "The assumption that diagnostic categories are distinct, when in fact psychiatric disorders show very high comorbidity with each other, is simply spurious" (Pihl and Nantel-Vivier p. 96). For example, the term "schizophrenia" and its diagnosis is highly controversial, contested by clinicians, and variously defined in the literature, making it an extremely inexact term, and therefore nearly impossible to connect to any genetic causal factors (see Johnson et al. pp. 448–55; Kingdon & Turkington; Maj et al.).

Colin Ross, Clinical Associate Professor of Psychiatry at the Southwest Medical Center in Dallas, Texas, and Alvin Pam, Assistant Professor of Psychiatry at the Albert Einstein College of Medicine in the Bronx, New York point out that the common belief that biological psychiatrists have made many important recent discoveries about mental illness is simply false. Despite hundreds of millions of dollars in research funding, bio-psychiatry "has not made a single discovery of clinical relevance in the past ten years" (p. 116). Since their book was published in 1995 this figure can now be expanded to "in the past 20 years." The Director of Professional Information of a major pharmaceutical company and himself a medical doctor puts it this way: eighty years of research into the genetics of so-called mental illnesses has led to nothing "except utter confusion" (Weiner p. 200). And once again, it is simply not possible to find the gene responsible for causing an "illness" which is a non-biological, non-material entity. No genes can be held responsible for the beliefs, values, fears, and assumptions that constitute an individual's mind.

In the chapter titled "Genetic Vulnerability to the Development of Psychopathology," Lisa Doelger, doctoral student in Developmental Psychology at Arizona State University and Kathryn S. Lemery, Assistant

Professor of Psychology at Arizona State University and co-director of the Wisconsin Twin Project write that their research has shown that "genetic influences are probabilistic, and we should guard against explaining psychopathology in a reductionsitic 'genetic engineering' manner. Quantitative genetic liabilities to a specific temperament, disorder, or disease alter risk but rarely determine outcome" (p. 187).

A discussion of genetics would be incomplete without at least a mention of the discoveries being made in the new field of "epigenetics" which are completely altering our beliefs of the relationship between human beings and their genes. Recent developments in the field of epigenetics have added a whole other dimension to the discussion of genes: the fact that genes are themselves affected and altered by the environment of their host. In other words it has been discovered that the successes, the failures, and the suffering in an individual's life, rather than being caused by their genes, actually function as a subtle but substantial gene-altering mechanism. Epigenetics is finding that genes are not simply permanent biological units that control human mental and physical development. Genes are not passed unaltered from one generation to the next. Geneticists have found that the individual's total lifestyle actually alters their genetic makeup which is then passed on to the next generation. According to psychiatrist Norman Doidge, author of the book *The Brain That Changes Itself*, when we learn, "we alter which genes in our neurons are 'expressed,' or turned on" (p. 220). In other words, the relationship between human beings and genes is reciprocal: genes do indeed have an influence on us, but we also have a significant influence on our genes. This means that nurture is of much greater consequence in the development of the human individual, and unborn future generations, than previously believed. It is the mind, and not merely inherited genes, that causes individuals to be who they are, to do what they do, and to share who they are with their offspring. Professor of Psychiatry Joel Paris explains that brain activities are influenced by many genes which can be turned on or off by epigenetic mechanisms. So it's not surprising that "expectations that specific genes might be discovered that would account for the development of any mental disorder have not been met" (p. 16).

One final point regarding assumptions about the relationship between the biological brain and the mind: Psychiatrist and Nobel laureate Eric Kandel taught his students that when psychotherapy changes people, "it presumably does so through learning, by producing changes in gene expression that alter the anatomical pattern of interconnections between nerve cells of the brain" (p. 460). What Kandel is talking about is not only epigenetics, but also "neuroplasticity"—the fairly recent discovery that neuronal connections in the brain are not fixed but can be altered and renewed by the very thoughts a person has. The claim I made earlier that you can change your mind but you can't change your brain is not entirely accurate. It is in fact possible to change your brain's neuronal makeup in a way similar to the way you change your mind: with your thoughts (Horstman p. 11). Furthermore, the findings of Daniel J. Siegel, Clinical Professor of Psychiatry in Los Angeles, show that nature and nurture are not the only factors affecting human cognitive development. In his book *The Developing Mind* Siegel explains how important interpersonal experiences are in creating vital connections in the brain. This "interpersonal neurobiology" is a factor at work in all human interactions, including those between counselors and their clients and therapists and their patients. Psychiatrist Susan Vaughan maintains that so-called talk therapy works by "talking to neurons," and that an effective counselor, psychotherapist, or psychoanalyst is a "microsurgeon of the mind" who helps patients make needed alterations in neuronal networks (p. 45). Perhaps a more precise way to make this point is to say that talk therapy can help the patient alter his or her beliefs, values, fears, and assumptions which then, in turn, modify the neuronal networks of the brain.

When properly understood, the mind is not the same as the brain; it is simply the sum total of an individual's thoughts: their beliefs, values, fears, assumptions, and so on. These are non-material, non-biological personal contents that are specific and unique to each individual. Mental suffering and distress is caused by both external life situations and by "internal" or personal beliefs, values, and assumptions. To say that Marta has a mental illness when she is upset would make no sense. It would be like saying Marta has a belief illness, or a value illness, or an assumption illness. Connecting the words "belief" or "value" or "assumption" with the word "illness" makes the phrases incomprehensible.

Furthermore, to say that Marta has a predisposition to mental illness, such as depression, would be like saying Marta's genes have predisposed her to have bad beliefs, bad values, and so on. If Marta had such a genetic weakness it would mean that she is more vulnerable than most people to bad beliefs and bad values. This is simply meaningless when the mind is understood to be non-biological. The idea of genetic predisposition or genetic weakness to anything mental is also incomprehensible in light of the fact that no one would say newborns arrive with their beliefs, values, assumptions, and fears already in place in their genes. Beliefs, values, assumptions, and fears are not genetically inherited. This means that problems which arise from beliefs, values, assumptions, and fears—i.e., problems of the mind—cannot be linked to a genetic predisposition or weakness.

It also makes no sense to treat mental problems as though they were medical problems of the organic brain for several reasons: (1) the diagnostic criteria that define various mental illnesses are ambiguous, vague, equivocal, contradictory, overlapping, and vary across cultures; (2) there are no reliable, transparent, medical tests for mental illnesses like there are for somatic ailments; (3) the psychotropic medications in use today are, in many instances, no better than placebos in that they treat symp toms but don't address the actual cause of distress; (4) psychotropic medications don't treat specific illnesses but act only in general ways on the entire brain; (5) and these drugs come with a long list of undesirable side effects.

Mental confusion and emotional distress are not organic pathologies. There is no "medical model" of the treatment for so-called mental illnesses because: (1) there are no biometrics that reveal mental illnesses; (2) diagnoses are always only subjective symptomatic interpretations, and can vary substantially from one diagnostician to the next; and (3) treatment protocols are inconsistent among clinicians because of the previous point about the subjectivity of diagnoses. Not only does a medical model of mental illness not exist, a mental illness itself doesn't exist until a clinician pronounces it as "discovered" in the patient. Today, the primary alternative to the standard, problematic, "medical model" approach to treatment of so-called mental illnesses with medications is psychotherapy, often referred to as "talk therapy." But exactly what is talk therapy?

THREE
Contemporary Modality

The first time Samantha came into my office she looked like she had been crying. Sam told me she was in her late thirties and still single. She began her story by saying she lacked meaning in her life. She wanted to know what the meaning of life is. That's why she had come to me, knowing that philosophers talk about "that kind of stuff." She said her mother and father felt that a family is the only thing that brings meaning. She said they were very disappointed in her for not yet being married at her age and not having the children, the grandchildren, they had been looking forward to. She explained again how everyone in her family always expected so much from her. She was seen as the strong and capable one, the one who took care of things and looked out for all the others. But when her doctor put her on anti-depressants it sent the message to everyone in her family that she was no longer the super woman they had been looking up to. Sadly, her admission of her vulnerability did not get her the emotional support she was hoping for. Instead there was disappointment from her parents for her weakness, and silent condemnation from her siblings for her failings.

She told me she had lost several close friends to cancer over the past year or so. She said she had been working at a dead-end job, then found herself a better job, only to have to deal with dishonest employees who were stealing from the company. After finding and quitting several more minimum wage jobs she decided to open a small business with a friend. But the friend fell in love and abandoned her by fleeing the country with her new boyfriend, leaving Sam with enormous bills to pay off all by herself. She said she had been able to deal with all this and still keep smiling until her favorite aunt, whom she had been very close to, died unexpectedly.

Sam said that her deceased uncle had been abusive to her aunt, and had sexually molested Samantha when she was a child. She said when her poor aunt died she was no longer able to be happy. She had been struggling with taking a course at university but couldn't see the point of it any longer. Her medical doctor diagnosed her as clinically depressed and immediately put her on anti-depressant medication. But the drugs didn't help, and Sam tried to commit suicide not long before she came to see me.

We talked about a lot of negative things that had already happened to her in the past, and I tried to have her see that much of it was what others had done to her, and was really no fault of her own. She agreed that for most of her life she had been defined by others, and that she was expected to be the person whose happiness was often sacrificed for the benefit of others. I explained to her that in philosophy this is called a utilitarian approach—where it's acceptable to sacrifice the happiness of one person for the benefit of others. But philosophers know that the theory of utilitarianism only seems reasonable when you're not the one being sacrificed. She said she used to be a very giving person, but she couldn't be that way anymore because so many people had taken advantage of her. Her father demanded she share the burden of caring for the family. Her mother had come to depend on her to be the care taker of her younger siblings, as well as being the strong one she could lean on for emotional support. And while she felt she had been doing her very best her mother had expected better of her. I couldn't resist asking her what it means to do better than your best. Of course there is no answer to this question. Samantha had grown weary of the heavy burden she was carrying. She had collapsed under its weight, and was now guilt ridden for no longer being able to continue. Sadness and hopelessness seemed to be the only emotions she could find in herself in response to the misery that had been her difficult life thus far. This had led her to trying to end it all.

I asked her what had prevented her from killing herself. She said she felt it would be too hard on the few people who still cared for her. She had voluntarily admitted herself into a psychiatric ward, and was put on more medications. The clinical psychiatrist assigned to her case pronounced her "too stressed out to get anywhere" and simply gave up trying to help her, other than by giving her prescription drugs.

During one of our sessions, Samantha told me something very surprising. I have had clients tell me about all sorts of diagnoses with which various psychotherapists and clinicians have labeled them. But Sam had received a diagnosis I had never encountered before. She told me that the therapist who had caused her the most unhappiness, and the most distress, was the one who had told her he believed Sam was suffering from demon possession. That was his professional diagnosis, "Demon Possession." Sam explained how this frightening diagnosis had made it impossible for her to discuss the meaning of life, or anything else for that matter, with this therapist. She decided not to go back again to him. But then she asked me hesitantly if I thought that, perhaps, this diagnosis might be accurate. Could her suffering be due to some other-worldly demon inhabiting her? Of course the question circling in my mind was "What would possess a psychotherapist to diagnose a distressed patient with demon possession? What sort of training would lead a psychotherapist into such a controversial area of metaphysics?" One can only hope that none of the various methods or schools of psychotherapy would endorse such a diagnosis.

In his book *The Use and Misuse of Psychiatric Drugs*, Joel Paris, Professor of Psychiatry at McGill University in Montreal, Canada, writes that the most important and most under-utilized alternative to psychotropic drugs is psychotherapy in the form of talk therapy. He points out that psychotherapy has an enormous research literature demonstrating that talk therapies are efficacious and effective in treating a wide range of psychological symptoms (p.133). But what is it that psychotherapists do when they practice "talk therapy"?

It is estimated that there are at present anywhere from two hundred to four hundred named and unnamed methods of psychoanalysis, psychotherapy, and counseling available to the North American public (Corey 447). It is difficult, if not impossible, to determine the exact number because of significant overlaps in theories and methodologies. Many of them are virtually indistinguishable from each other except for slight differences in emphasis. But the number continues to grow as various "new" psychotherapeutic treatment methods continue to be developed to address the needs of a pluralistic culture in a technological age. Some psychotherapies are focused on the internal psychological state of the individual, others concentrate on family dynamics within which the suffering individual is located, while still others take a broader "systems" approach that views the individual as within a community that is part of a culture embedded in a political system operating in a global village. Some psychotherapists encourage their patients to reenact terrifying events like rape or gun violence; others advocate the use of powerful, debilitating psychotropic medications to supplement their form of talk therapy; still others recognize "demon possession" and the lingering after-effects of past lives as legitimate diagnoses. Why are there so many forms of counseling and therapy on offer? One of the main reasons is because there seems to be an urgent need for them. The current rate of mental illnesses, especially in North America, is the highest it has ever been in all of recorded history.

Recall from chapter 1 that between 1980 and 1990 the diagnosis of Attention Deficit Hyperactivity Disorder (ADHD) jumped from 400,000 to 900,000 cases in the US alone (Bakan p. 73). And since the year 2000 the diagnosis of pediatric bipolar disorder in the US—mania and depression alleged to co-exist in infants—has increased 44 times from the previous decade. A survey published in the *Journal of the American Medical Association* in June, 2004 reported that an estimated 26.2 percent of Americans ages 18 and older—or about one in four adults—suffer from a diagnosable mental disorder in any given year. This amounts to almost 80 million people. In the spring of 2012 the Canadian Broadcasting Corporation (CBC) reported that, according to the Canadian Mental Health Association, more than 50 percent of the Canadian workforce are suffering from a diagnosable mental illness. A news report on the same network announced that in 2013 one in five Canadian students are said to be suffering from at least one mental illness. The numbers in both the US and Canada are expected to continue to rise in the coming years. It is also predicted that depression alone will soon replace heart disease as the leading cause of morbidity worldwide (Radden p. 4).

These astonishingly high statistics, along with the associated public appeals from mental health agencies for both governmental and public assistance in doubling efforts to help the many suffering individuals in society, have generated the invention and development of countless counseling methodologies and therapies. But while there is agreement among practitioners that there is indeed a great need, it is not clear exactly what is needed. Treatment methods present a wide variety of possibilities: everything from powerful brain-altering drugs to conversations over a cup of coffee. Psychotherapy claims that patient improvement occurs because of a combination of the science, the medicine, and the discussions or talk therapy. The problem is that in essays on how to "treat" or "cure" mental illness in psychotherapy journals and books the authors often conflate those three perspectives—science, medicine, and discussions or talk therapy—and treat them as though the differences don't matter, or as if the differences don't even exist. That's why it's common to find psychotherapy essays discussing treating a mental illness something like this: "it's an illness arising from a disordered *mind* that requires *medication* to correct the *brain chemistry* to help the individual cope with issues arising from difficult *life circumstances*." In order to take any sort of logical approach in a discussion of treatment in psychotherapy it is first necessary to come to an agreement on which perspective is going to be discussed. Is it going to be about its scientific theories, its biomedical treatments, or its so-called talk therapies?

SCIENCE, MEDICINE, OR TALK THERAPY?

Clinical understanding of psychopathology, and theories advanced for the treatment of so-called mental illnesses are based, first of all, on the science of psychology which is the study of a range of subjects such as human biology, sensation, perception, learning, memory, cognition, language, emotions, human development, personality, and disorders (Bernstein et al.). It includes the laboratory investigations of brain states, and the exploration of neuroanatomy and neurophysiology. The medical aspect of treatment for so-called mental illnesses intersects with the field of science and involves biomedical research into the human brain in the attempt to gain a better understanding of its normal and abnormal functioning via a number of areas in the neurosciences such as neuroendocrinology, the use of neuroimaging, and pharmacological experiments on both animals and humans. It is also concerned with determining diagnoses for physiological abnormalities of the brain and suggesting appropriate treatments. The medical aspect of psychotherapeutic treatment is a very contentious issue because of the disagreements among researchers and practitioners about whether "mental illnesses" are in fact biological pathologies of the brain or difficulties in the reasoning mind. If a diagnosed "mental illness" were in fact discovered to be a brain problem then medical intervention, in the form of surgery, radiation, or chemotherapy would be an appropriate treatment method. But mental problems have not been found to be brain problems. And psychotropic medications meant to "treat" mental problems have been found to merely bring symptomatic relief without directly addressing the causes of any so called mental illnesses. Furthermore psychoactive drugs are not disease specific, they create numerous side effects, and some have been prescribed for years before being discovered to have no more beneficial effect that placebos. (Paris p. 57, 73, 85) With all this uncertainty about the efficacy of drug therapy many psychotherapists are calling for increased attention to the benefits of the many different talk therapies. It is impossible to discuss all of the many talk therapies available in North America except to say that they all necessarily involve the counselor or therapist having discussions with the patient or client. Even those therapies whose titles don't seem to suggest discussion at all, such as Dialectical Behavior Therapy, Acceptance and Commitment Therapy, and Schema Therapy are described in their web sites as offering "cognitive" therapy, or discussions about thoughts and thinking as part of their method. Below is a very brief description of some of the foremost psychotherapeutic methods. Notice that what transpires in these therapies is very similar to both the subject matter, and the discursive strategies in philosophy.

Psychodynamic Therapy

The therapeutic practices in the field of mental healthcare in the twenty-first century are directly descended from the theories and methods developed by the Viennese neurologist Sigmund Freud (1856–1939). Of course Freud was not working in isolation. He developed his ideas and advanced his practices in tandem with the theories and practices of other healthcare professionals of his, and previous, generations such as Jean-Martin Charcot, Pierre Janet, Josef Breuer, and Wilhelm Fleiss. But the is not much in what constitutes contemporary mental healthcare that can't be traced back to Freud's pioneering work in seminal psychiatry and classical psychoanalysis. Although generally considered to be the father of psychoanalysis, many professional clinicians no longer consider Freud's quasi-medical psychoanalytic approach very effective given how the term "mental illness" and its treatment is understood today.

While Freudian psychoanalysis attempts to alter the personality characteristics and behavior patterns of the patient, psychodynamic therapy is generally focused on solving life problems. Psychoanalysis is analogous to major surgery, while psychodynamic therapy is consider to be less invasive and somewhat closer to supportive first aid (Gaylin p. 245). Psychodynamic therapy is based on Freud's orientation and his theories in regards to mental healthcare. But it also includes what is called "object relations." This is the recognition that the individual's relationship to family members, members of the broader community, and cultural norms are extremely important factors in the development of the individual's personality and in the evolution of mental distress and diagnosable disorders. This broader familial and social perspective is missing in both psychiatry and classical Freudian analysis which typically focuses on the specific psychopathology within the individual patient. The task of psychodynamic therapy is therefore not only to help individuals discover how their past influences their present, but also how their current relationships—their ecological personal environments—and their extended cultural and political environments have shaped their personality and continue to influence their day-to-day thinking and behavior (Ivey et al. p. 97–99). Contemporary psychodynamic therapists also consider it important to teach their patients the meaning of psychodynamic processes so that in the future they will achieve greater autonomy in being able to arrive at insight into their own problems without the aid of professional clinicians. The inclusion of a broader perspective as well as the attempt to teach patients reasoning skills and life strategies clearly shifts the method of psychodynamic psychotherapy away from the biomedical diagnostic and treatment models. Even classical Freudian psychoanalysis is now described as being concerned with the resolution of immediate problems along with its original aim, the long-established exploration of the unconscious and the transformation of personality (Ibid p. 123). But while both psychoanalysis and psychodynamic psychotherapy have moved far into the realm of talk therapy, a growing number of potential patients looking to resolve difficult life issues still avoid the services of psychodynamic therapists. They associate this form of therapy with psychiatrists who are perceived to be "too quick to resort to drug therapy rather than talk therapy" (Schill & Lebovici p. 85).

Clinical and counseling psychology

The word "psychology" refers to the science or study of human development, mental processes and cognition, behavior, affect or the emotion, interpersonal interactions, and so on. It involves observing, recording, and interpreting so that, like in all scientific fields, predictions about human beings can be made with greater accuracy than by simple guess work. As with any science, psychologists are engaged in research, testing their hypotheses in order to verify them and reach a relatively definitive conclusion. The science of psychology is instrumental in many different areas of human life. Neuropsychologists use tests to determine the extent and location of brain injuries and abnormalities; health psychologists and clinical psychologists help patients deal with medical issues such as surgery or chronic medical problems; forensic psychologists assist courts and individual lawyers in dealing with legal cases; sport psychologists help athletes to enhance the performance of both individuals and entire teams, and so on.

The area of psychology most closely related to therapy for "mental illness" is clinical or counseling psychology. Here psychologists focus on the human being in his or her social environment. They help their patients deal with both interpersonal and intrapersonal issues. Their focus is on all areas of human experience: cognition/thought, affect/emotion, and behavior. Clinical and counseling psychologists provide counseling and psychotherapy to people suffering from emotional problems, adjustment issues, and diagnosed mental illnesses or disorders. They employ many different written or verbal tests to determine what the mental problem might be, assign a diagnosis, evaluate various treatment options, and then offer a variety of psychotherapeutic methods such as Freudian, Jungian, Cognitive, Existential, Behavioral, and so on. In the US anyone using the title "psychologist" must have a PhD or PsyD degree and several years of training. But these academic doctorate degrees do not qualify or permit them to prescribe or administer medications in most jurisdictions. Their main treatment method is talk therapy which includes discussions about the individual's problems at home, in school, at work, in church, and so on. The aim of clinical and counseling psychology, as in all forms of psychotherapy, is not only to ameliorate life problems but enhance the patient's quality of life.

Adlerian Therapy

Alfred Adler (1870–1837) moved away from Freud's biological, unconsciously "instinctual," and deterministic view of human behavior. While he believed, as did Freud, that the first six years of life do indeed significantly influence what sort of person the adult will become, he also believed that being influenced by the past is not the same as being conpelled to act. A person's perceptions and beliefs about past events do not have the same causal efficacy as do unconscious or instinctual drives that are said to trigger predictable behaviors. Adler believed human behavior is purposeful and goal-directed; and people are motivated primarily by social urges rather than Freudian sexual ones. He held that people are the creators of their own lives, not helpless victims of hidden passions. They are therefore responsible for their own thoughts and actions. The center of personality is not the unconscious but consciousness which allows for choice, responsibility, meaning in life, and the purposeful striving for success or the ideal. The feeling of inferiority present in all individuals is not a psychopathology that needs to be eradicated, but is rather a motivating force that moves individuals toward creativity and self-development. Heredity and the environment which the person is born into are not unalterable determining factors in the formation of a human being.

Adler believed we have the desire and the ability to make many choices which shape life's circumstances and allow us to become the kind of person we choose to be. This freedom negates the limiting effects of supposedly deterministic factors such as where we are born, what sort of attributes and features we are born with, and any supposedly unconscious forces. To overcome potential limiting factors, Adlerian therapy is focused on the reeducation of the individual, on reshaping the person's external environment, and on improving society. Adlerian therapists help their clients (not "patients") deal with their issues and problems by means of an examination of their values, beliefs, attitudes, goals, interests, and perception of reality. Adlerian therapy is phenomenological in that the therapist attempts to understand the client's subjective reality—how the client believes and perceives life to be, regardless of how it might be defined from the authoritative perspective of so-called objective reality.

Adlerian therapy replaces the Freudian deterministic explanation of human behavior with teleology. It understands actions as being intentional and goal-oriented. Individuals are seen as having developed a uniquely personal way of thinking and acting in relation to a goal that is consistent even when it is flawed or problematic. Adler stressed that every individual has the desire to be part of the larger society around them. This "social interest" or "Gemeinschaftsgefühl" is often considered to be Adler's most significant and distinctive concept. Mental health is not dependent on the correction of the individual's problematic psychology or mental illness, but rather on helping the person establish interconnectedness and interdependence with others in order to reduce feelings of inferiority and alienation. Adler's theory on the importance of birth order in influencing personality and personal lifestyles is yet another perspective on the social interaction he believed was instrumental in influencing how adult individuals perceive themselves, relate to each other, and respond to events in the world.

Adlerian therapy is said to be a collaborative effort between the therapist and the client to identify and explore mistaken goals, misguided perceptions, and faulty assumptions. The client is helped to increase self-awareness by means of examining and modifying fundamental premises, life goals, and basic concepts. In other words clients are helped to develop new ways of looking at themselves, others, and the world around them. This process includes providing information, teaching, guiding, and offering encouragement to build the self-confidence and courage necessary for healthy and happy living within society. Adlerian therapists believe that people tend to have problems in life because they do not recognize the errors in their thinking and behavior, do not know how to think or behave differently, and are fearful of having to adopt new and unfamiliar patterns while leaving behind old and familiar ones. They are afraid to relinquish their "private logic" which is their personal philosophy on which their lifestyle is based, even if that philosophy is making life miserable for themselves and others. Adlerians take a primarily cognitive approach, looking for major mistakes in the client's thoughts and values. The therapeutic process involves two main steps: identifying major patterns that emerge in the family-constellation questionnaire the client fills out, and interpreting the client's recollection of early childhood events. This gives the therapist a sense of the client's current beliefs and values as compared to social interest concepts. It also provides a "target" for the therapy. Adlerians do not focus directly on the subjective feelings of emotional suffering; they avoid addressing the symptoms. Instead they examine the beliefs and convictions which are the underlying causes of the emotional disturbances and behavioral difficulties. The client's acquired insight and self-understanding is then employed in the development of constructive concrete strategies for future action in everyday life. The Adlerian therapist believes that a change in thinking can lead to a change in emotions and behavior. In short, Adlerian therapy helps the client to improve his or her thinking processes in order to feel and act in way that is more conducive to living a good life (Corey p. 133–38).

Existential Psychotherapy

Existential therapy draws from a major orientation in philosophy, and consists of many different streams of practice. It arose in the 1940s and 1950s in part in reaction to the ennui and nihilism—the feeling that life meaningless—that had arisen in Europe as a result of the horror created by the widespread death and destruction of the two world wars. It considered a philosophical approach that has no single school, method, or techniques, and no individual originator. This approach is based on philosophical views about the nature of human existence; it resists an concept of an essential nature of human beings. It is therefore said have brought the potency of the individual back into central focus. E rejecting the deterministic view of human nature, the Existential therapist avoids blaming the past as the cause of present troubles. It assumes instead that individuals, as well as composite groups, are free to act as they will. But this freedom of will is accompanied by responsibility for choices made, and actions taken. Humans are the active authors of human life, not the helpless victims of either unpredictable life circumstances or their unconscious. A characteristic theme of existential literature is that it promotes the "reality" that people are free to choose among alternatives and therefore have a significant role in shaping both their own fate and the destiny of the world. However, existentialism understands that it is possible to avoid this reality by making excuses. The French existential philosopher Jean-Paul Sartre (1905–1980) wrote that human beings exist first of all, and then are required to define themselves or their "essence" as part of the willful activity of becoming fully human. Human beings, he wrote, are "condemned to be free" and the knowledge of this freedom and contiguous responsibility can cause a terrible anxiety. He referred to the avoidance of responsibility through excuses as "self-deception," and outright avoidance as "inauthenticity" or living in "bad faith" (1997, p. 30–62, 147–59). For existentialists, then, being free and being human are identical; and being born human already always includes bearing responsibility for the eventualities in one's own life (Corey p. 174). The main aim of this therapy is encouraging clients to reflect on both their own lives and on life in general, to become aware of the alternatives open to them, to help them make the best choices from among them. The ultimate goal is to act authentically in line with personal beliefs and values.

Viktor Frankl (1905–1997) named his form of existential therapy "Logotherapy." The process of searching for the value and meaning of life is central to his method. This therapeutic process is aimed at challenging individuals to find meaning and purpose through, among other things, suffering, work, and love. It also includes exploring what clients believe they value, how these beliefs affect everyday life, and to what degree the client is actually engaged in doing the things that he or she values. The central concern of Logotherapy is helping clients examine the difference between beliefs about how life ought to be lived and the existential reality of a client's life as it is being lived. This difference is then challenged in order to help clients begin living "authentically" (Bugental). Its focus, as in all of existentialism, is on the capacity for self-awareness, the freedom to make autonomous choices, and the responsibility that comes with this freedom of choice. Frankl promoted both the creation and development of one's own identity as well as the establishment of meaningful relationships that maintain supportive environments. His philosophy was significantly influenced by his imprisonment during the second world war in a German concentration camp. Logotherapy has become synonymous with the search for meaning, purpose, value, and goals in life, and dealing with the anxiety produced by the awareness of death and nonbeing. By means of positive suggestions, the Logotherapist provides the conceptual framework for helping the client both challenge the currently accepted meaning, and establishing a new meaning for his or her life (Ivey et al. p. 266–67).

While Sartre spoke of an "existential angst" or anxiety that accompanies the realization of human freedom and responsibility, Existential therapy differentiates between normal and neurotic anxiety. Neurotic anxiety is seen as out of proportion to the actual situation, whereas normal anxiety is considered to be an appropriate response to a life event. Normal anxiety does not have to be medicated or repressed; it can instead be used to motivate personal change and growth. According to Existential therapy, dealing with existential anxiety involves viewing life as a challenge or an adventure, rather than as a threat requiring avoidance or protection (Deurzen-Smith p. 38–48). Existential therapist Emmy van Deurzen-Smith details the four "existential dimensions" to a person's life with which Existential therapy is concerned: the physical dimension which involves the individual in his or her environmental context; the social dimension which is about being with others; the psychological dimension which is about being with oneself; and the spiritual dimension which includes purpose and meaning in life without the requirement of religious affiliation (Ibid p. 103–30). When the Existential therapist helps the client to become more self-confident, any anxiety that results from an expectation of defeat or catastrophe will decrease. The ultimate goal of Existential psychotherapy is to help the client face life's anxieties and engage in actions that are based on the authentic purpose of creating a self-valued existence (Ivey et al. p. 233–84).

Gestalt Therapy

Gestalt therapy is also an existentialist, as well as a phenomenological approach. It is based on the premise that people must accept personal responsibility for the decisions they make and the life they are living. Only in doing so will they achieve the autonomy associated with the concept of human maturity. Its originator, Frederick Perls (1893–1970), saw phenomenological self-scrutiny as helping individual clients and groups become aware of who they really are and what they actually want. By achieving an awareness of what they want and what they are doing clients gain self-understanding. This leads to a more comprehensive knowledge that they are responsible for what they think, feel, and do, and that therefore making life changes is within everyone's power. This therapy is phenomenological in that its focus is on an examination of the client's subjective perceptions of reality as a significant influence on individual behavior. The Gestalt therapist concentrates on how an individual client behaves in the present rather than looking for childhood causes that might be blamed as eliciting a particular behavior. This therapy peutic method is existential because its emphasis is on the present rather than on the past, and on clients taking responsibility for the choices they have made that established the direction of their own lives. The approach is experiential in that clients are encouraged to be aware of what they are thinking and feeling in the present moment of discussion with the therapist, rather than merely engaging in an abstract conversation. Gestalt therapy focuses much more on the process within the therapeutic encounter than on an expert therapist's interpretation of hypothetically hidden psychical forces within the client's unconscious. The awareness developed by the client within this form of therapy includes knowledge of his or her social and natural environments, and insight into personal life problems or issues that can result in a reconciliation and integration of sometimes conflicting beliefs and emotions. This process fosters a self-acceptance that supplants a negative self-image, allowing the client to acquire or improve the ability to connect with others in a meaningful way. It also leads the client to develop an awareness of personal responsibility for choices that have been made in the past and that need to be made in the present. It brings together aspects of the self that may have been cut off from the unit or "gestalt" that constitutes the total person, and reintegrates them back into a unified whole. Its main focus is therefore on integrating or reintegrating the previously troublesome parts of the client that have been intentionally split off, lost, or abandoned (Ivey et al. p. 275).

Gestalt therapy is based on the foundational belief that people are capable of dealing with most of their problems themselves, rather than focusing on what they should have done, what others say they ought to be doing, or who they have been persuaded to be. When the day is filled with regret for past mistakes, or fear of possible outcomes in the future, the opportunity for change in the present is eclipsed by pointless ruminations. So this form of therapy is based on the theory that change is only possible when there is an understanding and appreciation, through observational awareness, of what present psychological and physical circumstances are actually like. Gestalt therapists therefore ask more "what" and "how" questions than "why" questions because these intensify any immediate feelings about the present situation. They consider "why" questions to lead to unnecessarily unhelpful rationalizations and self-deception about the reality of the present, or endless agonizing about the unalterable past. The therapist helps the individual shift attention from merely talking about feelings to actually being aware of them and experiencing them in the moment in order to understand how they are affecting life in the present.

In Gestalt therapy, any past issues that are seen to be causing problems in the present are actually brought into the present therapeutic situation by means of a reenactment fantasy—a dramatization also called a "Gestalt experiment." This "reliving" brings relief from pain and can bring a change in understanding and a resolution to confusion and suffering. Gestalt therapists believe that such an exercise brings unexpressed feelings to the surface and prevents the possibility of physical symptoms arising from unresolved internal conflict. Expressing feelings within the therapeutic sessions that have been previously experienced but rejected and disowned, such as anger or jealousy, allows the integration of those feelings as part of who the client is. This in turn enables the client to get past this "stuck point" or impasse that prevents the client from making desired changes and experiencing personal growth.

Frederick Perls likens the adult personality to the layers of an onion. In order to reach psychological maturity five layers of neurosis must be peeled off: the phony which is inauthentic or stereotypical behavior; the phobic which involves denying aspects of one's true self due to fear of what this might suggest; the impasse where the individual feels no more change or growth is possible due to unalterable life circumstances; the implosive which is the act of experiencing and acknowledging the impasse; and the explosive which is the energy released when the phony is abandoned and one's authentic nature is allowed to blossom forth.

Gestalt therapists believe that there are five ego-defense mechanisms that prevent individuals from being authentic: introjection, which is the tendency to uncritically accept the beliefs and standards of others; projection, where certain aspects of oneself are disowned and attributed to the social environment; retroflection, in which the person directs against himself or herself feelings or impulses that are actually meant for someone else; deflection, which is an avoidance of direct contact with others by means of humor, abstractions, and so on; and confluence, which is an avoidance of authenticity by simply "going along with the crowd."

A major part of the therapist's role in assisting the client is creating a safe climate in which the client can try out and experience new ways of being. The therapist encourages the client to make statements rather than ask questions, to use self-determining language free of what they believe others think they should do, and to flesh out the meanings of single words or brief phrases that suggest a larger story. The client is helped to critically appraise the beliefs, behaviors, and values of others rather than simply accepting and incorporating them into his or her own life. In other words the client is helped to question the unsanctioned authority others may exert against him or her. And unlike the approach in psychoanalysis in which dreams are believed to explain past conflicts, the Gestalt therapist sees the client's dreams as metaphorical representations of present aspects of the client's life world and self. Much like the Socratic method in philosophical discourse, Gestalt therapists claim that their method contains no pedagogic element, that it only facilitates the client's own process of discovery and development rather than teaching them outright. There are many clearly defined techniques in this form of therapy some that can seem rather confrontational, but all are aimed at the reinvention of the client's autonomy and authenticity (Corey p. 222–56).

Person-Centered Therapy

Carl Rogers (1902–1987) also based his approach on the philosophy of existentialism as well as what came to be known as humanistic psychology. It is not considered to be a comprehensive method because Rogers offered his theories and approaches only as starting points on which other therapists could build their own styles of practice. Person-Centered therapy assumes that people are capable of understanding themselves, have the potential to solve their own problems, and have an innate need for growth and self-determination. It was originally known as "Nondirective counseling" in a reaction against traditional directive psychoanalytic approaches. It then became "Client-Centered therapy" when its focus shifted to the therapist's attempt to understand the client's phenomenological perspective of life or subjective world view. When the emphasis shifted to the process of "becoming the self that truly is" and "becoming one's experience" it became known as "Person-Centered therapy." This approach is experiential and relationship-oriented, in that the therapist creates an atmosphere in which the client comes to experience a trusting relationship with the therapist. The therapist must also trust the client's ability and capacity to make positive choices leading to personal growth, allowing the client to enter into the experience of exploration and discovery on his or her own, albeit with the therapist's support. The existential aspect of this approach emphasizes freedom in general, freedom from the therapist's interference, the client's right to make autonomous choices, attention to both the client's and society's values, personal responsibility for decisions and actions, the client's general autonomy in both life and therapy, the client's right to determine his or her own purpose, and the acceptance that personal meaning need not be universal.

Existentialism maintains that being free to make life choices creates anxiety in a so-called meaningless world where there is no essence of the "I," no objective "real me," that a person ought to strive toward becoming. On the other hand the humanism on which Person-Centered therapy is grounded is more positive in that it credits individuals with having the potential capability of choosing and becoming who or what they want to be. Contrary to Freud's focus on psychological pathology, and the attempt of the authoritarian therapist to adjust the patient to conform to the norm, Client-Centered therapy focuses on the ability of the client to make self-directed changes from their own locus of power. It is also based on a relationship of equality in which therapists don't conceal their knowledge or techniques from discovery by their clients in order to maintain the illusion that they possess mysterious healing abilities and medical secrets.

Through patient and empathetic listening the therapist enters the client's own phenomenological world and frame of reference, and assists clients in seeing possibilities other than those which are habitual to them. This helps their clients' growth process so that they are better able to solve their own current problems and those they might encounter in the future. The relationship between the client and therapists is one of mutual trust and respect, which facilitates the efforts of clients to define themselves and select their own goals. The heart of Person-Centered therapy is not the therapist's knowledge, theories, diagnostic abilities, or remedial methods but rather the therapist's authentic listening to, "being with" and caring about the client (Corey p. 197–217).

Reality Therapy

Control Theory-Reality therapy is similar in many ways to Existential therapy, Person-Centered therapy, and Gestalt therapy in that it stresses the subjective, phenomenological world of the client, focusing on the way in which the client perceives and reacts to their world from an internal locus of evaluation. Reality therapists hold that individual behavior is often influenced by the way people believe the world exists from their point of view, and how they believe they are acting within it, rather than on how the world actually is, and what their behavior is actually like. This therapeutic approach therefore focuses on the reality of the individual's actual behaviors and their resulting real-world consequences (Ivey et al. p.220). It also makes use of cognitive and behavioral techniques by shedding light on what clients are thinking and what they are doing in the moment in order to change how they are feeling and what they are experiencing physically. William Glasser (b. 1925), the originator of Reality therapy, claims that behavior consists of four elements: doing, thinking, feeling, and physiology. In effect thinking and feeling are "doing something." And if thinking and feeling are indeed "doing" then thoughts and feelings can be changed by the individual.

In Reality therapy the therapist at times takes a directive and educative approach, challenging the client to examine what they are doing (in the broad sense which includes thinking and feeling). Clients are questioned in order to create an awareness of immediate thoughts and physiological states in order to facilitate change in their current condition. Glasser taught that it is pointless to dwell on trying to change either feelings or physiology because they can't be changed or manipulated directly, independently from what one is feeling or doing in the moment. Glasser argues that in Reality therapy, "we focus on helping people choose or change the only parts they can change, which are their actions and thoughts" (p. 5–13). People often find it easier to consider themselves to be victims of a "mental illness," such as depression or anxiety, because this allows them to believe that making any attempt to change their situation is a waste of effort and time. But Reality therapy holds that emotions, as well as so-called psychotic or neurotic behavior, psychosomatic disorders, and addictions, do not simply erupt from within the physical body, victimizing the host like some sort of disease. They are in fact part of the human range of behavior. People choose to have certain painful emotions such as anger or depression for several reasons: to keep their emotions under control; to control themselves, others, or the world; to indirectly ask others for help; or to simply cover up an unwillingness to expend the effort to do something more positive and constructive. Of course this completely rejects the medical or biological model of "mental illness" which portrays human beings as victimized by mental pathologies.

Control Theory-Reality therapy emphasizes the development of so-called positive addictions such as running and meditation. It also promotes taking personal responsibility for behavior that can fulfill one's own needs without obstructing the needs of others. The events in a person's past are characterized as evidence of their ability to succeed in spite of hardships and setbacks, rather than as a collection of failures that need to be revisited and expunged. The focus in this form of therapy is primarily on the problems that are experienced in the present, even though they may be the result of what has occurred in the past. The client is encouraged to not only look at him- or herself, but also to consider the self within the social and environmental context. As clients are helped to become more aware that their ineffective behaviors and distressing feelings are in fact self-inflicted, this non-critical therapeutic approach teaches them how to be more effective in dealing with both their own lives and with what the world throws at them. In a sense the therapist is both a teacher and a role model. The therapist teaches the client, who may be struggling with a serious problem such as alcoholism, a more effective process of self-evaluation in order to help them recognize the self-destructiveness of their behaviors. The therapist develops a warm and trusting partnership with the client, using questions to help the client see the reality of their thinking, behavior, and life situation. According to Glasser human beings are motivated to change when they are convinced that their present thinking and behavior is not getting them what they want. Change becomes appealing when clients come to believe that they can in fact choose other, more effective, behaviors that will lead to their desired goal and an improved life (Corey p. 258–77). When the time is right—that is, when the client shows a willingness to change—the therapist will give directive instructions that provide the necessary tools and skills to make that change.

Behavior Therapy

Many of the techniques in Behavior therapy, especially those developed in the past two decades, emphasize cognitive processes. While its origins lie in classical and operant conditioning that are used to reinforce or extinguish behaviors as developed in the 1950s by B.F. Skinner, contemporary Behavior therapy now includes attention to the individual's emotions, thinking processes, meaning, and the client's ability to learn. Behavior therapy has evolved from pure behaviorism to a much more humanistic methodology. It has been developed with the assumption that individuals are not simply passive, organic mechanisms controlled by their environments but are instead active agents, free to control and alter their circumstances. Therapists in this field are now attuned to how stimulus events are mediated by the person's cognitive processes and private subjective meanings. In other words, the questions "What do you think?" and "What does this mean to you?" have become important too for the therapist. And the client's answers to these questions have become an important part of diagnosis and treatment. Because of its reliance on the therapist's observation of the client's cognitive and behavioral patterns, and because of its focus on current problems and real-world issues, this method may be categorized as both a phenomenological and an existential approach.

Behavior therapy is often relatively brief in comparison to other methods because it focuses on the client's current problems and the present factors influencing them rather than delving into the distant past. The approach contains a significant educational element in that the general goal is to create new conditions for the client's learning. This comes from the belief that learning can ameliorate the client's problematic behavior. Teaching involves helping clients learn to manage their own lives by instructing them in the very cognitive skills and behavioral strategies that are employed by the therapist. This fosters self-reliance by reducing the client's need to rely on an expert or authority figure to solve future problems. Clients are taught strategies and skills for dealing with their troublesome situations, and are then encouraged to use what is learned in their daily lives. The aim is to increase the client's awareness of the alternatives, options, and choices that are available. Clients are helped to freely pursue their own goals as long as they are consistent with the general good of society.

There is a collaborative relationship between therapist and client, with the therapist taking on the roles of teacher, mentor, and role model. This means that Behavior therapists are active and directive, functioning as consultants and problem solvers for their clients. Arnold Lazarus (b. 1932) who developed the form of Behavior therapy referred to as "multimodal therapy" discussed below, advocated the employment of any techniques the therapist deems useful in helping clients. Because it has become so flexible and versatile in its approach, contemporary Behavior therapy is considered to be far more eclectic, and much more inclusive and attentive to the client's thoughts and emotions than it was in its original conception in the 1950s.

Cognitive-Behavior Therapy

The best known of the cognitive-behavior set of therapies is Rational Emotive Behavior Therapy (REBT) devised by Albert Ellis (1913–2007). Ellis based his approach to therapy on the idea that "neurotic symptoms and psychological problems spring from an irrational philosophy: irrational beliefs that are the result of 'philosophical conditioning'" (Corey p. 318). Ellis, like the stoic philosopher Epictetus of the first century CE, held that it is what people believe about the situations they face—not the situations themselves—that determines how they feel and behave (Velasquez p. 34). It is seen as a highly rational, persuasive, interpretive, directive, and philosophical approach that stresses thinking, judging, deciding, analyzing, and doing.

REBT became a general school of psychotherapy aimed at providing clients with the tools to restructure their philosophic reasoning styles as well as their behaviors. Ellis knew that the interrelationship among cognitions, emotions, and behaviors had already been noted long ago by several ancient Eastern and Western philosophers. He acknowledged his debt to the ancient Greeks, especially the Stoic philosopher Epictetus, who is quoted as having said, in the first century A.D. that people are disturbed not by things, but by the view which they take of them (1989).

The basic assumption of the REBT approach is that people contribute to their own psychological problems—which may then be labeled as specific diagnosable symptoms—by the way in which they approach life events and situations both in the present and in an imagined future. REBT assumes that a reorganization of one's self-statements will result in a corresponding reorganization and alteration of one's behavior. Thinking is seen as a behavior that can be changed and improved; psychological distress is seen as being relived by means of attention to disturbances in cognitive processes. This method in psychotherapy is based on a psychoeducational model that uses teaching strategies to persuade and actively teach clients the skills and tools they need to restructure their philosophic and behavioral styles. The therapist helps clients to change for the better what they believe and what they do. REBT acknowledges the importance of working with their client's goals, purposes, values, and the various meanings in human existence. It also sees human emotions stemming mainly from beliefs, evaluations, interpretations, and reactions to life situations in both the present and the imagined future. So while it is a cognitive therapy that aims at thoughts, REBT is also recognized as beneficial in the amelioration of emotional distress.

REBT is based on the belief that we originally learn irrational beliefs, negative values, and inappropriate or self-defeating behavior from significant others during our childhood. We reinforce these harmful beliefs, values, and behaviors by habit, repetition, and an inability to see better alternatives. Living with absolute cognitions such as "shoulds," "musts," and "oughts" demands and commands creates self-defeating disturbances. Individuals feel the way they think, and emotional reactions such as depression and anxiety are initiated and perpetuated by the self-defeating belief systems based on irrational ideas adopted from others, or simply self-invented. The REBT therapist helps clients to recognize that they have the capacity to evaluate these cognitions, as well as their own goals and values, and change them if necessary.

Through teaching and bibliotherapy REBT clients learn how to differentiate rational from irrational beliefs, logically and empirically question the dysfunctional beliefs, and argue effectively against them. This method of psychotherapy is a reeducative process whereby the client learns to apply logical thoughts to problem solving and emotional change. The restructuring of dysfunctioning personality traits and problematic life philosophies replaces inappropriate beliefs and values with appropriate ones. While this method of psychotherapy confronts the client's nonsensical thinking, socially harmful behavior, and self-destructive lifestyle, the therapist shows full acceptance of each client by refusing to evaluate or criticize them personally. The fundamental premise in this eclectic and flexible approach is that human emotional, and so-called psychological problems are philosophically rooted (Ivey et al. p.152–89, 196–205).

The Cognitive therapy developed by Aaron Beck (b. 1921) is similar in many respects to REBT with a few differences. Both take an educational approach, but while REBT can be confrontational and directive, Beck's method uses Socratic dialogue, posing open-ended questions to help clients discover misconceptions for themselves and arrive at their own conclusions. Beck's clients are invited to evaluate faulty beliefs by comparing them to empirical evidence and contradictory reasoning. Rather than Ellis's focus on irrational thinking, Beck sees faulty beliefs as being functional within the client's worldview rather than incongruous with reality, and therefore as merely problematic rather than irrational. In the philosophical context of Beck's cognitive therapy, clients are encouraged to critically evaluate the rules they live by. Suggestions of alternatives to harmful or self-defeating beliefs are offered less forcefully than in REBT. In Beck's cognitive therapy, as well as in many others, the constructivist approach is gaining increasing importance as a way to facilitate change in clients in a collaborative environment. It helps clients to evaluate current personal perspectives and create new ones, without imposing the therapist's beliefs and values (Corey p. 318–46).

Feminist Psychotherapy

Psychotherapist C. Peter Bankart explains that sexist bias against women is still fairly pervasive in both our society and in psychotherapy. For example, in 98 percent of the advertisements for psychotropic medications in commercial medical publications the physician is male, while in 78 percent of the ads the patient is female (p. 363). The ideal of the healthy mature adult in the psychotherapeutic literature is still the male adult (p. 347). Psychoanalytic psychotherapist Charlotte Prozan points out that psychoanalytic theory has represented an exclusively male view of personality development, despite the fact that the field has had some important women contributors (p. 344).

Four general areas in which sex bias and sex-role stereotyping tends to occur in psychotherapy are (1) fostering of traditional gender roles; (2) therapist bias in expectations of women, and in devaluing women; (3) sexist use of standard psychoanalytic concepts; and (4) therapists responding to women as sex objects (p. 361). Bankart writes that "it is unclear whether something clearly identified as 'feminist psychotherapy' really exists as an alternative to traditional forms of psychotherapy" (p. 370–71). Much like existentialism, so-called feminist psychotherapy is more a description of the therapist's value system than it is a set of principles or a specific method of practice (Rigby-Weinberg). Professor of Counseling and Human Services, Gerald Corey explains that feminists come from all cultures and may be conservative, liberal, Marxist, Zionist, Christian, radical, and lesbian separatist (Corey p. 414). In his book he discusses feminist therapy under the general heading of "Psychotherapy with Families." This is not uncommon in the clinical literature.

The practice of psychotherapy by feminists is complicated by the variety of approaches among women who call themselves therapists and feminists (Prozan p. 181). Prozan explains that early in the women's movement, the focus was on eradicating barriers of the past and promoting equality between the sexes. Inspired to some degree by the Civil Rights movement, women decried all forms of discrimination, and urged acceptance of women into all aspects of society (p. 99). Questions such as why women collude in their own depreciation and limitation, why boys and girls play differently, why men and women seem to have different needs in marriage, and why women appear to be more depressed than men and men more violent than women, have all been addressed from women's perspectives under the general heading of "feminism" (Ibid).

Feminism sees mainstream clinical psychology as holding the problematic assumption that biology is an essentialist determinant of human behavior and values. Feminism also sees as problematic the assumption in psychodynamic psychotherapy that the root of unhappiness is within the woman's psyche (Bankart p. 371). American ethicist, and psychologist Carol Gilligan has noted that developmental psychologists from Sigmund Freud to Erik Erikson, Jean Piaget, and Lawrence Kohlberg had based their theories on male populations. They assumed either that women's maturation was similar to that of men or that women were insignificant statistical exceptions to the male norm (Corey p. 415).

Feminist psychotherapy requires that therapists don't employ biasing sexist thinking; that conformist or stereotypical sex-role behaviors are not prescribed to patients; and that sex-role non-conformity is not diagnosed as pathology. Feminist psychotherapists understand that marriage is no any better for a female than a male, and that marriage can often be a form of oppression for women, especially in some cultures. They also hold that it is acceptable for males to be emotional, expressive, and tender, and for females to be strong, autonomous, and assertive (Bankart p. 366).

There are two main streams of feminist thought in psychotherapy today. In the first, feminist therapists like Nancy Chodorow have tried to rewrite psychoanalytic theory to make it reflect the experience of women. They have tried to create a psychodynamic understanding of women that does not see men as the standard, and that recognizes the powerful bond between women and their mothers. Other psychologists in this tradition, such as Karen Horney and Carol Gilligan, have focused on developmental patterns that are unique to women. Still others have challenged the value of any "therapy" based on the assumption that women's distress is rooted in the female psyche (Bankart p. 346). Social context (the woman's situation in family and society) and the oppression of women and other minority groups are particularly key issues in feminist therapy (Ivey et al. p. 331). Major areas of feminist therapy are egalitarian relationship, valuing pluralism and difference, the external genesis of personal problems due to sexism and oppression, getting support from community groups to counteract isolation, an active, participatory counseling style, giving information for personal changes, and personal validation of the value of being a woman (Ivey et al. p. 333).

Feminist psychotherapy is different from more traditional alternatives because it holds that whatever oppresses the client must be changed, that the therapist/client relationship is between two competent adults, and that the goal of therapy is the empowerment of the person seeking help (Bankart p. 347). Prozan points out that the listening styles of the early psychoanalysts were distorted by a considerable patriarchal bias. But she sees this as having been corrected, under the influence of the new feminism, the sex researchers, and unbiased child observations. She now sees modern psychoanalytic theory-building free of the former patriarchal distortions (p. 336).

Eclecticism or Multi-Modal Therapy

The term "multi-modal therapy" is typically used in reference to the comprehensive, systematic, holistic approach to Behavior therapy first developed by Arnold Lazarus. It is an open system that encourages "technical eclecticism," meaning that it is acceptable for therapists to use a variety of treatment strategies with their clients, recognizing the fact that clients present a multitude of problems that require different approaches. It allows for the integration of multiple techniques and strategies from variously named methods to meet unique client needs. In order to help the client acquire new skills, the therapist will teach, coach, train, model, and direct the client during a counseling or therapy session. In this approach the therapist makes an effort to avoid "pigeonholing" or fitting the client into a predetermined treatment strategy. It is multi-disciplinary in that it integrates or converges varying theoretical orientations and diverse approaches, based on the belief that no one orientation can adequately guide therapists in all their clinical work. Eclectic therapy is premised on the belief that human personality is complex and comprised of seven major areas: behavior, affective responses or emotions, sensations, images, cognitions, inter-personal relationships, and the physical which includes biological functions, drugs, medications, nutrition, and exercise. Eclecticism or multi-modal therapy recognizes that psychological disturbance can be the product of a number of factors such as conflicting or ambivalent feelings, misinformation leading to irrational beliefs, lack of interpersonal skills, negative or traumatic past experiences, external stressors, self-concept and self-esteem issues, existential concerns, and lack of meaning (Fay & Lazarus p. 33–39). Therefore comprehensive therapy must necessarily include a number of activities: the correction of irrational beliefs, deviant behaviors, unpleasant feelings, bothersome images, stressful relationships, negative sensations, and possible biochemical imbalances. In this approach the cognitive modality deals specifically with insights, ideas, opinions, self-talk, judgments, and personal philosophies that are the basis of the client's values, attitudes, and beliefs.

The therapist may use any number of different techniques, such as behavioral rehearsal, biofeedback, communication training, contingency contracting, modeling, social skills, assertiveness training, thought stopping, and bibliotherapy. Systematic eclecticism remains theoretically consistent in that it borrows techniques from diverse sources without necessarily subscribing to any one individual theory. For example, there may be an examination of the client's childhood experiences without adopting the psychoanalytic theory of the deterministic unconscious or psychosexual developmental stages. Eclecticism or multimodal therapy is not meant to be yet another distinct form of therapy (Ivey et al. p. 220).

These then are twelve of the main therapeutic modalities in brief about which future counselors, therapists, social workers, and other caregivers are generally educated. They are the core psychotherapeutic approaches taught to students which they may use in helping individuals in personal distress and misery, or diagnosed with serious, or so-called "clinical," mental illnesses. Students are taught the basics of Freud and Jung, perhaps some biographical information about the originator of the particular method they're about to study, a bit of the genesis of that particular method, perhaps a comparison of a few selected methods in order to illustrate their differences, and then how to apply each method in helping a patient or client. But there is an essential educational element that the vast majority of psychotherapy and counseling students are never offered.

Professor of Child and Family Studies, Eileen Gambrill points out that there are numerous common reasoning errors that can lead clinicians astray, and yet little attention is devoted in professional training programs to a discussion of how to recognize and offer a cogent response to those reasoning errors (Gambrill p. ix). For example, while the techniques of talk therapy are discussed in a course on counseling and psychotherapy, rarely are students taught to be aware of many informal fallacies, or errors in logic, that can arise in any form of talk therapy. These fallacies can lead to questionable discursive strategies, such as relying on traditional beliefs, arriving at conclusions based on generalities, or basing an assumption on too little information. Furthermore, training courses in psychotherapy and counseling are also largely devoid of instruction in ethical theories, moral decision-making, and how to avoid the trap of moral relativism. A psychotherapy or counseling student may also benefit from at least a cursory understanding of various political issues, not necessarily in terms of the functioning of national governments, but in reference to family dynamics and inter-personal power relations. Religion is also a topic that arises in psychotherapy, and the student therapist would be well served with at least a rudimentary grasp of topics in religion and spirituality. This is not to say that counseling or psychotherapy students ought to be trained in theology or pastoral counseling, but simply that a knowledge of basic issues in religion and spirituality would enhance these students' abilities to be helpful to their clients who are struggling with issues or problems in those areas. Furthermore, the counselor or therapist who is familiar with the area of philosophy known as metaphysics will be much better able to help the patient who is struggling in an attempt to decide what is and isn't real. These are not esoteric subjects; they are at the heart of many of the troubling life issues presented by patients engaged in sessions of talk therapy. And yet students of counseling and psychotherapy are rarely, if ever, taught anything about these topics.

No doubt anyone educated and trained in philosophy will easily recognize the philosophical elements that already exist in the methods or "schools" of psychotherapy, both in those described above and in the many others that have not been discussed. This strongly suggests that students who want to be proficient in any of these methods ought to be taught not only the practical techniques of these methods but also the philosophical content and the discursive practices of philosophy that informs them. For example, *Psychodynamic therapy* is generally focused on solving life problems. It involves an investigation of the individual's relationship to family members, members of the broader community, and cultural norms that may have contributed to the client's mental distress and diagnosable disorders. Psychodynamic therapists also consider it inportant to teach their patients so that in the future they will able to arrive at insight into their own problems without the aid of a therapist. These are the same activities found in a philosophical investigation of an individual's life and world.

In *Clinical and Counseling Psychology* the focus is on all areas of human experience: cognition/thought, affect/emotions, and behavior. Largely unconcerned with deterministic unconscious motivating forces, the main treatment method is talk therapy which includes discussions about the individual's problems at home, in school, at work, at church. *Adlerian Therapy* is a primarily cognitive approach. Adlerian therapists help their clients (not "patients") deal with their issues and problems by means of an examination of their values, beliefs, attitudes, goals, interests, and perceptions of reality. It includes a collaborative effort between therapist and client to identify and explore misguided goals, erroneous perceptions, and faulty assumptions. This method includes providing information, teaching, guiding, and offering encouragement to build the self-confidence and courage necessary for a healthy and happy life within society. The Adlerian therapist believes that a change in thinking can also lead to a change in emotions and behavior. Again, this is exactly what is done with philosophical inquiry and discussions.

Existential Psychotherapy is undisputedly modeled after a major orientation in philosophy. The main aim of this therapy is encouraging clients to reflect on both their own lives and on life in general, to become aware of the alternatives open to them, to help them make the best choices from among them, and then to act authentically in line with personal beliefs and values. *Logotherapy*, also closely parallel to existential philosophy, has become synonymous with the search for meaning, purpose, value, and goals in life, and dealing with the anxiety produced by the awareness of death and nonbeing. Another method based on existentialism is *Gestalt Therapy*. Its emphasis is on the present rather than on the past, and on clients taking responsibility for the choices they have made that established the direction of their own lives. The client is helped to critically appraise the beliefs, behaviors, and values of others rather than simply accepting and incorporating them into his or her own life. In other words the client is helped to question the unsanctioned authority others may exert against him or her. Much like the Socratic method in philosophical discourse, Gestalt therapists claim that their method contains no pedagogic element, that it only facilitates the client's own process of discovery and development rather than teaching them outright. This is exactly what Socrates claimed for his philosophic method.

Person-Centered Therapy is also based in part on the philosophy of existentialism. The emphasis in this method is on freedom in general and freedom from the therapist's interference. The client is understood to have the right to make autonomous choices that may be influenced but not driven by society's values. This therapy involves accepting autonomy as an essential part of a definition of "person," and the recognition that personal meaning need not be universal. Similarly, in *Reality Therapy* the client is encouraged to look not only at him or herself, but also to consider the self within the social and environmental context. The therapist may take a directive and educative approach at times, teaching clients how to be more effective in dealing with both their own lives and with what the world throws at them. In this sense the therapist is both a teacher and a role model. Socrates and most contemporary philosophers would easily fulfill this role.

While *Behavior Therapy* was originally based on a mechanistic theory of a person, it now includes attention to the individual's emotions, thinking processes, meaning, and ability to learn. "What do you think?" and "What does this mean to you?" have become important tools for the therapist. The aim of this method is to increase the client's awareness of alternatives, options, and choices that are available. This is exactly what is entailed in the practice of philosophy, both in the past and in its contemporary form.

The offshoot from Behavioral therapy, *Cognitive-Behavior Therapy* (CBT) is seen as a highly rational, persuasive, interpretive, directive, and philosophical approach, that stresses thinking, judging, deciding, analyzing, and doing. Its developer, Albert Ellis, readily acknowledged his debt to the ancient Greeks, especially the Stoic philosopher Epictetus. This method is used to actively persuade and teach clients the skills and tools they need to restructure their abstract philosophy of life and concrete behavioral styles. In fact Aaron Beck's method uses Socratic dialogue directly, posing open-ended questions to help clients recognize problematic thinking habits, discover misconceptions for themselves, and arrive at their own conclusions. The connection of CBT to philosophy could not be any more obvious.

And finally, the theory behind *Eclecticism or Multi-Modal Therapy* is that no one method alone is appropriate for all types of problems presented by clients and patients. The eclectic counselor or psychotherapist tries to utilize a number of different methods that include teaching, coaching, training, role modeling, and directing. There is an adage which says that to a man with a hammer everything tends to look like a nail. Unfortunately the same can be said of the clinician trained in only one psychotherapeutic method to so-called mental illness: to a clinician trained in behaviorism all human problems are seen as behavioral; to a clinician trained in biopsychiatry all human problems tend to look like biological pathologies; and so on. This adage can be adapted to any one of the many methods in psychotherapy. So-called Eclecticism or Multi-Modal Therapy has been developed to counteract this biasing influence. But while eclecticism and multi-modality are presented as methods in psychotherapy, they are in reality the same open-ended and open-minded approach that is the basis of philosophy. Philosophy has always been eclectic and multi-modal. So, of all the various psychotherapeutic modalities, Eclecticism or Multi-Modal Therapy may be said to seem the most overtly philosophical in their approach.

The observation that is being made in this chapter is that in very many respects all the various methods in psychotherapy not only resemble, but are based in large part on, the content and practice of philosophy. And yet there is rarely if ever any reference made in the current psychotherapeutic literature advising students of counseling and psychotherapy to study some of the vast quantity of philosophical textual material readily available today, or to learn the method of open philosophical discourse.

Unfortunately, philosophy is often erroneously perceived to be merely textual information and arguments. But if psychotherapy resembles philosophy, and if philosophy is not merely a body of knowledge, then exactly what else can the word "philosophy" refer to? There are many ways to describe it. It is described in one text as "the systematic, critical examination of the way in which we judge, evaluate, and act, with the aim of making ourselves wiser, more self-reflective, and therefore better men and women" (Wolff p. 6). Another source says that it is "the evaluation of beliefs to determine whether they are true and the evaluation of practices to determine whether they are sensible and ethical" (Shipka & Minton p. 2). In fact philosophy consists more in the activity of philosophizing than in the theories that might result from our reflections. "It is about expanding our minds and seeing things from a new perspective in order to reach our full human potential" (Stumpf & Abel p.1, 2). It is "the contemplation or study of the most important questions in existence, with the end of promoting illumination and understanding" (Pojman p.1). In his book *The Problems of Philosophy*, the famous British philosopher Bertrand Russell argued that philosophy is studied, not necessarily to find answers, but for the sake of the questions themselves.

> Philosophy, though unable to tell us with certainty what is the true answer to the doubts which it raises, is able to suggest many possibilities which enlarge our thoughts and free them from the tyranny of custom. (1912)

To sum it up succinctly, and at the risk of perhaps being too meager, it might be said that philosophy involves examining the reasons we have for the values we hold as good and the beliefs we hold to be true so that we can free ourselves from blindly following traditions, slavishly obeying authority figures, acting only on our feelings, or yielding to habitual modes of thought and reasoning. This synopses of philosophy reveals that it is clearly at the heart of all psychotherapeutic techniques discussed above, and the many more that were not mentioned. It is present in what transpires in absolutely every psychotherapeutic encounter, not just the few discussed above.

The point is that since psychotherapeutic "talk therapies" consist of significant levels of philosophical discourse it only makes sense that students of any method in psychotherapy ought to be educated and trained in philosophy as well. And students would gain the most benefit in learning not only the discursive techniques developed by philosophers but also in attaining an understanding of the many insights about beliefs and values that philosophers have recorded over the centuries. This may at first seem revolutionary, but the use of philosophy in therapeutic discussions meant to help resolve the difficult life circumstances experienced by ordinary citizens, and to mitigate distressing human emotions and turmoil, is not a new activity. It reaches far back into the earliest moments of recorded history.

II

Philosophy as Therapy

"Philosophy has no direct influence on the great mass of mankind; it is of interest to only a small number of intellectuals and is scarcely intelligible to anyone else."
—Sigmund Freud (1856–1939)

FOUR
Past Precedence

For a while I had the offer on my website to answer questions by e-mail. I didn't keep the service going for very long because I couldn't keep up with the flood of messages I was receiving. This is just one of the many e-mails I received:

> My girlfriend and I've been arguing a lot lately but I don't really know why. I don't think the fights are all that serious, just a lot of yelling about what we think the other person ought to do, stuff like that. But she's talked me into going to see a woman who thinks the problems my girlfriend and I are having is because of our past lives. She said me and my girlfriend need to know who we were a long time ago. Maybe if we knew who we were in ancient Greece or Rome it would help us figure out our problems. She wants us to do past life regression with her. What do you think of past life regression to help me and my girlfriend get along better?

In ancient times, the past was considered to have an influence on the present, but it was not believed to have a direct causal effect on one's current life circumstances. Philosophy at that time referred to any attempt by human beings to know themselves as they experienced the immediate self through their bodies and minds, to comprehend the structure and functioning of the contemporary world they lived in, and to understand the relationship between the interior self and the exterior world. Furthermore it included an effort to improve all areas of life that were considered unhealthy or just troublesome before the advent of so-called psychotropic medications. In fact the etiological roles of both innate and environmental factors in the onset of depression have been discussed since depression was first described more than two thousand years ago (Nestler et al.).

When we talk today about philosophers such as, for example, Socrates and Plato it is inaccurate to say they were doing philosophy as we understand it in the twenty-first century. In their day philosophy was the inquiry into absolutely everything: biology, astronomy, geometry, medicine, law, psychology, society, family, politics, and even religion. Rather than say Socrates and Plato were doing philosophy, it is more accurate in our modern languages to say they were engaged in scholarly activities or academics. The early philosophers did not specialize as do their modern-day counterparts. They were as interested in the sciences as they were in the arts, and as interested in mathematics as they were in discussions about the nature of love. Given the fact that philosophers studied everything, with the ultimate goal of the betterment of the human condition, they included in their studies the attempt to define mental health, and the alleviation of its opposite: mental distress and suffering. In his book *Therapeia: Plato's Conception of Philosophy* Robert E. Cushman argues that Plato was a philosophical therapist who taught that learning how to apprehend "the good" was a means to salvation from psychological, social, and political turmoil and distress. Philosophy, as it was practiced in the ancient world, helped individuals to refocus issues of life when they were perplexing, and rediscover meaning when it seemed lacking. Professor of Philosophy at Sheridan College, Oakville, Ontario, Anthony Falikowski reminds us that

> the therapeutic role of philosophy is neither new nor innovative. . . . To neglect the practical contributions of the ancients, and to ignore the enduring influence of their therapeutic mission is, in fact, to provide a distorted (twentieth century) picture of what the history of philosophy is all about. (p. 17)

There were many "schools" of philosophy, many ways of apprehending, defining, and striving for "the good." Some schools focused more on societal and political conditions while others focused more on the individual: his internal conditions and the condition of his personal relationships. Philosophy was not employed only to critique or analyze. It was seen as having the power to bring about change in the circumstances of both the individual's life in the world and in the functioning of the world itself. Philosophers have recognized the healing and therapeutic powers of philosophy since the beginning of recorded history. When the word "*therapeia*" was first used it referred more often to ministering to the mind—what the ancients sometimes referred to as the "soul"—than to physical therapy for the body (Ibid p. 16). Before scientific discourse became the dominant activity in academic philosophy in the 1950s many theories were formulated as a means for understanding the complexity and meaning of the human predicament. The purpose of philosophy was to promote more effective, more informed, and simply better living. Unfortunately, these concrete projects of applied philosophy, that were once eminently useful to human beings, have become very rare in light of the segregated specialization that is now the accepted norm in most university philosophy departments. The original intent of philosophy—to develop a broad understanding of life which could then be offered in service to the public—had all but disappeared, that is, until recently (Deuzen-Smith p. 131).

Most early philosophers, who lived before philosophy became an exclusively academic occupation, understood that philosophical discussions can have a significant positive impact on people's lives. They knew this because they themselves had experienced it first-hand. Even after philosophers locked themselves into the academic ivory tower many of them wrote—albeit from a distant perspective—about its practicality and usefulness in every-day situations.

The prevailing interests, activities, and preoccupations of most twenty-first-century philosophers is with theoretical philosophizing: the discussion of hypothetical scenarios and "what-if" fictions that are invented for instructional purposes, but which may not have any direct connection to the realities of life. Without a knowledge of the practical application of philosophy that was commonplace in the distant past, a modern-day discussion of philosophy's practical and therapeutic function will appear strangely new and innovative (Falikowski p. 17). But history clearly shows that the therapeutic application of philosophy to helping people who are suffering from life's difficulties is not at all a new invention of the current generation.

This chapter is not an exhaustive exploration of every ancient or historically significant philosopher who may ever have mentioned that philosophy can be therapeutic. This can be done by another author in a different volume. This chapter contains only a brief overview of some of the most well-known and notable practitioners of philosophy who advocated philosophy as therapy for what ails you, and sometimes even as a "cure" for serious mental suffering.

PHILOSOPHICAL THERAPY IN ANTIQUITY

Psychotherapist Martha Nussbaum points out that from Homer on we encounter, "frequently and prominently," the idea that *logos* is to illness of the soul as medical treatment is to illness of the body. She translates Epicurus' use of the word *logos* as meaning therapeutic philosophical discourse. But she points out that it is more broadly used to refer to speech, discussions, and arguments of many kinds, religious utterances, and even friendly advice (p. 13 n. pp. 1, 49, 50). Philosophy's claim to be the therapeutic "art of life" is a significant claim: it is the claim that it can do more to alleviate the suffering of distraught individuals than any of the other available specialized resources because it is capable of dealing with all the vicissitudes of human life.

Various ancient practices were called *therapeia tēs psuchē*, translated as "cure of the soul" (C. Gill p. 307). In translating the Greek word *psuchē* from the ancient texts the word "soul" is often used. But this does not mean that it implies any particular metaphysical or religious standpoint. *Psuchē* is simply a term used to differentiate the physical body or material organism that is the person from his or her state of awareness or consciousness (Nussbaum 13 n. 2). *Psuchē* is just as correctly translated into the word "mind." By replacing the word "soul" with "mind" in the translations of ancient philosophical texts it quickly becomes clear that, rather than as some sort of path to spiritual enlightenment, philosophy was believed to be an appropriate method for healing suffering and distress of the mind. In her highly regarded book on the ancient Hellenistic philosophers, *The Therapy of Desire,* Martha Nussbaum often uses the words "soul" and "mind" interchangeably. She notes that the Stoics viewed the *soul* not as a religiously significant aspect of the person, but rather as a spacious and deep place within the individual where much that goes on is unnoticed. Their idea of learning is, in part, the *mind's* repossession of its own experiences from the fog of habit, convention, and forgetfulness which fills that spacious and deep place. The soul or mind is not an inaccessible pit. The person is challenged by the Stoics to "investigate these depths and to gain mastery over them" by means of self-scrutiny. At other times she broadens the word "soul" to include thoughts, fears, anxieties, emotional desires, and bodily desires (pp. 340, 269 n., 37, 270). This illustrates that, although a term like "healing the soul" may be used in a modern exegesis of an ancient philosophical text the context often shows that, rather than the religious meaning of "soul," what is actually being referred to is what we would generally refer to as healing or therapy for the mind.

There were many ancient practices originating from medicine, religion, and philosophy that were called "cures for the soul or mind" (*therapeia tes psuchēs*). The philosophy of antiquity was not nearly as theoretically oriented nor as abstruse as it is today. And it was never a "system" or methodical arrangement of ideas. As Professor of Hellenistic and Roman history Pierre Hadot points out,

> philosophy appears not as a theoretical construct, but as a method for training people to live and to look at the world in a new way. It is an attempt to transform mankind. . . . First and foremost, philosophy presented itself as a therapeutic, intended to cure mankind's anguish. It was meant to be a method for achieving independence and inner freedom. (pp. 107, 266–7)

Philosophy was a way of life, both in its practice and in its more esoteric goal of achieving wisdom. The striving for wisdom was not seen as the mere part-time or casual collecting of facts; it was understood as an activity which could itself significantly influence humans to "be" in a different way (Ibid p. 265). But if philosophy was meant to help individuals in antiquity to overcome mental distress and to live a good life, there must have been some agreed-upon conception of what mental health and good life actually are. The answer was simple: if an intolerably crippling condition of the body could not be defined as physical "health," then an unacceptably monotonous, impoverished, painful, or distressing way of life could not be defined as what mental health and a good human life are (Nussbaum p. 22). A good life then was conceived as the absence of both physical and mental suffering.

Hadot explains that in antiquity philosophy as therapy appears originally as intended to deal with the passions which includes the emotion, thoughts, and way of being in the world. Each "school" had its own unique therapeutic approach or practical method, but all of them "linked their therapeutics to a profound transformation of the individual's mode of seeing and being" (p. 83). And while these schools disagreed, and often even competed, with each other they held one belief in common: that philosophy could be helpful to ordinary people in resolving both every-day life problems and the many deeper, more philosophically profound issues that often haunt and distress the human mind. As Professor of philosophy, Anthony Falikowski puts it, "The therapeutic dimension of Hellenistic philosophy points again to philosophy's surprising practicality in real life" (p. 17). People in antiquity were just as filled with anguish about the political events in their world, the social events in their communities, and the personal events in their lives, as we are today. Like us, the ancients were burdened with the nagging baggage of their individual pasts, the demands of the ever-evolving present, the uncertainty of the ever-receding future, the fear of the certainty of inevitable death, and the uncertainty of what may lie beyond. The ancient philosophical schools essentially sought to provide a remedy for the troubles and fears in life. They were therapies intended to provide a cure for the anguish that is often mistaken to be "just part of life." They were meant to bring freedom from the tyranny of tradition and convention by enhancing self-mastery and restoring the self-confidence that is an essential part of a good life. Their goal was to allow people to free themselves from both the past and the future, so that they could live within a more rewarding, and less stressful present (Hadot p. 221–22).

In her book Martha Nussbaum examines three major schools of philosophy in the early Greek times. She finds that the Epicureans, the Stoics, and the Skeptics were all concerned with the practice of "compassionate 'medical' philosophy"—that is, philosophy applied specifically to the alleviation of human mental suffering (p. 40). She explains that the Hellenistic thinkers "see the goal of philosophy as a transformation of the inner world of belief and desire through the use of rational argument" (p. 78).

The idea that a philosopher could use his knowledge and skills to cure the soul or mind (*therapeia tes psuchēs*) emerged in the late fifth and early fourth century BCE. Philosophers in ancient Greece were very much concerned with psychological well-being; they sometimes even called themselves doctors of psychic diseases. For example, more than two thousand years ago Antiphon (5th century BCE) founded a discursive cure that was a psychological analogue to medicine. Democritus (c. 460–c. 370 BCE) claimed that, while medicine heals the body, wisdom (or philosophy) frees the psyche from passions (*pathē*), and releases mankind from despair (*dusthumia*) (Gill p. 320). These were the earliest practitioners of psychotherapy. But their methods were certainly nothing like the prescription of brain-dulling medications that is central to the relief of human mental suffering today.

Socrates (c. 470–399 BCE) wrote nothing down. His philosophical practice consisted exclusively of verbal discussions. His personality and his philosophizing are known to us primarily through the written works of Xenophon and Plato. Socrates is described by them as insisting that the young and old reflect on their way of life, and assisting them in doing so. Socrates encouraged those with whom he held discussions to conduct a self-conscious self-scrutiny. He challenged them to assess their remembered past, evaluate their lived present, and critique their imagined future. He counseled that instead of "being carried away" by an "unknown" self that was formed by tradition, conventions, and habit, people ought to become self-aware and self-determining beings. He "guided the young in the art of living by giving meaning to the burdens of life" (Schuster p. 37). And he disseminated the idea that a more self-conscious lifestyle is possible by questioning traditional values, religious beliefs, and the various assumptions that comprised the long-held values, the fashionable beliefs, and the political status quo of their contemporary society.

On the last day of his life Socrates instructed those gathered around him to let no day pass without discussing the meaning of goodness and all the other philosophical subjects about which they had heard him speak. He reiterated that examining oneself and the philosophies of others is not only the very best thing that a person can do with life but that it is also essential to actually living a good life. Socrates then made one of the most famous statements in all of recorded philosophy when he said that a life without this sort of philosophical inquiry is not worth living (*Apology* 38a). He meant this not only as a statement of his own values but as a call to action to all his students and followers.

Plato, like Socrates, lived at the end of the fifth century BCE. (428–347 BCE). He argued that just like there is both a cleansing or purifying of the external body with bathing, and a healing of the body internally with medicine, there is also a purification of the intellect and a "taking away of evil" from the mind. This, he says, is done with reasoning or philosophy which includes gentle advice, admonition, and pointing out contradictions in beliefs (*Sophist* 227–30). Plato saw philosophy as a kind of medicine, sometimes combining this idea with the claim that the Socratic style of questioning dialogue (*elenchus*) is the most effective method in curing illnesses of the mind. In *Charmides* Socrates is presented as a special kind of doctor who refuses to cure the body alone without addressing the problems of the psyche or mind (Gill p. 321).

> If the head and the body are to be well, you must begin by curing the soul [mind]—that is the first and essential thing. And the cure of the soul [mind], my dear [youngsters], has to be effected by the use of certain charms, and these charms are fair words, and by them temperance is implanted in the soul [mind], and where temperance comes and stays, there health is speedily imparted, not only to the head but to the whole body. (*Charmides* 157)

Aristotle (384–322 BCE), like his teacher Plato before him, also used the medical analogy to depict a philosophical approach to ethics that is practical, fruitfully related to human hopes and beliefs, and responsive to the complexities of the case under consideration (Nussbaum p.69). In the *Eudemian Ethics* Aristotle argues that in the study of ethics philosophy must go beyond mere theory; it must have a practical goal and an application to the realities of a lived life.

> For we do not wish to know what bravery is but to be brave, nor what justice is but to be just, just as we wish to be in health rather than to know what being in good health is, and to have our body in good condition rather than to know what good condition is. (1216b, 22–25)

The Stoics rejected Aristotle's notion of a non-rational (innate) aspect of the soul or mind that could be taught and corrected through force—something like the modern approach to behavior modification called operant conditioning. Chrysippus and other Stoics compared the deficiency of character, which they saw as being at the root of defective morality, with bodily diseases. The illness of the soul was seen as the soul's troublesome passions that are caused by emotional disharmony. Problematic impulses and passions were seen as produced by some sort of flaw in the ability to reason properly. Accordingly the Stoics thought that people could be improved or cured through the education of their reason. To the Stoics mental health is attained by a rational evaluation of matters that are causing problems. When knowledge of the good is employed in transforming inconsistent and hesitant opinions it creates inner harmony (Schuster p. 76). The fourth book of Chrysippus' treatise on the passions is called *The Therapeutic Book* because it provides cures for life's emotional maladies (Inwood p. 128–52). British philosopher Bertrand Russell characterized the Stoic attitude as the "acceptance of the unavoidable with fortitude." He considered Stoic self-discipline more appropriate to the alleviation of mental distress and confusion than many twentieth-century psychotherapeutic methods (p. 110).

The Stoics, like Plato, did not accept the notion of the absolute dichotomy between sanity and madness that existed in their contemporary society. They were operating with conceptions of "psychic sickness" as a matter of degree, and cure that consists of corrective thinking. This is significantly different from the view of both ancient and modern medicine (Gill p. 322). And unlike the current trend in modern biopsychiatry, they saw a clear distinction between illnesses of the body and distress of the mind. Mental illness was not confused with biological brain disorder, nor was it routinely treated with medications as is the standard practice today. The Stoics were perceived by some thinkers as "philosophical practitioners" par excellence. For example, the French philosopher François-Marie Arouet, better known as Voltaire (1694–1778) considered the Stoic Cicero (106–43 BCE) to be an exemplary advisor. The Stoics declared explicitly that philosophy, for them, was an activity in the service of humanity. In their view, philosophy did not consist in teaching abstract theory; much less was it seen as merely an exegesis of written texts. They saw it rather as completely entwined with the art of living. For them philosophical activity is not situated merely on the cognitive level, but includes the physical self and one's being-in-the-world. They taught that philosophy is a process which enables us to exist more fully, and makes us better human beings. It raises the individual to an authentic state of life—a life lived in accordance with their own beliefs and values—in which distress and confusion is alleviated, and self-consciousness, an exact vision of the world, inner peace, and freedom are readily attained (Hadot p. 83).

Registered psychotherapist Donald Robertson explains that modern psychotherapists are often surprised by how relevant to their own practice, and how strangely familiar, the ancient Stoic ideas actually are. He says that many modern theories of psychotherapy, counseling, and personal development "are ultimately indebted to this age-old but virtually forgotten therapeutic tradition. Stoicism is the forgotten ancestor of our own psychotherapeutic tradition" (2005, p. 1). He argues that Stoic philosophy proves significantly more relevant in today's treatment of mental distress and emotional suffering than the much more recent theories of Freud and others (p. 9). He points out that the three main surviving primary sources of Stoic philosophy seem to represent three distinct modalities of philosophical psychotherapy:

> Seneca's letters illustrate the individual mentoring of a student, the transcripts of Epictetus record group discussions, and Marcus Aurelius' private journal records his personal Stoic regime of contemplation. These modalities can be seen, respectively, as analogous to individual

psychotherapy, group therapy workshops, and self-help journals or workbooks in modern times. (p. 48)

In all the ancient schools of philosophy—with the exception of Skepticism—philosophy was held to be an exercise consisting of learning to regard both society and the individuals who comprise it from a universal point of view. This was meant to shift the focus away from a simplistic and atomistic conception of the human experience as individualistic and in self-serving isolation. This was accomplished partly with the help of a philosophical view of nature in which human beings are just one interdependent element among many. But above all it was done through moral and existential exercises. The goal of such exercises was to help people free themselves from the self-centered desires and passions which troubled and harassed them. It was thought that self-interested needs and desires were not natural to human beings, but were instead imposed on the individual by both cultural conventions and socially produced cravings of the body. The goal of philosophy was to help individuals come to see the artificiality of these drives, to free them from their tyranny, and consequently to desire nothing other than that which is natural (Hadot p. 242). Philosophy was regarded as the means for the relief from the oppressive torment of traditions and the controlling urges of desires. "The Hellenistic philosophical schools in Greece and Rome—Epicurean, Skeptics, and Stoics—all conceived of philosophy as a way of addressing the most painful problems of human life." In short, there is general agreement that in the Hellenistic period the central motivation for philosophizing was the pervasiveness and extent of human suffering, and that the goal of philosophy was, and still ought to be, *eudemonia*—human flourishing (Nussbaum p. 3, 15).

In his *Letter to Menoeceus* the philosopher Epicurus (341–271 BC) characterizes the study of philosophy as caring for the well-being of the soul or mind. He points out that the arguments of philosophers are just empty and meaningless if they do not relieve any human distress or suffering. He wrote,

> Empty is the argument of the philosopher by which no human disease is healed; for just as there is no benefit in medicine if it does not drive out bodily diseases, so there is no benefit in philosophy if it does not drive out diseases of the soul. (Inwood p. 99)

Nussbaum translates this passage slightly differently as, "Empty is the philosopher's argument by which no human suffering is therapeutically treated" (p. 13). For Epicurus and his followers philosophy was clearly thought, and taught, to be a therapy. He taught that, besides helping others, we must also concern ourselves with the healing of our own lives by means of a personal practice of philosophy. People's unhappiness, for the Epicureans, does not always come from actual occurrences of unfortunate events but also from what people believe, value, assume, fear, and so on. Unhappiness is the result of the fact that people are often afraid of things which they only imagine might happen in some negative conception of the future that is beyond their control. It also comes from a desire for things which are not actually needed for happiness, and which are beyond their ability to acquire. Consequently, their life is consumed by worries over unjustified fears and unsatisfiable desires (Hadot p. 87). Of course this is not to say that some fears are not at times justified, and that it's unacceptable to desire anything. It is certainly acceptable to desire things which might actually make life better, such as freedom from poverty and oppression. What Epicurus encouraged was a reasonable view of life, free from what today may be called anxiety, depression, pessimism, defeatism, materialism, egotism, and so on.

In 45 BCE, writing about how people should learn to deal with their own mental distress, Cicero said in his *Tusulanae Disputationes*,

> There is, I assure you, a medical art for the soul (mind). It is philosophy, whose aid need not be sought, as in bodily diseases, from outside ourselves. We must endeavour with all our resources and all our strength to become capable of doctoring ourselves. (Nussbaum p. 14)

Of course doctoring is not an easy task. It is even more perilous to be one's own physician for any number of reasons. But in the absence of any objective source of evaluation and critique of one's life, becoming self-aware and practicing self-scrutiny can have very beneficial results. Of course someone else's assistance in examining one's own life can often prove to be an even more beneficial approach in philosophical therapy. In his *Therapeutae* Philo Judaeus of Alexandria (c. 20 BCE–40 AD) describes a Jewish philosophical community. He wrote that philosophers of this community practiced a healing art that was superior to that of the medical doctors practicing in larger urban areas. He noted that the physicians cure only the body while these Jewish philosophers

> treat also souls that are mastered by grievous and virtually incurable diseases, inflicted by pleasures and lusts, mental pains and fears, by acts of greed, folly, injustice, and an endless multitude of other disturbances and vices. (Winston p. 42)

Around the beginning of the Christian Era Seneca (c. 1–65 CE) wrote in his *Letters to Lucilius*,

> Shall I tell you what philosophy holds out to humanity? Counsel. One person is facing death, another is vexed by poverty. . . . All mankind are stretching out their hands to you on every side. Lives have been ruined, (philosophers) that they look for hope and assistance. (Borowicz p.7)

In the Ancient world it was commonly understood that there were events and circumstances over which a mere human being had no control. But it was also accepted that philosophy could in fact offer hope and tangible assistance in coping with many of life's contingent eventualities.

THERAPEUTIC PHILOSOPHY IN MORE RECENT HISTORY

Also writing in the first century CE, Celsus saw a clear connection between the health of the body and the state of the mind. He advocated reading literature to medical patients in order to bring them back to both physical health and mental rationality. He urged physicians to discuss with their patients any topics that were of interest to them. Lacking any specific interests, he suggested that the patient be asked about trivialities or engaged in games that stimulate the mind. Celsus advocated a kind of therapy for the soul or mind that was very much in line with the teachings of many of the Hellenistic philosophical therapies.

Caelius Aurelianus, of Sicca in Numidia was a Roman physician and writer on medical topics. Writing in approximately the fifth century CE, he was among the earliest advocates of the use of psychological treatment for mental disturbances in physically ill individuals. He recommended that patients attend philosophical discussions because "philosophers remove fear, sadness, and anger by their words, and this helps to provide a considerable improvement in the bodily condition" (Gill 1985, p. 318). In his essay titled "Ancient Psychotherapy," Christopher Gill writes that "philosophers were very much concerned with the area of the psychological, and sometimes claimed to be 'doctors' of psychic diseases." This theme of dialogue as a cure for suffering patients was prevalent in most of the ancient schools of philosophy (1985, p. 317–20).

In his *Eight Chapters on Ethics* Moses Maimonides (1135–1204 CE) wrote that just like the body, the soul or mind can also be either healthy or unhealthy. While medicine is the appropriate treatment for bodily ills, the appropriate therapy for an unhealthy soul or mind is both the improvement of moral discipline and the cultivation of the intellect. He explained that immoral behavior that causes harm to others also causes injury to the intellect of the wrongdoer. He maintained that the suffering soul or confused mind of either a victim or a perpetrator can be relieved by means of study. To this end Maimonides recommended the study of Aristotle's *Physics* and *Metaphysics*. Once good moral behavior is learned through study and discourse, the practice of good moral behavior can lead to the actual living of a better life (Bakan p. 46).

The belief in the practicality of philosophy carried across medieval and Renaissance scholasticism into the seventeenth century. Philosophers René Descartes (1596–1650) and Baruch Spinoza (1632–1677) remained faithful to the ancient definition of philosophy as therapy of life, and therapy for a good life. For them, philosophy was both living a moral life according to good reason, and the practice of wisdom in everyday affairs

(Hadot p. 272). British philosopher David Hume (1711–1776) held that less abstruse, non-academic philosophy, which he called "easy and obvious," is useful to society because it enters everyday life. It can mold the heart and affections, and reform individual conduct by "touching those principles which actuate men" (Flew p. 54). The writings of German-born philosophers Arthur Schopenhauer (1788–1860) and Friedrich Nietzsche (1844–1900) are also invitations to radically transform one's way of life for the better. Both men were steeped in the practical tradition of ancient philosophy as a life-altering activity (Hadot p. 272). In fact many of the leading figures of modern philosophy, such as Søren Kierkegaard, Karl Marx, William James, John Dewey, Bertrand Russell, Jean-Paul Sartre, and Michel Foucault, all accentuated the practical aspects of philosophy, although not always using the word "therapy" in reference to it (Schuster p. 31).

The Viennese-born philosopher Ludwig Wittgenstein (1889–1951) was critical of the newly developed therapy called psychoanalysis as Freud practiced it. Wittgenstein's project was to rid humankind of suffering from the distress brought on by the most profound philosophical questions by means of the utilization of clear thinking and discussions. Professor of philosophy James Peterman explains that the therapeutic aspect of Wittgenstein's project becomes clear in his *Philosophical Investigations*. There he makes the analogy between philosophy and therapy. Philosophical problems are likened to forms of physical illness that require medical treatment and healing. Wittgenstein explains that the general form of philosophical illness is not knowing one's way about; it is a confusion or lack of clarity. This lack of clarity gives rise to deep disturbances, sometimes referred to as "mental cramps." The cure comes when one finds the right way to clarify what has become puzzling, and thereby bring peace to one's thoughts. In the *Tractacus* and *Notebooks* he is concerned with the problems of whether life has meaning, whether life is worth living, and how to be happy and content in the face of the awful things one must endure in life. Peterman argues that Wittgenstein must be understood as setting for philosophy the task of healing individual human beings through clarification (p. 17).

The sickness of a time is cured by an alteration in the mode of life of human beings, and it was possible for the sickness of philosophical problems to get cured only through a changed mode of thought and life, not through medicine (Wittgenstein p. 132).

Peterman asks rhetorically, if a philosopher could discover a conceptual reform that would increase the health of a culture and so of its members, why should he or she not do so? In fact that seems to be what Wittgenstein himself was doing in advocating philosophical discourse as a kind of therapy (p. 117).

At this point a question may arise about how philosophers of the past were able to deal with a patient's emotions, or indeed if they even could.

Where is there room for the emotions when philosophy is typically conceived to be about rational thinking, theorizing, and playing with word concepts, and ideas? How can the quest for "wisdom" alleviate emotional suffering? Recall that the Ancients, and even more recent philosophers, promoted an idea very contrary to the contemporary conception of philosophy as primarily a specialized theoretical academic activity. It is said to be therapeutic for individuals who are suffering from life's many troubles. Therefore this therapy must necessarily include taking care of unsettled and unsettling emotions. The French existentialist philosopher, Jean Paul Sartre argued that the emotions serve a function, and that one can understand emotions only if he looks for a signification (1997, p. 23, 216). He explained that while it is commonly believed that an emotion an unreflective and spontaneous eruption from within, it seems obvious that a man who is afraid is afraid *of something*, a woman who is distressed is distressed *about something*, a child that is traumatized has been traumatized *by something*. An emotion has meaning to the one who is experiencing it, and it seems to always be accompanied by a belief about a particular circumstance. An emotion is therefore a phenomenon of belief. In that way the emotions are very closely tied to what transpires in the mind. This is very similar to what the Stoic philosophers had argued so many centuries before Sartre. Sartre wrote that it is a mistake to see emotions as simply passive disorders of the organism and the mind that are caused by external disturbances to the psychic life. There is an internal element to the emotions, a connection to the individual's consciousness, that must not be disregarded in the face of precipitating external events. To understand the emotional process clearly, with consciousness as the point of departure, it is necessary to bear in mind the twofold character of the body, which is, on the one hand, an object in the world and, on the other, something directly lived by consciousness. Consciousness does not limit itself to projecting affective signification or emotions upon the world around it. It lives in the new world which it has just established. Emotion is a mode of existence for consciousness, one of the ways in which it understands the life-world (in the Heideggerian sense of "Verstehen") its "being-in-the-world" (1997 p. 223, 238, 240, 250). And because emotions come from one's understanding, both the understanding and the subsequent emotions can be affected and altered with discussion. In other words, according to Sartre, philosophical discussion can help to alleviate an undesirable emotion by addressing whatever is in the individual's mind that is causing the distress.

Martha Nussbaum reminds her readers that the aims of both medicine and philosophy are the same: to bring about some change for the better in a person's circumstances, "to answer people's needs" (p. 23). The ancient traditions that employed philosophy as therapy in the distant past can work equally well today to bring about the emotional change requested by suffering individuals. And more than that, philosophy can also provide guidance in the development of a therapeutic human relationship with oneself, with members of one's family and community, with other human beings in general, with the natural world, and even with the infinity of the cosmos (Hadot p. 274).

Of course it could be argued that just because a treatment approach to mental suffering and distress, that is today called "mental illness," has a long history connected to the ancient past doesn't necessarily justify the belief that it is an effective treatment for today's mental maladies. After all that would be committing the logical fallacy of appeal to tradition. Exorcism has also had a long tradition, but it is no longer considered an effective therapy for mental suffering. In fact it is not considered to be very helpful at all anymore, except by a very few very religious people for a very few, very specific, and very controversial "spiritual" problems. But while the majority of psychotherapists have abandoned exorcism, they have adopted—or some would argue they have appropriated—philosophy wholeheartedly, and are employing it extensively in their daily professional practices. Professional clinicians may not often acknowledge philosophy's central role in psychotherapy, or even know that it exists, but the evidence is clearly out there.

FIVE

The Clinic's Appropriation of Philosophy

I could hear that the young woman who had phoned to ask to come an talk with me was crying. When Ally arrived the next day she explaine how she felt she was being pulled in a number of different directions b her family. Her father, a successful businessman, set very strong guid lines as to what courses she should take; her "career-woman" older sist tells her what clothes she should wear; and her friends tell her who sh can, and can't, be friends with. She said her thoughts were complete muddled, and that even thinking about her family gave her a headach. She confessed that she does what others tell her to do because wheneve she has made her own decisions things have always turned out badl. Her father allows the older sister to smoke, but not Ally. Her fathe favors her older sister, and allows her so many things he would not grar Ally, like much later curfews, more money and gifts at birthdays, smol ing, and so on. So Ally has secretly at times stolen cigarettes from he older sister's bedroom even though she doesn't enjoy smoking at all. Al confessed that she has also occasionally stolen items from local store But what is worse, she said, when she feels bad she goes shopping an spends a lot of money, money she doesn't really have, on clothing tha she doesn't even wear. Ally went so far as to steal a shirt from her sister closet. She said when her father found out he "beat me up, and m mother never protected me." The situation at home became so tense tha Ally ran away from home and lived a miserable life on the streets fc several months. When she finally returned home her mother had to cor vince her angry father to let her stay. Her mother then secretly paid fc Ally to visit a psychiatrist. She immediately put Ally on a combination f anti-depressant and anti-anxiety medications. Ally explained that "the don't really help me figure things out," and that "the side effects ar awful." After a number of sessions with the psychiatrist Ally came to enjoy talking with her. Ally found her to be genuinely caring, and said that she often said things about life in a philosophical way. But when Ally happened to mention to the psychiatrist that she was in fact also going to talk with a philosopher (me), the psychiatrist immediately told Ally that she would not work with her anymore if she continued to come and see me. Ally was hurt and confused by this. She wondered aloud whether this is what all psychiatrists are like: do they all worry more about possibly losing their patients to the competition than they do about their patients' feelings?

In chapter 4 of his book titled *Group Psychology and the Analysis of the Ego* Sigmund Freud wrote the following: "In its origin, function, and relation to sexual love, the 'Eros' of the philosopher Plato coincided exactly with the love-force, the libido of psychoanalysis" (1987 ed. p. 119). Notice that Freud (or his translator) didn't write it the other way around like this: "In its origin, function, and relation to sexual love, the love-force, the libido of psychoanalysis coincides exactly with the 'Eros' of the philosopher Plato." Writing it this way would have made a significant difference by highlighting the fact that Freud's psychoanalytic model was based on Plato's, and not the other way around. Credit is due to Plato for Freud's conceptualization of the libido. Freud also borrowed the concepts of a tripartite unconscious from the same ancient philosopher. His "id," "ego," and "super ego" coincide exactly with Plato's much earlier conceptualization of "appetitive," "rational," and "spirited" parts of the soul or mind. And contrary to what many students believe, although Freud was the originator of the concept of a dynamic unconscious, he did not invent the concept of an unconscious per se. Edward Erwin points out that "those who argued in support of the unconscious included the psychologist Herman von Helmhotz (1821–1894) and the philosophers Arthur Schopenhauer (1788–1860), Friedrich Nietzsche (1844–1900), Eduard von Hartman (1842–1906), and J. F. Herbart (1776–1841)" (2012, p. 59).

As mentioned in the third chapter of this book, many of the contemporary psychotherapeutic methodologies contain significant elements of philosophy—sometimes dating back to the ancients—although contemporary practitioners rarely acknowledge this, or are simply unaware of it. Psychotherapy did not emerge in a vacuum; it was born of both the science of psychology and of the reasonings of philosophy. Many of the early developers of the various psychotherapeutic techniques were in fact educated in the history and content of philosophy, and trained in the art of philosophical discourse. They employed their knowledge of philosophical themes, and their philosophical reasoning abilities, without hesitation in the treatment of their patients. Unfortunately, at the time that psychotherapy was being rapidly developed as an alternative to psychoanalysis, philosophy had already acquired the reputation of being nothing but a useless and frustratingly abstract academic diversion. Therefore few psychotherapists ever openly admitted their debt to philosophy. And yet the early psychoanalysts clearly recognized the value of philosophy, although not in its academic form. In his 1942 introductory address at the Conference for Psychology in Zurich, Switzerland, Carl Jung told his audience,

> I can hardly draw a veil over the fact that we psychotherapists ought really to be philosophers or philosophic doctors—or rather we already are so, though we are unwilling to admit it because of the glaring contrast between our work and what passes for philosophy in the universities. (1957, p. 47)

The point Jung was making is that philosophy lost its way when it stopped being of service to humanity, when it denied its practical nature, and when it instead became something only done by academics with an eye for other academics. He understood that when psychotherapists are helping their patients deal with their problems they are in fact practicing philosophy, but that psychotherapists dare not call themselves philosophers because of the bad reputation that philosophy had gained due to their self-imposed specialization in mere abstract speculations. This raises the question, "Why was it that those professionals who were trained in psychology, and not philosophers, were doing philosophy with their patients in the first place?" The answer is because at that time in history academic philosophers were unwilling to help ordinary people deal with their non-theoretical emotional distress and troubling life problems.

In the seventeenth century the Western natural sciences and the medical sciences developed and diverged out of philosophy as separate disciplines. Natural scientists left the theoretical and abstract reasoning about any sort of non-material reality to both religious leaders and philosophers, and focused their attention instead on the substance, the organization, and the functioning of the material world. Medical doctors turned their attention to suffering that was located more in the physical body than in the numinous soul. But with all this attention on physical reality, the mind was separated off as a largely unfathomable realm. It was officially disconnected from the material world by Descartes and others, thereby allowing defenders of the scientific worldview to simply ignore what goes on in the mind as being outside their area of expertise and interest. Medical doctors, whose training was in chemistry, physiology, surgery, and so on, had no idea what to do with individuals who were suffering from emotional distress and mental pain. So with burning at the stake no longer an acceptable form of treatment for people with so-called mental problems, people whose thinking was deemed abnormal were instead now removed from contact with the others in their community and locked away in prisons, and later in so-called insane asylums (Foucault).

During this blossoming of empirical or scientific reasoning, philosophy was slowly being crowded out of the discussion. Since philosophers were no longer needed to think about and discuss problems in empirical areas such as biology, geometry, or medicine they found themselves being relegated to meaningless questions such as the ubiquitous, "How many angels can dance on the head of a pin?" Philosophy was a sort of catch basin for discussion about all those abstract, theoretical, and even religious issues which no longer held any interest for the majority of other scholars, most students, or the general public. In other words, philosophy was well on its way to becoming a purely academic exercise, enjoyed by those with lots of money and time on their hands, and a useless waste of time to the rest of the world.

In the late nineteenth century it was becoming obvious that one area of human suffering was being largely ignored: the mind. I use the word "mind" loosely here to include suffering that some would say is actually located in the soul or the heart. It was discovered that many of the people locked away in insane asylums were not the victims of some biological malfunctioning of the brain; their minds were not deranged. Instead they were distracted by hunger, distressed by poverty, distraught by abuse, and dispirited by the hardships of life. In fact there were also many wealthy individuals who were not in asylums, and were not at all lacking in physical comforts at home, who were likewise suffering from mental pain. It was to these well-off individuals that the scientific and medical establishment first began to turn their attention.

Neurologist Sigmund Freud became one of the most famous medical doctors to turn his scientific gaze on the so-called mental problems of the rich. Freud, Jung, and others attempted to treat their patients by transforming the ancient therapy for the soul into what they believed to be a medical science, which they called psychoanalysis. The foundation upon which psychoanalysis is built is the belief that each human being is controlled by wishes and desires stored in the dark, mysterious, and largely unfathomable unconscious basement of the mind. Psychoanalysts believed, and still do today, that, in order to live a happy, normal life, the dark matter of each individual's unconscious must be removed by the surgery-like procedure of analysis. Freud was eventually forced to revise many of his early theories when he realized he was having only minimal success treating his own patients. But his attempt to discover, and explain in scientific language, what the mind is and how it works, and even the technical idioms of psychoanalysis itself, have had a tremendous impact on what people think and how they talk about the human condition today. Not all of his contemporaries agreed with Freud that every distressed patient was in need of his deep psychoanalytic "surgery." In fact some therapists who were thoroughly trained in psychoanalysis rediscovered philosophy as an effective method of treatment.

The members of the research group at the Chair of Philosophy at the Swiss Federal Institution of Technology in Zurich, Switzerland recently wrote,

> We believe that the rise of psychotherapy at the end of the 19th century is a reaction to the tension between the public want for philosophical therapies and the academic refusal to work on them. Parallel to psychotherapy, therapeutic conceptions of philosophy became influential at the end of the 19th century: in the thoughts of Schopenhauer, Kierkegaard, Nietzsche, Emerson, and Thoreau. (http://www.phil.ethz.ch/en/research/philosophy-as-therapy.html)

At the end of the nineteenth century, philosophical influences on psychology and psychiatric thought were numerous. Psychology found itself embracing either mechanisms inspired by materialist philosophies or organic teleologies, to which Hegel had given the greatest impetus (Bergo p. 340). In the Preface to the book *Rethinking Mental Health and Disorder*, Professors of Psychology Mary Ballou and Laura Brown point out that after World War II, when psychology became identified with the treatment of human distress, psychotherapists "began to accept, with little question, medical constructions of distress and disorder. These two trends—the narrowing of epistemologies and the focus on disorder—have characterized mainstream psychology" (xix–xx).

During the 1950s, with the rapid advancement of computer languages and technology, Western philosophy fell into a kind of second Dark Age with the invention of what was termed "logical positivism." Logical positivism was the pseudo-scientific combination of hyper-rationalism and empiricism. It was an attempt to bring certainty into what was regarded as the perennial uncertainty inherent in the discourse and language of philosophy. The central notion of the logical positivists was that only the material world can be known to exist, and that therefore the only reliable knowledge available to humanity is that which is based on either mathematics or empirical evidence. Language was considered to be too ambiguous for certainty, so symbols were created to represent words and statements which could then be manipulated like mathematical equations to determine the ultimate truth or falsity of any proposition. The philosophers who promoted logical positivism felt that "truth" in areas such as metaphysics and moral philosophy was unverifiable and therefore meaningless, so discussion in these areas was seen as pointless and was subsequently simply abandoned. By making philosophy so obscure in its technicality that only specialists could deal with it, and so removed from the affairs of everyday life that it was completely impractical, these logical positivists succeeded in condemning philosophy to function only within the sterile discourse of exclusive academic departments.

At this same time behaviorism was the leading theory in psychology. Its proponents regarded not only animals, but also human beings as essentially nothing more than simple mechanistic organisms whose actions were merely the automatic responses to the various stimuli in their environment. Everyone is familiar with the dog used in a laboratory experiment by the Russian physiologist Ivan Pavlov. He rang a bell whenever he brought food for the dog. After a while the ringing bell would cause the dog to salivate in anticipation of the food. This, he claimed, proved that dogs don't reason; their salivation is merely an automatic (autonomic) response to stimuli. The problem with this experiment of course, is that it is based on the assumption that dogs don't reason and don't anticipate—an assumption which anyone who has ever had a dog as a pet knows to be utterly absurd. Unfortunately, Pavlov's sort of mechanistic, deterministic reasoning was applied to the human "animal" as well. Behaviorist psychologists believed humans merely acted in response to stimuli and therefore, like dogs, could be trained to be better persons by means of manipulating their responses with rewards and punishments. Behaviorism's approach to human improvement was given the clinical-sounding labels of "operant conditioning" with "positive" and "negative reinforcements."

This reductionist, mechanistic, cause-and-effect, stimulus-and-response description of intelligent beings, both animals and humans, fit well with psychoanalysis. Freud and others had argued that human beings were somewhat like machines, which *believed* they had will and intention but were, unfortunately, simply driven by mysterious—mostly sexual—desires hidden in the remote unconscious. In other words, a person was understood to be nothing more than an organic response machine whose actions were triggered by the hidden causal apparatus within the brain. But when psychoanalysts were challenged, even by skeptical colleagues, to prove the existence of the id, ego, and super ego that were said to comprise the unconscious, their response was that these terms were metaphorical; they were never intended to describe actual ontological elements in the brain. Of course this raised the question, "then what sort of things did these metaphors represent?" This is a question psychoanalysts have still not answered adequately to this day.

Freud did not begin his studies with psychology. He began his intellectual life with a passion for philosophy. In a letter to a friend in 1885 Freud wrote that "under Brentano's fruitful influence" he had decided to take his Ph.D. in philosophy and zoology (Boehlich p. 95). There is a remarkable connection between Freud's passion for philosophy, his debt to a few specific philosophers such as Immanuel Kant, and his well-known psychological interpretation of what was then called "hysteria." Freud owed a significant debt to Kant's influential "transcendental logic." In brief this was Kant's claim that an individual's understanding is equipped with "a set of *a priori* concepts or categories, including substance and causality, which are required for knowledge of an object or objective realm" (Honderich p. 878). For Freud the investigation of the troubled mind of his patients would include a search for those *a priori* concepts or categories on which the client's thinking and behavior were based.

Freud's debts are arguably to both Kant and Leibniz. They are debts because these philosophers formed the conditions of possibility for Freud's theoretical models of mental life: Leibniz, for the notion of unconscious thoughts; Kant for the transcendental strategies. Some scholars believe that Freud also derived his concept of *katharsis* (psychical "purification") from a superficial reading of Aristotle (Robertson, 2005 p. 2). And, as mentioned above, his concepts of id, ego, and super ego are almost identical with Plato's notions of the three parts of the human soul. But by the 1920s Freud obscured his philosophical aspirations behind the naturalistic empirical model which he attempted to apply to his development of psychoanalysis. English-speaking philosophers, both analytic and continental, have recently reconsidered Freud's work from the perspective of him as a philosophical thinker (Bergo p. 338, 339, 341).

In his book *The Therapeutic Dialogue* Sohan Lal Sharma points out that Freud said psychoanalysis "neither has nor can have a philosophical standpoint. In reality psychoanalysis is a method of investigation, an impartial instrument like, say, infinitesimal calculus." But in reality most of Freud's writings do not support this position. He could not distance psychoanalysis from a discussion of values and ethics, which are undisputed philosophical themes (Sharma p. 61). As Professor of Philosophy and Mental Health Bill Fulford put it, psychiatry is "more value laden than any other branch of medicine essentially because it is concerned with areas of human experience and behavior in which human values are particularly diverse" (2004, p. 227). A practice that is value-laden can't be the objective, neutral, or scientific discipline which Freud had been trying to make of psychoanalysis.

The reductionist, mechanistic theory of the 1950s, that human behavior is controlled by nothing more than chemical and electrical reactions in the brain, led to the gradual development of the idea that anyone suffering from mental distress was in all likelihood suffering from some sort of biochemical malfunctioning within the organic brain. In other words it was argued that the factors that bring about the onset of a mental illness are the same sort of organic determinants as those that lead to a physical illness. In fact any student wanting to become a psychoanalyst had to qualify for a medical license first. This biological perspective in turn led to the development of a vast quantity and array of medications called psycho-pharmaceuticals. It also brought about both the clinical assertion, and the intense commercial marketing, of the idea that these chemical products were the most efficient and effective forms of treatment for so called mental illnesses.

In the meantime, also beginning in the 1950s, psychoanalysts such as Albert Ellis, Viktor Frankl, and others came to believe that human beings were not simply controlled by their unconscious, they were not merely reaction machines, but were capable of choosing how to act and what to believe. In other words some psychoanalysts acknowledged that individuals were in fact able to think for themselves at a much higher level than behavioral scientists were claiming. They came to accept consciousness and intentionality as foundations of human behavior. These psychoanalysts had studied philosophy either privately or as university undergraduates, and they realized that philosophy could be useful to their patients because the thoughts and behaviors of their patients were motivated by meaningful beliefs, values, fears, assumptions, and so on. They also saw that the academic philosophers working exclusively in universities—and heavily influenced at this time by logical positivism—were not at all interested in helping ordinary people resolve their real-life problems. So they developed therapies based on philosophy that were far more engaging of the thinking patient than allowed by psychoanalysis. Methods such as Rational Emotive Behavior Therapy, Logotherapy, and Existential Therapy, were based on philosophical discussions, but their developers aligned them with psychology in order to distinguish them from both the obscurity of academic philosophy and from the dependence on the unconscious that is crucial to psychoanalysis. Treatment consisted of a therapist having a carefully reasoned philosophical discussion with the patient. Their methods and techniques were then taught to psychotherapy and counseling students in universities.

Unfortunately, while students of psychotherapy were being taught the treatment methods and techniques of psychotherapy, they, unlike their teachers, had little if any understanding of either the content or the practice of philosophy. The same is still largely true today. So while many psychoanalysts gave up the Freudian approach in favor of the emerging practice of psychotherapy, and were applying philosophy as a central element of their practices, they were in turn not requiring their students to take the philosophy courses that had been so instrumental in the development of their own methods.

Cognitive, existential, and humanistic psychologists and psychotherapists seem to have only very recently come to recognize that their treatment modalities resemble philosophy in some respects (Schuster p. 108). And beyond merely recognizing that the techniques they employ were based on philosophy by their originators, contemporary psychotherapists are in fact intentionally borrowing many useful bits from philosophy, and incorporating them into their many practices. Even after only a cursory inspection it is easy to see that the specific psychotherapeutic modalities that are commonly referred to as "talk therapy" are clearly and unapologetically the practice of philosophy under various psychological-sounding labels. These psychotherapies are centered around the concept that the essence of being human is the right and capacity of self-determination, and that people are guided by purposes, values, meaning, and options. These are all human elements that are irrelevant within the mechanistic, biological model of human behavior, but are highly regarded in philosophy (Schill & Lebovici p. 132).

THERAPEUTIC PHILOSOPHICAL CONTENTS

In their book the *Oxford Textbook of Philosophy and Psychiatry*, philosophers Bill Fulford, Tim Thornton, and George Graham write that nowadays professional mental health practitioners as well as users of mental healthcare services are actively interested in a wide range of philosophical topics (p. 4). The following are just a few examples of how the various psychotherapeutic methods employ philosophy.

Psychoanalysis: is said to have "touched on *philosophy*, psychology, sociology, art, and literature" (Meissner p. 110). Freud and Jung were both thoroughly educated in philosophy.

Freud references Plato when describing dream work, and follows his lead in describing the mind as tripartite (1957 p. 153). Carl Jung relies on the philosophy of Nietzsche's *Zarathustra* to understand unconscious aspects of his patients and the drive to transformation and self-overcoming.

Psychoanalysts such as Rollo May were routinely using philosophical techniques and ideas as a part of the counseling process as early as 1953. May appeals to Descartes, Mill, Kafka, Nietzsche, Heidegger, and Sartre as he describes his therapeutic method as one in which the client comes to a "consciousness of self-identity" (May 1953). Erich Fromm uses Marx and Hegel as a springboard to an understanding of the human condition, so-called sick individuals, and sick societies (Fromm 1962). In another work he appeals to Aquinas and Spinoza to reinforce his perspective on human struggles and human desire (1976). R. D. Laing references Sartre, Heidegger's *Self and Others*, and Kierkegaard's *Divided Self* (Laing 1990, 1990b) as he explains how human sorrow is the result of "the creation of a false self" rather than living authentically.

The French philosopher Henri-Louis Bergson has had an effect on the psychological theories of schizophrenia originating in France. The writings of German philosophers Wilhelm Dilthey, Edmund Husserl, and Martin Heidegger have been instrumental in the development of phenomenological psychiatry. Psychiatrists Adolf Meyer, Norman Cameron, and Harry Stack found valuable insights in American pragmatism. In fact the two philosophical positions that had the most influence on Western psychiatry in mid-twentieth-century United States are phenomenology and pragmatism (Morris p. 52). Psychoanalytic authors such as Winnicott, Minkowsky, Horney, Kohut, Langs, and even Freud are considered to have existential elements in their theories even though their work dealt with psychoanalytic concepts (Deurzen-Smith p. 139).

Edwin Hersch, a practicing psychiatrist and psychotherapist, explains that in his own practice he has found some of the insights of the phenomenological philosophers in particular to be "enormously useful when it comes to appreciating clinical phenomena and understanding the people who come to me for help" (p. 5). Before entering clinical practice, he studied the works of the phenomenologists in the disciplines of philosophy and psychology. He has no doubt that these have deeply influenced his thinking, despite his substantial subsequent training in a variety of more traditionally psychological, psychiatric, psychoanalytic, and psychotherapeutic approaches. He often finds himself referring or appealing to ideas and concepts found in philosophical literature. But he points out that philosophical literature is often so difficult that it is largely unavailable to most clinicians (Ibid).

In her book *The Philosophy of Psychiatry*, Jennifer Radden writes that "Psychiatry, it seems fair to say, is a branch of medicine and a healing practice with a subject matter and presuppositions that are deeply and unavoidably philosophical" (p. 3). Many contemporary psychiatrists have argued that philosophy, and specifically continental phenomenology, is essential to psychiatry and ought to be part of any psychotherapy training curriculum (Parnas; Hersch).

Adlerian Therapy: Adler abandoned Freud's basic theories because he believed that Freud was excessively narrow in his stress on biological and instinctual determinism. He agreed with Freud that a child's early years are influential, but he believed, contrary to Freud, that human motivation was based more on social influences rather than sexual urges. He also felt that behavior is purposeful, and life is guided by consciously goal-directed choices, rather than simply driven by unconscious desires. Adler was influenced by the philosopher Hans Vaihinger's view that people live by normative fictions which are beliefs of how the world should be organized or how life ought to be lived (Corey p. 134–36).

While Adlerian therapy is described as a predominantly psychological approach it includes many philosophical elements such as exploring mistaken goals and identifying faulty assumptions. Psychologist Richard Watts explains that the epistemological roots of Adlerian theory is primarily found in the critical philosophy of Immanuel Kant and the "as if" philosophy of Kantian scholar Hans Vaihinger. Adler acknowledged the influence of Karl Marx and Friedrich Nietzsche on his theory, gleaning ideas such as the socially embedded and fictional nature of human knowledge, the abilities and creativity of human beings, the necessity of egalitarian relationships and equal rights for all persons, and the socially useful and socially useless political and power issues involved in human relationships (Watts p. 139, 140).

Existential Therapy: arose spontaneously among different schools of psychology and psychiatry in the 1940s and 1950s. It is built on the belief that people are not simply helpless victims of their past. It does not focus on uncovering the past. Existential therapy is not designed to cure people in the tradition of the psychiatric medical model. It does not frame the individual's shortcomings and doubts as psychopathology, and has no well-defined technique which the therapist must follow as in psychoanalysis.

According to Professor of Counseling and Human Services, Gerald Corey, Existential therapy can best be described as "a *philosophical approach* that influences a counselor's therapeutic practice" (p. 170). The existential-phenomenological approach to treatment for so-called mental illnesses reconsiders the whole of human existence from a philosophical rather than a medical perspective (Deurzen-Smith p. 158). It rejects the orthodox psychoanalytic and radical behaviorist, deterministic view of human nature. It emphasizes that human beings are free of the restrictions of the unconscious, irrational, and instinctual drives as postulated by psychoanalysis, and free from the social conditioning that behaviorists say simply causes people to act as they do.

Existential therapy presumes that many mental problems can be categorized into one of two existential crises (Prochaska & Norcross p. 108). These crises involve self-identity and the meaning of life, fundamental issues at the core of the "philosophies of being." These have been elucidated by several existential philosophers of the nineteenth century, and most notably by the twentieth century French philosopher Jean-Paul Sartre. Existential therapist and professor of psychotherapy Deurzen-Smith explains that Existential psychotherapy has been practiced since the beginning of the twentieth century and has been one of the most consistent and enduring alternatives to psychoanalysis. Existential and cognitive therapies have drawn explicitly from themes from classical philosophy. For example, when existential therapists, following Heidegger, discuss the importance of an "authentic being-toward-death," they are perpetuating one of the central methods of ancient philosophical therapy, the *melete thanatou* or "meditation upon death," dramatically portrayed in Plato's dialogues on the last days of Socrates (Deurzen-Smith p. 3).

Ludwig Binswanger was one of Freud's esteemed colleagues. He was a member of a family that had a long tradition of psychiatry; his grandfather and father had both been medical directors of the Kreuzlingen Clinic in Switzerland. He became the first existential practitioner to write elaborate case histories that demonstrated not only the application of philosophical concepts to psychiatric work, but also the effectiveness of his philosophically informed methods. He attempted to make the philosopher Heidegger's work the foundation of his practice, calling his existential method "Daseinanalysis" (Deurzen-Smith p. 146).

Medard Boss, trained as a psychiatrist and psychoanalyst, collaborated for over a decade with Carl Jung, using the work of Binswanger as an inspiration. Eventually Boss turned to the work of the German philosopher Heidegger, and established a collaboration with him that lasted more than ten years (Deurzen-Smith p. 150).

Viktor Frankl began his career in psychiatry with a psychoanalytic orientation, but eventually reacted against most of Freud's deterministic notions. Existentialism rejects the deterministic view of human nature held by orthodox psychoanalysis in which freedom is restricted by unconscious forces, irrational drives, and past events. Frankl's Logotherapy promotes the existential concept of the human freedom to choose a state of mind, even in situations where physical freedom is greatly restricted.

Karl Jaspers was a German-born research psychiatrist and philosopher. He was one of the foremost existentialists of his generation, both as a philosopher and as a psychiatrist. He not only taught psychiatry and philosophy at the University of Heidelberg from 1921 to 1937, he also wrote many books in both fields, some of which became enormously influential. His writings on psychiatry were deeply influenced by his philosophical knowledge, especially his reading of Spinoza, Kant, Kierkegaard, and Nietzsche. In 1913 his two volume *General Psychopathology* was published. It soon became a classic in psychiatric literature. In the following years his four volume opus *Great Philosophers* was published (the last two volumes posthumously) which discussed the individuals whose thoughts had the most significant impact on philosophy. He clearly saw the importance of philosophy to psychiatry. He argued that since the original aim of philosophy was practical, it is especially useful to the field of clinical psychology and therapy for "mental illness." (Deurzen-Smith p. 69).

One of Karl Jaspers' best known students was Ronald David Laing, more commonly known as R.D. Laing. He is regarded as the most significant promoter of Existential therapy in Britain. In his autobiographical book, *Wisdom, Madness, and Folly: The Making of a Psychiatrist,* Laing wrote that in his early years he had read the philosophies of the Skeptics, Epictetus, Montaigne, Voltaire, Kierkegaard, Marx, and Nietzsche. Then while serving in the army he had read the phenomenology of Heidegger, Sartre, Merleau-Ponty, Husserl, and Wittgenstein (Laing pp. 63, 66, 89). The movement of anti-psychiatry that he engendered was based to a large extent on the writings of Heidegger and Sartre. Rather than psychopathology, Laing saw the symptoms of "mental illness" as potentially understandable and meaningful. He considered insanity to often be a function of the life context in which the patient is situated, or the structure of the family or organization the diagnosed person belongs to (Deurzen-Smith p. 166). Laing references Sartre, Heidegger and Kierkegaard as he explains how human sorrow is the result of the creation of a "false self" rather than living authentically. In 1964 Laing, together with psychiatrist David Cooper, wrote and published an authorized précis of Sartre *Critique of Dialectical Reason* and *Saint Genet*.

The sometimes perplexing work of Jacques Lacan and his followers in France is an example of a psychoanalytic school that has been heavily influenced by philosophical writings, even if Lacan does not always directly embrace or credit these sources (Hersch p. 266). Lacan is indebted to the philosophies of Heidegger and Sartre (Deurzen-Smith p. 140).

Existential psychiatrist Irvine Yalom holds that the vast majority of experienced therapists, regardless of their theoretical orientation, already employ many of the existential themes he discusses in his books whether they are aware of it or not (Corey p. 172). But Existential psychotherapist Emmy Van Deurzen-Smith laments the fact that, while contributions by American psychotherapists like James Bugental, Carl Rogers, and Eugene Gendlin have done much to make the existential approach concrete and accessible, the underlying philosophical context often gets so diluted that the original project of the approach is lost (Deurzen-Smith p. 158).

Gestalt Therapy: is considered to be phenomenological because of its focus on the client's perception of reality. The approach is existential in that it deals with the present, and it emphasizes every individual's responsiblity for his or her own destiny (Corey p. 224). The "here and now" philosophy of Gestalt therapy is a figure of speech which is a translation of the Latin *"hic et nunc,"* one of the key themes of Stoic philosophy meaning returning awareness to the present moment.

The originator of Gestalt therapy, Frederick Perls left behind his psychoanalytic training, and separated himself completely from the psychoanalytic tradition when he came to the United States from Vienna in 1946. He established the New York Institute for Gestalt Therapy in 1952. He believed and taught that self-awareness and growth comes from genuine contact between two people, and from the type of discussions that resemble philosophy rather than a therapist's clinical analysis of a patient's thoughts and behavior (Corey p. 223–24).

The Gestalt therapist Richard Erskine writes that, when it comes to relieving shame, typical Gestalt psychotherapy methods will do more harm than good. Instead he suggests that the greatest benefit will come through the use of "methods that emphasize respect, the therapeutic dialogue, and gentle inquiry" (p. 108–17). He explains how the psychotherapist should discuss the phenomenological experiences to which the client has been subjected, and to make an effort to understand what the client is wishing, feeling, and thinking. But notice that these techniques don't sound at all like the psychoanalytic search for unconscious causes. They sound much more like a philosophical inquiry.

Person-centered Therapy: is described as "a humanistic approach that grew out of the philosophical background of the existential tradition" (Corey p. 199). The originator of person-centered therapy, Carl Rogers challenged many of the therapeutic procedures of his time including di agnosing, analyzing, and interpreting. He omitted diagnostic concepts and procedures from his therapeutic approach because he was convinced they were inadequate, prejudicial, and often misused (Corey p. 198). Constantinos Athanasopoulos identifies incongruence in self-identity as a key area of Carl Rogers' system of psychotherapy. He considers it so important that all philosophical practitioners ought to be aware of it. This incongruence is the clash between social values, the socially lived identity, and the "self-projected self" (p. 236). Patients or clients must be helped to achieve congruence by discussion which clarifies current values and beliefs, and creates a coherence between the adopted value systems and honest self-perception.

Reality Therapy (RT): is concerned with teaching people more effective ways to deal with the world. The reality therapist functions both as a teacher and a role model (Corey p. 267, 273). During his training in psychoanalysis William Glasser began to become ever more aware that there was a vast difference between what he was being taught to do, in following the Freudian model, and what seemed to work. Glasser found classical Freudian psychoanalytic concepts and techniques ineffective, and developed a therapeutic technique that was antithetical to Freudian psychoanalysis in many ways. A major difference between Glasser's Reality therapy and Freudian theory is that Glasser held that individuals do not have to be victims of either their unconscious or their past (Corey p. 258). He held that transference is a misleading concept that allows the therapist, who remains hidden as a person, to implant ideas into the minds of their patients. The approach to the patient in Glasser's form of therapy is much more like an open-ended and respectful philosophical discussion than a psychoanalytic analysis.

Behavior Therapy: was first developed by clinical and experimental psychologist Arnold Lazarus. It is a radical departure from the dominant psychoanalytic perspective which rests on a deterministic assumption that humans are a mere product of their sociocultural conditioning. The main premise of this therapeutic method is that behavior is motivated by cognitive processes and private or subjective meaning. It is a rejection of a traditional intrapsychic or medical model of behavior. It holds that psychological disturbances are a product of factors such as conflicted feelings, misinformation, lack of interpersonal skills, external stressors, and existential concerns. This is a philosophical perspective of the person that dismisses the Freudian unconscious as the source of mental control and conflict. It stresses changing specific problematic behaviors and developing problem-solving skills. And contrary to Freudian psychoanalysis in which the analyst is required to adhere to a carefully defined method, behavior therapy allows for therapeutic flexibility and versatility to meet various patient goals. (Corey p. 300, 305, 307).

Cognitive Therapy: Aaron Beck was trained in psychoanalysis and was a practicing psychoanalytic therapist for many years. He also came to find Freud's approach lacking. For example he discovered that client dreams were less about retroflected anger, as Freud had theorized, and much more about biased and negative automatic thoughts that persist even in the face of contrary objective evidence. Cognitive therapists are known to cite the famous quotations from the *Manual* of the ancient philosopher Epictetus in which he says: "It is not things themselves that disturb people but their judgments about those things" (Epictetus p. 5). The cognitive therapist helps individuals examine the disturbing beliefs, values, fears, and assumptions that trouble their lives, and then develop more rewarding alternatives.

Cognitive-Behavioral Therapy (CBT): is considered to be "highly rational, persuasive, interpretative, directive, and philosophical" (Corey 318). The cognitive-behavioral approaches are considered to be the most cost effective method by the current managed-care health insurance companies (Ibid 353). Donald Robertson, an integrative psychotherapist and trainer, has a background in philosophy and has authored a book titled *The Philosophy of Cognitive-Behavioral Therapy (CBT)*. It details the tremendous influence Stoic philosophy has had on this technique in psychotherapy (2010). It, and Rational-Emotive Behavioral Therapy (REBT) are perhaps the only two psychotherapeutic methods that openly acknowledge their philosophical foundations.

Rational Emotive Behavior Therapy (REBT): is said to combine humanistic, philosophical, and behavioral therapy (Corey p. 224). As well as being heavily influenced by the ancient philosophy of Stoicism, it "owes a philosophical debt" to a number of other sources that have influenced its development such as the writings of philosophers Immanuel Kant, Baruch Spinoza, Arthur Schopenhauer, Karl Popper, and Bertrand Russell (Dryden p. 4).

Psychotherapist Albert Ellis, who originated REBT in the 1950s, came to the conclusion that psychoanalysis was a relatively superficial and unscientific form of treatment. Rational Emotive Behavior Therapy departs radically from the psychoanalytic system in that it sees focusing on both the client's past history and the supposed unconscious as a mistake. REBT is antithetical to the psychodynamic approaches in that it accepts the fact that a person's past can influence their behavior, but it does not cause or drive the person to act. It holds that individuals have the potential to make decisions regardless of the circumstances of their past. It also sees the supposed necessity to have clients recognize, express, and ventilate feelings, and to relive past distressing or traumatic events as ineffectual, and possibly harmful. REBT has been shown to be effective in treating so-called serious or clinically diagnosable mental illnesses such as personality disorders, depression, anxiety, obsessive/compulsive disorders, eating disorders, psychosomatic and psychotic disorders, and addictions.

Ellis openly acknowledges his debt to the ancient philosopher Epictetus, the author of the therapeutic *Manual* of Stoicism. Ellis points out that "much of the field of psychotherapy always has been and still is admittedly philosophic" and that his own approach "stems directly from philosophic positions—particularly the outlooks of Epictetus (c. 33–c. 135 CE) and the ancient Stoics, and of the more recent phenomenalists, existentialists, and pragmatists" (1976 p. 49, 50). Many students of REBT become somewhat aware of its connection with philosophy during their training, but lack the comprehensive understanding of philosophy that Ellis brought to his own practice. REBT employs the sort of critical and creative thinking strategies found in informal logic courses that are now part of any college or university philosophy department's undergraduate curriculum.

Feminist Psychotherapy: As mentioned in chapter 3, so-called feminism in psychotherapy is much like existentialist philosophy, in that it is more a description of the therapist's value system than it is a set of principles or a specific method of practice (Rigby-Weinberg). In promoting equality between the sexes, and in condemning the segregation or oppression of any minority group, not just women, feminism is clearly in line with the concept of respect for all persons that is central to the ethical reasoning promoted in philosophy. Like philosophy, feminism values egalitarian relationships within pluralism and difference. Feminism and philosophy alike recognize that personal problems arising from sexism and oppression are externally generated, and are not simply the products of "mental illness." Feminism, like philosophy, promotes a participatory counseling style, a therapist/client relationship that is conceived as a collaborative effort between two competent adults. The goal of feminist psychotherapy is to offer support and information to the person seeking help as a means to personal empowerment.

A final word about methods: one of the most recently developed and expressly identified "methods" in psychotherapy is commonly referred to as *Eclecticism*. It consists of the therapist's decision not to stay with one method for all patients, but instead to apply different methods to different patients, depending on what their personal concerns or problems call for. Eclecticism also involves using different methods with the same patient in a single session. The point behind Eclecticism is for the counselor or psychotherapist to choose a method appropriate to what is transpiring at any given time in the therapeutic relationship. This makes Eclecticism seem even more like the open approach in philosophy than any one of the other methods or techniques discussed above.

The examination of the various methods or schools of psychotherapy clearly shows that psychotherapy was a large-scale abandonment of the beliefs in unconscious causation, the basis of Freud's psychoanalytic approach to human suffering. In its place is the belief that people have the capacity to think about things, to discover meaning, to value, and to choose to believe or doubt. These are conscious and intentional acts of which all human beings are capable when they are not afflicted by physical or mental difficulties. It is because of the fairly recent professional acknowledgement of human rational autonomy that philosophy has become so important to all the many methods in counseling and psychotherapy. But beyond benefit to the practitioners of counseling and psychotherapy, philosophy is of significant benefit to the practitioner's clients or patients as well.

THE THERAPEUTIC BENEFITS OF PHILOSOPHY IN PSYCHOTHERAPY

Psychotherapy is sometimes referred to as "iatrology" meaning healing with words. Healing begins when a troubled individual feels the need to visit the psychotherapist. This recognition by the individual—that it might be beneficial to him to find help—is the first step in the attempt to improve a difficult or distressing life situation. Psychiatrist John Paul Brady believes that most people who consult therapists are in an unsatisfactory, and often unhappy rut: "Their restricted or faulty thinking limits their freedom of choices so that their actions, feelings, sensations, creative outlets, and personal relationships are often conglutinated" (p. 161).

In their 1950 essay titled "Techniques of Therapeutic Intervention" Dollard and Miller point out that an advantage of a skillfully asked question over a direct assertion is that it encourages "the patient to respond by thinking and seeing relationships for himself. Thus he is . . . more likely to learn to think." Questioning can be likened to the well-known concept of the "midwifery" of ideas Socrates mentioned when he explained that he helps others to "give birth" to their ideas. Dollard and Miller see the ultimate goal of therapy as being the patient eventually asking the right questions for himself or herself (p. 62). The therapeutic process as they describe it is both philosophical and educational.

Psychoanalyst and physician Franz Alexander argued in 1963 that the therapeutic process in psychoanalysis should best be understood, and could best be described, in terms of learning theory. This is very different from Freud's conception in which learning occurs primarily within the activity of, and for the benefit of, the analyst. Freud's goal was "abreaction" in the patient; he saw no need for his patients to learn to fend for themselves. In Alexander's approach, during psychoanalytic treatment the patient unlearns old patterns and learns new ones. He points out that psychoanalysis ought to contain both cognitive elements and the client's learning from actual interpersonal experiences which occur during the therapeutic interaction. He believed that in the 1960s psychoanalysis was seeing "the beginnings of a most promising integration of psychoanalytic theory with learning theory" (Alexander p. 75–6). This was at the time when the philosophical approaches in the many newly devised psychotherapeutic methods was beginning to conspicuously overshadow Freudian psychoanalysis in terms of popularity among patients.

One of the most obvious benefits of philosophical or cognitive forms of counseling and psychotherapy is that medications are not required to supplement the discussions. But while elimination of a dependence on medications may be desirable when a client enters this type of therapy, it is obviously not sufficient in itself to resolve the client's problems, alleviate distress, or motivate a change in the client's approach to life. People who are suffering from so-called mental illnesses must be given a suitable substitute of some sort when the use of medications is eliminated. Philosophy is such a suitable substitute because it replaces the pharmaceutical management of symptoms with a discursive elimination of the existential causes of those symptoms.

Deurzen-Smith writes about an experiment she attended in England in the 1960s, in which people who had been diagnosed with serious "mental illnesses" were allowed to simply experience their disturbances in a free environment without medical interference. But, while there was some improvement, the experiment was eventually deemed unsuccessful due to the fact that "they failed to provide [the patients] with the alternative philosophical examination of their predicament, leaving them to flounder in an often negative and destructive cycle of depression and anxiety" (p. 163). Addictions are a compelling example of the need for alternatives because recovering addicts will inevitably return to the palliative effect of the addictive substance if no other alternative is recognized as offering relief from their existential suffering and distress. It is not the addictive nature of the substance that keeps the individual "hooked" or causes relapse, it is the lack of an alternative form of relief from painful life circumstances.

Self-actualization or self-motivation for change is now a common concept in, and goal of, psychotherapy and counseling. This represents a radical departure from the psychodynamic tradition developed following World War II which held that an expert and authority figure is always required in rooting out unrecognized negative influences on the patient's thinking and behavior. Whereas psychodynamic and behavioral therapy often viewed humankind as the unknowing pawn of unconscious forces and environmental contingencies, the new self-determining methods of psychotherapy stress the idea that humans can take charge of their own lives, and much of life in general, by making independent decisions and acting decisively on the world (Ivey p. 237). The attainment of personal autonomy—thinking for oneself, and being responsible for oneself—are particularly strong themes in both philosophy and most forms of psychotherapy.

The thinking or philosophical part of therapy involves getting the client to focus his attention on the messages he incorporated into his personal beliefs as a child, and on the reasons he had for the decision that he made in the past. The therapist challenges the client to look at the various choices that are now seen as having been problematic, and to make the necessary revisions that will allow a better life in future. But the client is not only asked to review the decisions of the past, he is also encouraged to learn different, more beneficial, decision-making strategies that will help avoid future emotional turmoil and concrete life problems. And rather than focusing exclusively on feelings, the therapist focuses on getting the client to understand consciously how early childhood and young adult experiences and beliefs have affected his life, and are still influencing him today. The therapist questions the path that has led to the conclusions to which the client has come about himself, others, and life in general. The emphasis is on learning to think rationally rather than harboring beliefs based exclusively on emotions. The therapist does not impose her version of what may constitute the client's faulty, irrational, or dysfunctional thinking, but instead engages in Socratic questioning to lead the client to evaluate his own thinking processes and conclusions. New thinking strategies, and the revision of assumptions about others and about life in general are the basis of all the philosophically driven therapies, and especially Existential therapy and the Cognitive therapies (Corey p. 492, 493).

Psychiatrist John Paul Brady views the therapy that transpires in his own practice as one in which "the client can try out new ways of thinking, feeling, and behaving" (p. 157). Psychotherapist C. Peter Bankart maintains that the task of the Cognitive Behavior therapist is "to act as diagnostician, educator, technical consultant, assessor, gadfly, coach, and mentor." (Socrates also used the term "gadfly" in referring to his role in Athens of persistent questioner.) Bankart sees his therapeutic role as enabling the client to "design learning experiences that may ameliorate dysfunctional cognitions and the behavioral and emotional patterns that accompany them" (p. 263). Psychoanalyst Stephen A. Applebaum maintains that "change in psychoanalysis is chiefly identified with understanding, learning the underlying meanings of thoughts and behavior, and making the unconscious conscious through insight" (p. 145). These perspectives on psychoanalysis and psychotherapy shed a bright light on both the philosophical content and discursive strategies that psychoanalysts and psychotherapists employ.

In his essay "Ancient Psychotherapy" Christopher Gill, of the University College of Wales, Aberystwyth, points out that the "searching dialogue" which can help locate the root of a person's life problems, and even cure them, "is a dominant theme in one ancient discipline: philosophy" (p. 320). But he also argues by way of a caution that philosophical dialogue, especially of the Socratic type, is very different from the techniques of modern psychotherapy in two ways: first, philosophers such as Plato and the Stoics were operating with a conception of psychic sickness and cure that is significantly different from the so-called medical model used by psychotherapists today (p. 321). The most obvious difference is that the ancient approach to mental distress did not include anything like Freud's theory of the unconscious, which is still believed by many of today's psychotherapists to significantly influence the behavior of their patients. Therefore the ancients made no attempts to probe into any sort of unconscious realm with an examination of dreams, fantasies, or verbal associations to uncover what Freud believed to be hidden desires and fears. And yet, even while modern psychotherapy still preserves a tenuous place for the hunt for unconscious motivating forces, like ancient philosophy it also holds dialogue to be the central means by which to help the individual examine him- or herself, and to thereby improve his or her aptitude for autonomous living.

Second, Gill argues that modern psychotherapy is different from what the ancient philosophers practiced because there was no attempt made in the ancient variety of philosophical therapy, as there is in modern psychotherapy, to create a morally neutral "free" space for discussion with the patient (p. 324). But this raises the question, Does modern psychotherapy actually function in a morally neutral "free" space? Morality, briefly put, is the attempt to avoid harming others with what we say or do. If psychotherapy were in fact morally neutral then there would be no limiting factors to what the psychotherapist would be willing to help the client come to believe or do. One of the primary functions of psychotherapy is to help prevent the patient from inflicting harm on either him/herself or on others. This cannot be done from a morally neutral therapeutic stance which would disallow a moral evaluation of the client's speech or actions. While Gill claims that modern psychotherapy attempts to create a morally neutral "free" space for clients, it is doubtful that such a space does, or even could, exist in any professionally responsible psychotherapeutic relationship. But a non-neutral, and beneficially morally active psychotherapeutic stance requires the therapist to be educated in ethics, and trained in helping the client to apply ethical theories to moral decision-making. The therapist must be knowledgeable of ethical theories, and adept at moral thinking if he is to enhance the client's ability to live morally. Furthermore, in order to help clients think morally the psychotherapist must also have been trained in the ability to think critically and creatively. This can only come about with a solid education in philosophy.

In his book *Reason and Therapeutic Change* Windy Dryden, Professor of Psychotherapeutic Studies at Goldsmiths, University of London, gives examples of what he calls "illogicalities." They include all-or-none-thinking, jumping to conclusions, disqualifying the positive, allness and neverness, minimization, emotional reasoning, labelling and overgeneralization, personalizing, and perfectionism (1991). These "illogicalities" have long been discussed in philosophy classes under the term "fallacies," and are a staple in most university undergraduate philosophy curricula. Eileen Gambrill, Professor of Child and Family Studies in the School of Social Welfare at the University of California has published an entire book dedicated to psychoanalysts, psychotherapists, counselors, and social workers that draws extensively from this area of philosophy titled *Critical Thinking in Clinical Practice* (2005). Its aim is to improve the quality of judgements and decisions made by mental healthcare workers. The author's focus is on one of the oldest fields in philosophy: informal logic more commonly referred to as critical thinking. She begins the first chapter by stating that decision-making is at the heart of clinical practice, and then asks the reader, when assessing a client's depression "what sources of information will you draw on and what criteria will you use to evaluate their accuracy?" (Ibid p. 3). She suggests that a thorough knowledge of critical thinking skills will enhance the quality of services offered by the clinician, and help him or her to avoid many reasoning errors that can negatively affect treatment such as jumping to conclusions, confusing correlation with causation, confusing naming with explaining, and so on (Ibid p. 29, 412). Gambrill also emphasizes that critical thinking includes creativity. Creativity, she says, goes hand-in-hand with reasoning "especially in areas such as clinical decision-making, which involves unstructured situations in which needed information is often hard to get or missing, and in which there may be no one best solution" (Ibid p. 65). Critical and creative thinking classes have been a staple in undergraduate philosophy curricula for many decades.

Donna M. Orange, faculty member and supervising analyst at the Institute of Psychoanalytic Study of Subjectivity in New York, and a training and supervising analyst at the Instituto di Specializzione in Psicologia Psicoanalitica del Se e Psicoanalisi Relazionale in Rome has authored a book titled *Thinking for Clinicians: Philosophical Resources for Contemporary Psychoanalysis and the Humanistic Psychotherapies* (2010). The book is based on the assumption that at least some background in the history of Western philosophy will help psychotherapists to better understand psychotherapeutic sources such as Freud, Fairbairn, Kohut, Loewald, and the Gestalt psychologists Mitchell and Stolorow, whose writings reflect many of the themes in Western philosophy (Ibid p. 1). Orange also makes the argument that a knowledge of the philosophical theories about psychotherapy is not only extremely useful in, but essential to, the practice of psychoanalysis and psychotherapy. In her book she explains how an understanding of the insights of five important twentieth-century European philosophers can greatly improve the clinical work of the psychotherapists who study them. She details the works of Martin Buber, whose words caution the clinician not to objectify their patients as "other" or different than oneself. He "challenges the clinician to meet the other as another human being, as a dialogic partner, and not as an instance of any category" (Ibid p. 9). Ludwig Wittgenstein was deeply engaged with Gestalt psychology and with Freudian psychoanalysis. Orange explains how his writings are cautionary about the "reductionism of scientific rationality" and show us instead "the philosopher at the everyday dialogic work of finding meaning situated within contexts" (Ibid p. 10). While Maurice Merleau-Ponty, the French phenomenologist, appreciated Freud, Orange points out that "he led us beyond Freud in the directions that relational psychoanalysis and intersubjective systems theories have since gone." His "body-subject engaged in the world is another neglected resource of therapy and practice" (Ibid p. 11). She writes that Emmanuel Levinas argues that the therapist's responsibility to the patient is "a forceful challenge to the contemporary focus on the psychoanalyst's or therapist's subjectivity" (Ibid). And she presents Hans-George Gadamer whose "philosophic hermeneutic has provided clinicians with a fallibilistic, dialogic, and open-spirited concept and model for clinical understanding." Siding with Gadamer, Orange argues that "dialogic philosophy is a better resource than 'postmodernism' for our clinical practice" (Ibid p. 12).

In his book *Philosophy for Counselling and Psychotherapy: Pythagoras to Postmodernism* Alex Howard reviews thirty two of the best known and influential philosophers from antiquity to the twentieth century. He argues that "just listening" is not only an impossibility but also inadequate when the counselor or therapist has a sincere desire to help the suffering individual before him or her. He argues that "talking treatments currently practice on inadequate foundations" (p. ix), and that in order to be truly helpful, it is important to have a knowledge of the ideas, values, and life experiences discussed by the many philosophers who have walked this earth in the past. He maintains that there is a wide range of thinkers "far removed from here and now, who still have a great deal to offer on the subject of identity, co-operation, meaning, love and wisdom" (Ibid p. x). In each chapter he first reviews the main ideas with which we tend to identify the various philosophers. Then, in a section titled "Application" at the beginning of each philosopher's chapter, he explains how a knowledge of the main theoretical arguments of each of these philosophers can improve the clinical efficacy of any therapist or counselor.

Donald Robertson is a psychotherapist who has published the book *The Philosophy of Cognitive-Behavioural Therapy (CBT)* (2010). He points out that psychotherapists who study philosophy are likely to discover new practical techniques, strategies, and concepts, such as critical thinking, and the Socratic discursive method. He says these are consistent with modern therapeutic techniques and methods but are neglected by many practitioners. He connects modern psychotherapy with the practices of the Ancient philosophers to illustrate what contemporary psychotherapists have to gain by studying what and how the Ancients practiced philosophy.

The above are just a few examples of contemporary psychotherapists who have written books explicitly recommending the study of philosophy to students and active practitioners of psychotherapy. Authors of texts on counseling, such as, for example, Susan Day, also often suggest students learn the fundamental skills of good reasoning in order to avoid "mental mistakes" that cloud judgment and lead to poor performance. Skills such as "single-cause etiologies," "availability heuristics," "confirmatory bias," "fundamental attribution error," and "illusory correlations," already are, or should be, taught to help students organize their thoughts "free from the prejudices and hasty conclusions rampant in everyday life" (p. 39). She seems to suggest that avoiding faulty reasoning is based on "a strong background in psychological theory," when in fact the good reasoning skills mentioned by Day are common fallacies taught in most undergraduate *philosophy* courses. And similar to so many other counseling and psychotherapy texts, Day's book also contains a chapter on ethics which she says serves as a background for much of a counselor's or therapist's decision-making (p. 43). A knowledge of ethical theory, and a skill in moral decision-making not only serves to enhance the counselor's or therapist's own moral reasoning, it also allows the practitioner to help the client or patient learn the same. Unfortunately, many counseling and psychotherapy books simply don't allocate adequate space for a thorough discussion of both ethical theory and moral decision-making strategies. But such in-depth discussions are readily available in undergraduate philosophy texts, and clearly ought to be part of the curriculum for any students of counseling or psychotherapy.

Other than writing complete books on the value of philosophy in psychotherapy, many psychotherapists have discussed individual techniques, strategies, and concepts that are indistinguishable from the ancient philosophical practices. Yet they don't always acknowledge the connection with philosophy. For example, Aaron Beck offers a list of six "common distortions that a cognitive therapist should listen for in a patient's description of life" that are very similar to the fallacies common to informal logic: his "arbitrary inference" is like the fallacy of hasty conclusion; "overgeneralization" is also a fallacy by the same name in philosophy; "magnification" is the fallacy of exaggeration, while "minimization" could be the fallacy of oversimplification (of course both are simply misrepresentation of facts); "personalization" is a fallacy by the same name in philosophy; and "dichotomous thinking" is also known as the black-and-white, all-or-nothing, and either/or fallacy in philosophy (Bankart p. 278). Cognitive psychologists are also sometimes taught to recognize all-or-nothing thinking, and generalizations. These are simply called "faulty cognition" or "cognitive errors" in the psychotherapeutic literature (Prochaska & Norcross 2010, p. 313). Again, these have long been known and identified by philosophers as logical fallacies. Under the heading "Finding Connections Between Active Events, Beliefs, and Consequences" in their book *Cognitive Therapy of Schizophrenia* psychiatrists David Kingdon and Douglas Turkington explain that cognitive errors are central to delusional beliefs. They maintain that it is important that the psychotherapist recognizes errors such as the following: personalization (taking things personally); selective abstraction (getting things out of context); arbitrary inference (jumping to conclusions); minimizing; maximizing (making mountains out of mole hills); overgeneralization; and dichotomous reasoning (all-or-nothing thinking) (p. 102). These are, again, the sort of logical fallacies familiar to most students of philosophy. Philosophy recognizes more than two hundred fallacies, many of them encountered almost daily in ordinary conversation as well as in counseling and psychotherapy such as faulty analogy, false or questionable cause, slippery slope, red herring, bandwagon, appeal to tradition, appeal to practice, begging the question, circular reasoning, improper appeal to authority, two wrongs, straw man, poisoning the well, guilt by association, and so on. This raises the question, "Why are students of counseling and psychotherapy taught so few of these errors in reasoning or fallacies?" And, furthermore, "Why are the identical fallacies given names in psychotherapy that are different than in philosophy?" Nevertheless, counselors and therapists will be much more helpful to their clients or patients if they have first gained a thorough knowledge of all the fallacies available from philosophy, regardless of what psychological-sounding names the fallacies are given.

As can be seen from the above discussion, while philosophers may undoubtedly learn much from therapists, psychotherapists have much to learn from philosophers (Deurzen-Smith p. 173). As registered psychotherapist Donald Robertson puts it "the many ways in which modern therapists are indebted to ancient philosophy would fill a book by themselves. . . . All therapists, for the most part unwittingly, operate in the shadow of a very ancient therapeutic model" (p. 3).

Various professionals in the many fields of mental healthcare have commented in their writings that philosophy already is, or ought to be, part of all the various methods of therapy. For example, August G. Lageman, Director of the Hartford Pastoral Counseling Service in Bel Air, Maryland, explains that two of Socrates' best known and most basic ideas, "know thyself" and "an unexamined life is not worth living" are fundamental to all of psychotherapy: "Socrates' unrelenting commitment to questioning has been expanded by the family therapist, particularly of the Milan approach, who asks questions [of his clients] designed to evoke possibilities" (p. 222). Psychiatrist and psychotherapist Edwin L. Hersch points out that some psychological theorists, especially in recent years, have made valiant efforts to venture into more traditionally philosophical domains. Terms such as epistemology, hermeneutics, historical versus narrative truth, relativism, objectivism, constructionism, postmodernism, deconstruction, and so on are appearing more and more often in the psychological literature, and especially in the psychoanalytic field (p. 10).

Professor of Sociology Allan Horwitz writes that psychotherapists use symbolic systems to heal the minds of sufferers that are "rooted in philosophical and religious systems of healing" (p. 182). Hersch writes that philosophy is unavoidable, because we always operate from within a context of beliefs, presuppositions, and background understandings.

> I believe that Freud . . . was quite wrong when he claimed in his Weltanschauung lecture that "philosophy has no direct influence on the great mass of mankind; it is of interest to only a small number even of the top layer of intellectuals and is scarcely intelligible to anyone else." On the contrary, philosophy has a great influence on all of us. (p. 345)

Furthermore, he maintains that all practitioners in the field of psychotherapy are already dealing with philosophical questions all the time. He argues that no one working in practice in this field or as a theoretician can possibly avoid it. "The real issue," he says, "is whether a given practitioner is doing so consciously and explicitly or only implicitly (i.e., without being aware of it)" (p. 267). He explains that while many psychotherapists and psychologists are beginning to integrate philosophy into their practice, they are "merely dabbling around the visible surface of a sort of "philosophical iceberg," and lack an appreciation of it as a more substantial albeit largely submerged whole" (p. 10). An appreciation, and working knowledge of philosophy can only be gained through a proper education in the discipline. So does the adage that a little knowledge can be a dangerous thing apply in this case? Or is a little familiarity with philosophy better than none whatsoever?

K. W. M. Fulford, Professor of Philosophy and Mental Health in Warwick, UK, explains that it is not necessary, nor indeed desirable, that every psychiatrist should become a philosopher. "But if philosophy is to make a substantial contribution to the subject, all psychiatrists should have some exposure to philosophical thinking in their training" (1995, p.19). He argues openly, like only a very small number of other clinicians have, that in the treatment for mental health problems, what is needed along with the science of psychology is the theory and practice of philosophy (2003 p. 24). Whether it is called philosophical counseling, philosophical therapy, or psychotherapeutic philosophy its practice offers the patient or client the best of both worlds.

SIX
Psychotherapeutic Philosophy

On the day that twenty-three-year-old "Alanna" was supposed to come to her third counseling session with me over the course of three weeks, her brother "Gregg" came to see me instead. Alanna had been bright and cheerful during our first two meetings. I could tell she hadn't felt ready to get to the heart of what was troubling her, but I was careful not to be too insistent. Sometimes a client will take a session or two to sort though and emotions into a meaningful story, so I was willing to be patient. But Gregg told me that the previous afternoon Alanna had gone to the hospital and slashed her wrists with a razor blade "right there in front of all the people in the waiting area." He said the nurses patched up her wounds, gave her some pills, kept her overnight, and then sent her home by taxi the next day. Gregg said his sister does this for attention; she loves the care and concern she gets from the nurses. She likes having women tending to her, and looking after her. Gregg said Alanna is "a talker and loves telling the nurses all about herself." Alanna often likes to talk about suicide, but Gregg has tried to discourage her from doing so. Gregg worries that Alanna hadn't told me about her "real problems" yet. He said Alanna wants to have a relationship with a woman, and to have "an older woman take care of her" but this would be very upsetting to their devoutly religious parents who would certainly see this as sinful. Gregg worried about how Alanna's needs seem to be connected with some sort of lesbian feelings, and that Alanna seems to be expressing these feelings in ways very destructive to herself. He wondered how Alanna can possibly meet her needs, given her parents' uncompromising attitudes. He also wondered if Alanna's very specific desire for the attentions of an older woman may not be homosexual feelings at all but rather, in fact, be an expression of her desire to be loved and accepted by her disapproving mother. Gregg said he is very puzzled and concerned. He wondered

Alanna's "problems" are just a childish desire for attention. Otherwise, how would it be possible for her to reconcile what seems like her lesbian sexual feelings for other women, with the desire to be loved by her own mother? I could see that Gregg was completely puzzled about what it was his sister wanted, what she might need, and what she "really ought to be getting."

WANTS AND NEEDS

People want and need many forms of comfort: physical, mental, emotional, spiritual, rational, and even logical. At first it may seem odd to list rationality and logic among forms of comfort. But rationality and logic furnish some very important elements to life. People want and need events and human behavior, in both their private lives and the public sphere, to be reasonable and consistent, to make sense within their conception of life—to be rational and logical. When things make sense there is a feeling of security because it is possible to predict reasonably well what will happen from moment to moment, and day to day. Being able to predict events, even at a rudimentary level, allows for plans to be made, goals to be aimed for, and for hope to endure. Both natural events and human behavior that fail to make sense initially create discomfort, which can worsen to worry and fear, and so on down a slippery slope to panic and despair. The resulting emotional distress and suffering then often leads to the clinical diagnosis of mental illnesses. Many distressed individuals go to counseling or psychotherapy for axiological clarification and advice because of ethical and moral conflicts that have created difficulty in their lives. They hope that therapy will, first of all, illuminate the values that they actually have, and by which they have been living their lives. They also hope that the counselor or therapist will help them to reorient any of their values that are at the root of their problems (Sharma p. 76). But there are many other reasons why individuals consult counselors and therapists. Below are just a few of the issues individuals might present:

- They don't know what to do or think about any number of issues. For example, about changing jobs, whether to have an "open" marriage, bad dreams, their responsibility to a loved one, coming across a so-called mental illness on the Internet that seems to apply to themselves, giving to charity, military service, and so on.
- They're afraid of doing or thinking the "wrong" thing. This may be as serious as a legal issue, or as personal as the desire not to live in opposition to family values or the values of the community—whether ethnic, religious, professional, social, and so on.
- They need someone to just listen because they feel the need to divest themselves of an emotional burden such as the suffering

brought on by the loss of a loved one by a terminal illness, divorce, abandonment, and so on. It may include a "negative" emotional burden such as the loss of self-esteem, or a "positive" emotional burden such as a feeling of guilt brought on by a life decision that was made.

- They want to know what emotions are appropriate for their situation: Is it OK to be angry? Or should I be sad instead? Is it OK to feel I deserve an apology? Is it OK to feel confused by the facts? Am I too optimistic about everything? Am I silly for feeling alone in a crowd? Am I abnormal for feeling nothing when others are upset?
- They want help with evaluating a situation in retrospect. Is it OK to have done what I did? Was it moral? Am I now the good guy or the bad guy? This can come after a decision was made in haste, when there was inadequate time for a careful consideration of all relevant factors. It can also come on the heels of substantial disagreement or criticisms from others such as family members or work colleagues. The individual may be in need of relief from self-doubt or even guilt about the immediate or distant past.
- They want the approval of an authority figure for what they have done or are about to do. This is different from wanting a second opinion or an expert's perspective on a situation in order to make the most appropriate or beneficial decision. The individual already believes what they have done or are about to do is the right thing to do. What they simply want from the counselor or therapist, for whatever reason, is uncritical expert endorsement. This can be problematic since the counselor or therapist may find the client's actions, or plan of action, morally unacceptable, or simply unwise.
- They want help in understanding someone else's actions or thinking. This can involve difference in cross-gender, cross-generational, cross-cultural, or cross-denominational behaviors and perspectives. It may also concern the individual's struggle to understand some professional's, or a superior's, actions or perspectives that differ from their own point of view.
- They want help in convincing someone else of something. This may be a request for strategic advice in either dissecting the "opponent's" position or in fabricating a robust counterargument. The situation may also be more benevolent such as, for example, when the individual is trying to help a loved one make a decision they believe will be most beneficial to them.
- They want help in developing a worldview. For example they may want to reevaluate the direction of their own life after a particularly devastating or disrupting life event such as a divorce, the death or injury of a loved one, being the victim of crime or oppression, or a loss of faith. They may want to develop a more satisfying understanding of the vicissitudes of life, and to avoid a sense of futility

about events beyond human or individual control such as a natural disaster or a terrorist attack, and to develop a worldview that accounts for them. They may also want life to be less futile, more fulfilling and meaningful.

- They want help in defining themselves in contrast to how others have defined them. This is often especially true of women who have been in abusive and controlling relationships. But it is also an issue for men who have lived a life expected of them which has been demanding and unrewarding. Defining oneself involves not only stereotypical gender issues, but also questions such as, Should I be more independent or more family or community oriented? What do I owe the older and younger generations? What is my duty to others and to myself? Can I be what I desire to be, given the circumstances in which I have been born, raised, and now find myself?

- They don't only want to know *what* to think, they want to learn *how* to think. Advice is very easy to come by, but following it can create a dependency on the thinking of others. Connected to the point above, defining oneself in such a way that one's personal life improves requires the ability to reason well. Sometimes individuals come to the realization that both the advice from others and their own reasoning capacity have reached their practical limits. They come to counselors and therapists to learn to think better for themselves. This is when the philosophically trained counselor or therapist acts as both a Socratic "midwife" helping the individual "give birth" to their own thoughts, and also as an educator imparting knowledge and reasoning skills that will improve the breadth and depth of their thinking.

- They want professional support for their perception of reality and their functioning within it. This often involves an individual who is trying to defend their perception against the accepted "norms" of family, friends, and society. It may also involve an individual's struggle against the metaphysical position inherent in the family's religious orientation.

- They want to find out if they have a diagnosable "mental illness." They want a perspective—other than medical—that will explain their mental distress. This may involve the individual's prior "assessment" by some other counselor or therapist based on the *DSM*'s criteriological diagnostic categories. It makes a significant difference in a person's life to know whether feeling distressed is appropriate in their circumstances or if it can be labeled as a so-called mental illness. This is often based on the erroneous assumption that a "mental illness" can unexpectedly victimize an individual independent of their current life situation. For some people the clinical diagnosis of a mental illness can actually be comforting because there is little, if any, personal responsibility or guilt associated with being victimized. For others such a diagnosis can be devastating, both emotionally and socially. The individual's primary underlying question is, "Is my distress abnormal?"

The *Oxford Textbook of Philosophy of Psychiatry* explains that mental disorders include disturbances of emotion, volition, desire, appetite, motivation, perception, behavior, and thought (p. 10). Although of significant concern, none of these disturbances themselves, nor any of the above issues, nor any others presented by individuals to their counselors and therapists, must necessarily be diagnosed as physical brain problems requiring medications. Such a diagnosis is also generally inadvisable because of the fact that in sentient beings the mental supervenes on the physical: the person's reasons, not the body's or brain's physical properties, are what motivate thinking beings into action. For example, a man buys flowers for his wife because it is her birthday, not because the image of a bunch of flowers stimulated the photoreceptors of his retina causing the neurons in his visual cortex to activate the muscles in his limbs into purchasing mode. Alternately, the woman is sad because she believes her husband has forgotten her birthday, not because seeing the empty flower vase on the table caused her to be sad. She has probably seen the vase empty many times during the previous year without ever feeling as sad as she does on this one particular day. Saying that the woman's seeing the empty vase caused her to be sad leaves an explanatory gap that can only be filled with her reasons for feeling this way. If the physical cause—perceiving the empty vase—were sufficient explanation for the woman's sadness then, logically, a blindfold over her eyes should alleviate her sadness. A simple experiment like this can easily demonstrate the flaw in the physicalist reasoning which seems to claim that emotional suffering and mental distress are caused by retinal stimulation or brain activity alone.

Individuals struggling with emotional suffering and mental distress want more than the medical alleviation of their physical symptoms. They are looking for a more informed perspective than the one they already have; they want to find a wise position to take. A positive outcome requires that the clinician possesses the sort of expert knowledge and discursive skills fundamental to, and characteristic of, good philosophy. The intention of the philosophy contained within any one of the many contemporary psychotherapeutic models, is not to diagnose and prognosticate. It is "to let philosophical reflection on the human condition throw light on the specific problems in living that arise in individual situations" (Deurzen-Smith p. 132) and then to help the individual resolve those problems in a life-enhancing way. For example, Marvin graduated near the top of his high school class a year ago. He says he has been fired from three similar manufacturing jobs since then because he can't concentrate on his work. His self-esteem has taken a serious hit, and he worries that there's something wrong with his brain that keeps him from being able to focus for very long on the job at hand. In fact at the last job his loss of focus resulted in a machine's costly breakdown. Marvin said his medical doctor suggested he may be suffering from ADHD, and offered to write him a prescription. Marvin declined the offer but now wonders if he should see a psychiatrist and maybe get that medication. But during discussions with a philosophically trained therapist, who does not search for a "mental illness" diagnosis, it turns out that Marvin is simply too bored to concentrate for very long on repetitive and unchallenging production line work. Marvin and the therapist came to the decision that the solution to Marvin's problem is for Marvin to find more mentally stimulating work. The solution seems to be to find work that suits the man, rather than trying to make the man fit the job. This philosophical perspective avoids the use of medications, and all the attendant side-effect problems that can make life even more difficult. Beyond the resolution of immediate life problems, philosophy can also be learned as a skill by the interested client or patient whose desire includes acquiring the ability to solve future problems without having to rely on a professional counselor, therapist, or other sort of clinician.

WHAT IS PHILOSOPHY?

The word "philosophy" is used in a variety of ways: as a position held by an individual on various issues or life in general, as a body of knowledge, and as an activity. It's not uncommon to hear someone say, "my philosophy is to always tell the truth." What the individual means is that she lives according to a personal code, an arrangement of values and beliefs which leads her to tell the truth. While having a personal philosophy seems admirable, such a personal philosophy might be neither benevolent, coherent, nor rational. Very few individuals ever take the time to examine their philosophy; and rarely are their philosophies so well organized or developed that they can, in actuality, be systematically examined. In fact it's not uncommon for a person to live with a personal philosophy that is internally contradictory, potentially problematic, and even harmful to both that individual and to others. For example, one element of a personal philosophy might be to always tell the truth. But is telling the truth always the best policy, one that avoids unnecessarily hurting others or oneself? There are many examples of life situations in which not telling the truth leads to the best, most moral, outcome. Obviously, what is most important to living a good life is to live according to a philosophy that is helpful to both oneself and others, not just any sort of philosophy at all.

The classical definition of philosophy is that it is the pursuit of "Truth" with a capital "T." But this is unhelpful because it leaves the unanswered question, "truth about what?" Also, in order to pursue the Truth the pursuer must already have a prior knowledge of what the Truth is. If it is unknown then how does the pursuer know when he has come upon it? But this creates a paradox in which the pursuer must already know what he is attempting to find.

Philosophy has also been historically defined as "the love of wisdom" based on its Greek etymology. This is likewise unhelpful because, if philosophy is an activity, then to say that it is the love of wisdom is no explanation of what it means to practice philosophy, to be engaged in doing philosophy, or to be an active philosopher. The explanation that philosophy is the love of wisdom can be found in most introductory philosophy course texts, as well as in many other books where philosophy is discussed or even just mentioned. For example, in his book *The Philosophy of Cognitive-Behavioural Therapy* psychotherapist Donald Robertson says that the ancient Stoics differentiated between "mere rhetoric or word play" and "*practical* philosophy, or genuine love of wisdom" (p. 49). He emphasizes the word "practical" but still identifies philosophy as the act of loving wisdom which does not seem very practical at all. Also, if a philosopher is simply a person who loves wisdom, and surely everyone would say they love wisdom, then does that mean that everyone is a philosopher? Clearly the classical definitions are not very enlightening. So what is philosophy, and how does it enhance the practice of counseling and psychotherapy?

Philosophy, beyond a personal code of behavior, includes accurate empirical knowledge, a knowledge of the history of ideas, critical and creative thinking skills, the capacity for good judgments, the ability to make moral decisions, on-going self-scrutiny, and a respectful discursive style. The philosopher Immanuel Kant called this "practical philosophy." It "originates from goals and motivations, similar to activity, which arises from its goals, not from causalities" (Schrank p. 137). Practical philosophy involves a paradigm shift. It is "a practice connected to daily life, learning how to think and to live a good life rather than simply gathering information or transmitting knowledge. And it is mainly based on the history of ideas (Millon p. 410). Furthermore, it involves examining what we consider knowledge to be. The philosopher and psychologist William James describes it as "an unusually stubborn effort to think clearly" (p. 296). He should have added "and the application of the results of that clear thinking to one's behavior and actions." Philosophy has often been described as "open," that is, open to disagreement, open to self-doubt, open to being proved wrong, and open to new ways of looking at things. "Philosophy recognizes that our definition of abstract knowledge is open to critical questioning and reflection, as are the underlying conceptual foundations of our empirical or scientific knowledge claims and activities" (Kendler and Parnas p. 389). This is not the sort of position that is normally championed in contemporary psychotherapy with its rivalry between theoretical orientations and methodologies.

University course texts describe philosophy in many different ways—sometimes very obscurely and sometimes more clearly. For example, it has been characterized as a value orientation and "a generalized and organized conception, influencing behavior, of nature, of man's place in it, of man's relation to man, and of the desirable and non-desirable as they may relate to man-environment and inter-human relation" (Parsons and Shils p. 411). A simpler explanation comes from the text by Manuel Velasquez who starts with the well-known adage that philosophy begins with wonder. The goal of philosophy, he says, is to get us "to make up our own minds about oneself, life, knowledge, art, religion, and morality without simply depending on the authority of parents, peers, television, teachers, or society" (p. 4). He points out that philosophy deepens our awareness of both ourselves and the world we live in, which in turn "gives us the ability to deal with and slough off encumbrances to freedom." He says it also exposes us to the history of thought, gaining us an insight into a world of contrasting, and sometimes conflicting ideas that lead us to be more tolerant, humble about our own intellectual abilities, and less biased. Philosophy helps us to "refine our powers of analysis, our abilities to think critically, to reason, to evaluate, to theorize, and to justify" and to "apply them constructively to our own affairs" (p. 34). John Chaffee maintains that philosophy provides individuals with the motivation and the intellectual abilities required to explore life's most challenging issues. It helps us to be more thoughtful, more open-minded, more attuned to the complexities and subtleties of life, more willing and better able to think critically about oneself and life's important issues: "The conclusions we reach by thinking philosophically have direct application for how we live our lives in the real world" (p. 4, 5). Thomas Shipka and Arthur Minton characterize philosophy as "the evaluation of beliefs to determine whether they are true, and the evaluation of practices to determine whether they are sensible and ethical" (p. 2). And Paul Wolff explains in his book that philosophy is "the systematic critical examination of the way in which we judge, evaluate, and act, with the aim of making ourselves wiser, more self-reflective, and therefore better men and women" (p. 6). There are, of course, many more ways to describe philosophy other than the simplistic "pursuit of Truth" or "love of wisdom." Most importantly for this book are three primary functions of philosophy: first, philosophy can help the philosophical thinker overcome emotional suffering and mental distress, and thereby live a better life; second, the philosophical thinker can use his or her abilities to help someone else overcome their current suffering and distress; and third the philosophical thinker can teach someone else to become a more philosophical thinker who will then be better able to overcome their own future difficulties.

From the earliest days of recorded history philosophy concerned itself with attempting to better understand the human condition and human concerns, for the purpose of more effective, better informed, and more rewarding living. It is "a demanding activity" that, like any other worthwhile practice requires the practitioner to work on both himself and his proficiency (Millon p. 409). Philosophy was originally committed to having a broad understanding of life, and to put this at the service of the public. Unfortunately this practical application was seriously eroded over the centuries, until philosophy became nothing more than abstract and hypothetical disputation. But by the beginning of the twentieth century a revival of philosophy as a practice was taking shape. This led to philosophical works in various areas such as existentialism and ethics being recognized by a few clinicians as essential addendums to the practice of counseling and psychotherapy. This resulted in the work of a number of practitioners over the past century "addressing human difficulties as problems in living rather than as medical conditions." Many of these practitioners were trained as psychiatrists or psychoanalysts. But they discovered the limitations of their discipline and turned to philosophy as a better alternative to the purely psychological approach to mental suffering and distress (Deurzen-Smith p. 131–32).

Philosophical discussions sometimes help individuals to gain a unique or at least different way of looking at things. For example, a philosophical discussion may illustrate how it is possible to have a perspective on the rights of women or men that avoids common stereotypical generalizations; it can lead to a recognition of personal biases about religion, child rearing, relationships, and so on; or it might lead to a startling factual realization such as, for example, that evolution is not the process of natural "selection"—an action taken by nature—but simply the inability of some species to adapt to environmental changes. Philosophy is unavoidable, because everyone is always operating from within their own context of beliefs, presuppositions, social conditioning, and background understandings. These are "the total set of one's own philosophical beliefs, values, and assumptions including those which one may have adopted without being explicitly aware of them" (Hersch p. 8, 362)

But how can philosophy be therapeutic when it is often described as the pursuit of Truth with a capital "t"? One way to respond to this perspective is to actually ask the thought-provoking question, "Truth about what?" This focuses thinking or discussion on a particular issue, the nature of Truth, rather than a grandiose generalization about some nebulous pursuit or quest. Another response is that there is indeed a true or false answer to many particular types of questions such as, for example, "Am I, or are they, living a good life?" The answer to this question can indeed be evaluated as either true or false. To claim that a monotonous distressing, impoverished, fearful, or painful way of life is a good life is just false. So philosophy's "pursuit of Truth" might include the pursuit of truth about someone's life as that person is living it, with the recognition of the fact that only a life which fosters human flourishing and happiness is truly a good life.

Another way of looking at the "pursuit of Truth" definition is that it may have been accurate at the time of Socrates and Plato to describe philosophy as the pursuit of Truth when philosophy still dealt with questions such as "Why is a tree leaf green?" "How distant is the next continent?" "How do you calculate the area of a circle?" or "How many stars are there in the universe?" For these questions there are true and false answers, even if they are not actually available to us at this time in history. But these kind of empirical and mathematical questions are no longer part of philosophy. They have been removed from philosophy and segregated into their own fields. The famous nineteenth-century German philosopher Friedrich Nietzsche complained that philosophy in his day was nothing more than a very boring academic pastime. He said he was waiting for a "philosopher physician" who would have the courage to recognize that what was at stake in all philosophizing was not at all so-called truth but something more like health, growth, power, and life. The twentieth century's most influential philosopher, Ludwig Wittgenstein, saw the study of philosophy as useless if all it does is enable students to talk with some plausibility about some abstruse questions in logic, and so on, and if it does not improve thinking about the important questions of everyday life. John Dewey, the highly regarded American philosopher of education, wrote early in the twentieth century that philosophy would show its true value only when it stopped being what it was—a device for dealing with the problems of philosophers—and become instead a method, developed by philosophers, for dealing with the problems of men. So what has philosophy become? Since 1981 some philosophers, who call themselves philosophical counselors, have willingly accepted the challenge to take philosophy out of their university lecture halls and offer it as a kind of therapy to the real world. And psychological counselors and psychotherapists are beginning to recognize the value of applying philosophy overtly in their various practices.

Philosophy in counseling and therapy involves helping individuals to examine the reasons they have for the values they hold as good and the beliefs they hold to be true. Such an examination can free individuals from blindly following tradition, slavishly obeying authority figures, or acting only on their feelings. This has been simplistically called "thinking about thinking." In the language of academic philosophy it's called "metacognition" which refers to a set of processes by which people think about their own thinking and feeling, as well as those of others. It marks a "set of capacities for self-reflection as well as reflection about the thoughts and feelings of others" (Lysaker and Lysaker p. 169). Metacognition, the examination of one's own beliefs, values, fears, and assumptions, and those of others, is not simply a philosophical diversion; it is a important ability in the avoidance or mitigation of the distress and suffering that can lead to a diagnosis of so-called mental illness. While th ability varies greatly among individuals, the study of philosophy ca significantly enhance anyone's reasoning "tools," and thereby the meta cognitive abilities which are typically acquired from family, peers, and standard pre-university education. As Martha Nussbaum puts it,

> Philosophers claim that the pursuit of logical validity, intellectual coherence, and truth delivers freedom from tyranny of custom and convention, creating a community of beings who can take charge of their own life story and their own thought. (p. 5)

When philosophy is defined in this way it leaves no doubt that it perfectly suited as treatment for the more common "mental disorders such as depression, anxiety, and mood swings. However philosophy ha also been demonstrated to alleviate the suffering of those who have bee diagnosed with "serious" or "clinical" mental disorders that were on considered organic brain diseases such as "clinical" depression, schizophrenia, paranoia, and more. In his essay titled "Philosophy and Therapy: Professional Training and Certification" Sam Brown references R. I Laing's research and writes that "there is good reason to believe that philosophical approach can be effective even for schizophrenic sy dromes" when the philosophy "is rooted in existentialism rather tha conceptual analysis" (p. 161). Over the past two decades many treatme outcome studies have shown that the so-called "talk therapies," whic are modeled on philosophical discussions, are the most effective in n only resolving seriously troubling issues, but in long-term effect and be efits (Enright p.1811–1816; Frank p.219; Rothbaum p. 123, 132, 143, 16 204, 208, 254). In fact these philosophy-based therapies are even better l themselves than in combination with SSRI-type drugs (Simpson & Lieb witz p.143). For example, for a discussion of CBT as the best treatment f depression, social phobia (SP), obsessive-compulsive disorder (OCD panic disorder (PD), and post-traumatic stress disorder (PTSD) see *Path logical Anxiety: Emotional Processing in Etiology and Treatment*, edited b Barbara Olasov Rothbaum (p. 123, 132, 143, 160, 204, 208, 254). (See al Gerald Corey's *Theory and Practice of Counseling and Psychotherapy*, p. 170 CBT is also considered "the gold standard" for treatment of panic diso ders (Allen & Barlow p. 172). Elizabeth Hembree, with the Department (Psychiatry at the University of Pennsylvania School of Medicine, an Norah Feeny with the Department of Psychiatry and Psychology at Ca Western University report that "numerous studies have found CBT effe tive in reducing Post-Traumatic Stress Syndrome (PTSD) and associate symptoms, making it the most empirically validated approach among th psychosocial treatments for PTSD" (p. 204, 208). John Hunsley an

Catherine M. Lee, Professors of Psychology at the University of Ottawa, cite extensive research from both the US (e.g., Merrill, et al.; Persons et al.) and the UK (e.g., Cahill et al.) into treatment outcomes in numerous countries which have shown that the cognitive-behavioral type of treatments—which are the psychologized practice of philosophy—are more efficacious for individuals of all ages than were other treatment approaches.

> For most conditions, the outcomes of different treatments are not equivalent, and at present, there is strongest support for the efficacy of CBT ... for common psychological disorders—mood disorders, anxiety disorders, eating disorders, sleep disorders, sexual disorders, and substance-related disorders. (p. 660)

Again, a "mental disorder" is not an organic problem of the material brain; it is instead a problem within a person's mental narrative, within the mind's propositional content which are beliefs, values, fears, assumptions, and so on. So it is no wonder that talk therapies, and especially CBT, have been found to be as effective, and in some cases more effective, than medications—and without the horrible side effects. And these talk therapies are all just philosophy under different, psychologically sounding names. Philosophical issues are never really far from the clinical work that is called counseling or psychotherapy. The counselor's or psychotherapist's explicit awareness of those issues, found in what their patients or clients tell them, will help them in their practical therapeutic endeavors (Hersch p. 296). Nussbaum calls the philosophy that is practiced in counseling and psychotherapy "medical philosophy" which delves deep into the patient's psychology, and ultimately, if need be, challenges it, and helps to change it (p. 35). Edwin Hersch points out that philosophy is extremely relevant to the field of counseling and psychotherapy because philosophical awareness changes the actual practice in indirect ways.

> What we see and how we experience the interactions in our psychotherapy encounters will necessarily be different (and hopefully enriched), after we arrive at an understanding of "the philosophical anatomy of the psychotherapeutic situation," or more explicitly increase our own self-knowledge of our underlying philosophical paradigms. (p. 346)

In psychotherapy, the question "Why?" initiates the often medical search for what caused the patient's thinking, with the assumption that this cause is organic or somehow genetic. This can then lead to the diagnosis of a "mental illness," resulting in the shame associated with the belief that a label of a mental illness is indicative of that individual being defective. On the other hand, in philosophy the question "Why?" is asked in order to discover the reasons behind the person's thinking. The reasons may be vague, ill defined, confused, and even irrational. But these are just problems in reasoning and logic; they're not "mental illnesses." Problematic reasoning and faulty logic are not shame-inducing when they are discovered in a respectful discursive environment. They can be "fixed" with a little effort, and do not result in some life-long "disorder" label.

Because philosophy is a non-psychological approach to mental problems, it is sometimes accused of not being able to deal with emotions, and of dealing merely with cognitions. But emotions don't appear out of a vacuum. According to contemporary cognitive theories in psychology, "an essential property of emotions is that they are intentional states, typically either a belief or judgment, which entails that they are about or directed at something or someone" (Atkinson p. 548). The Stoics taught their students that many centuries ago. Philosophy is extremely well suited for an examination of beliefs, judgments, values, assumptions, and fears that can lead to a relief of unwanted negative and painful emotions.

Furthermore, emotions are very important as the primary factor in initiating any sort of philosophical thought or discussion. Mary Gick and Robert Lockhart explain that research has shown that the emotions or "the affective component" may play a major role in motivating the individual to locate the problem in the first place. Emotions also play a significant role in the individual's decision to go ahead and examine the problem. They maintain that the emotions can signal that there is something curious that invites a second look, or that there is something wrong that needs to be scrutinized more carefully. The discovery of a problem may leave the individual with a nagging feeling of not knowing, and therefore wanting to know more (p. 203). These are affective (emotional) motivating factors which every philosopher experiences before the personal decision is made to philosophize. Emotions play a central generative role in philosophy whether philosophers are willing to acknowledge, or are even aware of, this fact or not. To state it more simply: rational philosophical inquiry comes only after a feeling that something needs to be inquired into.

A slightly different perspective on emotions is discussed by the seventeenth-century British philosopher David Hume. In a conference presentation paper titled "The Case of Hume's Self-Cure through a True Philosophy" Heebong Choi gives a detailed account of how Hume went from despair, and what might be called a minor mental breakdown, to revise and improve the way he did philosophy. In "section vii: Conclusion of this book" Hume argues that a purely intellectual or reason-based philosophical inquiry can lead to serious melancholy, despair, mental misery, and a so-called "overheating of the brain." Hume decided to change his approach to include "sentiments and the indulgence of these sentiments, which would be "emotion-based philosophy." This constitutes "true philosophical inquiry" or at least a better, healthier form of it than a pure intellectual activity. Choi concludes that "philosophers are recommended to indulge their emotions when they are doing philosophy," so as to temper their reasoning with good emotions (p. 322, 324).

The belief that a philosopher is always someone who teaches in an institution is a fairly recent development within human history. In fact, as discussed in chapter 4, philosophy did not begin as an academic subject at all. It was originally considered a practice, a way of life, or a means by which to help people live better lives. Recall that around the beginning of the Christian Era Seneca wrote in his letter to Lucilius,

> Shall I tell you what philosophy holds out to humanity? Counsel. One person is facing death, another is vexed by poverty. . . . All mankind are stretching out their hands to you on every side. Lives have been ruined, lives that are on the way to ruin are appealing for some help; it is to you that they look for hope and assistance. (Borowicz p. 7)

But today few people facing death or vexed by poverty would imagine that they could find hope, assistance, or even simple comfort in a visit to an academic philosopher. Academic philosophy has gained the reputation of being dry, abstract, lacking in empathy and human compassion, more interested in tidy hypothetical cases than messy real-life problems, largely unconcerned with women's issues, and generally focused on technical trivialities. The so-called practice of philosophy in many colleges and universities has deteriorated into debating specialized terminology and determining the veracity of symbolized premises. The typical position of the academic philosopher is exemplified in Bertrand Russell's Lowell lectures delivered in Boston in 1914. He said that the aim of philosophy is the *theoretical* understanding of the world, which is "not a matter of great practical importance to animals, or to savages, or even to most civilized men" (1993 p. 36). This may have been true of his day, but today philosophy is in fact a matter of great practical importance when it is applied in counseling or psychotherapy.

Philosophy is of course taught and practiced best by philosophers. And yet while many scholars study philosophy, few trained philosophers actually offer their knowledge and expertise to the public as a practice. And those who do — for example by moderating a philosophy café — rarely, if ever offer their services directly to the so-called mentally ill. One of the characteristics of the university is that it is made up of professors who train students to become professors, professionals who train their apprentices to become professionals, and specialists who mentor their cohorts to become specialists. In the twentieth century philosophy is solidly linked to the university classroom. It is an academic discourse that is no longer linked to "a way of life" as Hadot puts it (p. 270–71). Arthur Schopenhauer put it this way: "University philosophy is mere fencing in front of a mirror" (p. 163–64). The concern among some psychotherapists is not that there is a new method of counseling on "the market" that will compete with theirs. It's more a worry about philosophers calling themselves "philosophical counselors," when the stereotypical philosopher is the solitary individual with few social skills, who enjoys theorizing, whose discursive approach is confrontational and combative, and who would rather bury his or her nose in a book than have an empathetic discussion with a suffering human being.

The practice of philosophy is in actuality neither mere solitary self-scrutiny nor teaching in a classroom. In the same way that teaching law is not the same as practicing law, and teaching medicine is not the same as practicing medicine, teaching philosophy is not the same as practicing it. The problem is that philosophy has for so long been identified with the exclusively academic activity—one knowledgeable person passing that knowledge on to others—that it's very difficult for some individuals to conceive of it in any other way. But the proffered practice of philosophy may rightly be compared to the practice of law and medicine not in order to superciliously elevate the status of philosophy in some way, but to demonstrate how the word "practice" is commonly used—as one person assisting another with his or her specialized knowledge and skills. Practice, when it means assisting, is very different from the practice of teaching. It's true that philosophers often write that philosophy is practiced alone, that it's a solitary discipline. But no lawyer would say that to practice law means to defend only oneself; and no physician would say that to practice medicine means to heal only oneself. If counseling is a practice between two people then the practice of philosophy as counseling or therapy is clearly not a solitary endeavor. How odd it would be if philosophically trained counselors and psychotherapists only treated themselves. Recall that Socrates compared the practice of philosophy to that of midwifery because, as he put it, philosophy helps people give birth to their own ideas. Being a midwife is clearly not a solitary activity.

To practice, whether it be law, medicine, or philosophy, actually always involves two important elements: first, at least two people—the patient or client and the specialist or expert; and second, a vested interest in the outcome held by both the patient or client and the practitioner. This second point is a crucial difference between the practice of philosophy and its academic pursuit. In academia there is no vested interest in the outcome of discussions about biomedical, business, political, ethical, or metaphysical issues. Of course, students do their best to resolve the philosophical issues presented in class by the teacher or textbook, but there are no real-life consequences for the student produced by the discussion's conclusion, except perhaps as indirectly reflected in the student's end-of-semester grade for the course. On the other hand, in counseling or therapy both the client and the philosophical practitioner do their utmost to come up with a fair, moral, and acceptable resolution to the issues under discussion, and then decide on an equally acceptable course of action. They do this with great care because the client will have to live with the long-term consequences of her subsequent action.

COUNSELING AS PHILOSOPHICAL THERAPY

Today the term "Philosophical Counseling" primarily refers to the use of philosophical discourse as a specific approach to, or method in, counseling; a therapeutic practice. Philosophical Counseling is also often referred to as Philosophical Practice. But beyond a name for yet another counseling or therapeutic method, the term "philosophical counseling" can also refer to any type of counseling that utilizes both the content and the skills of philosophy. For example, a counselor or therapist may carry both the title "Philosophical Counsleor" and also be a "philosophical" counselor while being a specialist in, say, Rational Emotive Behavior Therapy (REBT) because of his or her use of the insights and discursive skills gained from a comprehensive education in philosophy.

While psychotherapy is often primarily concerned with cataloguing a patient's symptoms in order to establish a diagnosis, philosophy goes directly to the heart of philosophical issues and concerns that are not merely of academic interest but of personal relevance and significance to that particular individual. It offers both the best available theoretical information as well as the most practical approaches to individuals searching for relief from the difficulties of their own real-life situations. And because a counselor who employs philosophy does not diagnose life problems as psychopathology—by not labeling those who are troubled as having a so-called mental illnesses—philosophy can be far more helpful in some situations than many of the various standard forms of counseling and psychotherapy where the presence of philosophy is merely incidental.

Contrary to criticisms from some academic circles, just because philosophy is used by a counselor dealing with a client's deeply emotional and very intimate personal issues does not mean the counselor is therefore not doing "real" philosophy. Every question the counselor asks of a client and every suggestion he or she makes is informed by a philosophical consciousness and methodology every bit as rigorous as those of his or her academic colleagues. When philosophy is employed in counseling and therapy it does not replace either psychotherapy or academic philosophy. Instead it augments the meager contents of what passes for "talk therapy" with the knowledge and skills prized by academics that have been developed by philosophers for more than two thousand years.

Philosopher John Davis writes that philosophy is a therapy when it provides the conditions for the progressive growth of what is distinctively human; when it assists in "the continued development of the constructive potentialities of the individual and the maximal fulfillment of the individual life" (p. 13). Philosophically trained counselors and therapists are free from the mandatory adherence to the specific techniques required by the various "schools" of psychotherapy. They employ the unrestricted approach of philosophy in helping the people who come to them. Psychotherapists, on the other hand, are constrained in dealing with their patients not only by exclusionist methodologies but by science and medicine which harbor numerous problematic assumptions and theories about the organic brain that are ambiguously attributed to the non-material mind.

Although reflection and insight by the patient or client are important aspects of almost every form of counseling, analysis, and therapy, counseling with philosophy is not psychoanalysis. The philosophical counselor does not attempt a "cure" by trying to make conscious so-called "unconscious motivations," or by trying to bring "new material" to the surface from an assumed unconscious by means of an analysis of random thoughts produced in "free associations." It is important to note that while the foundational theory guiding all forms of psychotherapy rests on supposed insights into a concealed unconscious, philosophical counselors hold that what often passes for the unconscious may be better described as an individual's accumulated, socially transmitted, and personally generated beliefs, assumptions, values, fears, and norms which influence but don't determine his thinking and actions. When their influence is not noticed by the individual, it is not because his brain has hidden them from himself but because they have been taken for granted, ignored, or forgotten (Sartre argues the impossibility of hiding thoughts from oneself in his book *Being and Nothingness*). Yet, even given this substantially different description of mental functioning, counseling with philosophy is not completely dissimilar to the many forms of cognitive therapy. Psychotherapist Albert Ellis argues that if a client's emotional upset stems directly from events that occurred in the past which can never "unoccur" then it seems logical to assume the client will necessarily always remain disturbed. Yet, as his many years of helping disturbed individuals with REBT has shown him, clients can and do get over past unchangeable life events. The question is, "How and why?" Ellis maintains that individuals undo the influence of earlier life events by means of a guided examination of those events. This modifies the ways the individual thinks, feels, and acts in relation to those events. He holds that there is an interaction which occurs in counseling both between client and counselor, and within the client. Ellis claims that this "interactionism" is central to any discussion of how counseling works.

> Interactionism implies that cognitions, emotions, and behaviors significantly overlap and interact with and affect each other. Therefore if we change any of these processes we tend to modify the other two. Also, biological and environmental factors reciprocally interact. In this kind of interactionism, thought, feeling, and action continually influence each other and are never completely disparate. (1989, 92, 139)

But Ellis is one of only a few psychotherapists who hold that cognitive restructuring or re-thinking of past events is generally sufficient to effect a "cure." Many believe that their patients must also release their pent-up emotions in the presence of a trusted therapist. This may involve acting out distressing past events (abreaction), or relating to the therapist as though the therapist were somehow responsible for those events (transference). The necessity for emotional release through so-called abreaction and transference has not been established with research, and is still a contentious issue. But since counseling with philosophy is not psychotherapy the question remains, "What is it that makes it so effective?" and "What needs to happen during the philosophical examination of a life for that life to be once again deemed worth living by its owner?"

Perhaps one of the first things philosophy can do for a distressed individual is help them to recognize their blind spots, their invisible biases, problematic beliefs, hurtful values, baseless or incorrect assumptions, unreasonable fears, and so on. Case studies presented in the "Philosophical Counseling" literature, as well as the experiences in my own practice, indicate that there are a number of necessary elements inherent in any successful examination of a life, i.e., in any examination which ameliorates the suffering and distress of the patient or client. These include the client's recognition that there is a problem, coming to trust the counselor, dealing with troublesome emotions (affects) in a non-psychoanalytic manner, insight into the issues or problems and their resolution, the discovery of alternative perspectives and actions, teaching and learning (heuristics), and a discovery or creation of meaning.

RECOGNITION

Individuals come to counselors and therapists voluntarily. Unless they are in an institution, people are not forced by others into counseling or therapy. Of course they may have been persuaded or coerced by family members, but generally individuals who become clients or patients have recognized that a problems exists for them that they are unable to resolve on their own or with the help of family and friends. But a recognition that a problems exists does not automatically lead to insights into what that problem actually consists of. Friends and family are often able to help resolve many of life's complications and disturbances. But when these consist of a complex of multiple interacting layers the attentions of someone trained in philosophical investigation generally results in the best outcome.

One of my clients who had experienced the loss of a number of significant people in his life to fatal illnesses felt helpless and ineffective in his attempt to live a happy life. It seemed every time a friendship deepened the friend died from some terrible disease or accident. He came to see me because he believed his approach to making and keeping friends was no longer working. He was so despondent he admitted to having had suicidal thoughts. But during our philosophical discussions he came to recognize that he had only actually lost a few close friends, and that he had pushed the rest away from him for fear of having to suffer their loss as well. He also came to see that the individuals he chose to be his friends were invariably people who made him feel needed because they were already suffering from various chronic illnesses or emotional difficulties. He came to understand that while he believed he was having a negative effect on others the truth was quite the opposite: the needful others he brought into his life were having a negative effect on him. A philosophical exploration helped this person to recognize the complex problematic beliefs he had about himself and others. It helped to diminish his painful emotions, to learn a new way of seeing his own actions, and to develop a different, more rewarding approach to personal relationships.

TRUST

The examination of a life is best done with the help of another person who is willing to act as an impartial but empathetic observer: someone who will listen non-judgmentally, can propose meaningful alternate perspectives on problems, and is willing to offer viable suggestions for their mitigation. The study of philosophy creates more competence in these areas than the study of psychotherapy alone. It helps the counselor or therapist to be a more capable facilitator in the examination of the client's personal life problems, and life in general. Of course, the counselor's or therapist's warmth, genuineness, care, and connection with the client, stemming from a thoughtful understanding of the client's values and goals, also helps to build trust. But the counselor's familiarity with philosophical themes and her analytical skills can create in the client the feeling—and legitimately so—that he is being helped by a competent partner. The counselor makes her expertise in philosophy readily available to the client as a resource in his battle with life's uncertainties against a background of a hostile world, or within the foreground of a dysfunctional family situation. It can lead to the client gaining significant relief from the depression brought on by the futility of indecision in dealing with complicated life problems. I have had clients say to me, "It feels good to know there's someone on my side; an educated person who I can trust not to diagnose my problems as mental illnesses."

The first step in establishing trust is making the counseling relationship a safe place. The philosophical attitude of the counselor or psychotherapist trained in philosophy ensures that there is physical, emotional, and intellectual safety in the physical space, the emotional interchange, and the philosophical discourse. The concept of intellectual safety is central to the Philosophy for Children movement's "Community of Inquiry" concept.

> In an intellectually safe place there are no putdowns and no comments intended to belittle, undermine, negate, devalue, or ridicule. . . . The group accepts virtually any question or comment, so long as it is respectful of the other members of the circle. (Homma p. 141)

Psychiatrists and other psychotherapists have been known to put their patients down—both intentionally and unintentionally—by maintaining a superior position of authority over them; by belittling their patients' theories about the origins of their so-called mental illnesses; by undermining their patients' hopes of recovery and cure; by negating their patients' subjective reports about their "conditions"; by dismissing their patients' complaints about the side effects of their medications; by devaluing their patients' interest in psychiatric and psychotherapeutic procedures; and by ridiculing their patients' desires for philosophical discussions. Not only does this create a negative emotional relationship between the counselor or therapist and the client or patient, it creates a counter-productive therapeutic environment by undermining the trust necessary for effective therapy. A philosophical attitude, on the other hand, avoids all of these "unsafe" practices.

Trust within a counseling relationship can strengthen the client's anticipation of operative help, and the possibility of improvement. The client knows the philosophically trained counselor has at her disposal a wealth of information, abilities, wisdom, and resources the client lacks. This raises the justified expectations in the client that the care being received includes an active attempt on the part of the care-giver to actually alleviate the pain of his suffering, and not simply to administer palliative comfort. Furthermore, the counselor's reassurance that she is on the client's side, and is a thoughtful partner in a therapeutic alliance, creates hope in the client that this team work will eventually be successful. Hope is also generated by the counselor offering examples from the history of philosophy of how individuals have overcome great personal difficulties, perhaps similar to those of the client, by means of philosophical contemplation and discussions. This leads to the client's trust in the very process of philosophical inquiry. It also leads to the client's recognition of the possibility that difficult life experiences are not inescapably permanent, but are merely indicators of a period of transition that will be overcome. The expectation of help and the hope for relief in the future are intrinsic catalytic therapeutic elements which can motivate the client to maximize his own efforts at self-transformation.

Another important aspect of trust is the fact that a philosophical approach in counseling allows the individual who has been defined by family and friends as "the strong one" to admit to weaknesses, to unload the burden of being the one who is always ready and able to help others, and to accept help from someone else without the risk of appearing weak and incompetent. It also allows the one who has been defined as "the weak one" or "the black sheep" to gather strength and self-confidence in both a supportive and learning environment focused on the client's strengths and positive characteristics.

The counselor's role in the examination of a troublesome life does not end at the door. Philosophically trained counselors are able to offer both confidential emotional support and comprehensive learning resources that the client may call upon at any time. This can afford the client relief from both intellectual isolation and emotional suffering.

EMOTIONS (AFFECT)

The examination of a life by means of a philosophical discussion allows for the expression of various emotions in a safe and non-judgmental environment. This helps to reduce daytime worrying and also enables the client to achieve a better night's sleep because it diminishes stress and its attendant wakefulness and nightmares. This in turn leads to an improved condition such as healthy blood pressure, a better appetite, a more cheerful disposition, and a better all-around physical state. Stress relief leads to a decrease in the feeling of helplessness and despair when life seems overwhelming. In my own clients I have seen stress relief manifest itself as a marked reduction in stuttering, fidgeting, facial tics, searching for words, worrying about "what ifs," anger, regret, guilt, fear, shame, frustration, sleeplessness, nightmares, fatigue, and crying. Relief from stress has led many of my clients to once again enjoy life rather than merely enduring it. The relief of stress by means of counseling with philosophy sets into motion an important phenomenon that may be called an *internal therapeutic circle*: stress relief allows for greater clarity of thinking which produces more stress relief which allows for greater clarity of thinking, and so on. And the improvement of the client's disposition by means of the philosophical discussions changes for the better his interactions with the individuals in the world around him, which in turn improves his disposition, and so on, in a second *external therapeutic circle* between the client and his world. While in psychoanalysis change is said to occur within the individual, or intra-psychically, and existential therapy maintains that change occurs "outside" or "in-between," at the point of the person's involvement with the world (Cohn 1997), the counselor or therapist trained in philosophy sees change as activated from both inside and outside the individual.

Counseling or therapy with philosophy achieves in the client or patient what may be called a "philosophical disposition." It leads to a welcoming of the inevitable, a calm acceptance of those things which can't be changed such as natural events, relationship transformations, and personal death. It relieves the client's fear of being at the mercy of either hostile hidden forces within himself or harmful forces targeting him from without. It helps the client understand that his fear of what may possibly occur can be alleviated by a rational consideration of its probability. It relieves the client's concern that his problem is trivial, that his suffering and confusion is unique and abnormal and therefore irresolvable, that his situation-specific problem is chronic, that nothing can be done about it, and that he will either have to suffer at the present level of distress for the rest of his life or end his life to find relief. The philosophically trained counselor relieves the client's fear of being less than perfect, and the despair of having to rely on someone else for help in dissolving what the client (and perhaps significant others) believed to be a "silly" problem, or worse, a "mental illness." The very fact that counseling with philosophy consists of a philosophical discussion rather than the clinical "treatment" of a putative mental illness, and the fact that the counselor is a philosopher rather than a clinical psychologist, psychiatrist, psychoanalyst, or psychotherapist, substantially reduces the feelings of fear, shame, and guilt which keep many people from seeking professional psychological help in the first place.

The term "internalization" comes from psychology but applies equally well to counseling with philosophy. When a client internalizes insights about life which have been arrived at in a philosophical dialogue he is engaged in the process of trusting those insights and accepting them as his own. Internalization comes from reflection and being not merely intellectually convinced but emotionally satisfied. It is the client getting "a sense of his own" about the epistemic and axiological perspectives reached during the counseling process. Internalization ultimately includes the client's ability to put both reasons and feelings into his own words and in accord with his own values. It is a willingness to put the resultant insights into practical use in his own life. For example, a person may have made the life decision to study medicine and become a doctor because he has been convinced by his parents that he ought to be doing something with his life that helps other people. His studies are thereby the result of external influences, not internal conviction. But if he comes to the conclusion one day that being a doctor and helping other people is what he really *feels* is the right thing to be doing with his life then he has internalized his parents' values. In a sense internalization is finding not only intellectual justification but affective gratification from adopting what may have begun as an alien value or external point of view.

A philosophical examination of life also helps alleviate feelings of frustration, anger, self-damnation, and blaming of others by helping the client come to understand the difference between *blame*—when an undesirable event occurs due to a lack of care or conscientiousness—and *responsibility*—when an undesirable event occurs despite good intentions and best efforts. It helps the client to determine the appropriate level of the feeling of responsibility for a negative life event, and perhaps accept complete responsibility for events for which she may have (rightly) refused to accept blame in the past. It also helps the client evaluate the validity of "pop" psychology maxims, such as "you can't blame the parents for everything" when in fact parents may have been abusive or neglectful. And it helps her avoid the trap of simply accepting the corporate/medical position that faulty brain chemistry is to blame for her suffering and confusion. Clarification of the feeling of responsibility also includes the client's learning to clearly differentiate between endogenous or internally generated suffering resulting from personal beliefs, values and so on, and life's exogenous or externally caused suffering such as familial expectations, sociocultural restraints, religious fears and prohibitions, work-place demands, crimes, accidents, poverty, and so on.

Philosophical introspection, the examination of a life, is, to borrow from Michel Foucault, "a critical ontology of ourselves" (1984, 34). In counseling, philosophy helps the client to be introspective about how he or she feels about life, and learn not only which feelings are justified but how appropriate the existing feelings are within a given context. Martha Nussbaum observes that philosophy as therapy is asked not simply to deal with the client's or patient's invalid references and false premises, but to grapple as well with crippling emotions such as irrational fear, unjustified anxiety, and excessive love (p. 37). Introspection about emotions and feelings is especially effective in male clients who deny their feelings or have difficulty identifying exactly what sort of feelings they are in fact experiencing. Understanding feelings leads to the ability to have not only appropriate feelings but the pertinent degree of those feelings. A philosophically informed discussion of feelings leads to the ability to recognize the thoughts that caused inappropriate actions or undesirable feelings, and aids in changing the thinking patterns and habits which brought them on. In both men and women introspection can also lead to a better understanding of their own lives in terms of their values, hopes, fears, and so on. This can improve the client's ability to protect him- or herself against emotional or intellectual assaults from others, and leaves him or her less vulnerable to emotional coercion and intellectual manipulation.

Counseling with philosophy helps the client shift the locus of self-evaluation from outside to inside the self, and to shift the locus of power from other-centered to self-centered, in the positive sense of that term. It thereby helps the client achieve a feeling of greater control over life, greater freedom, self-reliance, and self-trust both intellectually, spiritually, and emotionally. The counselor's provision of success-experiences for the client—such as, for example, helping the client conduct a satisfying examination of her own assumptions and values, and helping her come to her own insights—raises the client's confidence in herself, in the counselor, and in the philosophical process. It reduces her feeling of helplessness, confusion, and depression. It encourages the client to see herself as an effective human being rather than merely a "patient" or "client" under someone else's care.

The use of philosophy in counseling involves the "semiotic being"—the person for whom meaning matters—and the meaningful thoughts which generate the emotional domain of that human being. The person's beliefs, values, fears, and assumptions are the fertile mental ground from which feelings emerge, and within which problems sometimes develop. For example, a person might believe that his wife is being unfaithful. He has based this belief on the fact that she has been absent from home on a number of evenings. (The truth is that she has been secretly spending money from the household budget to attend a weight-loss group, but is too embarrassed to tell her husband about it.) When he asks her where she has been in the evenings, she is evasive and makes up a story he knows is not true. The husband now has the justified but false belief that his wife is cheating on him. This can create feelings in him of sadness, hopelessness, low self-esteem, and so on. His situation has created what psychology refers to as "cognitive dissonance"—a troubling conflict of beliefs, values, and assumptions. False or troublesome beliefs which are not resolved can become so powerful that the suffering individual may in time stop enjoying living a "normal" life. This then can lead to the diagnosis of any number of so-called mental illnesses, such as depression, anxiety, and so on.

A criticism raised in ancient times, and occasionally even today by psychotherapists, against those who use philosophy as therapy is that philosophy is an exclusively intellectual and logical approach and is therefore inadequate in dealing with the emotions. It was believed back then, and to a large extent still today, that emotions such as anger, grief, and fear erupt from the irrational animal parts of the human psyche and have nothing to do with reason and belief. They are believed to be bodily reactions to stimulus; unlearned and innate. Unlike beliefs, emotions are thought to be unaffected by teaching and argument. Aristotle did not hold these beliefs about emotions, which were common in his day, and are still prevalent as clichés today. He held that emotions are forms of intentional awareness, a point of view or belief directed at or about objects or people. He saw the importance of emotions in living a good life, but he also recognized the harm they could cause. In his *Nicomachean Ethics* Aristotle taught that emotions are not to be eradicated by reason but cultivated by reason so as to avoid excess (1179b).

Emotions may be appropriately assessed as rational or irrational, and also as true or false, depending on the character of the beliefs that are their basis or ground. All emotions are to some degree rational in a descriptive sense—all are to some degree cognitive and based upon belief, and can be modified through reason, teaching, and argument (Nussbaum 79–81). In his essay *The Passions of the Soul* René Descartes explained that the passions or emotions cannot be directly altered by simple force of will. But they can be changed indirectly by addressing the representation of things connected to the emotions which we wish to avoid arousing. He gives the example of how it's not possible to reduce fear and be bold by just deciding to do so by force of will. What is required, he said, is taking the time

> to consider the reasons, objects, or precedents which persuade us that the danger is not great; that there is always more security in defense than in flight; that we shall gain glory and joy if we conquer, whereas we can expect nothing but regret and shame if we flee; and so on (Cottingham et al. 235).

Therapy helps the client shift his perspective, from believing that he is simply the passive victim of active emotions to the realization that experiencing an emotion is an action, that emotions are under one's control and can be either reasonable or unreasonable, fitting or inappropriate to the situation. Philosophy as part of counseling and therapy is not mere intellectualizing because the emotions and the intellect cannot in fact be so easily separated into distinct objects of attention. In his book *What Would Aristotle Do?* Elliot Cohen, Director of the Institute of Critical Thinking in Port St. Lucie, Florida, and one of the pioneers in using philosophy in counseling, deals extensively with the interplay between reason and the emotions (2003). He explains that an emotional experience

> embodies the interplay or back and forth between your thoughts, deeds, and feelings. This interplay ... often has a looping effect, which can sustain and intensify it. First, your premises lead to internal bodily changes (autonomic effects), which lead to bodily feelings, and then to actions (muscular contractions), which back up your (original) premises. (p. 44)

Once an individual is stuck in this type of vicious loop created by negative feelings an effort is required by that individual to rescue himself from misery. An examination of the thoughts or premises which produced the emotional pain will help to determine whether or not those thoughts (and thereby the feelings) are justified. If it is possible to refute the premises then the attendant feelings will be diminished or diffused entirely. If the premises are found to be true, or if the circumstances are beyond personal control, then the only available antidote to the misery may be to reframe the situation into a more positive light. For example, a young woman who dreams of becoming an actress attends an audition to be in a television commercial. At the audition the casting director tells her, "I'm sorry, you're too tall for the part." This rejection leaves her feeling hurt, and could lead her to think she's never going to make it as an actress. If she becomes too despondent about this rejection she may qualify for a diagnosis of a "mental illness" such as depression. But she can reduce her negative emotions by recognizing that being too tall for this particular part does not mean she is too tall for all parts that will come up in the future. This kind of logical reasoning will counteract the possibility of the unrealistic negative generalization that she is too tall for *any* part, or that she will *never* become an actress, and shift her emotions from disappointment to optimism about the possibility of successful future auditions. Her emotions have been altered by means of reasoning. Of course this is a simple example, but this is the sort of successful reasoning in which counselors help their client to engage. When a counselor helps a client feel less victimized by the disappointments and problems in life the client's sense of self-worth and her self-acceptance increase simultaneously. As psychologist Carl Rogers put it, "In successful therapy clients come to have real affection for themselves . . . a quiet pleasure in being one's self" (1961, 73, 87–103).

INSIGHT

A young woman told me that she was diagnosed by a doctor as suffering from OCD (obsessive compulsive disorder) at the age of five and put on medications. She told me this in support of her own argument that mental illnesses like hers are definitely biological and probably genetically inherited. My response was to point out that children are not born with mental illnesses, although mental illnesses are now being "discovered" in them by overly ambitious therapists. Then I asked her what she had been obsessive about. She said she had a terrible fear of germs, a "germ phobia." I replied that it seemed to me five year olds usually don't have a fear of germs because they don't have any concept of what germs are. I suggested that for her to have developed a fear of germs she must have learned about them, and especially learned to fear them, from somebody else. At that moment her eyes widened and it seemed like a light had come on in her head. I could tell that she had suddenly remembered an incident, and probably the person, who had been responsible for instigating that "phobic" fear of germs in her when she was that five year old. Then she told me about her memories of her aunt telling her how the germs on everything in her house were constantly trying to make her sick. This insight into her aunt's fear of germs led the young woman to gain a new perspective on a so-called mental problem she had believed to be a genetically inherited medical problem of her brain.

Jerome D. Frank, Professor Emeritus of Psychiatry, writes that a basic assumption on which all psychotherapies are developed is that "humans react to their interpretation of events, which may not correspond to events as they are in reality" (Schill p. 132). Every psychotherapist therefore works to help the patient develop "a favorable view of themselves, their relationships with others, and their system of values" (Schill p. 132). This work would be greatly facilitated by a thorough knowledge of philosophy. The ancient Stoic and Epicurean philosophers helped citizens who came to them for counsel to recognize that their existing desire, intuitions, and preferences are mainly socially formed and therefore not very reliable guides to a good life (Nussbaum, 1994). Today counselors and psychotherapists trained in philosophy help their clients investigate the epistemological assumptions and stratagems they have adopted in life. The client is helped to gain insight, that is, "to understand more fully, to move from a state of relative confusion to one of comprehension" (Dominowski and Dallob p. 37). The philosopher helps the client reflexively examine how he comes to justify what he believes, and what his cognitive stance actually is in his approach to justification. In other words, counseling with philosophy helps the client develop a normative epistemology, not only when evaluating his knowledge acquisition strategies but also when choosing the sociocultural standpoint in life from which he obtains knowledge. Counseling with philosophy helps to reconcile the disparity felt by many clients between their *a posteriori* or empirical knowledge and their *a priori* intuitional or reasoned knowledge. It questions the reliability and acceptability of the various sources of conative states (the will, freedom, action), affective states (emotions, feelings, moods), and cognitive states (beliefs, certainties, conjectures). It reduces the persuasive power of the ubiquitous "they" of peer pressure, authority figures, the media, tradition, and public opinion. It invites a careful reconciliation of moral intuitions and personal meta-ethical justification with sociocultural traditions and the demands of life. Furthermore counseling with philosophy helps the client conduct an axiological reinterpretation, that is, it assists the client in realigning his values in relation to any newly discovered personal rights, and unaccustomed obligations and responsibilities.

Counseling and psychotherapy with philosophy involves helping the client or patient see things *differently*, to develop a new perspective on the familiar patterns of their thinking, the long-established habits of their behavior, and the influential elements of their environment. It involves insightful problem-solving which includes productive thinking. The person is helped to "go beyond past experiences and overcome misleading situational influences to formulate a novel approach to their problems" (Dominowski and Dallob p. 59). For example, the counselor or therapist may help Shama to redefine herself in order to counteract the label of "stupid and ugly" she has been struggling with. Or Ricardo may be helped to accept the fact—and not merely think it—that, as a child, he could not have been responsible for his parents' divorce. Or Amanda may be made aware of the fact that just because a company posts a code of ethics on its website doesn't mean it treats all its employees or customers fairly. Or Beata may be helped to understand why her view that gay marriage should be put to a vote is problematic from a human rights perspective.

Counseling and psychotherapy also involves helping individuals to *just see* things in the first place, to actually become aware of the perspective they already hold, to view the contents of their thoughts, to witness the manner of their behavior, and to notice the elements within their environment which they allow to influence their thoughts and behavior. For example, the counselor or therapist might point out to Jaypreet that the way she talks about herself shows that she considers herself to be stupid. Or Marty could be helped to notice that he believes men and women have specific roles in society that are determined by their biology. Or Ilona could be helped to see that the financial investment she is contemplating may be unethical. Or the counselor may help Ullin to become aware of the fact that he assumes human rights are granted by governments, rather than always only being restricted by them. These missed perspectives may help the client find a totally novel approach to an intractable problem.

Articulating the problems in one's life to a counselor or therapist requires what amounts to a cooperative philosophical inquiry, regardless of how the method of that inquiry may be labeled. It involves sorting mental information into manageable fragments, communicating emotions, translating cognitions into words, and reassembling fragmented memories so that they may be viewed as an interactive whole. This process can greatly clarify problems which previously made life seem a chaotic and incomprehensible jumble. The philosophical examination of a life promotes the correction of past weaknesses and errors in beliefs, judgments, and actions. Martha Nussbaum's comments about Existential therapy, which she has called "medical philosophy," are equally relevant to counseling with all the various approaches. She writes,

> The diseases [medical] philosophy brings to light are, above all, diseases of belief and judgment. But to bring such diseases to light . . . is a large step toward removing them. Recognition of error is intimately linked to the grasp of truth. Thus philosophical procedure tends in its very nature to make things better, given this diagnosis of the problem. (1994, 488)

Although "truth" is very rarely the goal in counseling, thoughtful discussion in any counseling partnership helps the client discover reasons why life is sometimes full of upset and confusion. For example a client of mine wondered why it was that she felt an "irrational" surge of anger whenever someone spoke on a cellular telephone near her. Our discussion led her to see that she believed telephone conversations to be a very private activity. When someone spoke on a cell phone within range of her hearing she felt as though she was being forced to listen in on their personal conversation. The anger came from feeling manipulated by the cell phone user into an immoral activity—the invasion of someone else's privacy. This insight into her anger helped her to understand its source and thereby feel less victimized by what seemed to be the irrationality of her own emotions.

Counseling with philosophy does not merely attempt to remove symptoms (the focus of behavior therapies), it helps the client to understand the meaning of life's suffering within its existential context. Existentialist therapist Hans W. Cohn says a symptom is a phenomenon which needs to be interpreted hermeneutically rather than analytically. He gives the example of a client suffering from compulsive hand washing. The time the client loses in repeatedly washing his hands is an important theme for therapeutic exploration. Behavior counseling might convince the client to stop washing so often so as not to waste so much time. This is an analytic solution, and might work to eliminate the symptom, but "it is only one aspect of the total situation, and the disappearance of this symptom would leave many questions unconsidered" (1997, 120). Not knowing the meaning of the symptom, that is, not knowing why the frequent washing has arisen in the first place, and why it seems so important and necessary, can leave the client feeling powerless to stop its recurrence in the future. Similarly a client's symptoms of depression and anxiety may be dealt with simply by means of prescription medication. But this would leave the antecedent precipitants of these symptoms and their continued threat to the client, unaffected and still in place. Medication is notorious for removing immediate symptoms and leaving the troublesome causal factors in life intact.

A series of counseling sessions with philosophy can help a client develop a more coherent and satisfying conceptual life framework or worldview. Of course counseling may not lead to an absolute consistency among the many conative, cognitive, and affective elements in life, but then such perfection is not necessary for an individual to lead a more rewarding and fulfilling life. But insight into the client's worldview will certainly enable him to achieve a better match between his beliefs and actions, between his desires and responsibilities, between his means and goals, and so on. A session of counseling with philosophy often consists of a retrospective view from the client's actions to precipitating life circumstances that have created the actions' initiating beliefs. By examining the beliefs behind his actions the client is able to either accept or reject those beliefs and alter future actions accordingly. There is an old adage which maintains that "time heals all wounds." But in actuality time simply passes. Something else is needed to produce the healing. In his essay "Getting Into and Out of Mental Ruts" Steven Smith argues that

> contextual change, rather than time, per se, is needed to escape from mental ruts ... Taking time off and changing contexts can allow mental conditions to become more favorable for escaping a fixated mental rut. (p. 249)

At other times counseling or psychotherapy with philosophy focuses on an introspective view. The client is assisted in comparing his intellectual reasoning with the urgings of his emotions and intuitions to see if there is an acceptable correlation between them. He is helped in clarifying what internal and external factors trigger his various emotional responses, and in determining how to resist experiencing automatic reactions to those triggers. This helps the client to live a life that is self-motivated, avoiding what Jean-Paul Sartre calls acting in "bad faith" (1997), and to achieve what Martin Heidegger calls living life "authentically" (1996). Philosophical discussion can release the client from problematic emotions that are the product of circumstantial "programming" by helping him to notice the programming.

Beyond awakening insight, a philosophical discussion can bring emotional relief. A client once told me, "I've thought about the things we've been talking about many times, but nothing in life around me really changed. I just kept worrying about everything. But now that we're talking about my worries out loud I find that it really helps to reduce the stress I feel."

Why is it that the act of simply discussing the various events in life with someone else can be therapeutic? Perhaps it's because when a client explains herself to the counselor or therapist she is able to better hear what she believes to be true. With the counselor or therapist's help she may then also notice the inconsistencies in her beliefs, the contradictions in her values, the generalizations in her discontents, the negativity in her self-image, the naiveté of her life plans, and so on. These problem areas can then be changed for the better. The client's self-worth and self-acceptance are enhanced by the mindful humility of the counselor who presents alternative points of view or insights not as rigid dictates but only as so many possibilities.

And the counselor or therapist whose philosophical training has taught him to admit when he is wrong conveys to the client the message that the client's thoughts, although contrary to his own, are in fact worthwhile. By acknowledging his fallibility he shows the client that her own imperfections are not pathologies. Explaining a decision out loud to the counselor creates a tacit collusion between two active partners; there is a "strength in numbers" which helps to reinforce the client's commitment to both her newly discovered points of view and her long-held beliefs and values. Perhaps most importantly, the counselor's respectful listening and authentic responses help the client to realize she is not "crazy."

ANTIDOTE FOR GUILT, SHAME, AND STIGMA

One of the significant beneficial side effects of philosophy as therapy and counseling is that it eliminates the stigma—including the "self-stigmatization" (Boevink p. 25)—associated with treatment for so-called mental illness. There is no stigma attached to having a conversation with a philosopher; in fact, quite the opposite is true. One of the roles of philosophy in counseling and psychotherapy is the reduction or elimination of the stigma and shame that comes with being diagnosed with medical-sounding conditions, being labeled as having a "mental illness," and being treated with, and having to depend on, medications to remain "normal." Why is shame so prevalent among the patients of psychotherapists?

Before this question can be answered it's necessary to consider two earlier ones: What exactly is shame? And why is shame much less of a problem in counseling with philosophy? The following is a portion of an e-mail I received from a woman I shall name "Maggie" about her experiences with shame. I present a portion of it here with her permission.

> With mental illness, my first exposure to shame came with the disclosure by my mother to me that her mother had, what was called at the time, dementia praecox—nowadays referred to as schizophrenia. Now this was not shameful for me, I didn't feel a sense of shame personally, but I sensed that it was a shameful fact for my Mom because she rarely talked about it at all during our years together. And when she did so she seemed to be somewhat uncomfortable if not pained by any reference to the fact. But it was her virtual silence that effectively "told" me that there was something shameful going on there—her silence and the silence of all her family—their downcast eyes, their body language, the lowering of their voices if they spoke at all about the woman who was their mother. It seemed to me as a child, and it seems to me as an adult, that silence and shame have a solid partnership.
> My younger brother became mentally ill in his mid twenties. He had been at university on the east coast of Canada but moved to the west coast to be with his siblings. Shortly after he arrived he made a suicide attempt that landed him in a "mental institution." From there he lived on the edge of our society in poverty until his suicide in 2003. He suffered from paranoid schizophrenia and he didn't go out much as a result. I do remember one time he called me up to wish me a happy birthday and invited me out for coffee at a cafe near his apartment building. I was reluctant to go because, frankly, I had not much to say to him. But I accepted his invitation and met him at his apartment. We walked up the street together to a coffee shop he had been to on occasion. It was around 11 a.m. and the place was virtually empty except for the server. We sat in a table near the window. I remember feeling uncomfortable, as usual, since my brother looked his usual harried, slightly frightened self, and I knew I was going to have a hard time relaxing and enjoying the occasion. Shame only came when the server arrived. I saw that the server "knew" my brother's "situation." It's a certain look we humans have and we all know it in each other. It's a demeanor that crosses all cultural and language barriers. A pulling away in spirit, a downcast or furtive eye, a cautious tone of voice. As a result, I immediately became ashamed that my brother was obviously

ill and here we were trying to pass as normal customers—who was I kidding?! Shame on him and shame on me! What was going on in my brother's mind that day I will never know because I didn't ask.

Maggie's e-mail raises a number of puzzling questions such as, If schizophrenia is in fact a legitimate illness, why is there so much shame surrounding it? Why are people ashamed of it but not of cancer or diabetes? One of the many websites on the topic explains schizophrenia this way: "In essence, this disease strikes profoundly at one's ability to think, formulate ideas, reason, remember or concentrate. It causes delusions, hallucinations, disorganized speech or behavior and a whole realm of negative symptoms." Note that it says schizophrenia *strikes* at one's ability to think and so on, and it *causes* delusions and all sorts of other problems. So despite the fact that schizophrenia is typically wrongly explained as an illness which causes suffering, its diagnosis does in fact cause the suffering individual and their family members to feel shame. Why is that?

The reason why the public readily accepts the disease or illness model of mental health problems such as ADHD, depression, and schizophrenia is because when a mental health problem is defined as a biological malfunction of the brain it *seems* to allow the sufferer to avoid the feeling of shame. But this is not in fact what happens. The medicalization of mental health problems has not eliminated shame; it has merely shifted it from the problematic functioning of body to the supposed malfunctioning of the mind. The shame appended to so-called mental illness comes in part from the habit of blaming the victim: seeing the sufferers as responsible for their suffering which is not typically the case with physical illnesses. The sufferer of a so-called mental illness is not only seen as somehow morally inferior or weak but also—and perhaps worse—as biologically defective, medically unsafe, and even socially threatening.

A diagnosis of "mental illness" brings with it the shame of being professionally described as having what is called a "genetic predisposition" or "genetic weakness" to the onset of mental illness. Unbelievably, professionals in various fields such as psychiatry, medicine, and even philosophy now routinely write that an emotion such as depression is probably endogenously produced by faulty genes, despite the complete absence of any corroborating evidence from medical research.

Furthermore, when symptoms are reified as pseudo-biological causes it permits the justification of the prescription of powerful psychotropic drugs (Jablensky and Kendell). The patient's regularly scheduled ingesting of medications leads to dependency, often for life, on both the drugs and the doctors who prescribe them. This dual dependency then becomes another source of shame.

Shame is an emotion. It is actually an emotional response that must be learned. It is generated in childhood by a gradual learning and internalization of familial and social values, which are in turn based on, and maintained by, the values of the wider community. This summer I noticed a little boy in our neighborhood playing with his older brother. The little boy's pants had fallen down. His brother was laughing at him because he was now standing there in his diaper. The little boy seemed puzzled by his brother's laughter. He had no shame about his own situation. But he was no doubt beginning to learn that there are times in his life when others expect him to feel ashamed. Psychologists Robin Grace and Beth Macgregor explain that no-one is born ashamed.

> It is a learned, self-conscious emotion, which starts at roughly two years of age with the advent of language and self-image. Although humans are born with a capacity for shame, the propensity to become ashamed in specific situations is learned.

In her e-mail to me Maggie makes a very similar observation:

> Shame is learned by children in dribs and drabs. One has to have the lesson at least several times and in different settings and for different reasons before one understands the common denominator. That is, someone else's opinion about an event or activity or person counts more than yours does and thereby, if the opinion is negative and if you had any part in perpetrating the event or activity, or had any even remote association with the person who is being scorned thereby, the shame is attached to you as well. Shame spreads like a stain through fabric, except that shame around mental illness can run through generations. I don't tell people that my grandmother had schizophrenia unless I feel in safe company because I know the power of shame.

The shame caused by having been diagnosed as mentally ill comes from the stigma surrounding it. In past history "mental illness" was believed to be demon possession. It was a mysterious affliction, and it was believed that only deserving people were possessed by demons. Today severe emotional suffering and mental distress are still seen as somehow being the suffering individual's own fault. And the resultant diagnosis of "mental illness" is still cloaked in a chilly fog of mystery. It's not perceived like "normal" sickness. There is, still today, enormous misunderstanding about it, and people tend to fear what they don't understand. The writers and film-makers of Hollywood today still represent the mentally ill as "other," as mysterious, alien, dangerous, even demonic.

A little attention paid to both public and social media quickly reveals that people in contemporary society commonly believe "the mentally ill" are some or most of the following: incompetent, needy, weak, unreliable, untrustworthy, dangerous, illiterate, less intelligent, unproductive, unemployable, useless, poor, lazy, contagious, incurable, unpredictable, disorderly, faking their symptoms, an embarrassment to family and society, not like us, and therefore shameful.

In writing on the Gestalt therapy approach to shame psychotherapist Richard Erskine maintains that whenever you define anyone, even if you do it accurately, you can devalue and humiliate them in the process. I suggest that it is fair to say that the diagnosis of a so-called mental illness always devalues and humiliates the one so identified. A counseling client of mine, Ariel, expressed an enormous amount of shame about being diagnosed as schizophrenic by her psychiatrist. And, because her medical doctor once offhandedly told her he doesn't think she has all the classic symptoms associated with "proper" schizophrenia, Ariel told me she feels ashamed for not being a "proper" schizophrenic.

Psychiatrist Judith Herman writes, "shame for a person diagnosed with a mental illness arises when that individual is treated not as a person but as a mental disorder." There is shame when a patient's diagnostic label is applied as though it were that patient's identity. We say, "she is schizophrenic," and yet we certainly don't say, "she is cancerous." Saying "she is schizophrenic" identifies, and even equates, the person with the diagnosis. It also places the blame on the suffering individual. The fact that the terminology used in mental healthcare has been altered actually makes it easier to blame. For example, it is no longer acceptable to use the words "mental illness." The officially sanctioned term now is "mental disorder." This small change makes a big difference. An illness is generally understood as a condition in which the sufferer was a victim of pathological circumstances. But to say "He has a disordered mind" implies personal responsibility in the same way as saying, "He has a disordered room." A disordered room implies a careless person; a disordered mind implies the same thing. It assumes an endogenous etiology; it locates the cause of the "disorder" in the careless personality of the sufferer.

A diagnosis of mental illness removes the ability to self-actualize—a trait greatly valued, especially in Western cultures. This loss of control over one's self-determination and self-definition is another one of the activating mechanisms of shame. There is shame in being unable to control the very basic elements of one's own life—such as finding employment, a place to live, or a life partner, choosing which medications to take or not to take—due to the barriers and restrictions to personal freedoms created by the stigma of mental illness.

People diagnosed as mentally ill can experience shame both when others are too distant, such as when family members shun or ostracize them, and when others come too close, such as when personal boundaries are violated by doctors and nurses. Shame is also brought on by the paternalistic/maternalistic treatment from all types of healthcare and social workers. They threaten punishment for disobedience—like warning the patient that they will be sent back to hospital if the prescribed medication protocol is not faithfully followed. There is shame and frustration in not being listened to, or their opinions not being taken seriously by mental healthcare workers and family members. And there is shame in the very fact of bringing shame on the family and the community.

And finally psychiatrist Judith Herman writes, "the shamed person feels ashamed of feeling ashamed and enraged, and then ashamed of being enraged." She calls this a feeling trap.

What can be done about all this shame surrounding mental illness? For those who are ashamed of their diagnosis it's not easy to even think about a solution. Shame interferes with the ability to think clearly. This confusion has been referred to as "cognitive shock" (Nathanson). For the patient in psychotherapy this mental confusion can be a serious dilemma. It may result in their being diagnosed with yet another psychological disorder (H. B. Lewis). The patient feels shame because she sees herself as weak, defective, and ineffective. Visiting a psychotherapist for help raises the feeling of shame just from the act of having to ask for professional help. Again, psychiatrist Judith Herman writes, "Because of the power imbalance between patient and therapist, and because the patient exposes her most intimate thoughts and feelings without reciprocity, the therapy relationship is to some degree inherently shaming."

In our society there is a long historical precedence, and therefore deeply ingrained belief, that it seems *appropriate* for a person to feel ashamed if they have to visit a psychotherapist for help in dealing with their psychological issues and problems. But shame is not expected of the person who visits a philosopher. After all, psychotherapy involves the attempt to treat illness, but philosophy is about the creation of wisdom.

At the end of a session with me, I accompanied the young woman who had come to talk with me, to the front door of the building. She hesitated, looking around to see if anyone out on the street would see her.

"Why are you being so cautious?" I asked.

She replied, "I don't want anyone to see me leaving your office."

She was obviously ashamed of being seen because of the stigma typically associated with having to go to therapy.

But then, to her surprise, I said, "But all my neighbors know this is a philosopher's office. If they see you they'll simply think you've been having a discussion with a philosopher."

This made a huge difference in her thinking, and from then on she always left my office with an air of poise and self-confidence.

ALTERNATIVE PERSPECTIVES

The examination of a client's life can develop in that person a sense of mastery of his inner experiences and emotions, of his external experiences, of his memories of the past, of his environment in the present, and of the contingencies of his future. It does so by helping him first disentangle, come to comprehend, and find meaning in the previously inexpressible and inexplicable elements of life. Then it helps him to find alternative perspectives where necessary. For example, a client is first helped to understand how he has been making moral decisions in the past, then he is helped to see why this approach is making his life so miserable, and finally he is taught how to improve his approach so that his decisions in the future will not leave him in the sort of problematic circumstances in which he finds himself in the present. The philosophy employed in counseling also helps the client put the unfortunate life decisions of the past "to rest," so to speak, by helping him to redefine himself by means of aligning himself with who he is in the present and who he wishes to become in the future. It helps the client to be better able to determine what kind of life he wants to live in the future, not only the distant future but the future in the next moment, despite the framework which has been seemingly forced upon him by his own past and by the others in both his past and his present.

A philosophical examination of motives can reduce the client's self-serving, and often immoral, self-interest, and increase his awareness of the many others with whom he shares his life. It helps the client to accept human fallibility and increase his social interest, moral consciousness, and personal responsibility. While the German philosopher Friedrich Nietzsche wrote about individuals striving to live *beyond* good and evil (1968), counseling with philosophy helps individuals to recognize that their lives cannot be neatly classified into good or evil, nor should they be. It also helps individuals to understand that life must be lived, not beyond, but within human society. Superheroes only exist in fiction; everyone else must learn to get along, cooperating with each other to fight the evil impulses of the misguided. Philosophical exploration and discussion reveals that most human beings live their lives somewhere in the very large region *between* good and evil. This can bring relief, reassurance, and comfort to the client who has been burdened by his belief that he is evil because he has not lived a life of absolute goodness. Jesus Christ sought a transformation of himself through suffering, the Buddha through an awakening, while Socrates sought it through philosophy. This is what these men inspired others to do as well. The counselor who uses philosophy demonstrates to the client that a philosophical examination of a life can positively transform the self without the dreadful necessity of physical suffering or the fortuitous experience of a spiritual "awakening."

The examination of life by means of philosophy creates in the client a sense of personal strength, an awareness of the power of her own thinking and feelings, and freedom from the coercive power of external influences of authority which demand unthinking obedience. It develops the ability to live life in a state of self-government that includes the freedom of inter-connection with others. The counselor or therapist who employs philosophy is careful not to take the place of the client's or patient's autonomy by giving explicit advice or instruction. He nonetheless offers suggestions, asks questions, and gives implicit guidance in a way that helps the client or patient develop her own autonomy (C. Gill, p. 307). Personal autonomy does not demand isolation; it allows for a level of *interdependence* among lives in which the interests and wills of individuals overlap and complement each other. The examination of life with philosophy helps the client understand that a range of human ways of being, a great variety of ways to live life, are possible and morally acceptable. One of my clients was concerned over her love of books and learning, afraid that if she "indulged" too much it would make her seem unusual because no one in her family was particularly "high-brow." But a philosophical examination of what she valued in life in relation to the rest of her family helped her to discover how she could live a life of intellectual autonomy which, though contrary to her family's behavior, did not actually contravene her family's primary value, that of "making something of your life."

So, in order for the examination of a life that seems not worth living to result in a positive outcome it requires, first of all, a recognition by the individual that problems are arising due to present beliefs, assumptions, and values, and due to current strategies employed in the way life is being lived. It then requires that individual to trust someone, such as a philosophical counselor, to act as an objective but empathetic partner who is willing to listen and to advise without being judgmental. Such an examination of life by means of philosophy can bring much needed emotional relief from feelings such as self-blame, regret, guilt, shame, and fear which are the result of painful life experiences and regrettable past decisions. The subsequent insights gained about the past, and the discovery of alternatives to current approaches to life, can make the examined life a life that is much more than merely tolerable; it can make life once again worth living.

As discussed previously, the employment of philosophy in counseling or therapy is based on four foundational premises: First, the mind is not the same as the brain. The mind is the contents of the brain, and those contents are propositional; they consist of beliefs, values, fears, assumptions, and so on. The mind is not a solid material object; it consists of narrative constructs or products of "the integrating activity of a concept using subject as a person in relation to others" (Gillett p. 34). Second, mental problems are not the same as organic brain problems: changing one's mind is not the same as changing one's brain. Third, a person's beliefs, values, and assumptions can cause mental distress, which in turn can cause a diagnosis of so-called mental illnesses. And fourth, good philosophical discussions can alleviate and then prevent much of this type of distress. So-called mental illnesses and emotional disorders are the result of life's conflicts and complications, and the associated beliefs, values, fears, and assumptions, etc. Therefore, good philosophical discussions in therapy are different from hypothetical academic discussions. When used in counseling, philosophy deals directly with personal life problems. Some problems may require changes in the person's life circumstances. Others require an examination, and perhaps an alteration of, the beliefs, values, fears, and assumptions which have led to those problems.

Philosophy can also be helpful to individuals who are not suffering from any specific diagnosable mental disorders, and yet are miserable. For example, one client explained to me that he had everything he could want—a house, money, a good job, and so on—but that he could be clinically diagnosed as depressed. He felt like his life was empty and meaningless. Over the course of just a few sessions we discovered that the many years he had spent in the financial world left him feeling like he had in fact accomplished nothing of value with his life. He had been so engrossed in his goal of personal enrichment that he had not even considered getting married. Now he was feeling well-off but lonely, accomplished but unfulfilled, secure but selfish. We eventually came to the decision together that the "treatment" for his so-called clinical depression should be for him to volunteer at a local charity, serving meals to the poor, and generally being helpful to the homeless and the destitute. This worked out very well because his acts of kindness for others eventually led to two good outcomes: his life felt much more meaningful to him, and he discovered a soul mate in one of the women volunteers.

MEANING

At a meeting of the American Medical Association in the 1950s Dr. Dan L. Farnsworth of Harvard University said that while medicine had made great strides in alleviating physical pain and prolonging life, it was now facing the task of giving meaning to life (Davis p. 20). Of course it has never been believed by anyone in the history of medicine that the job of the physician is to help the suffering person find meaning in life. That was usually left to religious leaders whose calling it was to relieve the afflicted of their spiritual pain and suffering. Then Freud came along and challenged the traditional roles of both physicians and of religious leaders. He began a movement in which psychology, and then psychoanalysis, attempted to develop theories for people's actions, and explanations for their motives, by postulating the building blocks of their personalities. Unfortunately little attention was given to the wider context of meaning in which those personalities develop. Early psychologists and psychiatrists had some interest in motivation, but very little grasp of why people behave and act as they do. Existential psychotherapist Emmy van Deurzen-Smith argues that it is high time psychotherapists take these "meaning–full" questions into acount when working with their patients or clients by taking a more philosophical approach. She insists that philosophy, in its classical interpretation, "can refocus issues of life and meaning in dramatic ways." (p. 184). Wilma Boevink explains that a essential part of recovery from so-called mental illness is for patients to look back on what has happened to them and create their own stories about it. "What is important," she says, "is that *you* [the patient], and no one else, give meaning to what has happened" (p. 21). Clinical psychologist Derek Bolton points out that the main philosophical effect of the congitive revolution in psychotherapy and counseling on "the science of psychopathology" is that explanations which include a consideration of meaning are just as much scientific causal explanations as are explanations of physical or chemical pathology (2003 p. 121).

Beyond helping a patient or client find higher meaning in their so-called mental illnesses, and in the mundane activities of daily living, philosophy can also help to elevate the very fact of being alive. It can help the suffering individual find meaning in the very experience of life itself. As philosopher John Davis puts it, "Philosophy is not merely a method for removing intellectual rubbish . . . it may also be a set of meaning giving sustenance to life" (p. 14).

"CLINICAL PHILOSOPHY"

In his book *The New Image of the Person*, published in 1978, philosopher Peter Koestenbaum explores the theory and practice of what he calls "Clinical Philosophy." Clinical Philosophy, he says, is the use of philosophy as a healing art. He defines it as "the confluence of a combined phenomenological model of being and existential personality theory with depth psychotherapy." He points out that since many problems brought to physicians, psychiatrists, and psychologists are more philosophic than psychological or medical, a therapist trained in clinical philosophy will have "an above-average diagnostic grasp of a patient's condition and can therefore create deepened and innovative treatment strategies" (p. 523). He explains that psychotherapy is in fact the continual application of the principle of philosophical reflection: on the life that is already in progress, on past lifestyles, on behavior systems, on self-definition, and on personal history (p. 70). The value of philosophy, he says, comes from its use in reflecting on, distancing from, and assessment of the material developed within any psychotherapeutic technique. He goes on to say that, in order for clinical philosophy to be therapeutic, the ability to both *be* and *reflect on being* must be utilized consistently (p. 71). Therefore,

> Clinical philosophy requires a solid background in philosophy, especially what are [in this book] called the phenomenological model of being and the existential personality theory, and in psychology and psychiatry, especially clinical practice and experience in psychotherapy. (p. xv)

In their 2000 brochure, the Koestenbaum Center for Philosophical Practice offers "seminars and workshops for practicing psychotherapists who are interested in learning how to integrate philosophical issues into their practice." Unfortunately Koestenbaum's discussion of Clinical Philosophy seems to accept many of the problematic terms found in psychoanalysis and other standard forms of psychotherapy such as the client's "resistance," the patient's "projections," symptoms as preventing access to the "transcendental ego," and the "unconscious" of the therapist, just to name a few. As discussed in my first chapter of the current book, in today's field of philosophy of psychotherapy these terms are considered questionable, if not outright erroneous, characterizations of the constituents of the mind and mental activity. For philosophy to be "clinical" or therapeutic it need not incorporate psychoanalytic or psychotherapeutic hypotheses, nor their language.

Interestingly, and much like contemporary philosophers, Hellenistic philosophers considered their societies to be unhealthy, and people to be suffering from the evils inherent in their societal circumstances. They believed their societies fostered an unhealthy attitude toward money, promoted damaging competition, and encouraged the pursuit of fame and status. It would not be too controversial to claim that, today too, many people are in distress because society has infected them with the "sickness" of its various corrupting values and beliefs which are promoted continuously in the numerous forms of media. The philosopher's job therefore is to listen skeptically to what the client says because the client's statements originate from the problematic judgments and perceptions inherited from their ailing social environment. Therapeutic philosophy does not accept all perspectives on life as equally acceptable; it operates with a normative idea of the flourishing life that is reasonable, moral, and attainable. Just like the whole point of medical research and treatment is the attainment of a cure, so too the whole point of philosophy as therapy is the attainment of human flourishing. Nussbaum writes,

> If the diseases that impede human flourishing are above all disease of belief and social teaching, and if . . . critical arguments of the kind philosophy provides are necessary and perhaps even sufficient for dislodging those obstacles, then philosophy will seem to be necessary, perhaps even sufficient, for getting people from disease to health. (p. 4)

Psychotherapy has at times been criticized as often being "too persuasive" and even "manipulative," as though it is used to maneuver the client or patient into accepting and obeying the status quo (e.g., Al-Shawi). Philosophy, on the other hand, is not based on promoting any specific worldview as right, the best, or the one that ought to be lived. It is open to various interpretations of "the good" and even allows the client to question and disagree with the very process of philosophical discussion underlying the therapy itself. This is generally not welcomed in most forms of psychotherapy. In fact questioning the process of any psycho therapeutic method can easily be diagnosed as "resistance," "denial," or even some form of "mental illness." Therapeutic philosophy is centrally concerned with helping the client or patient locate and then attain the many "goods" attainable in life. Any therapeutic philosophy depends in part on a conception of human flourishing and the human good (Peterman p. 17, 18). The therapeutic arguments employed by counselors and psychotherapists who use a knowledge of philosophy have a practical goal intended to help make the client feel better. Therapeutic arguments are what Martha Nussbaum calls "value-relative" in that, at some level, and in contradistinction to academic arguments, they respond to the deep wishes and needs of the client. The appropriateness of each therapeutic philosophical argument is assessed according to its success in meeting the client's individual requirements (p. 46).

Generally, the client is at least vaguely aware of the conflicting motives and values, contradictory attitudes and behaviors with which they are struggling. Therapeutic philosophic discussion sharpens and clarifies this awareness. This leads to the client accepting full responsibility for his behavior, rather than relegating his actions to some uncontrollable unconscious forces. In this way the choice and direction of the client's life can be more under his or her own control (more intentional) (Sharma p. 55).

But counseling with philosophy, while therapeutic, is not time travel. If the client's birth family was dysfunctional—if there was emotional mistreatment of family members, abandonment, or physical abuse—it is not possible to go back and "fix" that damaged and damaging past with counseling or psychotherapy of any sort. I tell my clients I'm willing to help them achieve any goal that is morally permissible, reasonable, and possible. Of course it's morally permissible, and reasonable to want the past to be different; but it's not possible. So how can counseling help when the past is painful? The past can't be changed; it is what it was. But a person's beliefs about the people and the events of the past can be examined and changed if necessary. And a person's beliefs about who they are, and their level of responsibility for past events, can be scrutinized and changed if necessary as well in order to be more in tune with who they actually are, and wish to be, in the present. These sorts of changes can be immensely therapeutic. For example, I've had many clients who felt that as children they were somehow responsible for their own mistreatment. We examined this belief about themselves, and their beliefs about the others in their lives, to see if those beliefs are at all justified. What we often found, of course, is that children mistakenly blame themselves for the terrible wrongdoings of their parents and other adults. While this belief remained with them well into adulthood in the form of guilt, regret, and low self-esteem, counseling or therapy with philosophy proved to be very liberating.

Philosophy in counseling and therapy acts not only to liberate the individual client or patient from their present suffering and distress, it can also help prepare them to be better able to deal with troubling future circumstances once they arise. Philosophy can be taught as a kind of "inoculation" that will help the individual guard against and avoid having any issues become "serious mental problems" in the first place.

SEVEN

Preventive (Prophylactic) Philosophy

A documentary on the "Discovery" TV channel in 2011 presented the story of a young girl who had been a very active and happy child. She was only a little unusual because of the fact that she was heavily involved, and fairly successful in soap box derby car racing. But when she came into her teen years her mother and father said she became a different person. She often stayed out past curfew or didn't come home at all; she began frequently using alcohol and drugs, and was discovered cutting herself. The parents took her to see a doctor who told them that the cause of the young woman's problems was depression. So she was given anti-depressant medication which her sister said "turned her into a zombie." The doctor's professional opinion had been that the "mental illness" of depression was causing her troubles. The mother told the television reporter that her daughter had shouted at her one day, "You should know why I'm feeling this way. You should know!" But the mother insisted she had no idea. The young woman was then sent to a psychiatrist who said that what was in fact causing her problems was that she was manic-depressive or bi-polar. So he put her on a different medication meant to treat that "mental illness." But soon after an argument with her mother the young woman committed suicide by hanging herself in her closet.

Notice that the medical doctor and the psychiatrist said that the cause of the young woman's distress were two so-called mental illnesses: depression and bi-polar disorder. Notice also that the young woman had, in a sense, accused her mother of being well aware of what was causing her distress. What was that all about? This question was not answered in the program. While it seems obvious that the medications did not help to alleviate her anguish, could her unfortunate suicide have been prevented in any other way?

In his discussion of the essay "Cause and Explanation in Psychiatry" by James F. Woodward, Kenneth Kendler, Professor of Psychiatry and the director of the Virginia Institute for Psychiatric and Behavioral Genetics, explains why the biological perspective of suicidal ideation is a poor guide to choice of treatment. A suicide attempt may have a "higher order" explanatory variable: self-derogatory ideation. There may then also be a dozen or more biological explanations proposed by neuroscientists. Assuming that all the biological explanations "flow through" self-derogatory ideation, so that there are many different ways one's brain can get to the state of having self-derogatory ideation, then if intervention is on only the biological variable "the effect would be highly dependent (or nongeneralizable) because of the state of all the other complex biological causes." But if cognitive therapy were used to intervene on the existential level of the suicidal ideation "the impact would be more consistent and generalizable." In other words, in a case of a complex and interacting set of biological causes that "flow through" a simpler existential explanation, intervention at the existential level "will likely be more effective, generalizable, and just plain 'better'" (p. 134–35). But could this young woman's suicide have been prevented much earlier, long before she had even begun to have any suicidal ideation?

Compared with the mountain of literature on the diagnosing and treatment of "mental illnesses"—from the perspective of biological psychiatry, psychoanalysis, psychotherapy, counseling, and the field of mental healthcare in general—there has been relatively little discussion about preventing so-called mental illnesses in the first place. Academic psychotherapy books and journal articles have been published on the topic, and professional conferences have had "prevention" as the theme of their theoretical presentations, but prevention is almost completely absent from its practice. Yet it is not entirely surprising that schools of psychiatry, psychoanalysis, and psychotherapy don't offer public programs designed to help prevent "mental illnesses" given the ambiguity of the various definitions of "mental illness," their ontology, etiology, and prognosis, and the dispute between the biomedical and the sociological models of the so-called pathogenesis of mental distress.

The word "prevention" is a meaningless concept in the discussion of psychotherapy because the word "therapy" is by definition the treatment of an already existing illness or disability. Psychotherapy is restorative or remedial; it is not prophylactic. Therapy suggests attending to the amelioration of harm already done, not an avoidance of the possibility of harm. When prevention is discussed in the mental healthcare field it typically refers to averting onset of "illness" by means of early symptomatic diagnosis and intervention, or to the deterrence of relapse, which includes ensuring the patient's compliance with medication regimens, monitoring and managing pharmaceutical side effects, controlling comorbid symptoms, stabilizing the patient, supervising self-help recovery groups, and so on (Amering and Schmolke p. 43–47). This type of "prevention" is focused exclusively on avoiding the recurrence of so-called mental illnesses, relapse in individuals who have previously been diagnosed with "mental illnesses" and have often already gone through some sort of remedial therapy. There is very little discussion of non-diagnostic prevention of the initial onset of "mental illnesses." Part of the reason for this is because of the professional confusion about both the ontology and etiology of these so-called illnesses.

Research on relapse prevention indicates that a systematic program of instruction can help clients learn more from their therapy and maintain their recovered state for longer than if therapy only consists of standard clinical treatments after onset (Ivey et al. p. 185). But this raises the question, "Why are there no systematic programs of instruction to help people maintain a 'premorbid' or 'healthy' mental state in the first place?" While there is talk in the literature about promoting mental health by "strengthening the competence and responsibility" and "rediscovering and promoting personal resources, capacities, and abilities" that will help the individual "cope with the normal stress of life" (Amering and Schmolke p. 41–42), there is no explanation as to how the person's competence, responsibility, resources, capacities, and abilities will be rediscovered. What is the mechanism that would help the individual cope with the normal stresses of life, and avoid "mental illness"? There is very little discussion in the literature about how it's possible to help people learn to avoid the kind of mental suffering and emotional distress that can lead to the devastating diagnoses of so-called mental illness such as anxiety, schizophrenia, depression, and so on.

Parents typically tell their children, "Always look both ways before you try crossing the street." Good parents don't wait until after the child has been struck by a car before they offer this sort of life-saving instruction. There are many similar situations in which preventive information is proactively given in order to help the child avoid having to experience physical disaster. Likewise, parents give their children moral instruction by asking them to put themselves in place of others, by, for example, suggesting they think about how they would feel if the other child stole her favorite toy from her. This is the kind of practical instruction all good parents offer their children as protection from harm; it is what helps children go through life prepared for contingent eventualities about which they have had no previous experience. Good parents don't wait until their child has experienced pain before giving them the knowledge and wisdom to avoid it. Prevention builds resilience, which is "the process by which children, youth, and adults withstand sources of challenge," and the ability to overcome those challenges (Amering and Schmolke p. 27). Prevention is instruction that is always aimed at future possibilities and probabilities. In fact recent studies have shown that prevention programs which promote mental health can even avert the deveopment of physical illness (Ibid). So-called protective factors "are capable of diminishing and attenuating the effects of major stressors, traumatic events, and cumulative risks on a person" (Rutter p. 77).

Discussion about the prevention of the onset of so-called mental illnesses is extremely rare in both the clinical and theoretical literature. Attention in the last twenty years or so has been focused mainly on the "relatively new" idea of recovery. And the argument is often made that, while counseling or psychotherapy may be adequate for helping some sufferers overcome common mental illnesses such as "ordinary" depression, medications are essential for those afflicted with serious mental illnesses such as "clinical" depression. But medications serve only as treatments after the onset of the diagnosed clinical condition. There seems to be very little effort put into preventing the initial occurrence. This raises the question, "Why does our mental healthcare system put so little effort into programs aimed at prevention?" There is no compelling reason why the strategies employed in counseling and psychotherapy need to be focused exclusively on remedial treatments. In fact psychiatrists Michaela Amering and Margit Schmolke argue that recent studies have shown that the most powerful effects in the reduction of risk factors for so-called mental illnesses "tend to come from both reducing risks and increasing protection." They conclude that "it is much better to increase capacities to do well despite adversity than it is to treat individuals after maladjustment has crystallized" (p. 37). But what does it mean to "increase capacities to do well"? What are these capacities, and how are they increased? The answer to these questions lies in philosophy.

Philosophy as counseling or therapy doesn't need to be applied only retroactively as a "curative" remedy or treatment subsequent to some sort of mental catastrophe. It can be learned and applied as a preventive—a prophylactic—a kind of "inoculation" that will assist the individual in avoiding any diagnosable suffering in the first place. Prevention really is the best medicine when it is not merely employed as the avoidance of relapse. If people are taught good reasoning early in life then they're less likely to be led into the kind of emotional distress and mental suffering that can be diagnosed as mental illness. To put it more succinctly, if the knowledge, the critical and creative thinking skills, the capacity for good judgments, the self-scrutiny, and the discursive skills of philosophy are taught to students before university there are likely to be far fewer cases of so-called mental illness in our society.

As argued in earlier chapters, the term "mental illness" is completely misleading. Mental suffering and distress are not illnesses because they're not biological brain disorders. The idea that a person's emotional suffering and mental distress is "mental illness" is relatively new. As Deurzen-Smith points out, "It is only in recent centuries that we have begun to consider problems in living to be synonymous with mental illness [and] that we have relegated its cure to medical science." She goes on to say that when medical science turned its attention to so-called mental illnesses, it began to seriously impinge, and eventually take control over the area of psychological, personal, and relational difficulties (p. 131). This has led to confusion in diagnoses and problems in treatment modalities. This is because there is a noticeable equivocation in the psychotherapeutic literature that presents the mind and the brain as though they were one and the same thing, and treats them medically as though both were biological organs. Of course the brain is such an organ, but the mind is not. The brain is the biological container; the mind is the non-biological content. The mind is not material; it is propositional, consisting of beliefs, values, assumptions, fears, and so on. It is impossible to conceive of a program of prevention if mental suffering and emotional distress is erroneously defined as "mental illnesses" caused by endogenous chemical imbalances in the biological brain. For any discussion of prevention it is essential that a paradigm shift take place in thinking about the ontology and etiology of so-called mental illness. This in turn requires a paradigm shift from believing "mind" is just another word for "brain," to the understanding that "mind" is the propositional content of the biological container called "brain."

Eliahu Shamir is the chairperson of the NGO "Ozma," the Israeli association of families of people coping with mental illness. He writes that so-called "mental morbidity"

> affects all age groups, but the impact may be greatest on young people post puberty. In present-day societies, young people are subject to intense pressures, and too many of them fall behind. Those afflicted by mental illness are the extreme cases of this fallout. (p. 55)

Young people today are diagnosed as suffering from a "mental illness" when there are sexual identity issues, or when there is substance abuse, poor school performance, a negative body image, unhealthy eating habits, low self-esteem, physical, mental, or sexual abuse, depression, conflicts with parents, and suicide attempts. All of these troubling life situations and more can be found in the diagnostic manuals and psychotherapy literature as "mental illnesses" requiring treatment that often includes powerful, side-effect-laden psychotropic medications.

The first error that practitioners in the mental health field make is diagnosing common human suffering and distress as brain-generated "mental illnesses," and then treating them with powerful psychotropic medications designed to alter the brain. The second error that both practitioners and policy makers in the mental health field make is that they have been focusing almost exclusively on the intervention, treatment, and rescue of individuals who have already succumbed to emotional suffering and mental distress.

Why is it that our mental healthcare system seems to value alleviating harm more than preventing it? For one thing, there seems to be an "If ain't broke don't fix it" mentality: if there is no evidence of suffering then nothing needs to be done.

For another thing, the costs and benefits of prevention are difficult, if not impossible to calculate (Sanders et al. p. 416), while the data on the costs and outcomes of restorative treatments are fairly easy to come by. So treatment appears to be more cost-effective. Health insurance providers, including governments, typically don't recognize the value of preventive care. Their money is aimed toward treatment where the diagnosis is confirmed and the outcome of treatment methods is fairly well documented. Mental healthcare policy seems to be based on the rhetorical question, "If treatments are available why bother with the elusive notion of prevention?"

From the perspective of criminal justice, it has been discovered that crime prevention is a highly cost-effective alternative to the costs of crime to individuals, neighborhoods, and communities. In other words it's less costly—both economically and psychologically—to prevent crime than to deal with the numerous consequences to various individuals and communities in the aftermath of a crime. The same can be said about mental health: it's less costly to prevent so-called mental illness than to deal with the numerous consequences to various individuals and communities after onset. But does this mean that individuals should be given psychotropic medications even before they've been diagnosed with a so-called mental illness? That would be a valid argument if "mental illnesses" were in fact brain disorders treatable with chemical remedies. But they're not. So-called mental illnesses are in fact problematic and distressing beliefs, values, assumptions, and fears brought about by difficult life circumstances that can't simply be dispelled with drugs.

When it comes to physical health there is a movement in our society toward prevention: people are learning how to eat properly, participate in regular physical activity, get adequate amounts of sleep, and so on—in other words to take care of their bodies. This movement is driving people to health care professionals who practice preventive medicine, focusing on education as a means of preventing health problems from arising, rather than just treating the symptoms of already existing conditions.

Why can't the same proactive, preventive approach be followed in taking care of the mind? Philosophy doesn't need to be applied only retroactively as a "curative" or therapy antecedent to psychotherapeutically diagnosed "mental disorders." Why not offer philosophy as prevention rather than just intervention or rescue? Currently philosophy is being offered by some practitioners primarily as a palliative treatment after a distressing event. But counselors and therapists who have been educated in the content of philosophy and trained in its practice are also willing to teach their clients the knowledge and discursive methods they have employed to help them. This informal education promotes the client's autonomy and helps to avoid a dependence on the counselor or therapist in the event of future difficulties. Philosophy can be a heuristic treatment which encourages individuals to learn how to discover, understand, and solve problems on their own. The same is rarely true of psychologically oriented psychoanalysis and psychotherapy, and is completely absent from biological psychiatry.

If good reasoning is learned by students early in life then they are much less likely to be led into the kind of mental distress that can be diagnosed as "mental illness." An education in philosophy is the best precautionary training as a preventative against the effects of both undesirable events and manipulative individuals.

Elizabeth Flanagan, an Assistant Professor of Psychiatry at Yale University School of Medicine, and her colleagues write that research has shown that users of mental healthcare services "consistently asked for outpatient services that emphasized prevention and rehabilitation rather than just acute symptom management" (p. 267). In a different essay in the *Journal of Mental Health Counseling* the authors write that

> preventive counseling has been a defining characteristic of mental health counseling throughout the history of the profession. Yet a review of the literature suggests that prevention has rarely been emphasized in the training process or in the practice of mental health counseling. (Kinselica p. 102)

Unfortunately, almost the same thing can be said of philosophy. There is a "request only focus" in which philosophy is offered in counseling to individuals asking for relief from currently experienced suffering and distress. There has been almost no deliberate attempt made to teach philosophy proactively as a preventive measure against the future onset of so-called mental illnesses.

But teaching philosophy to young people at the pre-university level is a preemptive endeavor that anticipates the possibility that life stresses may result in what can be diagnosed by the medical establishment as "mental illnesses." Knowledge and reasoning capacities act like an immune system that help the "reasoner" avoid harm. Using philosophy to help someone overcome a problem they found insurmountable is like offering both a "cure" for the suffering, and an inoculation of knowledge and skill to help prevent the reoccurrence of the same problem. An immunization with philosophy averts dependence on an "expert" to solve each and every problem as it arises.

It might be argued that teaching philosophy as an inoculation against so-called mental illnesses is an unreasonably radical treatment when there are no means by which it's possible to determine which child or young person will in fact succumb to a so-called mental illness. But this raises the question, "Are irrefutable empirical data always necessary in support of taking a precautionary measure?" Christopher J. Rikard-Bell, Staff Psychiatrist with the Department of Child and Adolescent Psychitry, Prince of Wales Hospital, University of New South Wales, points out that the reasoning which says prevention interventions can't be put forward in the field of mental health until all the underlying causal mechanisms are known "is not consistent with prevention in other areas of health." He maintains that "effective forms of treatment and prevention have been developed, using aetiological hypotheses, without knowledge of aetiological mechanisms" (p. 434).

In discussing the role of precaution in public health, *The Lancet*—one of the world's oldest, best known, and most respected general medical journals—ran an editorial about what is known as the "Precautionary Principle" The author wrote,

> We must act on facts, and on the most accurate interpretation of them, using the best scientific information. That does not mean that we must sit back until we have 100% evidence about everything. . . . Where there are significant risks of damage to the public health, we should be prepared to take action to diminish those risks, even when the scientific knowledge is not conclusive, if the balance of likely costs and benefits justify it. (Horton p. 251–52)

What are the risks and benefits of teaching philosophy to pre-university students? There are few, if any, risks involved, while the benefits will no doubt appear in the future when the incidence of so-called mental illnesses declines. The ability to reason cogently—free of fallacies and biases—about difficult life issues is clearly of benefit to any student. Doing philosophy with young people is not only about preventing harm, it is also about enhancing their experience of life. Philosophy is not the mere transmission of facts. It can instruct, prepare, and forearm students against difficult and distressing life situations.

Some of the literature on harm prevention talks about three different types of prevention: Primary, Secondary, and Tertiary (see Brooks-Harris et al.).

Primary prevention includes efforts directed toward an entire population in order to improve resilience and optimize healthy functioning, and to reduce the risk for dysfunction or distress. In the case of mental health, primary prevention means providing philosophy programs for students in all schools in order to prevent the negative consequences of troubling life situations from resulting in distress that might be diagnosed as "mental illness." Although not focused specifically on the prevention of so-called mental illness, a well-known curriculum of philosophy for pre-university students is the "P4C" Philosophy for Children program developed by philosopher and teacher Matthew Lipman and his colleagues in the United States. This approach to doing philosophy with children uses the "Community of Inquiry" in the classroom. It is a "self-correcting process" where students discuss topics collectively with the aim of learning from each other, even from those with whom they strongly disagree (Lipman p. 72).

Secondary prevention targets groups within a population that have been deemed to have a higher probability of experiencing an incidence of specific dysfunction or distress. For example, secondary prevention efforts may include philosophical discussions about self-esteem and interpersonal relationships among a group of teenaged students who are more likely to experience feelings of depression than younger children. Secondary prevention may also include a focus on specific topics such as religion, drugs, ethics, or family politics for groups of students for whom a topic is of greater relevance than the general population.

Tertiary prevention is directed toward individuals or very small groups. This type of preventive effort is comparable to individual counseling with philosophy. The first two of these levels of prevention can easily be carried out by means of a program of philosophy in pre-university classrooms.

Under the heading "Preventing Problems" the authors of the book *Caring for the Mind: A Comprehensive Guide to Mental Health* suggest that some good ways to prevent mental illness are taking an occasional break, taking a short vacation, playing a musical instrument, or "allowing yourself small indulgences, like taking an extra five minutes in the shower" (Hales and Hales p. 792). This raises the question, how would taking a short vacation, playing a musical instrument, or taking an extra five minutes in the shower help prevent the mental distress caused by confusion about a problematic personal relationship, or a costly life decision? While a dose of warm water may be physically soothing, it certainly can't prevent the distress that may arise from troubling life issues. What young people require are the reasoning tools that will help them to comprehend, evaluate, and respond to the challenges of life. These are exactly the skills that may be gained from philosophy. And since emotions are typically precipitated by beliefs, values, fears, and assumptions, emotional distress can also be mitigated with philosophy.

Turning again to the field of criminal justice, crime prevention is said to be concerned with reducing the likelihood of an occurrence of an undesirable event within a population. It is understood that effective prevention must involve an entire population. The undesirable event to be avoided in the case of mental health is a diagnosis of so-called mental illness. The population is in fact partially responsible for the creation of so-called mental illnesses because an individual's beliefs, values, fears, and assumptions are generated and supported by the social environments in which that individual is situated. So how can an entire population be involved in the prevention of so-called mental illnesses?

In countries where education is freely available, student participation in philosophy is in fact an involvement of the entire *future* population of society. And the question of distributive justice that is so difficult to resolve in the field of medicine is a moot point in terms of an educational strategy for the reduction of so-called mental illnesses. When every child is freely given a metaphorical "philosophical inoculation" at school distributive justice will have been realized.

When considering the cost, to both societies and individuals, of treating and caring for those who have been diagnosed as suffering from "mental illnesses," it seems clear that a preventive program of philosophy in pre-university classrooms will benefit not only individuals, but entire future populations.

TEACHING (HEURISTICS) FOR PREVENTION

Mila was in her mid fifties when she came to see me because she was having difficulty with her two grown sons. She told me they are very critical of her for often being "absent," and at other times "cold" toward them. I asked her to explain what these accusations were based on. She told me that her parents were immigrants from communist Eastern Europe, that her mother was never very warm toward her, which was not surprising given that she had eight children to care for. Her father discouraged discussions, and especially arguments, among members of their large family. So Mila learned to "bite her tongue" whenever she was upset with something or someone in the family. She now realizes that she uses this same behavior with her own two children; she avoids conflict and argument by simply walking away. She supposed that this is what made her children see her as absent when they felt the need to engage in discussion or argument with her. She said that they see her as "cold" due to the fact that she does not feel the need to hug them as often as it seems "people want to hug each other these days." She said she couldn't understand why her children can't just accept that she loves them without demanding that she display her affection with physical contact. She asked, "Isn't my love for them obvious enough?"

After a number of visits with me this developed into a teaching situation. Mila asked to learn how to improve her participation in a discussion—especially one that escalates into an argument—without feeling the need to run away. She wanted to know how to make a strong point without offending others, or without attacking them personally; what to do about the "unfair" tactics her children sometimes employed. And she wanted to know if she was a bad mother for being so "cold." What is it that makes a good mother anyway? Does it require hugging her children at times when she really doesn't feel like it? What does it mean to love your kids? How could she avoid repeating the same problematic situations for herself over and over again in the future?

Education and learning does not necessarily have to remain confined to the early years of life. There is no reason why an individual can't learn as an adult what was missed in childhood, whether that be how to play a musical instrument, calculate a math problem, or practice philosophic reasoning and discussion. The practice of philosophy can be taught equally well to both young people and older adults.

Philosophy as a preventive measure includes not only teaching philosophy to individuals who have never been diagnosed as having a so-called mental illness, but also teaching it to current clients and patients, suffering individuals who are presently engaged in counseling and therapy, in order to help them avoid future problems. This is analogous to installing an anti-virus program after the removal of a virus from a computer in order to ward off future infections. In a study of the outcome of psychotherapy for clients, Strupp et al. found that patients in fact already view psychotherapy as an educational or re-educational process (Strupp et al. p. 14). Patients felt that they had learned from the psychotherapist how to deal with their immediate problems, and also how to live life so as to avoid similar instances in the future. It seems, therefore, that in psychotherapy the therapist is, either intentionally or unintentionally, cast into the role of an educator as well as that of a physician or healer (Sharma p. 57).

While psychiatry involves medical treatments for the brain meant to alleviate problems in the mind, the focus of psychoanalysis is "catharsis," the effort to release the patient's negative or unwanted emotions. Both these methods unhesitatingly advocate the prescription of medications as part of treatment. On the other hand, psychotherapy and counseling offer talk therapy which consists in part of what is sometimes called "edification." It involves helping clients or patients enhance their knowledge, their reasoning, their skills, and their general perception of, and insight into, life issues. Dr. Mike Slade, Professor of Health Services Research at the Institute of Psychiatry, King's College London, describes clinical work as "inherently a collaborative effort" in which the patient and clinician work to construct and reconstruct "more helpful understandings about the person and their world" (p. 91). The client of the counselor or therapist trained in philosophy is not simply a passive recipient of the philosopher's expertise. She is instead, in Martha Nussbaum's words, " emulate the philosopher, entering actively into the give and take of criticism, being not subservient but independent, not worshipful but critical" (p. 74). Psychotherapy and counseling are thereby not only a therapeutic practice, they are also a form of client education.

Psychotherapy claims to include "psychoeducation" which consists of "providing, or better still, eliciting from the person him- or herself psychological explanations for the symptoms," as well as helping clients and their caregivers to "know what's wrong with them, what diagnosis they have, and how their condition may have developed" (Kingdon and Turkington p. 83). But that seems to be as far as "psychoeducation" goes. In contrast, the counselor or psychotherapist who is trained in philosophy

phy, recognizes the need to "educate" the client by teaching him better reasoning skills as a preventive measure against a diagnosis of "mental illness." An education in philosophy is therefore not only of immense practical value to a counselor or therapist who will use this knowledge and skills to directly help the client or patient deal with life problems, it is also a transferable set of knowledge and skills—and ultimately wisdom—that the counselor or therapist can teach the client or patient. Teaching philosophy to the client or patient results in an enhancement of the client's autonomous reasoning and decision-making ability, and the development of a life less vulnerable to problematic reasoning and emotions, and thereby less dependent on the intellectual expertise and emotional support of counselors and therapists.

Unlike teaching in a classroom, philosophy in counseling is only occasionally concerned with the direct transmission of knowledge from an expert to a novice, or from the "knower" to the one seeking knowledge. Yet there are times when a client asks to learn from the philosophical counselor such things as critical and creative thinking skills, what famous philosophers have said on various issues, how to make an ethical decision, and so on. I have had clients literally say to me, "I want to learn how you helped me do that just now." Counseling with philosophy becomes teaching when the client asks to acquire knowledge and learn skills due to a desire for personal edification, or from what the Germans call the *Entwicklungsdrang* (literally, the urge to develop). The client's or patient's self-improvement will be enhanced when the counseling relationship is intentionally focused on the exchange of information and abilities.

"Constructivism" is a theory of learning and change which seems appropriate to the act of teaching philosophy during sessions of counseling or therapy. It says that a person will continue to act according to past behavior, think according to past beliefs, and cling to past values so long as those behaviors, beliefs, and values work in maintaining the desired lifestyle. Learning and change only occur when those behaviors, beliefs, and values are recognized as being no longer viable or beneficial by that person (Larochelle et al.). Albert Einstein is often loosely quoted as having wisely said that you can't solve a problem by using the same thinking that got you into the problem in the first place. Healing or therapy results when the distressed individual has been shown new approaches to resolving mental distress, and been taught new reasoning skills—and learned how to actually apply them—to resolve his or her own problems without having to depend on a counselor, clinical therapist, or medical doctor. Besides a growing trend toward integrating cognitive and behavioral methods to helping clients manage their own problems there is now also a related trend geared toward "giving psychology away." This involves psychologists sharing their knowledge so that mental healthcare services users can increasingly lead self-directed lives and not be dependent on the help of experts in dealing with their problems. Psychologists who share this perspective are primarily concerned with teaching people the skills they will need to manage their own lives effectively. Self-management is a relatively recent phenomenon in the fields of psychological counseling and therapy, and reports of clinical applications have burgeoned since the 1970s (Corey p. 296). But it is not at all new to philosophy in which, since before Socrates, philosophers have been helping people improve their own reasoning abilities in order to solve their own problems and to live better lives.

Since about the 1980s there has also been a growing interest in so-called self-help groups. Mental health associations, professional clinics, and individual therapists have been establishing self-help groups in growing numbers. These groups invite so-called mental healthcare "consumers" to gather together and share their stories of suffering and distress. The assumption about these groups seems to be that simply talking about their problems will help to improve the lives of participants. But such groups raise the question, "Just how helpful are they when this type of discourse takes place only internally, among a segregated gathering of variously distressed individuals?" Beside some emotional relief and the companionship found in such groups, how does sharing stories of their own misery help alleviate their distress or generate insight into the causes of their suffering? How is it possible for a brainstorming session or discussion within a "closed" group to generate new information and increase knowledge? Kenneth Gill, Professor and Chair of the Department of Psychiatric Rehabilitation and Counseling Professions at the University of Medicine and Dentistry of New Jersey, points out that "insider" status within a group does not automatically lead to insight into the group's concerns (Rudnick, 2012b p. 104). Some self-help groups invite speakers from the professional community to share their insights on causation and treatment for variously diagnosed mental distress. This can be helpful to some extent. But a one hour lecture by a professional on the "facts" about so-called mental illnesses is only minimally helpful if members of the group are then left to fend for themselves. Most individuals within a mental health self-help group are simply not up to the task of helping either themselves or each other because they lack the prior knowledge and practical skills required to do so. After all, it's often because of their lack of self-help knowledge and inadequate problem solving skills that they became burdened with a diagnosis of "mental illness" in the first place.

Groups consisting solely of individuals who have been diagnosed with so-called mental illnesses, which have no input from "outside" the group, find it difficult to progress toward alleviation of their diagnosed conditions. Such groups are analogous to a group of apprentices, in say a bakery, who come together to talk about how to bake bread and cakes without prior knowledge of recipes or the practical skills of baking necessary to produce results. While a self-help group can function somewhat in alleviating distress or suffering, there can be little, if any, progress toward recovery or cure without input and facilitative help from caring and knowledgeable individuals external to that group.

A more helpful approach than the conventional self-help group would be a "philosophy café" style of gathering that includes a facilitator who makes the effort to research the topic before discussion begins. A mental health philosophy café would have a facilitator well versed in both philosophy and the many issues involved in mental health and "illness" who not only encourages the sharing of personal stories but also maintains a "community of inquiry." This is a term used by Matthew Lipman and others in describing the style of discussion held in pre-university classrooms where there is "intellectual cooperation" among the participants without an authority figure or expert dominating or manipulating the discussion (Lipman p. 6). In a mental health discussion group the facilitator is also a resource for the participants in that he or she has available factual information about diagnostic criteria, medications, and other treatments options including the many philosophical topics that may arise in philosophical discourse. A mental health "community of inquiry" stimulates in the participants not only intellectual progress, by way of developing their reasoning about mental health and "illness," it also serves to aid in their recovery.

When a person cuts his thumb while slicing vegetables, the first thing we do is stop the bleeding by applying a bandage. But that's not the only treatment offered. We also discuss the situation with the suffering individual to find out what happened. Then we teach a safer method of knife handling: make your fingers into a claw, move them back, keep your thumb tucked behind your fingers, use a smaller knife, and so on. We make suggestions, we supervise for a little while, we educate. This is the approach also used in counseling and therapy with philosophy. Perhaps a bandage is necessary at times to first "stop the bleeding," but treatment for the painful cuts of life should never end with a simple bandage—such as psychotropic medications. It must include instructions on how to proactively avoid and prevent similar painful cuts in the future.

A serious shortcoming of psychoanalysis—and indeed in most of counseling and psychotherapy—is that it fails to provide prophylactic services. But unlike the field of psychoanalysis, philosophy does not preserve the knowledge and skills inherent in the field as an exclusive domain accessible only to practicing experts and professionals. The contents of philosophy, and philosophical discursive skills, are readily shared with all counseling clients. In fact, this sharing is entailed by the very definition of the term "philosophy." Effective "inoculation" against the onset of so-called mental illnesses requires explicit philosophical training for counselors and psychotherapists in order to "equip clinicians with the skills to recognize the limits of their own world view" (Slade p. 90). But an education in philosophy has at least three distinct benefits in the area of mental health care: it is not only a preventive measure to protect young people from unnecessary suffering and distress; it is a guard against unexamined assumptions about the nature of so-called mental illnesses, and thirdly, it can reduce the current "hyper-diagnosia" so pervasive in current clinical practice. Discussion in both academia and society must now turn to the question of what the content of an education in philosophy for young students, and counselors, psychotherapists, and other mental healthcare services providers ought to include.

III

Application

"Let no one delay the study of philosophy while young, nor weary of it when old. For no one is either too young or too old for the health of the soul."
—Epicurus (351–270 BCE)

EIGHT

An Education Plan

In December of 2012, shortly before Christmas, a young man shot and killed his mother in her home in a small Connecticut town. He then took his mother's two handguns and a semi-automatic rifle and drove to the local elementary school where he proceeded to kill several teachers and twenty little children in their classrooms. As the police arrived to stop him he took his own life. When the news of the massacre began to appear in the media one of the first questions that was asked by almost all reporters was, "Did this young man have a mental illness? Might it have been a 'mental illness' that made him do what he did?" No doubt this made television viewers wonder, "What about all those other mentally ill people running around loose in our society?" These questions are generated by the pervasive belief in our society that anyone who commits a horrendous crime must be "mentally ill" for the simple reason that normal people don't do such things. Behind this belief is the implied definition "mass murder is mental illness." In the philosophical field of informal logic this claim is called the "true by definition" fallacy. It ignores the fact that some people know they are committing evil, and understand that there will be dire consequences for themselves—either due to police response or suicide—but they are convinced that their harmful and destructive actions are worthwhile. And it is a second fallacy—called "circular reasoning"—to argue that "mental illness" is the cause of a crime, and the only proof of "mental illness" that is offered is the fact that a crime has been committed. Reporters, politicians, and media pundits all perpetuate these erroneous allegations by persistent association of sensational crimes with the assumption of "mental illness" despite the lack of evidence. In fact, and statistics show, that the overall risk of violent behavior among individuals classified as "mentally ill" is lower than the general population average, and that violence towards strangers perpetrated by people diagnosed as having serious "mental illnesses" is very rare (Shamir p. 47).

It seems obvious that the media, as well as the general public, need a greater awareness of the true nature of so-called mental illnesses. Counselors and therapists also need to be educated in the less harmful non-biological, non-pharmaceutical approach available in the use of philosophy in helping individuals to overcome their emotional distress and mental suffering and to live a good life, free from the personal impediments and social stigma brought on by a diagnosis of "mental illness." As psychiatrist and psychotherapist Edwin Hersch points out, philosophy is unavoidable in counseling and psychotherapy because everyone always operates from within a philosophical context of personal beliefs, professional presuppositions, and background clinical understandings. Recall that he says Freud was simply wrong when he claimed that philosophy has no direct influence on most people, and that only a small number of top intellectuals can understand it (p. 345). The problem is not that ordinary people are incapable of understanding philosophy, it's that the majority have never had a single course in philosophy as part of their education. And the same applies to professionals in the field of mental healthcare.

Many students of counseling and psychotherapy are never informed about two critical issues in the diagnosis and treatment of so-called mental illness. The first one, as pointed out in earlier chapters, is that there are egregious problems inherent in what students are taught about the ontology, etiology, diagnosis, and treatment modalities for so-called mental illnesses. The second is that there is an essential educational element that the vast majority of aspiring counselors and therapists are never offered: the rich discipline that is the framework on which all "talk therapies" have been built, namely philosophy. In their book *Psychotherapy as a Human Science* therapists Burnston and Frie argue that psychotherapy should not just be about treating symptoms. It should also enable patients to explore the reasons for their emotions so that they will come to understand what their emotions, and their emotional suffering, tells them about their current approach to life. The intention is to help the patient come to a greater self-awareness, and perhaps a better way of living and relating to others that is free from conflict and pain (p. 292). If psychotherapeutic practice involves an examination of the reasons patients have for the emotions they feel, the values they hold as good, and the beliefs they hold as true, and philosophy is concerned with exactly that, then it seems imperative that psychotherapists and counselors have a solid understanding of the theory and practice of philosophy.

At the moment the majority of students graduating with counseling psychology certificates and psychotherapy degrees have little if any explicit education in philosophy. Their expertise is dominated by knowledge of the various psychologically oriented treatment methods, such as

Existential psychotherapy, without any understanding of the wealth of practical applications that inhere in the philosophy of existentialism on which that approach is based. While today's counseling and psychotherapy courses offer an education in technique they often do so in a philosophical vacuum. In his book *From Philosophy to Psychotherapy* psychiatrist and psychotherapist Edwin L. Hersch argues convincingly that it is necessary to have a comprehensive and coherent philosophical foundation for any psychotherapeutic theory or method on which a practice is built. Hersch writes that some philosophical issues such as, for example, ontology and epistemology

> are so important to our understanding of the human condition that the underlying positions we take on them necessarily have profound implications for our psychological theories and practices. So we can't afford to be unaware of these issues. Philosophical issues such as those of consciousness, knowledge, validity, meaning, subjectivity, objectivity, values, morality, and reality are so intrinsic to the field of psychology that we seek to understand, that we should not ignore them, take them for granted, or leave them entirely to others to decipher. (p. 4, 5)

The therapeutic and counseling theories students are taught in their university psychology, counseling, and psychotherapy courses focus almost exclusively on technique or methodology, that is, the procedure of applying this or that approach to a diagnosed collection of symptoms. Students learn the technical "how" of various methods, and they learn "what" to say, without ever learning the meaningful "why" of the philosophy that informs those methods. They learn how to go through the motions of asking questions without understanding why some questions are better than others, and without knowing how to recognize the reasoning problems within the painful narratives presented by their patients and clients. They learn the techniques without recognizing the thought patterns that have led to the client's pain and suffering, and without knowing what issues to focus on in order to formulate the most helpful question, choose the most ethical course of action, locate the reasons for troubling emotions, and so on. Students of psychotherapy are not taught the philosophical disposition whose main feature is a respectful and open-minded consideration of points of view different from the "social norm." Instead they learn to promote the ideology of a particular time and place by attempting to reduce so-called social deviance, and thereby possibly also diminish their patients' uniqueness and creativity (Stein and Holland, p. 102). In this sense, psychotherapy is employed as a way to prevent "difference" from offending the community at the expense of the extraordinary individual.

While any number of counselors and psychotherapists, both past and present, have knowingly and unknowingly used philosophy to enhance their encounters with clients and patients, there are others who insist that the content of the therapeutic discussion is not nearly as important as the personality of the therapist. In his book *The Great Psychotherapy Debate: Models, Methods, and Findings* Bruce E. Wampold, Professor of Counseling Psychology and Clinical Professor of Psychiatry at the University of Wisconsin-Madison, argues that in talk therapies the "specific ingredients" of any therapeutic approach are not as important as the relationship between the therapist and client. But this conclusion is based on data gathered at a time when schools of psychotherapy were more concerned with a supposedly scientific approach to the patient as a bundle of symptoms needing treatment than as a human being asking for assistance. Until the late 1980s students of counseling and psychotherapy were taught "mirroring" and other techniques similar to the so-called neutral and zero-affect approaches to patients found in classical psychoanalysis. It's no surprise that in that cold, analytic, clinical environment patients would say that they found a friendly and congenial therapist to be more agreeable. But given that talk therapies are meant to be remedial—they are about talking with patients or clients in order to alleviate their emotional distress, clarify and resolve a life problem, or reach a moral goal that is agreeable to the patient or client—surely a background knowledge and a basic skill in philosophy would constitute a "specific ingredient" that is essential and perhaps more beneficial to therapeutic practice than the therapist's pleasant demeanor.

In their book *Persuasion and Healing* psychiatrists Jerome and Julia Frank point out that "among the focused therapies, none has yet consistently been shown to be more effective than any other" (1993 p. 19). Psychologist C. Peter Bankart also writes that the overwhelming statistical evidence shows that theoretical orientation, therapeutic method, choice of technique, and professional allegiance "are variables of almost no real weight in determining the degree of success a client will encounter in a course of psychotherapy." He goes on to say that virtually all psychotherapy outcome research agrees that only one variable predicts the relative success of the therapeutic process: "personality, personal style, and 'psychological presence' of the therapist." The research reveals that what helps the client most is "a caring, competent, and skilled practitioner." What does he mean by "competent" and "skilled"? Bankart then quotes Lipsey and Wilson as writing that "well-developed psychological, educational, and behavioral treatment is generally efficacious" (p.19). But it seems that Bankart is contradicting himself. On the one hand he says that theoretical orientation, therapeutic method, choice of technique, and professional allegiance make no difference in outcomes, and that the common factors of personality, personal style, and "psychological presence" are what make a good counselor or therapist. And on the other hand he argues that the practitioner requires competence and skill. Surely he can't mean that personality, personal style, and "psychological presence" are forms of competence and skill? But if he means competence and skill in psychological, educational, and behavioral treatment methods, then why does he say that only "personality, personal style, and 'psychological presence' of the therapist" predict the relative success of the therapeutic process?

In his essay titled "Philosophy and Therapy: Professional Training and Certification" Sam Brown creates a similar contradiction, arguing that most of the efficacy in counseling

> is attributed to the empathetic bond between client and counselor. The therapist, must, however, be well-trained in the theory and practice of their own modality. Outcomes improve with training and experience, regardless of approach. (p. 167)

Brown fails to explain why it is essential that therapists be well-trained in the theory and practice of their own modality when the method or approach is supposedly irrelevant, and empathy seems to be what is required the most for a good outcome. The focus on the personality of the therapist by both these authors leaves a huge explanatory gap as to why the therapist needs any sort of training at all, and can't simply rely on the beneficial effects of his or her empathetic personality. But most suffering individuals are probably able to find empathy among close family members and good friends. Why would anyone need to pay for visits to a counselor or therapist? Do therapists only see clients who have no one willing to empathetically listen to them?

Interestingly, John Hunsley and Catherine M. Lee, Professors of Psychology at the University of Ottawa, point out that more recent research data show that the alliance between the patient and therapist "accounts for only about five percent of the variability in the outcome of treatment" for both adults and youths (p. 659). This certainly calls into question the claim that the therapist's personality is what counts. The claim that no particular therapy has been shown to be more effective than any other is also contradicted by more recent research data. Recall that in chapter 6 of this volume Hunsley and Lee reported that recent extensive meta-analysis of a large amount of research data has shown that "the cognitive-behavioral set of treatments was more efficacious than were other treatment approaches," and that "for most conditions, the outcomes of different treatments are not equivalent, and at present, there is strongest support for the efficacy of CBT [cognitive-behavior therapy]" (p. 659). Furthermore, if it's true that all methods are equal, and "any kind of service provision is better than none" (Adeponle et al. p. 126) then why not sanction treatment protocols that undermine individual rights and empowerment, and practices that focus primarily on the pharmaceutical control of symptoms? Unfortunately, this is in fact what has happened in the mental healthcare field, in part due to the misleading claim that the data show no outcome differences in treatment modalities. This misinformation has greatly benefited the ascendancy of biomedical psychiatry as the dominant treatment paradigm. The oft-repeated erroneous claim that research shows method to be unimportant when all that is really needed is a therapist with an empathetic personality has left the door open for a clinical dismissal of all forms of talk therapy and the turn to an almost absolute reliance on pharmaceuticals as the standard treatment modality.

Since the literature claims that competence and skill of some sort, beyond personality, are in fact necessary to be an effective therapist it raises the question, What sort of competence and skill should counselors or therapists possess? Jerome and Julia Frank write that the similarity they see in improvement rates for all forms of psychotherapy suggests that there must be a common feature in all of them. But they don't suggest that empathy or a friendly bedside manner is this common feature (p. 19). So what might it be? Perhaps the feature that produces improvement, which was perceived by the Franks, is the therapist's philosophical attitude and philosophical discursive skill. An effective philosophical style would fit the criteria of a competence or a skill. And a philosophical style such as is found in the cognitive-behavioral set of treatments has been shown to lead to improvements in the client or patient (Hunsley and Lee). But a clinical approach that is very similar to, or fortuitously resembles, philosophy is not the same as the clinician's inclusion of philosophical content and a philosophically informed discursive method based on an education in the content and practice of philosophy. Is it possible that the lack of philosophical content and discursive style in the majority of psychotherapeutic methods might explain why "none has yet consistently been shown to be more effective than any other" and why there are similar improvement rates for all forms of counseling and psychotherapy? I suggest that a solid education in philosophy for all counselors and psychotherapists would make them more effective, and bring a higher rate of improvement in treatment outcomes. Perhaps it is the case that researchers attribute the effectiveness of counselors and psychotherapists to their personality, personal style, and "psychological presence" because, in searching for the best clinical traits in a psychotherapist, the psychologically trained researchers who collected the data were incapable of recognizing the *philosophical* knowledge and *philosophical* skills in those counselors who were in fact the most effective.

In his book *After Therapy What?* Thomas Oden, American United Methodist theologian and religious author associated with Drew University in New Jersey, noted that therapists often extend themselves far beyond their competence "into hidden or implicit moral, political, and religious judgments, precisely where their self-critical capacities and historical awareness are, by their training, extremely limited" (p. 32). Clearly personality, personal style, and "psychological presence" cannot compensate for a lack of competence in dealing with the many and varied philosophical issues that arise in counseling and therapy. The clinical effectiveness of some counselors and therapists must therefore result from something more than simply a nice bedside manner, to include their philosophical competence: their ability to ask meaningful questions, offer valuable insights, and make helpful, practical suggestions.

A former psychiatric patient and victim of past abuse explained that her madness was undoubtedly a reaction against her unhealthy familial circumstances. She wonders, "Why was I never asked about my circumstances? Why did no one ever ask, 'What was it that drove you mad?'" Such obvious questions are not usually asked in mainstream psychiatry. In psychiatry it is all-important for the expert to establish a diagnosis of the patient's symptoms without regard to whether this is meaningful or helpful to the patient or not. And once this diagnosis has been made, it is assumed to automatically provide answers—at least for the psychiatrist—to many pertinent questions (Boevink p. 21). But Existential therapist Emmy van Deurzen-Smith argues that "the enterprise of psychoanalysis, psychotherapy, and counseling, as it is currently conceived, could benefit greatly from more existential input" which would include the counselor or therapist asking the client the kind of obvious life questions mentioned above (p.286).

Bradley Lewis, Associate Professor of Medical Humanities and Cultural Studies at New York University, also maintains that the world of mental health work is "inescapably" a world of stories or narrative. Unfortunately, for the most part the narrative dimension of clinical work has been omitted in recent years as "the clinical literature has sought to be as scientific as possible through the pursuit of biological research, rigorous classification, and evidence-base therapies" (p. 148). What the different models of counseling and therapy have in common, according to Lewis, is that they work to re-work, or "re-author," the person's initial story into a new narrative that "allows new degrees of flexibility in understanding the past, and provides new strategies for moving into the future" (p. 153). The person's narrative consists of his or her beliefs, values, fears, and assumptions. These are also the basic elements of any philosophical discussion. It seems then that the psychotherapeutic "reworking" of the patient's or client's narrative is in fact philosophical work. This cannot be accomplished effectively by a clinician whose primary training has been focused on the biomedical model that dominates clinical psychology.

THE STUDY OF PHILOSOPHY

To become just another counselor, it's enough for a student to take a course in counseling. But to become a really *good* counselor it is essential for the student to study philosophy as well. A student of counseling or psychotherapy can be taught to treat clients using a step-by-step how-to manual; but understanding *why* a method says to do this or that makes a significant difference. That difference is the illuminating power of theory. If the counseling student is following prescribed steps, and one of the steps goes awry, knowing the principles on which the theory is based will help the student set the process right by initiating alternative techniques that remain consistent with both the theory and the desired outcome. If there is no understanding of the basis of the theory, a course correction is impossible (Day p. 23).

There is somewhat of a misconception that simply reading a philosophy book will make you a better counselor, or a better person. This is like believing that reading a book on how the chess pieces move on the board will make you a better chess player. Unfortunately, it's not enough to simply know how the pieces move, without understanding what constitutes a good move. It's crucially important to understand exactly when, in which circumstances—in what configuration of all the pieces on the board—one particular move is best. It takes many games of practice, as well as, ideally, some instructions from a stronger player, to become the kind of chess player who can judge which moves lead to advantage and which bring difficulty.

It takes three things beyond mere knowledge of the content of philosophy for it to have a positive impact on one's own life: first, a *correct* understanding of the content of philosophy—knowing what the various philosophers actually meant with their writings; second, the *will* to apply this knowledge to one's life; and third, a comprehension of how, where, and when it is appropriate to *apply* that knowledge. Then, in order to go one step further and use that philosophical experience in helping others, it requires not only the ability to judge when its application is appropriate, it also requires the personal *courage* to offer to do so. Training in philosophy prepares the counselor or therapist to take a different, more helpful non-biological approach to assisting those who have been unfortunate enough to be diagnosed as suffering from a so-called "mental illness." But it takes courage to deviate from the standard psychotherapeutic methods that are steeped in psychological and medical theories, and intentionally apply philosophy as the main treatment element.

There is a small but growing number of professionals in the field of mental healthcare who recognize and accept the fact that the mind is not the same as the brain, and that many so-called diagnosable mental illnesses are in fact not biological brain malfunctions requiring drug treatments. For example, the Royal College of Psychiatrists in London recently added to its curriculum for higher specialist training "a substantial section on philosophy, covering relevant areas of conceptual analysis, value theory, philosophy of science, philosophy of mind, and phenomenology" (Fulford et al. 2003 p. 2). They have come to recognize and acknowledge the value of philosophy in the professional treatment of so-called mental illnesses.

So much of what is done to patients today is still, unfortunately, based on the mistaken assumption that "mental problems" are somehow caused by the biological mechanisms or chemistry of the brain. What is often ignored is that mental health problems have to do with the non-material mind: the person's beliefs, values, fears, and assumptions. They are often complex life problems that are not at all easily fixed with only the help of family members or friends. But they are the sort of problems that are indeed fixable with the help of someone trained in philosophy.

An educational plan for students and mental healthcare workers needs to include both the theoretical content of philosophy as well as diligent practice in philosophical discursive skills if they are to become competent counselors or therapists. There is no clear separation between academic philosophy and clinical philosophy; the material covered in virtually all philosophy classes is useful in clinical practice. But a comprehensive education in philosophy for counselors and psychotherapists calls for a paradigm shift in the beliefs and assumptions most students initially bring to the classroom regarding what "mental illness" is, what causes it, and how it affects an "afflicted" person's behavior.

For example, as already mentioned above, students need to really grasp the fact that the mind is not the same as the brain. They need to be brought to an understanding of how so-called mental illnesses are neither medical nor scientific discoveries but rather are created by a popularity vote of mental healthcare workers. They need to be made aware of the fact that the distress and suffering that comes from difficult life circumstances are not organic pathologies; calling them "mental illnesses" is misleading. Students need to see that so-called mental illnesses are not discrete entities that cause suffering; they are labels attached to symptom clusters that are the result of suffering. They need to understand that so-called mental illnesses don't cause anything, but are instead the suffering caused by life circumstances that lead to mental and emotional distress. They need to comprehend that medications never address the actual causes of so-called mental illnesses: troubling life circumstances. They need to see that the very diagnosing of a "mental illness" brings them into being. Students need to learn that the definitional criteria for so-called mental illnesses overlap extensively with each other, and that both social convention and the pharmaceutical industry have a strong influence on the "discovery"—which is actually the fabrication—of "new" mental illnesses." They need to notice that the treatment of so-called mental illnesses does not conform to the medical model of patient care because of the indisputable difference in treatment modalities between medical care and what is done in psychotherapy. They need to learn, by means of their own research, that neither the diagnosing nor the treatment modalities for so-called mental illnesses are in any way informed by the medical science of genetics. And they need to learn that the use of philosophy as therapy has a long history that has been interrupted and appropriated by medical science; that the "talk therapy" part of psychoanalysis, psychotherapy, and counseling are built on a knowledge and practical skills originating with philosophy; and that the originators of many of the contemporary psychotherapeutic methods had a solid education in philosophy. A good place to begin the study of philosophy's role in psychotherapy and counseling is with an examination of the differences between them.

DIFFERENCES BETWEEN PHILOSOPHY AND PSYCHOTHERAPY

It's not uncommon for students to wonder whether there is actually any difference between counseling or therapy with philosophy and the many conventional methods in psychotherapy learned in other classes. After all, isn't counseling and therapy with philosophy just a kind of "talk therapy" not unlike so many others? Philosopher and philosophical counselor Shlomit Schuster cautions that true philosophical counseling "does differ significantly from the way philosophy is used by psychotherapists, psychoanalysts, and other mental healthcare workers, in terms of its methodology and content" (p. 108). Of course it's difficult for students to think of differences between philosophy and psychotherapy at the beginning of the semester when they still lack a comprehensive knowledge of what is entailed by philosophy. But many students find it useful to have a list of differences supplied to them early in the year to which they can later refer as they become more familiar with the contents and skills inherent in the practice of philosophy.

1. *Prevention:* Philosophy can be taught as a preventive (prophylactic) measure to help people avoid the kind of emotional suffering and mental distress that can be diagnosed as mental illness. On the other hand, the methods in psychotherapy are designed as treatments that are applied only *after* an official diagnosis has been made. It is not possible to teach psychotherapy to individuals as a preventive measure in the way that is possible with philosophy.
2. *Etiology:* the origin of so-called mental illness. Psychoanalysis depends on the concept of "unconscious" causality. Biopsychiatry takes a materialist/causal approach, claiming that so-called mental illnesses are generated endogenously (internally) primarily by chemical imbalances in the brain. Mainstream psychotherapy maintains that psychological problems create symptom groups which can be diagnosed as mental illnesses. But it is unclear what constitutes a psychological problem, and how to group symptoms into distinct illness categories. Philosophical counseling sees emotional suffering and cognitive perplexity as based on reasons, i.e., as precipitated by difficult, distressing, or problematic life circumstances. Blaming individuals in the past (such as parents), as is

done when the so-called unconscious forces are presented as explanatory causes, creates an infinite regress (from parents to grandparents, to great-grandparents, etc. ad infinitum). Although philosophy in counseling and therapy deals with the negative influences of the past on the present, it recognizes that while people may be influenced they are not controlled by deterministic forces from the past. As Professor Young E. Rhee points out, "Human actions cannot be reduced to physical events." Humans are intentional agents, and intentionality and consciousness cannot be described nor anticipated according to scientific laws (p. 59). Philosophy accepts the fact that human beings have the freedom to make life-altering decisions, and to shape a future that cannot be accurately predicted by means of scientific laws of causation. Philosophy helps people to use this freedom to good advantage.
3. *Blaming the victim:* Psychiatry assumes there are forces in the patient's unconscious that are causing the mental problems. Psychiatry, psychotherapy, and especially biopsychiatry, implicitly assume that the patient is the source of his own suffering. The patient's brain chemistry or genetic makeup are cited as the cause; causes are defined as endogenous, needing to be "rooted out" of the patient. There is no such assumption in philosophy. The philosophical counselor or therapist assumes that people are often negatively affected by external circumstances. The philosophical counselor or therapist knows that people want to live an enjoyable, rewarding, and satisfying life, and that therefore clients do not unconsciously instigate their own mental suffering. Nor is existential distress the result of biological malfunctions.
4. *Taxonomy:* Emotional distress and mental suffering is defined by psychotherapy as "abnormal" and as "mental illness" or "disorder." Philosophy defines distress and suffering as existential, part of the human condition and life circumstances. But philosophy also acknowledges that life can at times become so difficult and perplexing that help from others may be necessary to restore equilibrium and return life to a "good" state.
5. *Nosology* and *Diagnosing:* The field of psychotherapy, and especially biopsychiatry, suffers from a fatal ambiguity in its contemporary nosology: the knowledge of, and systematic classification of diseases. There are two "official" diagnostic manuals currently in use by professional clinicians in the field of psychotherapy (*DSM* and *ICD*). The diagnostic criteria in these manuals is under constant disputation and revision. There is no such manual in philosophy because it does not involve locking the counselor or psychotherapist into employing specific diagnostic criteria while seeing the client. Philosophical counselor Constantinos Athanasopoulos makes this point very strongly when he says, "The freedom of both

the client and the therapist/facilitator must be preserved at all costs. The practice contract should not be binding on the choices that both the client and the facilitator have" (p. 227). Furthermore, psychotherapy, and especially biopsychiatry, sees comorbidity—the diagnoses of multiple illnesses in one individual. Philosophy sees so-called comorbidity as a person struggling with troubling life issues and emotional suffering that need to be sorted out and dealt with. Psychotherapy, in contradistinction to philosophy, holds the belief that a diagnosis is true rather than simply being a hypothesis.

6. *Reification:* Psychotherapy, and especially biopsychiatry, reifies "discovered" or invented, and then labeled, symptom clusters. That is, psychotherapy defines various presentations of suffering as symptoms of an assumed illness, and then labels those symptom clusters as though they were natural disease entities. In this way psychotherapy creates the illusion of biological illnesses out of symptoms clusters. Philosophy does not consider mental suffering and emotional distress to be symptoms of any sort of illnesses in the mind.

7. *The medical model:* Psychotherapy, and especially biopsychiatry, claim to treat patients according to the medical model. But in fact the methods in psychotherapy do not follow the standard medical procedures of biological testing, standard diagnosing, and treatment according to accepted medical protocols. Philosophy does not make any claims to following any model, especially not that of medical treatment. Psychotherapy promotes itself as a practice within the field of medical science. Philosophy disputes this claim, and makes no similar claim for itself.

8. *Treatment protocol:* Treatment modalities vary widely in both biopsychiatry and psychotherapy. There are many "schools" in both psychiatry and psychotherapy which demand that their practitioners adhere to strict methodological protocols. Philosophy is open-ended, with no requirement for allegiance to any specific methodological schools of treatment. "The mental health professional has far less faith in the power of human rationality than his philosophical counterpart" (From the pre-publication version of the paper by Ellenbogen).

9. *Pluralism:* Cognitive pluralism is encouraged in philosophy but not in psychotherapy where treatment "schools" dictate specific treatment modalities. In psychotherapy the dialectical examination of alternative views of both symptoms and their treatment is discouraged. Since the 1950s psychotherapy has been a fertile field for the development of an ever-increasing number of ever-more specialized methods. But the limitations encountered in clinical practice by the exclusive use of one method over another, and what has

become the significant overlap of the elements of many methods has, out of necessity, led to what the literature refers to as "multi-modal" or "eclectic therapy." Eclectic therapy is the serial application of one specific method after another (serial methodology) as required by the circumstances encountered in the psychotherapeutic session. Philosophy as therapy has no segregated methods which compete with each other or overlap. It is completely open and inclusive of many approaches, and is thereby beyond eclecticism. It is, as Gerd Achenbach famously put it, "a beyond method method."

10. *Method:* Philosophy has always been "open." "The Philosophic Practitioner opens up the space of attention by refraining from knowing in advance . . . " (Lindseth p. 191). The Greek term *epoch*, the suspension of judgment, is often used to describe this philosophical attitude. Psychotherapy is "closed" in the sense that the patient or client is discouraged from questioning the assumptions held, and the goal set, by the therapist during the course of the therapy. Philosophy is open simply because philosophy allows everything to be questioned, including philosophy itself. "Insight-oriented psychotherapy results in a deceptive form of social control . . . . Insight-oriented psychotherapies are engaged in a process that subtly 'absorbs' clients into the therapist's epistemological-metaphysical-ethical framework. Insight-oriented psychotherapy "constructs and reconfigures clients along the lines of socially accepted norms and values" (Al-Shawi p. 159). No such manipulation occurs in philosophy. Philosophical counselors don't defer any one philosophical "method" over any other because philosophy is the means, and not a "method" in the strict sense of the word. M. R. Bennett, Professor of Physiology and University Chair at the University of Sydney, and P. M. S. Hacker, Fellow of St. John's College, Oxford put it this way: "Analytical philosophy is above all a conceptual investigation. . . . It is concerned not with matters of fact but with matters of meaning. Its province is . . . the domain of sense and nonsense" (Bennett and Hacker p. 399).

11. *Medications:* Psychotherapy always has a biological explanation close to hand, and often prescribes medications as the recommended treatment. But this creates a paradox: the prescription of medications for so-called mental illnesses assumes that the problematic life circumstances which have caused mental suffering in the non-biological mind can be altered with the administration of biological substances into the biological brain. Philosophy does not accept this paradoxical pharmacological approach as reasonable treatment. It sees the brain as a biological organ (the container) and the mind as non-biological, non-material, and propositional (the content). Philosophy does not treat the brain; instead it deals with

alleviating mental suffering, cognitive confusion, and emotional distress of the mind.
12. *Dream interpretation:* Psychoanalysis and other forms of psychotherapy assume that dreams give access to the unconscious—the deeply hidden mental worlds of their patients that are inaccessible by the patients themselves. Research in psychology has shown the hypothesis of an unconscious to be groundless. Philosophy makes no attempt to offer dream interpretation as a treatment modality, although a casual discussion of a troubling or puzzling dream can sometimes arise. A critique of the validity of dreams analysis, and an explanation of the role of the discussion of dreams in philosophical counseling can be found in *Issues in Philosophical Counseling* (Raabe; see chapter 19 "Dream Interpretation").
13. *Power structure:* The relationship in psychoanalysis is based on a power differential between the knowing and skilled authority figure—the analyst—and the helpless victim of unconscious forces—the patient. Most other psychotherapists are less of an authority figure but still generally considered to be the expert on diagnosing and labeling the patient's mental suffering. In philosophy the relationship is also not one of absolute equality because the philosophical counselor or therapist has knowledge and skills which the client does not possess. But the philosophical counselor or therapist considers herself to be a partner with the client or patient, and will readily admit to any shortcomings She will also unhesitatingly share both her knowledge and her expertise with the client. While the knowledge and skill relationship between the counselor and the client is uneven in philosophical counseling, the power structure is not.
14. *Neutrality:* There is an assumption and a claim in professional clinical circles that psychoanalysis and psychotherapy are neutral practices. Freud claimed at one time that psychoanalysis "is a method of investigation, an impartial instrument, like, say, infinitesimal calculus" (Sharma p. 61 n.) But Willard Gaylin, Clinical Professor of Psychiatry at Columbia College of Physicians and Surgeons, writes that the contention of psychiatrists that they are value-free in their practice stems from their desire to be members of the scientific community. He points out the unlikelihood of any human activity, scientific or otherwise, being completely value-free. "In the case of psychotherapy, where one is dealing with the behavior of the individual in his relationship to those around him, the assumption is patently absurd" (p.246). And yet the claim to neutrality in dealing with client or patient issues stands as part of psychotherapy. Philosophy does not demand nor assume neutrality, especially when the client's problems are in the realm of moral or "political" issues. Furthermore, by taking a neutral position the

counselor would reduce a human relationship to something quite non-human. The counselor who is merely a "mirror" to the client, parroting back what the client has said, asking vacuous questions, and refusing to answer questions asked by the client, is not behaving like a normal human being whose dialogue is expected to be both respectful and meaningful. Philosophical counseling and therapy involves compassion and empathy as an accessory to understanding the client. It also includes critical evaluation of life circumstances, and the use of moral stance in decision-making strategies both of which are discouraged in many forms of psychotherapy. As psychoanalytic psychotherapist Charlotte Prozan put it, "Self-destructive behavior, such as excessive drinking or drug use, suicide attempts, repetitive abortions, sado-masochistic or criminal activity. . . . is not a matter about which the therapist remains neutral" (p. 328). The philosophical counselor or therapist understands that it is sometimes imperative to take a moral stand on an issue. He will not help the client aim at either an immoral or impossible goal.

15. *Stigma:* The stigma of mental illness comes in part from the habit of blaming the victim for their suffering. The sufferer is not only seen as somehow morally inferior or weak but also—and perhaps worse—as biologically or genetically defective, and medically unsafe. Psychotherapy perpetuates this perspective, and both the self-stigma and social stigma associated with it, by defining emotional suffering and mental distress as endogenous illnesses or disorders. Philosophy does not see the person as the cause of the problem. The philosophical counselor helps the client to examine the reasons she has for the beliefs, values, and assumptions she holds, and advises her on how to change any that are creating problems for herself or others. The philosophical counselor also advises the client on what might be done to alleviate the negative effects she is suffering from troublesome social circumstances. And since the philosophical counselor is doing *philosophy* with his client, the client suffers none of the self-stigma or social stigma from the session that would result from a similar session of psychotherapy.

16. *Recovery and Cure:* A label of "mental illness" cannot be easily erased by the one so labeled. Alcoholics Anonymous (AA) promotes the fallacy of definition: "once an alcoholic, always an alcoholic." This same erroneous belief can be found in relation to so-called mental illness: once a person is diagnosed as being "mentally ill" it is widely believed by both clinicians and the general public that this person will always be ill and thereby physically or mentally defective. Until very recently psychotherapy has not held a concept of recovery from "mental illness." Today many psychotherapists still assume that so-called mental illnesses are permanent or

chronic conditions for which the prognosis does not include recovery (for a more comprehensive discussion of recovery and cure see chapter 11). Once a person has been psychotherapeutically diagnosed as mentally ill, treatment is focused on symptomatic "management" or "control," and patient "stabilization." On the other hand, philosophical counseling holds the belief that the individual can overcome distress and suffering, and achieve a cure that will include cogent reasoning, appropriate actions, and an improved quality of life. Recovery and cure are realistic goals in philosophical counseling and therapy.

17. *Involuntary treatment and institutional confinement:* Some professionals in the mental healthcare field have the authority to force treatment and/or institutional confinement on individuals deemed a danger to themselves or others. Unfortunately this power has been used to treat and/or institutionalize individuals who are not in fact a danger to anyone. They have simply resisted the authority of the clinicians assigned to their case, or have refused to take debilitating medications, or accept other forms of undesirable treatment that have been forced on them. Philosophical counselors disagree with the right of any clinician to exert this level of control over another human being by means of coercion and/or incarceration. And they certainly don't assume to have such power themselves over any of the individuals in their care.

18. *Training:* The psychotherapist is primarily trained in the science of psychology, thereby lacking the knowledge and skills of a counselor trained in philosophy. The philosophical counselor on the other hand has a deep and broad understanding of the content and practice of philosophy, and its application to both the mitigation of troubling life issues and their prevention. While a standard education in counseling and psychotherapy tends to focus on the scientific facts of psychology, and training is in interpersonal skills, students of philosophy are taught the theoretical contents of philosophy, and the skills of respectful discourse, cogent reasoning, and effective problem-solving.

19. *Self-transformative Aim:* The aim of the various schools of psychotherapy is primarily instrumental: treating so-called mental illnesses, changing socially unacceptable behaviors, and to a lesser degree, solving the patient's personal problems. Philosophy, on the other hand, helps the client to not only resolve his problems, it also facilitates a self-transformation. In his presentation paper titled "Voices of Philosophical Self-Transformation" Ran Lahav writes that the topic of self-transformation has a rich history in philosophy. Plato promoted leaving the "cave" of ignorance; the Stoics advanced the idea of awakening our inner guiding principles; Jean-Jacques Rousseau advocated the cultivation of the natural (as

opposed to the socially constructed) self; Friedrich Nietzsche called for self-overcoming; and Martin Buber endorsed the transition from the "I-You" relationship to one of a more respectful "I-Thou." Lahav explains that these philosophers all envisioned "a change from a narrow, superficial attitude to life to a richer and fuller attitude, one involving our inner depths, as well as wisdom and plenitude" (p. 455). While self-transformation is an implicit goal in many psychotherapeutic schools, it plays a relatively minor role next to the dominance of diagnosing and treating "mental illnesses."

20. *Philosophical Attitude:* The points below are adapted from the paper presented in 2012 by Ora Gruengard at the combined 11th International Conference on Philosophical Practice and the 4th International Conference on Humanities Therapies. She explains that the proper use of philosophy in counseling and psychotherapy involves taking responsibility for one's own words, as opposed to referring to some authority figure; authenticity in voicing one's own views; the ability to recognize and admit the limitations of one's own knowledge and expertise and be willing to admit being wrong; the willingness to confront immoral thoughts or behavior in the client and challenge its justification, and the suspension of judgment (*epoché*) which includes non-diagnostic philosophical assessment of the client's problems. None of this is possible in the psychotherapeutic methods which call for the therapist's personal "neutrality" and clinical objectivity. On the last point P. P. M. Harteloh adds that the philosophical practitioner questions his guest "without prejudice" in the way a doctor, psychologist, or coach would. The philosopher handles almost every statement of his client "in a reflective way." The philosophical practitioner or counselor employs a "Socratic attitude" in which there are no fixed beliefs or desires, and a "not-knowing" approach. This leads to open wondering about, and questioning of, the client's life and problems (p. 327, 330).

21. *Community of Inquiry:* The term "Community of Inquiry" was adapted from early pragmatist philosophers C.S. Pierce and John Dewey by Matthew Lipman, professor of Philosophy at Columbia University, and developer of the "Philosophy for Children" program. For the purposes of philosophy in counseling and therapy, a community of inquiry can be established in both the classroom among students of counseling and psychotherapy, and in group counseling or therapy sessions. A community of inquiry in the classroom involves discussions in which each student is encouraged to think for themselves while at the same time participating in class discussions. It promotes a range of thinking, critical and creative reasoning, and the recognition that learning often arises

from the viewpoint of other students with whom one strongly disagrees. The instructor does not direct discussion to a pre-determined conclusion, but works in tandem with the class to develop productive collaborative discussions; the instructor encourages the class to consider alternative explanations for the etiology of so-called mental illnesses, the contradictions and ambiguities in diagnostic categories, and the problems inherent in the routine use of medications as a standard treatment modality. The instructor is also willing to concede fallibility, and to consider the point of view reached by the class during discussions, including its evaluation of the community of inquiry itself.

In the counseling or therapeutic settings, discussions in the style of a community of inquiry distinguishes psychotherapy from philosophy in a number of ways. While the psychotherapist is understood to be the authority whose knowledge is employed in directing discussion within the patient group, in a community of inquiry the philosophical counselor works in tandem with the group to help its members develop the capabilities necessary for productive collaborative discussions. While the psychotherapist sees her knowledge of the etiology, diagnosis, and treatment of so-called mental illnesses as founded on the facts of empirical medical science, the philosophical counselor encourages the group to consider alternative explanations for the etiology of their emotional suffering and mental distress, the contradictions and ambiguities in diagnostic categories, and the problems inherent in the routine administering of medications as a standard treatment modality. While the typical psychotherapist is reluctant to admit fallibility due to her claim to authoritative knowledge, and is therefore often dismissive of the patient's point of view, the philosophical counselor is willing to concede fallibility, and to consider the point of view reached by the group during discussions, including its evaluation of the community of inquiry itself (adapted from Lipman 2003, p. 18–19).

Ora Gruengard offers an outline of the kind of activities that are, and should be, involved in counseling a troubled person when philosophy is the foundation of the therapeutic encounter. This is a recommendation of what ought to be taught to students wishing to become philosophical counselors or therapists. But she cautions that these are not to be understood as steps cut in stone, or a method that must follow one another in chronological order. She writes that, in general, philosophical counseling begins with finding out what the client feels is the problem that is bothering him. There is an inquiry as to what this problem means to him, and how it connects to his life. This kind of inquiry into real-life circumstances is not often encountered in academic philosophy nor in psychiatry or many of the other forms of psychotherapy. Then the counselor checks to make sure that the issues involved in the problem are actually philosophical rather than a lack of facts, or erroneous information, or a legal matter, and so on. She explains that the issue is philosophical when it involves conflicts and dilemmas with regard to beliefs, wishes, emotions, aims, values, or ideals. The counselor then has to identify the tacit philosophical presuppositions and dilemmas that may underlie the problem in general terms. The search continues with locating the client's tacit beliefs, values, or ideals that the client feels justify the sense of confusion, helplessness, frustration, despair, misgiving, shame, guilt and so on engendered by the problem. The counselor must verify that the client actually holds the presuppositions and dilemmas she assumed previously, and if not then articulate new ones that are actually in line with those held by him. Once this has been done to the client's satisfaction the counselor questions and challenges his assumptions that his presuppositions are obvious and his dilemmas are necessarily true. She does this by employing various philosophical tools and strategies, offering insights from what philosophers and other notable individuals have said on these issues, and helping the client find alternative perspectives and explanations for exploration. The final decision as to which alternatives are worth pursuing is left up to the client (albeit with the understanding that an alternative must be reasonable and morally permissible). At this point there are three possibilities: the dilemma may have already been dissolved in the very act of this philosophical discussion; a resolution may be decided upon; or the client may find that he will have to live without being able to change the situation. This last possibility can occur when the issue is a function of the client's life circumstances such as his familial, social, or political context. But Gruengard points out that a problem which may seem irresolvable on first attempt may become more tractable from a different perspective, so a second attempt is always justified. And finally she maintains that it may ultimately be possible for the client to live a good life despite negative circumstances or issues that are beyond his control (p. 380–81).

FINDING THE PHILOSOPHICAL ISSUES

Since the day I received my doctorate for my work in philosophical counseling, I've been astonished a number of times by both academic philosophers and philosophy students for their lack of an ability I took for granted. The ability I assumed all philosophy students developed and philosophers had, is that of being able to apply the philosophy they have studied in the classroom to an investigation of real-life problematic situations. But I experienced three different events that showed me my assumption was quite wrong: The first example is about a graduate student in philosophy who came to study philosophical counseling with me at my office. One of my counseling clients was kind enough to allow him to observe a number of our sessions. When I invited him to take over facilitating one of the sessions he was unable to apply his wealth of academic, theoretical philosophical knowledge to the issues presented by the client. This student eventually became frustrated and gave up on the idea of practicing philosophical counseling because he wasn't able to "hear" or "see" the philosophy in our counseling sessions. There was a perceptible disconnect between the philosophical knowledge he possessed and what he was able to do with his knowledge.

The second example comes from a third-year undergraduate course I teach titled "Philosophy for Counselors." The majority of students in this course come from faculties other than philosophy, such as psychology, social work, criminal justice, teaching, and nursing. The last thing we do in the second half of each three-hour class is discuss one or two relevant case studies from my practice. After the end of the third class, one student approached me at the front of the room. Looking clearly distraught, she told me she was very worried about the possibility of failing the course. I asked her why she felt this way so early in the semester. I assumed she was new to the study of philosophy. But she said she had already taken many courses in philosophy because this was her major, and she therefore thought this course would be an easy credit for her. But it turned out she was having an extremely difficult time applying her extensive knowledge of philosophy to the cases we were discussing. Interestingly, none of the psychology majors in this class were having any problems applying their fairly limited knowledge of philosophy to the same cases.

The third situation arose at a small conference in Ottawa, Canada, where I was invited to give a workshop on philosophical counseling. Among the dozen or so participants were two professors of philosophy. During the workshop I first discussed, and then presented for general discussion, a number of actual cases from my own practice. After we had finished examining only the first two of these cases, the two professors threw up their hands in frustration and said they'd had enough. They confessed that they felt completely unprepared to deal with the problems presented by the clients, and suggested that these cases were far better suited to psychologists than to philosophers—which, in my opinion, they were not.

After a number of similar instances, it occurred to me that there must be a serious problem in the way we're teaching philosophy in our colleges and universities. I'm still not exactly sure yet what the problem is. It may be that students are being taught too much about how to win a philosophical argument and not enough about how to apply the philosophical skills they've learned to resolving real-life problems. Perhaps they're being taught philosophy at such an abstruse theoretical level that they can't see its practical application. Or it may be that they're led to believe classroom philosophy learned from books is separate and distinct from everyday situations, and has nothing to do with real life.

Counseling and psychotherapy with philosophy includes helping the client or patient to recognize the issues that need to be dealt with in the long and often complex narrative he or she has presented. The person in distress will often not be able to overcome the emotional tangle and confusion of perspectives that always accompany distressing life circumstances. Helping the client sort this out, and clearly identifying the issues involved, is one of the first responsibilities of the counselor or therapist. But locating the issues in the patient's or client's narrative is no easy task, even for students educated in philosophy. While it is challenging for students, it can also be very difficult for academically trained philosophers who choose to turn their academic careers to counseling or therapy. It requires a different mindset from the normally argumentative approach to a discussion topic that is common in the classroom or at academic conferences. First of all careful attention must be given to what the client or patient is saying in order to "hear" the various issues contained in the narrative. Issues are often not clearly articulated, and must be discovered by means of an imaginative exploration of the narrative. Then the counselor or therapist must make tentative suggestions of possible branches that may be followed, in order to see which issues the client or patient feels are most relevant, and which will be the most useful to discuss in the alleviation of their current conundrum. In this way the "issues tree" will grow one branch at a time, and philosophy will serve to alleviate the suffering of the distressed and the confused.

In academia, philosophy students and academic philosophers typically agree on the issue on which they will focus during their discussion. For example, the instructor might say to the class, "Here is a case in which the man has to decide whether to report the illegal activities of his brother that have been supporting the family. What ethical theory would you use to make this decision?" No effort needs to be made to discover the issue before discourse begins because it has been clearly articulated. On the other hand, it is often very difficult for the therapist or counselor to determine exactly what the issues are in the frequently confused and stress-filled narratives first presented by the patient or client. It takes practice and a trained "ear" to detect the issues and establish with the patient or client which of them merit further clarification, or require resolution.

An issue can be defined in a number of ways: as the subject of discussion or interest, the theme, a topic, a question, a matter of importance, a matter in dispute, a point in question, the heart of the problem.

In reading case studies it can seem that issues are not that difficult to find. But this is misleading because the client session notes on which published case studies are based, and that counselors and therapists typically publish, tend to be linear and chronological. They go something like this: She said such and such, to which I responded so and so, then she said such and such . . . and so on. But this doesn't accurately reflect the "messy" process of the counseling or therapeutic encounter. This is not how patients and clients speak. It is not what the counselor or therapist hears. For any of us, if we have a problem or issue that is for us complex and complicated, we stop to organize our thoughts before we speak or write them out. But the problems and issues which a client or patient brings to a meeting with a counselor or therapist are not displayed as a tidy, carefully thought-out, linear list of separate and distinct beliefs, values, and assumptions. They are personal and stressful, often a very chaotic jumble of interconnecting, interrelated, and sometimes seemingly unrelated impression and feelings. In fact the client's distress comes in part from the recognition that his or her own narrative seems internally contradictory, and that associated emotions are interfering with intelligibility. This can lead to feelings of powerlessness and frustration. It often involves embarrassment, shame, and guilt which add still one more layer, yet another barrier, against a possible resolution of the perplexity or problem. But a lot has been written about how a client or patient is best approached, and what method should be used to help resolve the issues.

Since its early inception in Germany by Dr. Gerd Achenbach there has been much discussion about whether there is or ought to be a method in philosophical counseling. It has been suggested that philosophical counseling should not have a method, that it should be open-ended and beyond any method. But this creates a paradox: if a practice has no method then that practice may consist of absolutely anything. If philosophical counseling has no method then philosophical counseling may consist of absolutely anything. And yet I'm sure philosophical practitioners would be reluctant to call things like astrology, past life regression, or tarot card reading "philosophical" practices. While there is no formal method that must be followed in any philosophical practice, this does not mean that just any practice is philosophical.

It has also been argued that there should be no intention in philosophical counseling, no striving for a goal in the process. This raises the question: What then is the purpose of philosophical counseling? The answer to this question is normative and depends on the answer to another, more obvious question: Why has the suffering individual come to the philosopher? What does the client want?

In my experience there are three goals in any philosophical counseling relationship: first the counselor has the goal of helping the client achieve any goal the client wants, as long as it is reasonable, possible, and morally permissible. Second the client has the goal of achieving relief from emotional distress and mental suffering. But a client can't always explain the cause of their suffering in a clear narrative because the problem is often not manifest to them in propositional terms. It is typically experienced as a disharmony in some aspect of life, accompanied by a distressing complexity of emotions and a tangle of thoughts. This means that the counselor must have a third goal that actually precedes the mitigation of the client's problems: helping the client articulate the problem in the first place.

The task of doing that—of articulating the problem—has been expressed in a number of different metaphors, for example, a ball of twine. But I don't think the metaphor of untangling a ball of twine works very well because a strand of twine, no matter how tangled and tightly wound, is still linear, whereas I believe the encounters in a person's life are more aptly analogous to a net or web consisting of separate but interconnected strands.

Philosophical counseling has also been described as the counselor metaphorically approaching the client's life as a text. But I find this lacking as well. A text is a finished work while a life is not. When it is read, the text's author is typically absent, while a life's author sits before the counselor and continues to live that life from moment to moment, even as the living text is retrospectively expanded and investigated. The client's text will change even while it is in the process of being examined. Furthermore, unlike a completed text, the client's present moment is connected to any number of other moments in the past, and anticipated moments in the future in a clearly non-linear fashion.

Counseling work has also been explained as archaeological: digging up the past, unearthing matter that has been abandoned long ago. But illuminating the client's issues is not really a digging down into the depths, a sort of dissecting of a shadowy, primordial unconscious. It is more a matter of allowing the various issues to rise up and emerge into the light, not an unearthing in an archaeological sense but an engendering, enabling what the Germans call *Entwicklungsdrang*—the urge to develop. It is more like fostering growth, involving illumination and nurturing. While it is heuristic—a guided discovery—it is a discovery not of hidden labyrinths but rather of sprouting realizations and developing comprehension. This is why I prefer the metaphor of a growing tree.

The client asks the counselor, "Can you help me stop worrying about everything?" Please see figure 8.1.

The "Issues Tree" is not immediately evident to the counselor and client as a mature tree. It grows from a complex "seed" which is the complex, compact set of initial problems that have been articulated by the client. It continues to grow and extend various "branches" during the entire time of the counseling sessions. It is very difficult to predict which branches will grow new branches and which ones will reach a satisfying end point.

Every client's Issues Tree is different. Even if one client's initial "seed" seems identical to a previous client—such as when various clients all claim they want to know the meaning of life—the branches usually go off in very different directions. General themes can be identified ("this is

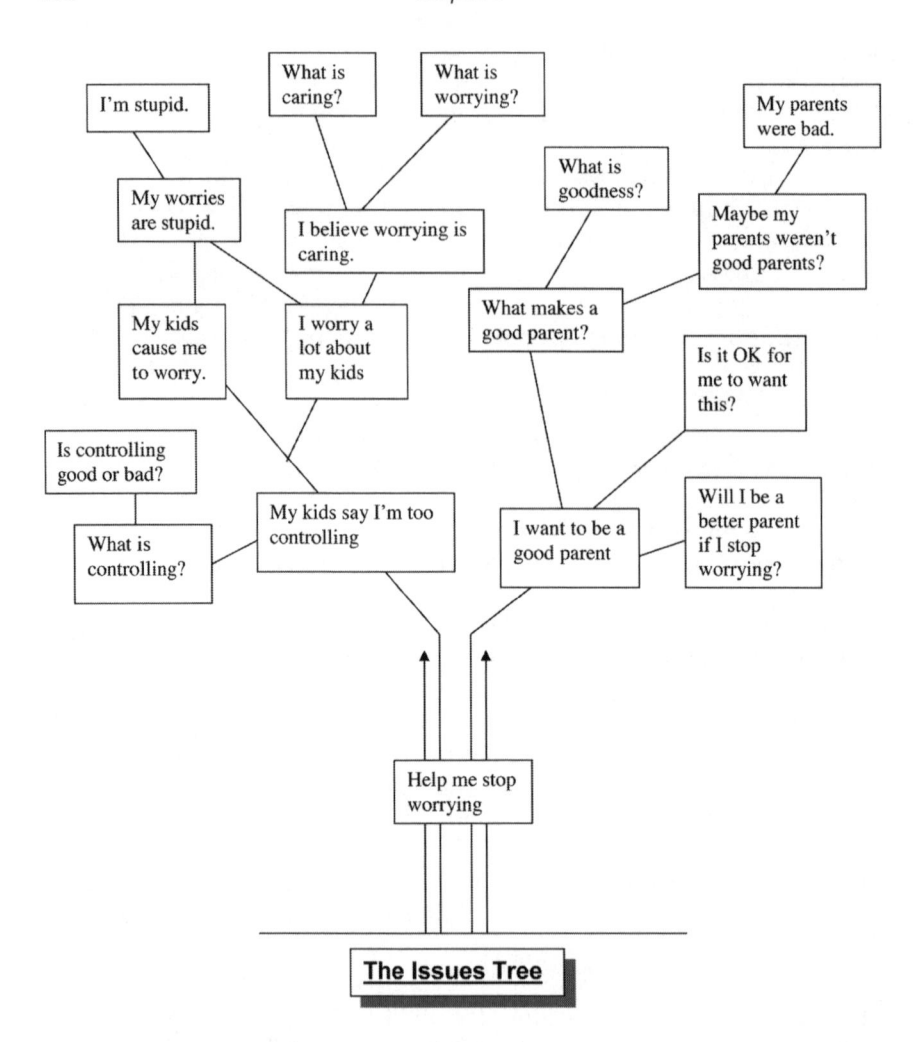

Figure 8.1. The Issues Tree

relationship problem") just like an actual seed can be identified ("this is a maple seed"). But while it is in the process of developing the eventual shape of the mature tree can't be predicted.

The duration of the counseling relationship depends on how many branches sprout on the Issues Tree, how complex the person's life situation is, and how many of the branches the person wishes to explore. The work that is done on each branch is cumulative with each singular elucidation adding to the comprehension of the entire, integrated tree.

The Issues Tree becomes a "Tree of Knowledge." And just like its Biblical prototype this tree of knowledge offers both good and evil. The process of philosophical counseling can bring both insight and further questions, both relief from distress and additional distress. For example, while the client may have felt he was acting with good intentions in a particular life situation, in counseling he may come to the realization that his actions were in fact self-serving, or that others saw his actions as interference.

Philosophical counseling and therapy means analyzing each branch in two ways. First, it is examined phenomenologically— what do we have here? Is it a belief, a value, an assumption? Is it a hope, a fear, an expectation? What is its origin? What observable effect does it have on this life? Second, it is examined hermeneutically—what does it mean? What does it mean to this individual? What does it mean to others? What does it mean morally, and so on? So while philosophical counseling is an exploratory process it is even more a generative process. The counselor and client generate new perspectives, useful insights, and fresh alternatives to the problematic elements that are confounding the mind.

It's not a subterranean investigation at the roots of the tree. Philosophical counseling and therapy is much more of an ascending search for where each issue branch leads, and then an unfolding of the leaf that is the end point. This leads then to the question, "How do you help the seed develop into an Issues Tree?" I offer my students six questions they can ask themselves during the counseling process.

1. What does the client say is the problem?

    For example: The client might say, "My problem is that I worry too much about my children. But they say I'm just controlling them. I don't want to be a controlling parent. I want to be a good parent. Can you help me be that for my kids?"

2. What else might be involved in the problem that was suggested by the client?

    For example: Was there a previous event with the *children* that led to this level of worry? Was there a previous event in the life of the *parent* that led to this level of worry? Is there only one parent in this family? What is the age of the children? How many children are involved? Does the parent worry equally about each child? If not why not? Has the parent talked with the children about the problem? Is the parent receiving criticism from others in the family or in the community?

3. Are there words or terms that need to be defined or clarified?

    For example: What is a "good parent'—according to society; according to the children; according to the parent? Is there a difference between a good father and a good mother? What is a child? What is the difference between a good child and a bad child? What is worrying? What does it mean to be controlling? Is caring the same as controlling?

4. What does the client assume to be true, good, right; or false, bad, and wrong?

    For example, the assumption might be: Worrying is a bad thing. It's possible for a parent to worry too much. A controlling parent is a bad parent. The parent should change. The children should change. The children should not complain. The parent should not complain. Talking to a counselor about this problem is bad, or good, or embarrassing.
5. Is there behavior that needs to be morally evaluated? (NOTE: Being moral is trying to avoid harming others with what we say and do.)

    For example: is there harm involved in worrying too much about your children? Is there harm involved in not worrying enough? Are the children behaving immorally by complaining about their mother? And lastly....
6. Where are the issues situated in relation to the areas of study in philosophy? For example:

    a. *religion:* are spiritual beliefs, teachings, and practices involved?
    b. *politics:* do they involve power, status, family relationships or group dynamics and decision-making?
    c. *morality:* are they about harmful or beneficial actions and behavior?
    d. *ethics:* are they about the general principles that guide actions and behavior, e.g. don't steal, be kind to others, always tell the truth, etc.?
    e. *metaphysics:* might they be concerning beliefs about what is and isn't real, the supernatural, personhood, the existence of mental illnesses?
    f. *epistemology:* what is believed to be true, what is assumed, what is or can be known with certainty about the issues?
    g. *logic:* is there a breach of rationality or reasoning, and does it include fallacies?
    h. *aesthetics:* is it about the beauty of life (or lack of it), or the sense of goodness?
    i. *existentialism:* does authenticity, autonomy, self-image, or self-esteem come into it?
    j. *feminism:* are we dealing with equality and respect between men, women, and children?
    k. *emotions, feelings, and intuitions:* what are their origins in relation to the issues, and are they reliable?

In training the students who want to become counselors and therapists I assign them the task of locating the issues in a number of sample case studies. Of course these case studies are not spoken narratives from live

clients. That would be much more difficult. To begin with I give m
students e-mails that I have received over the years from various indivic
uals looking for advice and help. Working in small groups, their task
only to find as many issues as they can in these pieces, and then diagra
them on a sheet of paper similar to the tree diagram above.

CASE #1

> I am a divorced mother of two boys. The three of us are survivors and as a team have overcome many obstacles to come out "on top." One son married two weeks ago, one is still with me but looking forward to traveling. One is a computer technician, the other is a chef in a well-known hotel. At 21 and 23, both are well rounded, productive young men. I have done my job. My problem is, now that the time has come that I worked so hard for I'm having a terrible time letting go. I have forgotten how to live for me because I've spent 23 happy years living for them. Searching for help on the internet concerning this topic has not been very successful. Any advice would be appreciated.

I ask students to notice that case #1 doesn't end with a question tha
might point the way to the main issue. And yet this woman is clearl
looking for some sort of helpful response. Students begin by looking fc
the possible issues. Here is a preliminary list of possible issues for discu
sion with this client that students typically compile: divorce; being
single mother; being the mother of only boys; and letting go of he
grown-up boys. Then, as discussion progresses, the students come to se
that there are deeper issues such as the question, What is a mother's jc
in relation to her children? What is a mother without her sons? Does
mean she is no longer a mother when her sons are gone? Will she eve
stop being a mother to her sons? Do her sons have any responsibilitie
toward their mother? Is it important for her sons to be "productive"?
so, why? What defines who or what we are? Are her sons in fact gone
What does it do to your self if you live only for others? What does it mea
to forget how to live? What does it mean to know how to live? What is
good life? Does life have to be happy to be good? Many more possibilitie
arise as these issues are discussed.

CASE #2

> A close native friend of my mothers lost her 20 year old son last year. He was found in a ditch in the far north (where he was working at the time) and his cause of death was left as undetermined. She was destroyed, as I imagine any mother would be. She was on a lot of medication at his funeral. We heard she was suicidal. I'm not sure what kind of counseling she was receiving. Less than 6 months later, she lost her fiancé, who supported her extremely well through the loss of her son, to a heart attack. Once again, she was back on heavy doses of medica-

tion. I'm not sure if she was off medication at all, actually. Now, she is attempting to return to her job and "normal" life. My question is if you think medication in this type of case is OK? I mean, obviously the medication was to numb her pain—of course she would have to deal with the pain, but does it get to a point where it's too much? Is it possible that she was physically not able to handle this kind of emotional pain? Do you think the medication allowed her to not commit suicide, or did it just prolong her extreme grieving feelings?

While case #2 ends with a question this may not be the only one that requires an answer. This case deals with many complex, and very serious, issues. Students initially have to be careful not to be overwhelmed by their emotions, or blocked by self-doubt when dealing with the seriousness of this case. The students generally begin by wondering if the writer of this e-mail is in fact herself the "friend" under discussion. Then the question arises, Does it matter? Of course the main issue that is noted is the advisability of medication as a treatment for grieving. This leads to questions about whether the woman asked for medications "to numb her pain," or whether her doctor simply deemed she should have them, by way of a standard medical protocol in the alleviation of suffering. They wonder what it means to live a normal life after such terrible losses. Is a return to normalcy possible for her, given that she can't live in the past prior to her experiences of those losses? They discuss the issue of whether medication can in fact prevent suicide. They discuss the relationship between emotional, mental, and physical pain. They imagine what they would say to the woman if she were in front of them in person. Does she think there is a level of emotional pain that her friend would not be strong enough to endure? Was she included in the decision-making process that has her on heavy medication? How can she help her friend deal with the pain of her losses? How can she help her friend avoid committing suicide? How can she help her to return to living a relatively "normal" life? The students always come to a point where they suggest that in order to clarify the issues that need to be discussed it would be necessary to have live conversations with both of these women—the friend who sent this e-mail request for advice, and the woman who lost both her son and her fiancé. The face-to-face conversations would allow the students to listen empathetically, ask questions for clarification and information, make suggestions, and so on, taking the discussion well beyond this exercise of impersonally analyzing discovered philosophical issues.

In actual counseling or therapy sessions, discovering the issues is an ongoing activity. It continues until the client or patient herself decides either that the issues which are being raised are trivial—too distant on a topic branch—and create little or no concerns, or that they can be handled by the client or patient on her own. In a session, after the initial goal of finding the most troubling issues has been reached, the counselor or therapist uses his or her reasoning skills to help the client deal effectively with those issues. But while the counselor or therapist comes into the therapeutic relationship with the ability to reason proficiently, many clients do not. If one of the goals of philosophical counseling or therapy is for the client to become better able to reason cogently about his or her problems, and to eventually do so autonomously, then one of the responsibilities of the counselor or therapist is to teach the client good reasoning skills.

NINE

Teaching "Sanity"

A man and his wife visited their family physician together. The woman had previously been diagnosed by a psychiatrist as suffering from depression. The doctor could see that the man was very angry. He openly accused his wife of being a "tart," and offered as evidence of his wife's infidelity the patterns of cars parked in the road near their home. His doctor referred the man to the psychiatrist who then diagnosed him with "Othello syndrome" or delusions of infidelity. But both doctors knew very well that the man's wife was depressed due to the breakup of an extra-marital affair she had been having (Fulford et al. p. 43). The decision by the two doctors not to tell the man of his wife's infidelity is based on their professional oath to protect their patients' right to privacy. But the man was diagnosed untruthfully, or actually misdiagnosed, in order to protect his wife's confidentiality. Was it a fair decision; was it ethical? This situation illustrates how complex some decisions, especially ethical ones, can be. The question of when and how ethical and moral reasoning ought to be applied in counseling and therapy will be discussed in greater detail later in this chapter. But the doctors' decision to remain silent about the truth, and to professionally diagnose the husband with a non-existent mental illness, also raises the question of how sanity and insanity are defined, and by whom.

At one time individuals suffering from emotional pain or mental distress were simply considered to be mad or insane for some unknown reason. Times have changed so that now clinicians claim they know the reason for the same suffering and distress: sickness in the mind, or "mental illness." But given that the mind has been defined as a person's beliefs, values, fears, and assumptions, it seems odd to say that the absences of emotional suffering and mental distress is "a healthy mind." What exactly is it that makes a mind "healthy"? Health and illness have historically been medical terms applied to the functioning of the biological systems of the physical body. But as argued in earlier chapters, the mind is not one of the physical body's biological systems. Therefore, rather than calling a non-suffering or non-distressed mind "healthy," it seems much more appropriate to simply call such a mental state "sanity." Sanity is connected with the concepts of rationality, emotional stability, clear thinking, wisdom, autonomy, and the ability to live in harmony with others in society. The use of the word "sanity" in the title of this chapter is not an attempt to turn back time to an earlier era in the history of mental healthcare. It is more to emphasize the non-medical aspect of its opposite, so-called mental illness.

Philosophy employed in counseling a client, or in psychotherapy, does not necessarily include lessons in the history of philosophy. It does not require the practitioner to have memorized the names and birth dates of famous wise men, nor does it involve being able to quote passages from philosophical texts. The main focus of the *practice* of philosophy is on respectful inquiry and discussion, critical reflection, "metacognition"—the self-critique of beliefs, values, assumptions, fears, and so on—and the search for conceptual definitions. But this doesn't mean that the students of counseling and psychotherapy, and those already employed in clinical practice, don't need to learn as much as they can of the content of philosophy. Everyone, by virtue of being able to reason and communicate can be said to be able to philosophize, but being able to philosophize is not at all the same as having learned to be philosophical in one's approach to specific issues and problems, or life in general. And being philosophical does not guarantee that the discussion will necessarily be helpful in restoring "sanity" to the troublesome and distressing life of the individual with whom the counselor or therapist is discursively engaged. The intention behind the philosophy in counseling and psychotherapy must be very different from mere casual or academic philosophizing. It must be purposefully directed at helping the client or patient.

A central assumption in any other form of "talk therapy" is that, apart from some initial hesitations, the client is capable of having a rational discussion. The therapist or counselor therefore enters into the discursive relationship assuming that client's approach to discussion will be logical, that she will listen politely, that she will respond thoughtfully, that she will disagree respectfully, and so on. But while it's true that many clients are willing to have this type of discussion, they are often unable to do so because they simply don't know how. Of course when emotions run high, logic becomes distorted, and thoughts come out jumbled. But even in a calm atmosphere people are often incapable of seeing the logical problems in their stories, arguments, and decisions. In fact many individuals become labeled as criminals because of the bad decisions they have made. Although some criminals come from law-abiding families and decide to break the law knowingly because they believe it's worth the personal gain, many others come from broken homes where they had poor role models and little instruction on moral behavior and "good" thinking. In other words they lack proficient decision-making abilities. They make bad choices early in life which lands them on the slippery slope to incarceration or worse. These unfortunate individuals have learned self-serving reasoning strategies, or they have learned to reason only defensively. And besides leading to criminality, poor decision-making can also lead to the kind of suffering and distress that can be professionally diagnosed as "mental illness." This can in turn lead to all sorts of personal difficulties including poverty, disintegration of the family unit, and social stigma. But poor decision-making and generally weak reasoning can lead to all sorts of other problems as well, such as relationship difficulties, being victimized by others, immoral behavior, and so on.

I wrote in my first book, *Philosophical Counseling Theory and Practice*, that a counselor can't undertake a rigorously logical discussion with a client who is in a serious crisis situation, because such a situation forces the client to base his thinking on the self-protective logic of prior experience. So what is one to do when a client's response to difficult situations is to go into an automatic "crisis thinking" mode? What I did with one client is point out to her, and let her see, that the crisis thinking she reverts to when life becomes difficult is actually part of her problem. I helped her to see that her crisis thinking leads her to avoid problems by both metaphorically hiding herself away at work (by avoiding confrontations with her staff), and by sleeping long hours to prevent thinking about them. She had learned as a child that when violent conflict arose in her family the only option open to her was to hide under the covers of her bed. But I also showed her that, while this may have been the only option available to her as a defenseless child, there are many more options available to her now that she is a strong and capable adult. I acknowledged that for the child, hiding in self-defense was the most logical response, but it is now hurting her relationships, her self-esteem, and even her business when she uses this same strategy as an adult. For the client, this recognition of her "crisis thinking" pattern of behavior, and the childhood self-preservation strategy she was still using as an adult was an amazing revelation. She hadn't considered the fact that avoiding arguments and disagreements with her staff was very similar to hiding under the covers of her bed. This insight was also a great relief for her because she had believed that her behavior was impossible to change because "this is just the way I am." We spent many weeks discussing ways to respond to various problematic situations, and then having her practice imaginary confrontations with defiant staff, difficult customers, and finally problematic family members. This led her to understand that the "crisis thinking" that she believed to be a fundamental flaw in her personality could in fact be brought to awareness, scrutinized, evaluated, and then substantially revised.

Many individuals have simply never learned how to reason cogently, how to argue convincingly, how to make a "good" decision based on selecting the best reasons others have given, or just how to be part of a sociable discussion where their contributions are taken seriously. Many people have been forced to defend themselves in a hostile, threatening, confrontational, competitive, and/or combative, emotionally disturbing discursive environment. This leaves them vulnerable to making poor choices, and completely unprepared for having a philosophical discussion. They are coerced, intimidated, or manipulated into agreeing with disagreeable premises. This leads them to subsequently regret their position because it does not reflect who they truly are. And it makes them unwilling to engage in discussions where disagreements might actually lead to insights. This type of client is perhaps mentally capable of having a philosophical discussion but emotionally incapable because of never, or rarely, having experienced a discussion partner who isn't trying to either "win" the argument, gain some advantage, convince her of something immoral, or attempt to inflict direct emotional or psychological pain.

While the counselor needs to learn about the client's problems, one of the initial things the counselor needs to do is teach the willing client how to engage in, and how to benefit from a discussion with a respectful discussion partner. As discussed in chapter 6, this requires, as the fundamental starting point, cultivating the client's trust. This can't be switched on at will; it requires time and effort. Before a helpful discussion can take place the client needs to trust that the counselor won't try to make her look stupid; that there will not be a demand for information which the client is not ready to disclose; that the counselor won't take control of the situation; and perhaps most important of all, that the counselor won't laugh or shrink in horror from anything the client reveals. These—and many more—are the negative events the client has come to expect due to her previous experiences with former non-philosophical discussion partners, all of which have no doubt contributed in some part to the problematic life circumstances that brought the client to counseling.

Furthermore the client then needs to learn how to argue without the use of the many fallacies so common in everyday discourse, such as generalizations, begging the question, hasty conclusions, and so on. While fallacies can be either unintentional or part of an intentional discursive strategy focused on "winning" an argument, they are counterproductive in a philosophical counseling or therapeutic relationship. Fallacies are abundant—with more than two hundred identified—and ubiquitous. Even well-educated people sometimes make them. In his book *What Would Aristotle Do?* Elliot Cohen discusses twenty-two of the most common ones and explains how they can cause personal emotional suffering and mental distress, as well as interpersonal relationship problems (see p. 73–115). The student learning the application of philosophy to counseling and psychotherapy must know how to spot any fallacies used by her client, and how to avoid making them herself.

The student must be taught that one of the counselor's primary jobs is to help the client experience an open, philosophical dialogue without the need to "win" the discussion—in fact with no hidden agenda at all—and to demonstrate to the client that the discussion is meant to be exclusively for her (the client's) benefit. This means that the philosophical counselor or therapist freely offers the client or patient the very same philosophical content and skills possessed by the clinician herself. This is not usually offered in a standard counseling or psychotherapeutic relationship.

At the 4th International Conference on Philosophical Practice in Korea, Isabelle Millon from France pointed out that for a person to be good at philosophizing requires possessing and learning two attributes: a philosophical attitude and competency in philosophical reasoning and discourse. Under attitudes she lists the following: *responsibility* (from Sartre): accepting responsibility for one's own words and choices in life; *authenticity* (also from Sartre): the position taken on a issue and the words spoken are in accord with what one actually believes and thinks; *settling down* (from Descartes and Spinoza): not giving in to instinctive or emotional responses, and not allowing emotional turmoil to dampen rational thought; *ignorance* (from Plato): recognizing and accepting the limits of one's own expertise and knowledge; *sympathy/empathy* (from Plato and Dewey): accepting that one's own ideas may be wrong or biased, and that ideas which are different from one's own are not necessarily wrong; *astonishment* (from Aristotle and Kierkegaard): accepting the fact that others may have a point of view or information previously unknown to oneself and yet very relevant to the issue at hand; *suspension of judgment* (from Descartes): putting aside one's own opinions, beliefs, and values and seriously considering a "foreign" point of view; *confrontation* (from Heraclites, Plato, and Nietzsche): accepting being challenged, and courageously and respectfully challenging others whose perspectives seem problematic. Under "competency" Millon lists the following: being able to *justify* the arguments produced; *explaining* difficult or "foreign" ideas to those who are less educated in philosophy; *analyzing* an idea "to make its content visible;" *synthesizing* in order to clarify the connection between ideas; *exemplification* to illustrate and give concrete substance to an abstract idea or concept; and *interpretation* to give objective or subjective understanding of the meaning of a proposition or argument (p. 411–12). These are, of course, attitudes and competencies required by all counselors and psychotherapists who want their practices to be philosophical. But they are also important attitudes and competencies for all clients or patients to learn and eventually employ in their own lives.

GENERAL COURSE CONTENT

The senior-level course titled "Philosophy for Counselors" that I teach at the University of the Fraser Valley is in part based on my book titled *Issues in Philosophical Counseling*. This book not only outlines a number of different issues a counselor is likely to encounter with a client, but also suggests ways of dealing with those issues. Issues discussed include free will, sexuality, the difference in communication styles between men and women, humor, medications, how to define "normal," the meaning of life, getting old, suicide, religion, dream interpretation, and self-esteem. There are, of course, philosophical books that go much deeper into each of these topics which students are urged to consult prior to a particular topic's discussion in class.

Philosophy in a therapeutic or counseling relationship involves helping the patient or client examine the reasons he or she has for the values they hold as good, and the beliefs they hold as true. This will enable them to free themselves from blindly following tradition, slavishly obeying the dictates of authority figures, or acting only on their feelings. But in order to help the patient or client learn how to conduct a beneficial examination of his or her beliefs, values, assumptions, and fears the therapist or counselor must first become thoroughly familiar herself with all the subtle nuances of the practice of a legitimately philosophical inquiry. One of the primary attributes that is enhanced in students who study philosophy is rationality. They not only apply rationality in their sessions with clients, they also help their clients to improve their rationality when discourse shifts to teaching the client philosophical skills and attitudes. In his essay "Mental Health as Rational Autonomy," Rem B. Edwards explains that rationality is comprised of seven main features:

> (1) being able to distinguish means from ends and being able to identify processes and manifest behaviors which will result in the realization of consciously envisioned goals; (2) thinking logically and avoiding logically contradictory beliefs; (3) having factual beliefs which are adequately supported by empirical evidence, or at least avoiding factual beliefs which are plainly falsified by experience; (4) having and being able to give reasons for one's behaviors and beliefs; (5) thinking clearly and intelligibly, and avoiding confusion and nonsense; (6) having and exhibiting a capacity for impartiality or fair-mindedness in judging and adopting beliefs; (7) having values which have been (or would be) adopted under conditions of freedom, enlightenment, and impartiality. (p. 55)

In my private philosophical counseling practice I apply all the different areas of rationality, and all the various topics in philosophy, to my clients' problems, many of which had previously been diagnosed as "mental illnesses." And I have at times been asked by my clients to teach them what I teach my students in class. In a single-semester course of philosophy for counselors and psychotherapists it's not possible to spend more than one or two classes on each area of philosophy. In my course there is an assumption that students have studied at least some of the topics in other full-semester philosophy courses such as ethics, critical thinking, or philosophy of religion. For students, the philosophy in a course for future counselors and therapists ought to be merely a review of material with which they are already fairly familiar. Typically, senior students whose major is psychology or social work will have already taken two or three philosophy courses before enrolling in my philosophy for counselors course. Therefore the focus in this course is less on new theory and much more on the application of their philosophical knowledge to case studies and so-called mental illnesses.

Some of the many topics that can be covered in a course on philosophy for counselors are the following:

Critical Thinking: Critical thinking, also called reasoning or informal logic, is first of all concerned with putting into practice a systematic way of looking at what's being said in order to make better sense of it. "Our authority over our reasons depends on our being able to say what they are; this requires attention, rather than searching for a hypothesis or making an observation" (Gordon and Mayo p. 62). Students are taught that after the client has been helped to recognize the reasons she has for her beliefs, values, and assumptions she is then helped to evaluate which of those are problematic and which both support her beliefs, and allow her to be the kind of person she wishes to be. This evaluation may lead the client to come to very different conclusions on any number of issues than were initially held. This is not only an intellectual or cognitive process, it also clarifies and examines the appropriateness of coexisting feelings and emotions. For example, a young woman is so shy she doesn't know how to live a "normal" life. This involves examining the reasons why she is so shy, what life circumstances have led her to both the shy behavior and her feelings associated with her shyness. Because of the volume of material available, this course is taught in two parts.

Critical Thinking I—The Basics

To begin with it's important for students to help each other define what philosophy is. It is also important to clearly define other terms that may come up in discussion so as to avoid the mistaken assumption that one definition is universally accepted. Then discussion can move to what distinguishes an opinion from an argument, and what sort of things constitute good reasons for a conclusion. From there students are engaged in defining critical and creative thinking; practicing breaking down arguments into the various underlying issues; identifying reasoning patterns, inferences, biases, and both implicit and explicit conclusions. Important as well is interpreting values and assumptions, identifying underlying ethical issues, and evaluating arguments and actions accordingly; recognizing and dealing with the most common reasoning errors or fallacies such as appeal to authority, stereotyping, irrelevant reason, red herring, straw man, equivocation, ambiguity, false cause, faulty analogy, ad hominem, slippery slope, and many more; and finding the elements of non-argumentative persuasion, such as threats, crying, or shouting. Important also is creativity which includes anticipating, predicting, and estimating outcomes and consequences. This is a condensed review of the sort of material that is commonly found in the many critical thinking, reasoning, or informal logic texts such as, for example, *Think it Through: Reasoning in Everyday Life* by Moira Kloster and Anastasia Anderson.

Critical Thinking II — Counseling Specific

This class focuses on applying what was learned in The Basics above to counseling case studies. Students are also encouraged to discuss their own past experiences and current life circumstances. This includes issues such as internally vs. externally generated problems; the effects of various factors on rational thinking and personal beliefs and values, such as culture, gender, education, religious beliefs, age, medication, stress, trauma, and so-called "mental illnesses." If possible, examples should be from actual case studies and students' lives. Students learn how to help clients recognize their reasoning errors and contradictions; and overcome poor listening habits. They are taught to recognize the importance of emotion and intuition in reasoning. Students are also encouraged to articulate and critique their own personal philosophies on various important issues. We sometimes evaluate letters to the editor of our local newspapers. Through this exercise they learn how to find the letter writer's values, beliefs, and assumptions even when they are unspoken and subtly hidden. This is not an easy task. And what they find even more difficult is to determine how those hidden values, beliefs, and assumptions can actually be phrased as arguments. For example, when the writer says, "Honesty is important" my students see the writer as meaning "I value honesty." But the next step is to imagine what argument lies behind that writer's brief statement of belief. It might be something like this: "I value honesty, and honesty should be valued by everyone, because it helps to sustain trust." Obviously, the hidden or unspoken value in this example is honesty. But what is not so obvious is the way this value becomes an argument when there is understood to be some sort of reason behind the value statement. A statement of value is only an opinion or conclusion, but it becomes an argument when this conclusion is supported by a reason, and especially when a "should" or "ought" is included to make it a normative assertion. The same thing happens with beliefs and assumptions. Of course this value statement about honesty was a simple example, and the imaginary argument may seem somewhat hasty given the very brief statement on which it's based. Students learn that in an in-person counseling or therapy session it's far better to ask the client or patient why she said that she values honesty, rather than simply imagining or assuming what her reasons may be. Bringing hidden or unspoken arguments to light is a very important part in a critical thinking course for students learning to become philosophical counselors or therapists because with this knowledge they can teach their clients or patients to do the same.

Metaphysics: This topic deals with the issue of what it means to say that something is "real." What exists? Why is there something instead of nothing? Does God exist in the same way as people exist, or does God exist merely as a concept? Does a concept, like love, have existence the same way an object exists? Can we be sure we exist and aren't just dreaming?

A client of mine felt that the characters in the books he reads, and the stories he himself writes, have more "reality" than he can find in the people around him in his life. It has led him to doubt his own physical existence.

A different client asked me, "Do you think there's intelligent life in the universe besides us here on Earth?" I used simple logic in order to assemble a metaphysical response. I replied, "If I were a Christian creationist I might give you one of two answers. First, I would point out that some people interpret the Bible as saying God only created humans. Others say there's nothing in the Bible that says God hasn't, or won't, go on to create intelligent life on other planets. So it's not really possible to go beyond guessing at an answer because the Bible gives us too little helpful information on the topic. On the other hand, an evolutionist might tell you to consider a slice of bread that has been ripped into a number of small pieces and placed on a tray in a dark, damp place like an old basement. There is potential for living mold to develop in a place like that because the conditions on all the pieces of bread are agreeable to it. The question is, on which piece of bread does the mold develop? The answer of course is that it develops on all the pieces. Similarly, scientists are slowly discovering planets in the universe that, like Earth, have the potential to engender living organisms. On which planet does it arise? It seems to me the answer is that it would arise on all the planets where the conditions are agreeable." This is using logic and the analogy of living mold to arrive at a possible answer.

The client then asked, "Well, mold is one thing, but intelligent beings are another. I'm not sure that was a good analogy. Could those living organisms on other planets be more than just mold? Could they be intelligent beings, maybe even more intelligent than us?"

My response was that it's unlikely the mold on all the pieces of bread would have begun at precisely the same moment, and developed at exactly the same rate. After a while, some of the mold on some of the pieces would be more advanced than others. The same might be true of intelligent life in the universe. Does this analogy hold? It is logical? Is it acceptable and fair? Perhaps or perhaps not. But it's a thought-provoking starting point for more discussions about life, the universe, and everything.

Clients sometimes wonder if there are many realities. Do people all live in their own reality that's not like mine? My response is always to point out that if everyone experienced a different reality then people would constantly be bumping into each other. In order to get along with each other we must be experiencing at least some common elements of reality. But this doesn't mean that there aren't many different realities in life. These are some examples:

Authoritative reality: The reification of a professional diagnosis which tells a person, for example, "You are a schizophrenic." This makes the so-called mental illness a reality for the diagnosed individual and anyone else who finds out about this person's diagnosis.

Situational reality: She's awkward within a group of strangers, but she's confident within a group of friends. A particular street is dangerous at night but safe in the daytime.

Assumed reality: A woman believes all men are the same. A man believes a government agent is spying on him.

Actual reality: A man denies that he is an alcoholic but he is unable to go even one day without several strong drinks. In actuality his behavior defines him as an alcoholic despite what he assumes.

Personal reality: I'm feeling hurt that she left me — or — I feel relieved about it. It doesn't matter that you think I'm an idiot for letting such a nice woman leave. In my reality she was not very nice.

Social reality: In their culture women may not own property or work at jobs, while in our culture women may own companies with many employees. The reality of everyone's life is heavily influenced by the society in which they live.

Virtual reality: A computer-generated gaming problem keeps him awake all night trying to come up with a solution.

Immaterial reality: The possibility that "things" exist which can't be empirically measured such as a soul, heaven, angels, demons, mind, love, courage, wisdom, etc. But the word "exists" is used equivocally in these examples.

Material or objective reality: We agree that objects in the world are external to us and "real" when we can perceive them. The problem is that our perceptions can be mistaken. When we see or hear what isn't "real" then we can be diagnosed with a "mental illness."

Another aspect of the question of reality relates to experiences that are believed, or feared, to be not real. For example, a client may be anxious about having heard his name called when he was tired when no one was around to call it, or had the sense that a room full of noisy people suddenly became quiet when he walked in because they had all been talking about him. One author describes these experiences as "attenuated (or near) examples of psychotic symptoms" (Kingdon and Turkington p.88). But these are common situations occasionally experienced by most people. They are not "real" in the sense that they were not actual occurrences. Clients who have been given a diagnosis of "mental illness" will wonder how to distinguish what a "real" experience is compared to what is a symptom of delusion or "mental illness." Some therapists argue that the definition of "reality" is based on social convention, or a community consensus. This means that anyone whose perception or definition of reality differs from the majority could be labeled "insane" (Szasz 1961). The question of whether what is perceived is real or not is a metaphysical issue that is sometimes difficult for individuals to resolve on their own without the help of an empathetic counselor or therapist. One of my clients wanted to know whether the music he could hear in his head at times was "real" and "normal," or whether he should be concerned about it. I told him I would ask my class. A quick hands-up survey in my class the next day revealed that most of my students at times heard music in their heads. When I shared this informal survey data with my client he was greatly relieved. And he was overjoyed when I pointed out to him that the history of music contains many examples of people who heard music in their heads, wrote it down, and became famous for doing so. In fact these "abnormal" people cannot be conceived of as experiencing reality in the same way that most of us "normal" people do. One student, who had been studying classical music most of her life, told the class that she perceives a piece of music as consisting of various shapes in all sorts of different colors. Is this normal?

The standard definition of metaphysics is the study of reality. But in considering its application in counseling and therapy, it's more useful to think of it as an investigation into what a person believes reality to be, and how that person came to that belief. Obviously, helping the client to differentiate between beliefs and facts is a very important part of counseling and therapy. So epistemology, the study of knowledge and how it differs from belief, is an important element in counseling and therapy.

Human beings in general, as well as most counseling and therapy clients, typically begin with the assumption that the understanding of reality is a given, that is, that what exists is the same for everyone all the time. But when a problem arises it can bring a person's conception of reality into serious doubt. And not only will that person doubt his or her understanding of reality, they will also often come to doubt their rationality as thinking beings, and sometimes even their character as moral beings. Here is an example of an e-mail on this topic:

> Hello, I hope you can help...
> For several months I've been suffering from a strange kind of anxiety. It seemed to come out of nowhere and has persisted since. I tried to put

my finger on what could be the cause with no success. There was no cause, but the feeling stayed. Eventually I began feeling strangely detached, something I have read is called- depersonalization. The strange detached feelings have, in recent weeks, evolved into a deep astonishment, that is to say, I am constantly in disbelief of reality. I feel that I need to understand it; I am always aware of things on a huge level; my mind is constantly on the universe, eternity, consciousness. . . . It all seems impossible and overwhelming; our existence seems impossible. I have been evaluated twice and told that I'm not going mad but suffering from obsession and anxiety, and that antidepressants would help. I know drugs are not the answer, and I feel this as being something bigger than just anxiety and obsession. Is it possible to find peace again? All I want is to take things for granted as I once did. Can it be that I crossed a threshold of awareness or questioning from which there is no return? Is this state I'm in something you have ever heard of? I know these are pretty big questions, but I hope you can help.

With an application of even just a rudimentary knowledge of metaphysics this e-mail reveals many metaphysical themes. Perhaps the easiest theme to spot is that of reality. But there are a number of other ones as well, such as, for example, fate, change, causation, existence, personal identity, the emotions, perception, consciousness, the mind, and of course the ontological status of a so-called mental illness. But the question remains, how can a counselor apply the academic study of so many themes in metaphysics to the task of discussions with a client? A good place to start is with reality assumptions. It's important to first of all find out what sort of reality assumptions a counseling client is bringing to the discussion. Here are a few examples:

- Because I've thought about suicide I'm mentally ill.
- Depression is caused by a chemical imbalance in the brain.
- Ghosts are real. Space aliens are not.
- He was in that store because I saw his car parked nearby.
- If you believe strongly enough, it will happen.
- Sometimes dreams predict the future.
- I'm a kind person with a good sense of humor.

Some of these reality assumptions may be true, and others may not be. It's important for the counselor or therapist to help the client decide which is which. For example, the mental health care workers of one of my clients—let's call him David—hold a very a dubious reality assumption about him. David has been diagnosed as schizophrenic, and he came asking me about the reality of his life. He told me that he's required to take a number of powerful medications, with terrible side effects, meant to counteract his supposed suicidal nature. When I asked him if he feels like killing himself he said, "Not at all. I've been enjoying my life for many years." So I contacted his case worker and she assured me that

David needs his medication because he is suicidal. I asked her why she believes this is true. She said that he had tried to commit suicide. I asked her when this happened. She said when he was a teenager. But David is now in his mid-fifties! The reality for David is that his care team still thinks of him in terms that are 30 years out of date, as though he's still the same suicidal teenager he was 30 years ago, and nothing has changed. The irony in this is that one of the symptoms of schizophrenia is described as a person losing touch with reality. This means it could be said that David's care team is exhibiting one of the symptoms of schizophrenia because they are 30 years out of touch with his present reality. The reality assumption about David's suicidal nature, which is 30 years out of date, prompted me to discuss with David the question of whether any of us are still the same person we were 30 years ago. And it made me wonder if it will ever be possible for David to escape the reality assumption that he's suicidal which is held by the professionals managing his life. David's case illustrates two problems that can arise when reality is defined by authority figures: first, the fact that a mental healthcare worker can instantiate the existence, or ontological status, of a "mental illness" by simple proclamation; and second, that the label of a so-called mental illness is inescapable.

Of course it could be argued that the reason David has not attempted suicide in the past 30 years is precisely because he's been on medications designed to prevent suicidal ideation. But this also assumes that in reality schizophrenia is a life-long illness from which the patient will never escape. This false reality assumption will be discussed in chapter 11.

What if the client says, "My dreams are so real I'm scared I'm not even really awake." This calls René Descartes to mind, and raises the question "How can we know we're not dreaming?" There are a number of answers to this questions that most clients can easily discover for themselves with just a little help from the counselor. For example, the counselor may rephrase the question and ask, "What are the differences between a dream and reality?" The answers to this question can be very reassuring. And any discussion of Cartesian references to dreaming always raises the question, "What are dreams all about?" Answers to this question are available not only from psychologists, but from many philosophers as well. And speculation about whether dreams can foretell the future raises the interesting metaphysical question of what time is, and how we might define the future, the present, and the past within different conceptions of time.

Some clients wonder about the power their own thoughts might be having on reality. William James said that we choose our own reality according to what is meaningful to us; we create the reality we want to experience according to our desires. This pragmatic perspective can be both comforting and horrifying at the same time, because it contains freedom and responsibility simultaneously. Of course this is connected both Søren Kirkegaard's and Jean-Paul Sartre's explanation of the consequences of existentialism. After existentialism, conversation with a client may also include the question of whether there is such a thing as fate, in which God runs the show, or determinism which suggests to some individuals that we can't have total freedom. Determinism can be very distressing when the client is convinced that we humans are purely material beings who are manipulated by cause-and-effect relationships. But a philosophical counselor knows that metaphysics offers alternatives to a deterministic reality.

What about the client who says, "But I can look at my life up to this point, and I can see that I'm on a path that's nothing more than a chain of causally determined events?" Or the client who believes that his life is set on an unalterable path designed by God? Again, this can be comforting or depressing, depending on what sort of path the client believes he's on. When this argument or complaint is made about a seeming lack of freedom, what can the counselor or therapist do? The first thing is to ask the question, "In which direction are you looking when you observe the path you're on?" The answer will be, "I'm looking backwards." So then the point can be made that the path is behind the client, like the tracks the client would leave having walked across a snow-covered field. And how was the direction of this path determined? By the client's own choices, of course. In other words, in looking backwards at his life the client sees a path, but the path is the self-made result of his choices. And just because a path of choices exists in the past, it does not at all prove that a path exists ahead, in the future, which the client is forced to take.

The intention of this section has been to illustrate how relevant the application of a philosopher's knowledge about reality is to the practice of philosophical counseling and therapy. The focus of this discussion has been on reality assumptions, kinds of reality, and the definition of reality proposed by a few philosophers. But in just this short time and space a number of other metaphysical themes have unavoidably arisen, such as ontology, materialism, Berkeley's idealism, God, Descartes, dreams, time, future, present, past, pragmatism, freedom, existentialism, fate, logic, realism, post-modernism, relativism, anti-realism, phenomenology, and feminism. And there has been no mention at all of perhaps the most controversial, and yet important, question within the general topic of reality: whether there really could be life after death.

Epistemology: While metaphysics deals with the question of what is real, and what actually exists, the focus of epistemology is on the lens or lenses through which we perceive reality, and which lead us to believe we know what it is. Questions about how we know what we know about reality, and everything else that counts as knowledge, is very important in counseling and therapy with philosophy. It includes an awareness of the difference between knowing and believing, between truth and conjecture, and between certainty and skepticism. It's not uncommon for a counselor or therapist to have a client who sees believing and knowing as equivalent without realizing what a huge effect this erroneous assumption can have on life. A common scenario reached in many counseling situations is when the client makes an assertion and the counselor feels compelled to ask, "But how do you know that's true?" A counselor may also find herself with a client unwilling to believe anything or anyone. Such skepticism may have been developed while growing up in a family where the truth was hard to come by. It can also come from having experienced difficult interpersonal relationships in which significant others were untrustworthy. The counseling or therapy student's knowledge of epistemology is an important tool in helping suffering individuals resolve troublesome issues surrounding belief and certainty. For example, a session might include a discussion with a client about how she can determine if her partner actually loves her. She believes and feels the love is real, but can she trust her belief and her feelings in light of her partner's often antagonistic behavior toward her? When a belief resembles something that is hoped for, then it is more of a wish than it is a fact, or true knowledge.

Epistemic issues often flow into the realm of metaphysics. For example, the counselor or therapist may have a client who, either through drugs or alcohol abuse, or due to disturbing life situations, has come to hold a "solipsist" position. The solipsist, who believes he is all alone and everything in the world is simply a product of his imagination (or fantasy), can be helped with metaphysical examination of the solipsist position. This is where the arguments against solipsism from an academic metaphysics course become useful. Epistemic questions would be based on why the client believes he is all alone. What evidence is there for this? The client can be asked how a person could acquire language if he were all alone. Where is his body located, what is he, if the world is only in his imagination? How could you learn things you don't already know? Where did you come from if not from another person (your mother and father)? And, if a second person also believes she is the only real person—if, like the client, she's also a solipsist—which one of them is correct?

If the client is not a solipsist he may perhaps believe, like the philosopher Bishop Berkeley argued, that the world and everything in it is just ideas in God's mind. Metaphysical reasoning will produce the following questions and perspectives for consideration: If the world is only ideas in God's mind, where does God exist, in what sort of context or location, what sort of reality? A reality that exists only in God's mind simply assumes God exists; what evidence is there that this assumption is correct? If it is accepted that God exists and all of what we experience as reality is just in the mind of God, it still leaves unanswered the question of where God came from. Also, if this world is just ideas in God's mind, then all the evil in this world must, unfortunately, also be ideas in God's mind. But isn't God supposed to be perfectly good? And if reality is just ideas in a thinking mind (God's) then what distinguishes creating from simply thinking? This makes the word "creating" seem meaningless.

Ethical Theories and Applied Ethics: The simplest way to define what it means to be an ethical or moral person is that it involves trying to avoid harming others with what we say and do. Students need to learn about the many ethical theories that have been developed by theologians and philosophers over the centuries. These theories were meant to help people actually be moral. Students and clients sometimes ask, "Why be moral? What's in it for me?" This is a good opportunity to point out that asking how one can gain benefits for oneself from being moral is a self-serving question which contradicts the point of morality: concern and respect for others. Students must also be made aware of an oft-neglected element of Immanuel Kant's categorical imperative which says that in order to be a help to others you must first take care of yourself. Individuals who care for others at the expense of their own physical or mental welfare risk losing the ability to care for others. It is also important for them to consider the argument that, due to the definition of morality — trying to avoid harming others — it is not possible to have immoral thoughts since thinking does not cause direct harm to others. But besides this information, students are also taught how to apply their knowledge in helping their clients to deal with their real-life moral problems. Any discussion of ethics and morality must also include a consideration and critique of both personal and shared social values. Examples given to students might focus on various individuals who are trying to decide whether to, and how to, be honest with a teacher, an employer, or a significant other.

I — Ethical theories (meta-ethics)

This includes a discussion of the pros and cons of the many ethical theories collected through the long history of philosophy: from the ancient virtue ethics to the modern ethics of utilitarianism and deontology; from pragmatism to the problems of relativism and psychological egoism; and postmodern ethics based on relationships, care, and discourse. In total some 21 ethical theories are discussed. But a moral decision can't be made by simply applying one of the ethical theories. This is for several reasons. First, theories sometimes conflict and result in contradictory conclusions. For example, one theory says lying is never acceptable, but another theory seems to lead to the conclusion that to be a good person it's sometimes better to lie than to tell the hurtful truth. Second, even though there seems to be an abundance of moral theories to choose from, they can't address all the various contingencies in life, nor all their subtle variations. For this reason, in order to be a moral person, the student must be both familiar with the theories, and also capable of rational and empathetic reflection on the issue at hand.

II—Moral Philosophy (applied ethics–counseling specific)

This applies the theories discussed in the "Ethical Theories I" class above to actual client cases. It includes how to make a moral decision that is both logical and caring; the relevance of emotion and intuition in ethical decision-making; how to help someone else make an ethical decision in light of conflicting values, the law, religious beliefs, family pressure, the power of superiors and employers, and so on. It also deals with the morality of suicide, and practical considerations such as, for example, how an individual's financial status can affect her moral behavior, and how a family's traditions can foster contradictory morality. Useful also is a discussion of how to make an ethical decision cooperatively with another person without infringing on their autonomy. The student's knowledge of these common situations will enhance their abilities to be helpful in counseling and therapy where moral issues come to the fore.

Existentialism: This includes how existentialism is defined by various philosophers; atheistic and theistic kinds of existentialism; the problem of uncontrollable natural and chance occurrences; existential ideals as a harmful Western male fantasy of absolute independence; the problems of thinking and acting alone; existentialism as social Darwinism; as the rejection of ideals and higher purposes; as the denial of social responsibility; as the freedom to create and be oneself; as freedom to choose, including our emotions; as the responsibility to choose or not choose; as the ultimate freedom as opposed to destiny; as freedom from religion; existential freedom as the cause of "dread" or "angst" or "nausea" or extreme anxiety; as sometimes fostering self-deception and denial; as humanity's absolute freedom and responsibility toward the environment and non-human life forms (what I call environmental existentialism); and as applied to a client's self-definition and personal problems. It also includes the social, economic, and legal constraints, and political barriers to personal freedom. The concepts of existentialism can be an especially practical tool for counselors and therapists in helping clients who feel trapped by oppressive current life situations, or limiting past circumstances. It is helpful to clients and patients struggling to redefine themselves as self-actualizing and free.

Feminist Philosophy: Counseling and therapy students are taught what the agenda of feminism entails. This includes feminist critique of the concept that the male experience of reality is the universal perspective; the political difference, and emotional relationship, between equality and sameness; the issue of human rights especially as it pertains to women and minorities; the impact of expectations regarding the stereotypical social roles of men and women; the issue of the relationship of human biology to male and female psychology; the question of the supposed innate nature of women; the issue of different capabilities in men and women, boys and girls; women's critique of the supposed need for absolute autonomy and individualism; the difference between male and female comprehension and applications of ethical theories; the problem of discrimination by gender, age, color, wealth, and so on; feminism's relationship to religion and spirituality; feminism's perspective on critical reasoning; differences between men and women's discursive styles in counseling and therapy; and the problems of paternalism and maternalism. Feminists also write about how often distress is not a symptom of "intrapsychic conflict" but rather a rational and understandable reaction to oppressive life situations. They also point out how a distinction needs to be made between this distress and biological diseases, and how human suffering that is a reaction to injustice and trauma should no longer be "medicalized" and treated as a flaw in the victim. Feminists argue that what is often termed a symptom can be a coping strategy, or a justified rebellion against an unjust status quo that is accepted as a societal norm. Examples for discussion could include the young woman who believes she will be a failure in love and life because she believes she is ugly; the black woman who has been a valued employee in a car parts store for many years but has never been promoted to manager; the woman who feels guilty about being "only a stay-at-home mom," and the case in a Middle Eastern country of a single woman who was raped and then sentenced to prison for breaking the law by having sex outside of marriage.

The Philosophy of Human Nature: This includes a discussion of the question of whether there is such a thing as human nature, and what elements of personality are inherent or intrinsic to a so-called human nature. This is in contrast, for example, to existential conceptions of human nature as chosen rather than inherent. It also includes discussions about the various aspects of the "self," and of what it means to speak of a collective human nature. This class would bring many of the topics from anthropology and sociology to bear on the discussions. An example for discussion might include the case of the man who wonders how he can make a significant life decision where the most profitable choice goes against what he considers to be his true, altruistic nature. It might also involve a consideration of the claim that humans are by nature greedy and violent, and are only kept in check by threats of retaliation or punishment. This philosophical topic includes two sub-topics:

1. Philosophy of human relationships:

This class examines various kinds of human relationships, such as parent/child, teacher/student, boss/employee, priest/parishioner, husband/wife; same sex relationships, and so on. It also considers the expectations, problems, and responsibilities inherent in the various relationships; the variations in power relations brought by gender, race, age, religion, social status, etc.; the concept of fidelity in friendships and love relationships; the problem of dependency. Also examined are internal and external pressures on relationships; the value and drawbacks of cooperation and competition within various relationships; the social variance in the concept of the "normal" relationship; the private, the public, and the media generated concept of the "ideal" relationship; the issue of changes, expectations, assumptions, growth, self-deception, self-denial, consensus, coercion, and development within a relationship; various endings to relationships such as mutual agreement, infidelity, mistrust, loss of interest, and death; and how to help a client deal with the after-effects of the various kinds of relationship endings.

2. Philosophy of human identity and self-development:

Areas to be discussed are the nature versus nurture debate, and the related problem of the reality of supposed "innate" traits; the question of whether human nature is static or constantly evolving. Also at issue is the question of ultimate human motivation: which of the many "Will to. . ." postulated by philosophers over the centuries is most convincing; the problem of the ideal of the independent self; the problem of accurate and fair self-scrutiny; the origin and basis of self-image; the problem of the client's self-deception, feeling of incompleteness, idealization, etc. in self-description; the influence of societal stereotypes of male and female social roles on human nature; influences on the development of human nature such as gender, religion, race, genetics, etc.; the effects of mental and physical illnesses, physical abuse, substance abuse, and medication on self-identity; the relevance of childhood to the nature of the person as an adult; issues around sexuality and sexual orientation; the question of how youth, maturity, and old age affect human nature; the issue of self-esteem; and the ethics of the counselor or therapist's influencing change in the client or patient. Philosophy can literally be life-saving by helping the individual recognize self-worth, and take the initiative to define him or herself anew.

Defining The Self

The theory of the "mental illness" labeled "multiple personality disorder (MPD)" was widely held at one time by psychotherapists. Then was thoroughly discredited not long ago. But normal individuals do in fact act in many different ways that might conceivably be mistaken for discreet personalities. For example, a person will use a different tone of voice and manner when speaking informally with a friend or spouse than when speaking formally with the head of the corporation they work for. Does this mean this person is "mentally ill" and may be diagnosed as suffering from MPD? Not at all. Philosophical counselors understand that normal individuals may act in surprisingly different ways at different times, but that these variations are completely appropriate to the situation at hand. That's because people see and define themselves differently, and therefore act or behave differently, depending on the social context in which they are situated at the present moment. While the individual acts as an equal with her friend or husband in one conversation, she behaves as a deferential employee in another, and as a commanding leader in yet another. People have many different ways of thinking about the "selves" that they are displaying at any given time. For example, the physical self: my body image and identity; the extended (field) self: what I perceive to be "my space" in a crowd; the temporal self: me over time and in the moment; the emergent/developing self: me as process oriented; the intellectual self: what I know and believe; the spiritual self: my transcendental nature, and so on.

The loss of self-esteem, and indeed the loss of the self, can happen very easily to the client whose relationships include individuals who feel it is their right to define who this individual is or ought to be. A diagnosis of "mental illness" and the ingestion of powerful psychotropic medications can also seriously alter both the individual's conceptions of himself as well as the way others perceive him. Medications and their negative side effects can seriously hamper the individual's ability to live life according to his own conceptions of what living a good life ought to be. For most individuals life is not just about amassing personal possessions, it also includes sharpening their perception of who they are, and then expanding and detailing their own definition of who they wish to be. The famous nineteenth century Danish philosopher Søren Kierkegaard wrote that "the greatest hazard of all, losing oneself, can occur very quietly in the world, as if it were nothing at all. No other loss can occur so quietly; any other loss—an arm, a leg, five dollars, a wife, etc.—is sure to be noticed" (p.32). The philosophical counselor is sometimes in the position of not only being asked to help the client maintain his "real" self, but also to actually find his "true" self among the various selves with which others have encumbered him. An example might be the young person enrolled in an academic or technical program as suggested by the parents, while the goal of the program is not in accord with that student's view of either his future or self-identity. Another example is the person who has been ascribed the label of alcoholic, or been diagnosed as being "mentally ill," who wishes to overcome the limitations of these problematic categorizing labels.

Meaning of Life: Some of my clients started their first counseling session by saying they would like to discuss the meaning of life. My response has always been to ask them why they want to discuss this particularly deep philosophical topic. For most of us, the meaning of life manifests itself precisely by virtue of escaping our attention. When life becomes difficult, complicated, or painful the question "What is the meaning of my suffering?" arises.

It turns out that all but one of these clients had some personal problem they wished to resolve or some emotional suffering they hoped to ameliorate. There was only one client who actually wanted to discuss the topic of the meaning of life in a philosophical way.

A legitimately philosophical discussion about the meaning of life can begin, first of all, with an examination of what philosophers have said about the topic throughout the history of philosophy. From there discussion turns to how the meaning of life is dealt with within various contexts such as academia, religion, and counseling. Also discussed are attitudes or stances in relation to life such as optimism, pessimism, "mesomism," nihilism, and absurdity. Other topics include the value of fantasy, imagination, dreams, and wishes; the question as being a non-issue or a "category mistake" which is a nonsensical question which cannot be answered rationally; the responses of behaviorism, determinism, and free will; existentialism as meaning-making; influences on meaning from cultural norms, family demands, personal goals and expectations; the influence of utopianism and ideals of "the perfect life"; the balance of freedoms and obligations in determining meaning; the difference between meaning and purpose; situational meaning as opposed to the meaning of the entirety of life; and the various ways of discovering or creating meaning in life for oneself. Examples can include the case of the wealthy retired man who, after a long life of running a very successful business, feels his life has been mostly empty of value and meaning; the woman whose husband has abandoned her for a younger woman and left her alone to care for their physically challenged child; or the family who comes home from a church charity event only to find that their house was burglarized.

Phenomenology and Hermeneutics: This topic considers two different ways of perceiving and knowing: the objective and the subjective. Phenomenology is described as the pure, objective description of observed phenomena, especially of one's own mind. It includes observational listening styles; counselor observations of client non-verbal communication; counselor self-observations; recognition of hidden values, biases, and assumptions. Hermeneutics is the search for subjective meaning, and an awareness of various interpretative methods. It examines the I/Thou and I/

relationships; the problems of perception created by cultural differences, gender, religion, and social status, etc. It is an analytical and critical listening style which sees the client's narrative as a "text" within a context. It also involves an interpretation of the meaning contained in a physical action or verbal assertion.

Postmodernism: This includes discussion of so-called postmodern thought which stands contrary to the certainty inherent in the positivistic, scientific, "modern" world view developed in the seventeenth century. It involves the problem of the loss of tradition, and the comfort of the familiar; the effects of postmodernism on philosophy, religion, politics, lifestyles, science, technology, and the media; the problem of postmodernism's abandonment of the concept of the absolute "Truth" about anything; the questioning of the authority of so-called experts; and postmodernism's effect on everyday thinking. It also deals with the problems of reification and realism in counseling and psychotherapy. Examples for this topic can include a discussion of the authority of psychotherapeutic assertions made about patients, and the validity of the diagnostic and classificatory criteria used in clinical evaluation of mental states.

Philosophy of Religion: This topic includes thinking about traditional values and their relationship to religious tenets; for example why homosexuality, divorce, masturbation, and sex out of wedlock, were all deemed sinful in ancient Judaism, Christianity, and Islam. It might also include an examination of the logic of religious commandments and their ultimate authority. For example, prohibitions: it is fairly well known why pork was prohibited in hot Middle Eastern societies. Not as many religious people avoid pork in modern times where refrigeration and microwaves are readily available. But the prohibition against masturbation is still fairly common in some religions. The religious commandment is kept, but the logic has been forgotten. In ancient times, up until the late medieval times, it was believed that the human being existed completely formed in microscopic form in the male semen. The woman was only the vessel in which the seed was planted and grown to be born into a human baby. The prohibition against masturbation was an actual prohibition against the murder of microscopic humans within the male semen. While today we know that semen contains only half the DNA for procreation, the prohibition against masturbation still stands in many religions, despite its being based on faulty biological reasoning. This discussion of reason and empirical evidence versus the authority of religious commandments can be very liberating for troubled clients and patients. Discussion may also include theological detoxification: the removal of beliefs that are simply harmful, such as oppressive prohibitions on women, the us-against-them mentality in some churches, a lack of human rights, disregard for civil laws, racism, homophobia, coercive retention of members, and fear mongering. An example may include the case of the young female member of a church who had a child out of wedlock. Church leaders have led her to believe she is worthless and will end up in Hell. A different case is the highly intellectual man whose extremely passionate worship of God has led to him being diagnosed with schizoid-affective disorder.

Social and Political Philosophy: This can also involve various moral issues. Included are the question of what makes a good nation, a good neighborhood, a good family. Why skin color, sex, age, and at times even species are an irrelevant criteria for the assignment of rights. Central are topics dealing with power issues in public arenas such as municipal and national governments, as well as questions of power allocation in smaller social groups such as families. The argument for and against the business concept that a corporation is a "person" with rights and obligations is also a topic in this area, especially as it concerns drug manufacturers and multinational corporations. Topics include the question of the cross-border reach of corporate ethics, the obligations, and the limits to those obligations, of the state toward those who have been diagnosed with so-called mental illnesses, the rights and obligations of individuals who are supported by the state, and state financial and legal support of corporations. A case for discussion might be the man who is trying to decide whether he should support a state sponsored free drug injection site, or a half-way house for "mentally ill" people in his community; or the individual who wants help in deciding what to think about legalized abortion, euthanasia, gay marriages, or marijuana use.

In My Class
I sometimes tell my students the story of a significant change in thinking which occurred in the sport of bobsledding. Some 30 years ago the Olympic winter sport of bobsledding ran into a problem that I think is similar to the one I became aware of not long ago in one of the courses I teach. The course offers philosophy specifically geared to students wishing to make a career for themselves in the field of counseling or psychotherapy. Everyone knows that in bobsledding a team of men (and now women too) push a sled as fast as they can, and then jump on it to ride it down an icy, twisting track. The team with the fastest time wins. The men who were pushing and driving the bobsleds were athletes who joined the sport of bobsledding because they enjoyed the speedy ride down the hill. One day there came a time when there was virtually no difference any more in the way the various countries designed and built their bobsleds. Because of this, all the sleds were going down the hill at pretty much exactly the same speed. Likewise, the drivers had all perfected their skill to the point where there was very little more they could do to make their own sleds go faster and cross the finish line sooner. It finally became

obvious to the coaches and trainers that the only possible way to go faster, and win races, was to train their athletes to push their sled harder and faster than the others at the very start of the hill. So they encouraged their bobsled team members to practice running harder and faster.

But the coaches found that most of their bobsledders were not runners, and it simply wasn't possible to get them to run much faster than they were already running. At the same time many of the bobsledders were not very happy having to practice running faster when all they really wanted to do was ride down the hill on their bobsleds. And so, because the bobsledders couldn't run any faster, the sleds didn't go any faster. This made the coaches very unhappy. Until one day one of the coaches had an idea. He wondered, Why are we trying to teach bobsledders to run faster? It just makes everybody unhappy. Why don't we find some fast runners and teach them how to ride on a bobsled? And so the coaches of the bobsledding teams found men who were willing to learn how to ride on a bobsled, and who were already national championship athletes in sports that involve running like track and field, soccer, and professional football. These men were able to push the bobsleds much harder and faster at the start of the hill which, in turn, made their sleds go much faster down the track. Bobsledding was improved by a change in thinking. It was by means of a minor paradigm shift: from trying to teach bobsledders how to run faster, to teaching fast runners how to ride on a bobsled. This story is a metaphor for my own paradigm shift in the way I teach philosophy. Instead of trying to convince philosophy students to learn the gentle art of counseling, like I did initially, I now find it much more productive to teach philosophy to those students who are already interested in counseling and psychotherapy. The course of philosophy for counselors I now teach at my university is aimed mainly at students who call the psychology or social work departments their home, and whose goal is to be helpful to individuals burdened by mental distress or emotional suffering.

In my "Philosophy for Counselors" course for senior students at the University of the Fraser Valley located in Abbotsford, British Columbia, Canada we use two textbooks. The first is simply titled *Philosophy* by Manuel Velasquez and the second is my book titled *Issues in Philosophical Counseling*. Students are generally required to read two chapters before every class, one from each book, in preparation for discussion. And the readings are assigned so that the chapters complement each other. For example, when the chapter assigned from the Velasquez text is on ethics, the reading from my book is on the ethical questions involved in the issue of suicide; when the Velasquez chapter discusses the metaphysics of reality, the chapter from my book is on dreams and their relation to reality. It's not possible to give all the many details of each class in the course (that would take another book), but here are some of the highlights.

I begin by helping my students understand what philosophy is all about. Remember, these are mostly psychology and social work students with little knowledge of how to apply the philosophy they have previously studied to counseling or psychotherapy. I tell them that philosophy in a counseling situation involves helping the client examine the reasons he has for the values he holds as good, and the beliefs he holds as true, so that he can free himself from blindly following tradition, slavishly obeying authority figures, or acting only on his feelings. I talk a little about how philosophy was adopted by psychology in North America in the 1950's, when dynamic psychoanalysts discovered how helpful philosophy can be to their patients. And then we get into discussing and practicing critical and creative reasoning skills which involve reality assumptions, value assumptions, fallacies, and so on as discussed above. The first case we discuss at the end of this class is about a 20-year-old woman who is very shy and lonely, and worried that this is a symptom of mental illness. There are, of course, small group discussions, as well as handouts, overheads, charts, videos, diagrams, and notes on the board in all of these classes.

In the second class we continue to focus on critical and creative thinking. We discuss the interpretation of the meaning of words, we do a group exercise where students discover their personal philosophies on the issue of lying and stealing, and we discuss how to find the philosophical issues in the problem a client may present. In this class we discuss two cases: the first deals with a man who loves a single mother, but he doesn't like her young son; and the second is about a client who sees reality as very strange but wants to avoid taking medication he was told would "correct" this. Students are not asked to try to resolve these cases. The point of the exercise is only to recognize and find the many philosophical issues in them.

The third class deals with the issue of human nature. In this class we discuss whether there is such a thing as human nature, what it means to be "normal," the fact that it's much easier to define "abnormal" than it is to define "normal," various ways it's possible to think of yourself, and some of the important differences between how men and women experience themselves and each other. The case we discuss is an e-mail I received from a woman in a psychiatric hospital who asks whether she should be worried about the struggles she's having with what seem like two opposing "selves" within her. At this time the first student essay is also due. They've been asked to give their philosophical thoughts about a woman who worries that she is genetically determined to become addicted to drugs because her mother is a drug-addict. The reading for this assignment discusses the issue of the relationship between genetics and so-called mental illnesses. This assignment leads into the following week's discussion of the metaphysical issues of free will and determinism.

In the fourth class, first of all we discuss the essays from the previous class which have now been marked and returned. Then we enter into metaphysics and the issue of reality. We discuss the various "kinds" of reality relevant to discussion that may come up in counseling. There is an introduction to various theories such as idealism, pragmatism, relativism, anti-realism, and so on. Finally we talk about what to make of dreams. The case we discuss at the end of this class is Jung's problematic analysis of a patient's dream found in my second book *Issues in Philosophical Counseling*.

The next class focuses on epistemology. We examine where knowledge comes from, how it differs from belief, what it means to be rational, and various theories of truth. One of the group exercises involves coming up with arguments against the theory of multiple personalities before a handout on this topic is circulated. This time the case discussion is about a young man who wonders about the value of doing a "past life regression" with a psychic to find out why he and his girlfriend are having problems in their relationship.

In the sixth week we cover various theoretical issues in ethics and morality such as psychological egoism, subjectivism, relativism, and the various theories on how to make a moral decision. The question of whether suicide is moral is first discussed in small groups and then by the class as a whole. This time the case study is about two brothers and a sister who wonder whether it is ethical to move their aging father out of his family home and into a professional seniors care facility. Students then have to go home and write an essay for the following week giving a philosophical perspective on the case of a young man who has become very bitter about his family's religious beliefs. This essay assignment leads into the next week's topic.

In class number seven discussion is all about religion and the various arguments for and against the existence of God. In their groups the students are asked to deal with the question of how religion affects even the non-believers in a community. The case we discuss in this class is that of a Catholic woman who feels overwhelming guilt for, as she put it, "living in sin" with her boyfriend.

Class eight covers the various issues that can arise when living within any human society. This is an overview of political philosophy. We discuss the relationship between morality and the law, human rights, war, education, feminism, and so on. The case study concerns a young man who agreed to meet with a woman as a potential marriage partner. In her many personal e-mails to him she had led him to believe that she was much prettier, and that she was much more submissive, than she actually turned out to be when they finally meet in person. This case covers a number of issues such as rights, obligations, contractual agreements, and of course honesty and deception.

Class nine deals with the meaning of life. We discuss a number of different answers to this question that have been offered over time by various philosophers. The small student groups are asked to discuss the possibility that life is simply meaningless. The case study involves using an assortment of possible approaches to a client who has been diagnosed with terminal cancer, has never been married or raised a family, and wonders whether there was any point to his life at all. A final essay is due the following week in which the students are asked to discuss the role of philosophy in psychotherapy and counseling in light of recent reports of significant developments in modern psychotropic medications for "mental illnesses."

Students are asked to prepare for the last class by reading chapters 1, 12, and 13 in *Issues in Philosophical Counseling* dealing with psychotropic medications and the attempt to come to a definition of "normal." They're also required to do an on-line search of the topic "anti-psychiatry," which will show them essays written by psychotherapists and psychoanalysts who are critical of the theories and practices in their own professions.

With two classes devoted to examinations, this is the structure of one semester of philosophy for students of counseling and psychotherapy.

Notice that each class deals with both abstract philosophical themes as well as actual "case studies" which are examples of problematic circumstances in the lives of suffering human beings. While students are encouraged to consider the emotions, feelings, and so-called psychological problems the client narratives present, students are also asked to deal with these on the level of the client's concrete or existential experiences rather than just in the abstract. The point is that these narratives are taken from the real life experiences of individuals, and are not contrived hypothetical cases whose resolutions have no real-world impact. Students are asked to situate the client's beliefs, values, fears, and assumptions within the client's lived experiences, such as their family arrangement, their financial circumstances, their social connections, their gender, their culture, their wider political situation, and so on. This shifts the focus from the client's troubles being merely some isolated issue—or "mental illness"—within the client to a more contextual consideration. And one of the most important aspects of the work the students do with these cases is to come to a concrete conclusion, and a variety of practical suggestions for course of action that may be helpful in reality to the suffering individual. This includes decisions about the placement of responsibility for past events in the client's life, accountability for the current state of affairs, as well as choosing a moral course of action for the future (Haas p. 190).

There are of course many more topics and issues that could be discussed with students during a longer semester. One semester isn't going to make expert philosophers out of students majoring in counseling or clinical psychology. And yet there is no doubt that this kind of philosophy course will serve to improve the abilities of every student working toward becoming a counselor or psychotherapist.

A Word on Non-Western Philosophy

Although I'm not an expert on non-Western philosophy, I have studied enough of it to know that its practice can be very different from that which is found in the West. Perhaps one of the main differences is the extremely individual orientation of Western philosophy when compared to the much more community-oriented or collective perspective in the East. Another significant difference is that the approach in Western philosophy, especially analytic philosophy, is very critical, that is, students are encouraged to disagree and critique the writings of the most respected members of their discipline. In non-Western philosophy the student is typically required to suppress his or her own thinking on matters out of respect for, and in deference to, the chronicled thoughts of the ancient wise ones. There is a big difference between learning what the "experts" or the "masters" suggest one ought to think, and thinking for oneself and disagreeing with traditionally honored beliefs and values. As the editors of a forthcoming textbook on philosophical practice so aptly put it, "we will try to think with Descartes rather than think about Descartes" (Harteloh et al. p. 81).

Those who practice philosophy in the typical Western tradition note that not all recorded ancient wisdom is still timely, accurate, useful, or even wise. They point out that even the experts or masters can be perceived as wrong on some matters. Philosophy students in North America are taught to be skeptical and critical of experts and masters, but in a respectful way. This questioning attitude is expected and even encouraged as the appropriate philosophical stance. In Western cultures the respect for authority figures that is common in Eastern cultures is often seen by Westerners as simple obedience. A counselor or psychotherapist trained in Western philosophy does not expect or want obedience from the client. For a Western philosopher respect means careful listening, careful consideration of what is suggested, the acceptance of disagreements during a discussion, and arriving at a mutually agreed-upon solution to a problem. It does not require the client's unquestioning obedience to the directives of the counselor.

For example, a wise man may claim: "To be honorable you must always tell the truth." But obedience to this can lead to immoral (harmful) behavior. Sometimes telling the truth is not an honorable thing to do. How is it possible to be moral and less than honorable at the same time? The directive to "always tell the truth" is a hotly debated topic in Western philosophy classes.

In North America we discourage students from including in their essays long quoted passages from experts or authority figures. This practice seems to be accepted and even required in some Eastern education institutions. In Western institutions students are instead encouraged to think for themselves, to speak for themselves using their own words, to make their own arguments with good reasons that support their conclusions, and to find and cite appropriate references which support the arguments. This same strategy is part of how philosophical counseling works as well. This kind of forthright disputation seems to be discouraged in more traditional Eastern cultures.

When there is only respect for tradition, and an obedience to authority, it is very difficult to encourage originality, and the progress the originality engenders. While it's true that the wisdom of the elders creates a foundation for later generations, it's also true that times change, and what is considered "wise" changes as well. It is especially true that over time our beliefs about what is moral have changed. In the distant past the wise ones of Greece and Rome felt it was moral to own slaves; and the ancient wise ones of most cultures saw nothing wrong with beating their wives and children. But we don't consider this behavior morally acceptable anymore because the ancient philosophers allowed their followers the freedom to question everything, including their own authority.

Any first year student of philosophy knows that a tradition cannot be called "good" simply because it is long-standing. The examination of ancient wisdoms and traditions extends even so far as the teachings of various religions. Morality supersedes religion. What is immoral is immoral not because religion says so, but because it causes harm. Conversely, what causes harm is bad because it causes harm, not because religion says it is bad. This point was already made centuries ago by the earliest philosophers. Students are taught that the philosophical counselor or therapist has no right to act like an authority figure. He or she should not tell the client what to believe or do; the counselor must not demand or expect obedience. The philosophical counselor helps the client to come to respect him- or herself. This respect means the client is helped by the counselor to come to trust his or her own thinking and decision-making ability in the way common to Western philosophy.

Learning requires more than just memorization. It requires thinking for oneself, and questioning one's beliefs. It also involves questioning others, even authority figures, which can lead to respectful but challenging discourse. This can in turn lead either to strengthening current beliefs or coming to new insights. There is no dishonor for the teacher who learns from the student. In North America optimal learning is believed to be a collaborative activity, a reciprocal relationship between the teacher and the student. Likewise counseling and therapy is ideally a collaborative effort between the counselor and the client or the therapist and the patient. Therefore, in Western cultures it is not uncommon for the authority figure, the counselor or therapist, to learn from the client during the discussions. It seems to me that this may be lacking in the practice of

Eastern philosophy. But the discussion in this section has focused on the practice of Western philosophy. While the practices inherent in Eastern philosophy may not be applicable to this style of counseling and psychotherapy, the content of Eastern philosophy can certainly help to inform those practices. But that is a topic for a different book. I apologize if this very brief discussion is found to be inaccurate, biased, or lacking in any way.

Social and Political Activism

Simply being right about the misconceptions and misinformation concerning so-called mental illness and its treatment is not enough to improve the deficiencies in its current theories and practices. It was only in 1992, after 359 years had passed, that the Vatican admitted it was wrong about the movement of the planets in our solar system, and that Galileo had been right. Authority figures and institutions don't like to admit they've been wrong. Changes in thinking about the nature of "mental illnesses" and their treatments requires concerted action. A paradigm shift requires a challenge to the status quo. Therefore, an education in philosophy for counselors and psychotherapists should also include teaching and promoting political activism on behalf of the many millions of people diagnosed as suffering from so-called mental illnesses. These people are caught in a system which typically begins their treatment with the assumption that recovery is unlikely, and a cure is impossible. Individuals diagnosed as mentally ill find themselves on a treadmill of dependency on both their medications and their care-givers. They become locked into a system which demands their compliance to a regimen of powerful mind-numbing medications in return for continued financial support. It is a system of so-called support and life management for the "mentally ill" which creates continued dependency and powerlessness. Therefore students of counseling or therapeutic philosophy should be encouraged to do the following:

- help clients to either change, or remove themselves from the vicinity of offending individuals and detrimental social environments that are the cause of their mental distress and emotional suffering.
- respond to problematic practices, such as the rampant over-prescription of psychotropic drugs, by requesting reduction or cessation of the use of medications for non-physical suffering.
- respond to the claim that medications are essential in the treatment of so-called mental illnesses.
- respond publicly and negatively to the announcements of "newly discovered mental illnesses" that are actually psychiatric inventions.

- publicly question the ontology and etiology of any new "mental illnesses."
- lobby physicians and psychotherapists to not diagnose mental distress and emotional suffering as biomedical conditions requiring treatment with medications.
- respond to professional misinformation about the nature, the causes, and the effects of so-called mental illnesses.
- respond to the media's perpetuation of the erroneous belief that the motivation for commission of terrible crimes is explainable by a diagnosis, or that these crimes must simply be due to a mental illness in the perpetrator. "People have the right not to be exposed to negative portrayals of people with mental illness in the media (Flanagan p. 266).
- cite statistical data on recovery and cures in order to change widespread negative stereotypes and beliefs that so-called mental illnesses are chronic, permanent, and incurable.
- lobby boards of education to include courses in philosophy as prerequisites for counseling certificates and psychotherapy degrees.
- lobby boards of education to include courses in philosophy in pre-university curricula to help prevent the kind of suffering and distress in young people that can lead to early diagnoses of mental illnesses.
- lobby practicing psychotherapists to update their knowledge and practical philosophical skills as a way to enhance their therapeutic competence, and at the same time reduce their dependence on prescribing drugs for their patients.

Biases about mental illnesses are "knowledge structures" that permeate society. They are very difficult to overcome, especially today with the proliferation of both public and social media that are frantically disseminating misinformation about the ontology and etiology of so-called mental illness, erroneous claims about the incurability of so-called mental illnesses, deceptive claims about medications, fears about "an epidemic" of mental illness, and the stereotypes they perpetuate. One example of media bias is presented by psychologist C. Peter Bankart who reports that while in 98 percent of the advertisements for psychotropic medications the physician is male, in 78 percent of them the patient is female (p. 363). A profusion of media messages about so-called mental illness can lead to the so-called "paradox of health." This is when societies with populations that are in fact healthy, and who are inundated with information about pathology, complain more about illness than unhealthy societies who are not inundated with similarly information of pathology (Stein p. 124). This "paradox of health" may in fact be operational in the United States, Canada, and other developed nations in which pharmaceutical industry advertisements about the pervasiveness of so-called mental illness—and therefore the need for medications—is absolutely rampant.

Recovery and cure of so-called mental illnesses is also difficult if the erroneous messages that permeate society about mental suffering and emotional distress lead to both social stigmatization and self-stigmatization. A professional counselor or therapist trained in philosophy must therefore be prepared to counter the influential elements out in the wider community, and also within families, whose negative effects on her client have led to the emotional suffering and cognitive distress that can lead to a diagnosis of "mental illness." Bankart put it this way: "I agree with my feminist colleagues who believe that we must . . . recognize the social, political, and economic sources of suffering and oppression" and then do something about them (p. 385).

The philosophically trained counselor or therapist must be ready to encounter new and sometimes puzzling cases with both the courage and the open-mindedness and compassionate curiosity of a true philosopher, using what she has learned from her study of the philosophers of the past (Nussbaum, p. 67).

Teaching reasoning to counselors and psychotherapists, who will in turn teach it to their clients and patients, requires the same sort of approach as teaching any other skill. For example, teaching someone how to replace a broken spoke in a bicycle wheel requires not only explaining how this is done but demonstrating how to do so: "You take out the old spoke like this; you thread the new one in like this; then you true the wheel like this. Now you try it." Philosophically ameliorating a problem in someone's life, like replacing a broken spoke in a bicycle wheel, is a skill that has to be taught with demonstration and learned with practice. This is why it is simply wrong to assume that learning academic philosophy in a classroom, or worse, just reading about philosophy in a book or online, is adequate training to become a good counselor or psychotherapist.

The education of counselors and psychotherapists should not stop at the "downloading" of information on how to apply philosophy to "cases." And the practice of counseling and therapy should not be limited to a one-on-one discussion between counselor and client. Therapists and counselors should become instructors, facilitating learning among the members of self-help and mental health support groups, and in the wider community, in order to help prevent their future dependence on experts and authority figures who claim to know what is best. Ideally an education in philosophy for future counselors and psychotherapists will lead to the establishment of clinics and private offices in which philosophy is the solid foundation for whatever counseling technique or psychotherapeutic method is practiced.

What's to Be Gained?

The distressed client, who has been diagnosed with a serious mental illness, asks, "How can I be sure I'm not dreaming right now?" This can be a difficult question for him to answer, given popular Hollywood movies that seem to show that reality is just an alien construction or a bad dream. But a philosopher can make the answer more attainable by revising the question into "What is the difference between dreaming and life when you're awake, or between a dream and everyday reality?" With the question formulated like this it's much easier to come to an answer. This kind of rewording of the question in order to help locate a path to its resolution is one of the helpful strategies philosophical counselors employ to assist their clients in finding their own solutions to seemingly irresolvable problems. It can also be learned in the classroom by students who have the goal of becoming counselors and psychotherapists.

Academically published information on the correlation between "mental illnesses" and both the family environment and interpersonal dynamics tends to not make it into public awareness. For example, a journal article will discuss the link discovered between family dynamics and schizophrenia but this will not become common knowledge (see Barham). One reason is because pharmaceutical companies publish rival paradigms, citing malfunctioning brain chemistry or faulty genes as the causal factor. This fits better into the agenda of those whose main aim is to sell their chemical products. A television news cast will report, for example, a study that shows the link between diet, disrupted sleeping habits, and ADHD in kids, but this report is rarely repeated, and the general public who did not manage to see it the first time it was aired will never be made aware of this information by other sources. Perhaps busy, overworked, and over-stressed parents don't actually want to believe that the convenient fast foods they have been feeding their child—high in sugar, salt, fats, color, and preservative chemicals—or the lack of a calm and quiet home environment during sleeping hours is behind the child's behavioral problems. It's easier and less guilt-inducing to live with the belief that factors out of the parent's control—such as the child's brain chemistry or a genetic weakness—are at fault. But philosophy does not condone promulgating the standard theories about "mental illness" just because they are profitable or less offensive than the truth.

A thorough knowledge of both the "hard" and social sciences of both normal and abnormal psychology, that is, an understanding of human development and behavior, is essential in philosophical counseling and therapy. For example, it is important to know that men and women communicate differently. Men's talk often involves the expectation of suggestions from the discussion partner. Women on the other hand often use talk as a way to diffuse strong inner emotion, which men rarely do (see Tannen). The philosophical counselor or therapist must understand the crucial difference if he or she is to approach the counseling or therapeutic relationship in a way that is beneficial to the client. This is information that is critical to becoming an effective counselor or therapist. While it is not necessary, nor indeed desirable, that every psychiatrist should become a philosopher, all counselors, psychotherapists, and psychiatrists "should have some exposure to philosophical thinking in their training" (Fulford p. 19). Martha Nussbaum argues that medical or therapeutic philosophy,

> while committed to logical reasoning, and to marks of good reasoning such as clarity, consistency, rigor, and breadth of scope, will often need to search for techniques that are more complicated and indirect, more psychologically engaging, than those of conventional deductive or dialectical argument. (p. 35)

In other words, while employing philosophical rigor, good counseling and therapy must use "gripping examples, techniques of narrative, appeals to memory and imagination—all in the service of bringing the [client's] whole life into the investigative process" (Ibid). This investigative process between the philosophical counselor or therapist and client is a transformative process that psychologist Michael Mahoney calls "autopoiesis." It involves the counselor/client or therapist/patient dyad searching for new insights, reaching for higher levels of self-awareness and understanding of the world, and inventing and trying out new approaches to solving stubborn problems.

Good philosophical counseling also requires what I call "philosophical maturity." This is includes not just an intellectual comprehension of the contents of philosophy, and not just the ability to imitate a philosophically discursive style. It requires an authentic appreciation for the power of philosophy as a preventive, recuperative, and curative agent in all the various forms of counseling and psychotherapy. This does not come after only a few courses in academic philosophy. It requires witnessing philosophical therapy in action, seeing its impact on suffering and distressed individuals, and recognizing that recovery or cure was not just fortuitous or accidental, but that philosophy actually had a significant beneficial effect. But what does the application of philosophy in counseling or psychotherapy look like? Case studies can give an introductory glimpse into how beneficial a philosophical discussion can actually be.

TEN
Three Case Studies

The following three case studies are examples of how I have dealt with three different individuals who contacted me for my philosophical assistance. They are idiographic accounts, that is they are concerning particular individuals within specific circumstances and contexts. These type of reports have often been criticized for being of limited interest or utility because, it is argued, the information in them cannot be generalized to a larger population. But that is a very meager perspective of these types of narrative accounts. While the information gleaned from them may not be absolutely universalizable, there is much in them that can in fact be applied in working with many individual clients. These three case studies are not meant to exemplify any "school" of counseling or psychotherapy. They are not meant to demonstrate an established protocol or method that must be closely followed. While there are books available about Philosophical Counseling, there is no manual or "how-to" book for counseling or therapy with philosophy whose author promotes, or worse, demands the strict adherence to a particular approach. These three cases are merely meant to illustrate the sort of philosophical questions I asked, and the type of suggestions I made during the discussions I had with three different troubled individuals. Other counselors or therapists may have approached these people differently, resulting in an equally satisfactory outcome.

The aim in any encounter with a client is for the counselor or therapist to be of help to that individual. Sometimes asking good questions is enough; sometimes just listening is all that is required. At other times, when the client can't produce any further insight, a respectful suggestion from a different perspective can be very helpful; at still other times the counselor or therapist may share his or her own experiences. This can be both comforting and instructive to the client. But these bits of information will not be new to practicing psychological counselors and psychotherapists. What will be new to those students who have studied philosophy on their way to becoming counselors and therapists is seeing the philosophical knowledge and reasoning skills, ones they have also acquired from their own study of philosophy, being put to use in real-life encounters.

The first case is offered initially in its entirety, although somewhat clarified from my scribbled session notes. Then it is presented again in segments with annotations which offer questions and insights. This is the story of a young man whose desire for the peace of spiritual contemplation is soured by the human imperfections of others who claim spiritual superiority.

CASE #1: "LUKE" THE DISGRACED MONK

'Luke" asked if I thought I might be of help to him. He told me he had been diagnosed with schizoaffective disorder and paranoia. The treatment he received first from his medical doctor and then his psychoanalyst had consisted primarily of powerful mind-altering psychotropic medications.

After I had spent some time researching the confusion, contradictions, and obscurity surrounding Luke's diagnosis of schizoaffective disorder and paranoia, I decided that my best course of action was to find out more about Luke himself, to try to figure out just how much of his diagnosis was based on actual organic pathology and how much of his distress was perhaps the result of his life's circumstances.

During our first session Luke told me that he was twenty-six years old, and that he was seeing a psychoanalyst who had put him on antidepressant medication. He said this psychoanalyst was unwilling to help him figure out what direction he ought to take in life because this is not what psychoanalysis is all about. I told Luke that I would be happy to help him but that I would first like to know a bit more about him. He told me his father and mother were very kind and supportive of him, as were both his younger and older brothers and sisters. He said his family was devoutly Catholic, and that his older brother is in fact an ordained priest whom he respects and admires, and with whom he sometimes has very stimulating theological discussions. Luke said he used to be "a party animal," but that he had gone to college and things had gone badly. He began to have paranoid thoughts, believing that people could tell what he was thinking. "Even now," he said, "it feels like people can read my mind." This was, of course, very troubling for him.

Luke used to work at a part-time job, and had lots of friends as well as a girlfriend, all of which he lost when he started to become paranoid. He now felt that everything positive is a lie, that there is sarcasm in every sentence, and that he has an "evil core." I wondered where this might have come from, so I asked him what he had done before he went to college. He told me that before he spent the two years as a student he had actually been a Catholic monk living in a monastery for four years. It was only after he had left the monastery and entered college that he was first diagnosed with schizoaffective disorder and paranoia. He told me he had decided to become a monk at his older brother's urging, but that he had eventually been expelled. I asked him why he had been expelled. What had happened in the monastery?

He told me that he had at times questioned and even criticized his superiors, and he was therefore accused by them of being dishonest, full of pride, and not sincere in his religious beliefs. He said that he had looked forward to the life of peace and contemplation his brother had promised would be his as a monk. In fact when he first got into the monastery he felt very much at peace. He firmly believed this structured and orderly life was indeed the perfect life for him, so that when he was expelled it made him feel like he was the worst sort of failure. With the approach of the end of our hour-long session I suggested we might want to discuss his self-esteem in a future conversation.

When he came to see me the following week he wondered aloud whether his self-esteem might have been damaged by having been expelled after four years in the monastery. He said he believed that he had gotten over it in about five months. Things had gone fairly well at his new part time job as janitor at a Catholic high school until he began to have a sense that people around him at his place of work were insincere and that they could actually read his mind. This same feeling then began to haunt him in college as well. I asked him whether this had ever happened to him in the monastery. He said it hadn't, but that he had gotten some bad feelings from some of the senior instructors there. He said they often spoke badly of the monks who had quit, explaining in detail to the classes how these deserters hadn't measured up spiritually. Luke remembered worrying that if he should ever leave the monastery he would then also be made into an example of a sinful deserter to be paraded in front of all the classes. Luke told me that some of the senior monks would pretend to be loving and kind and happy in their work when visitors came, but that in reality this was just a cheerful facade they put on and took off at will. They often made fun of visitors behind their backs, and they were openly disrespectful of their young students when there were no visitors about. Luke said it was this kind of hypocrisy which led him to question and eventually criticize the senior monks. He said his questions and criticisms were then turned back on him when the monks decided to define him as "a troublemaker" and "a problem in their ranks" that needed to be dealt with. When he was called into the Superior's office Luke was told that he was "prideful and weak" and that he had other shortcomings and failures that were sinful and reprehensible to God. But the Superior said he did not have the time to explain any further, and dismissed Luke from his office and from the monastery. Luke came to feel that these criticisms were not at all directed at his lack of effort in his religious studies; they were instead aimed directly at himself—at his spirit and his soul.

Luke's discussion with me about his experience of this cruelty from the Superior and the hypocritical posturing of the other senior monks made him think that perhaps his present feelings—that everyone around him is insincere and inauthentic—might be due to the negative experiences he had had in the monastery. He also came to see that life in the monastery had been so severely regimented that the senior monks would often know what he was about to do or say as though they could read his mind. He realized that this life in the monastery, and the brutal criticism from the Superior, had made him extremely self-conscious about a sinfulness in himself that God and all the other monks could see but which the Superior monk had refused to explain to him. So Luke asked me to please tell him if he should now take the way of Saint John of the Cross and simply accept a life of denial, suffering, and constant prayer. I suggested that before he does that he might want to think about what sort of God it is that would require him to endure such a difficult life.

When he came to see me next, Luke said he had had another paranoid experience in which he felt as though his thoughts had been broadcast on TV. He said he knew intellectually that this was not very likely, but he felt emotionally that perhaps God was doing this in order to "correct his thinking." I suggested that perhaps he was seeing meaning where there was none. I gave the example of a flower vase he has received as a gift which has no intrinsic meaning but in which he might see a great deal of meaning because of the personal value with which he had invested it. He agreed that this may have happened with his TV experience. He also said that his having been expelled from the monastery had led him to believe that this meant he was a bad person who had evil things hiding inside. So I suggested he consider for a moment the difference between the institutional rules that maintain the status quo in the monastery and his personal desire to remain true to his own spiritual principles. Yes, he had broken the rules but this didn't mean his personal spirituality was flawed or that he was sinful inside. And furthermore, while he had left his monastic studies did this mean he now had to enter a penitent's life of denial, suffering, and constant prayer as a form of punishment as suggested by the way of Saint John of the Cross? What sort of sadistic guy did he imagine God to be anyway? Would a loving heavenly Father send a misbehaving earthly child to hell to suffer for eternity? And would an all-knowing, super-intelligent being like God be forced to send people into purgatory because he can't make up his mind about them? These questions seemed to brighten Luke up, and we talked for quite some time about how Luke might imagine God to be, and about how, if God is a loving father, He may have meant for us to enjoy life here on earth in the present rather than living a life of denial and suffering in hopes of future rewards in heaven. I suggested he give this some more thought before our next conversation, but it turned out that this one would be our last.

He sent me an e-mail the following week in which he wrote in part,

> I am not going to be coming over this evening. The reason being, I figured out who God is for me, and the mind reading symptom has gone away. You were helpful with your advice, especially the advice about the flower vase, and me projecting meaning onto that vase, that it may have been my interpretation of things that led to my symptom of mind reading.

He later sent me another e-mail in which he said in part,

> I am at peace. I have no paranoia. . . . I can go places without worrying about what other people are thinking about me. And a lot more. You might be surprised but the thing that helped me the most from our conversations was the idea that I am free to believe what I want. Like the question you asked me, Who is God to you? I never thought I was "allowed" to do that. Growing up in a strict Catholic setting is restricting, and quite frankly, sucked big time.

And in another e-mail he wrote,

> You said in one of our conversations that me being a monk and facing rejection from the Superior may have been the straw that broke the camel's back. I am here to tell you that our conversations on the phone have not only restored everything broken but have set me on a path to transcendence and have opened me up to a world with infinite possibilities. I have never been happier.

Luke continued to occasionally touch base with me for several years after that just to let me know he was doing fine.

CASE #1: Annotated

The notes in *italics* below are topics or issues for possible further discussion, as well as various questions that arose but were never pursued during our sessions. Some occurred to me only after I had time to review my session notes. This doesn't mean that what was done was inadequate, only that there are various roads to the same goal. The particular choices I made resulted in a good outcome. Below are suggestions for alternative choices.

Luke said he was diagnosed with schizoaffective disorder and paranoia. After I spent some time researching the confusion, contradiction, and mystery surrounding Luke's diagnosis of schizoaffective disorder and paranoia, I decided that my best course of action was to find out more about Luke himself, to try to figure out just how much of his diagnosis was based on actual organic pathology and how much of his distress was perhaps the result of his life's circumstances.

What is entailed in a diagnosis like schizoaffective disorder and paranoia? What are the symptoms? How do the symptoms affect the ability to reason cogently, and how do they affect the emotions? What are the side effects of the medications he's taking? Does Luke have any medical conditions that might contribute to such a diagnosis? What is his life like now as compared to before the diagnosis? Is a diagnosis necessary for "treatment"? Does treatment have to be in the form of a medical approach? How else can schizophrenia be perceived and defined?

During our first session Luke told me that he was twenty-six years old, and that he was seeing a psychoanalyst who had put him on antidepressant medication. He said this psychoanalyst was unwilling to help him figure out what direction he ought to take in life because this is not what psychoanalysis is all about.

How does the anti-depressant medication alter how Luke feels? How does it make Luke feel when the psychoanalyst says, in effect, "I don't want to discuss what you feel you need to discuss"? What is psychoanalysis all about? How is "figuring out what direction you ought to take in life" accomplished? Does life have a direction? Can a person take life in any direction they wish? Is there only one "best" direction? What makes a direction good or bad? How does one choose which direction to take? What makes life good or bad?

I told Luke that I would be happy to help him but that I would first like to know a bit more about him. He told me his father and mother were very kind and supportive of him, as were both his younger and older brothers and sisters. He said his family was devoutly Catholic, and that his older brother is in fact an ordained priest whom he respects and admires, and with whom he sometimes has very stimulating theological discussions. Luke said he used to be "a party animal," but that he had gone to college and things had gone badly. He began to have paranoid thoughts, believing that people could tell what he was thinking. "Even now," he said, "it feels like people can read my mind." This was, of course, very troubling for him.

What does it mean to "be" Catholic? Does being Catholic make a person different from others? What is respect? Why do people want respect? Is respect something that everyone deserves? How does one get respect? Why does he respect and admire his brother for being an ordained priest? What does it mean to be a "party animal"? Why go to college? Is an education always a good thing? From metaphysics: what is the possibility or probability of mind reading? Would it be a good thing or a bad thing if people could read each other's minds? What is a mind? What is thinking, and how do we do it? Can only humans think? Would life be easier if we couldn't think, but only react to stimulus?

Luke used to work at a part-time job, and had lots of friends as well as a girlfriend, all of which he lost when he started to become paranoid. He now felt that everything positive is a lie, that there is sarcasm in every sentence, and that he has an "evil core."

What things in life are positive? How can something positive be a lie? This raises the question of the nature of the self: does everyone have a "core"? If so, where does it come from? Is it genetic or spiritual or both? Is this core a permanent thing, or can it be altered? If it can be altered, how would this be accomplished? What does it mean to have an "evil core"? What does it mean to be evil? What does it mean to be good? What are some of the ethical theories philosophers have devised to help people be good? What is it that makes you who you are?

I wondered where this might have come from, so I asked him what he had done before he went to college. He told me that before he spent the two years as a student he had actually been a Catholic monk living in a monastery for four years. It was only after he had left the monastery and entered college that he was first diagnosed with schizoaffective disorder and paranoia. He told me he had decided to become a monk at his older brother's urging, but that he had eventually been expelled.

Where do our ideas about ourselves come from, besides ourselves? How do this affect us? Which ones do we keep, and which ones do we disregard? How do we choose? What does it mean to live up to the expectations of others? Are the expectations of others always reasonable? Where do our own expectations of ourselves come from? Why do people go to college? What do they expect to get out of it? What are colleges meant to do? What do "schizoaffective disorder" and "paranoia" mean? What is their treatment and prognosis? Can they be defined and perceived any differently than by means of the so-called medical model?

I asked him why he had been expelled. What had happened in the monastery? He told me that he had at times questioned and even criticized his superiors and he was therefore accused by them of being dishonest, full of pride, and not sincere in his religious beliefs.

The topic of religious beliefs is enormous and includes everything from personal spirituality to the question of the nature of God, and to what religions are all about. Philosophy has a rich literature on religious topics. But here is a sampling of what can be discussed: What is the nature of the spiritual/religious self? What is the nature of authority in a religious system? When does authority become bullying? Do beginners, and should they, have the right to question superior monks? What is the purpose of a monastery? What is the goal of the person attending one? What is the difference between religious belief, indoctrination, and brain washing? Many religions say pride is a bad thing, but is it really? What does it mean to be sincere in your religious beliefs? Can you be spiritual without being religious? What does God want from us? What do religions want from believers?

He said that he had looked forward to the life of peace and contemplation his brother had promised would be his as a monk.

What does a life of peace entail? Does "peace" mean the same thing to everyone? How is a life of contemplation in a monastery different from contemplating elsewhere? How does expectation affect perception? How does reality compare to expectations? What are the different kinds of reality discussed by philosophers? Does everyone experience reality the same way? If not, then which one is the "real" reality? How do we know or judge what is real? What is the difference between reality and subjective experience? Is being a monk always the same experience for everyone? Is there only one road to every goal? What does it mean to be a monk and what is a monk's role? Are all monks the same? Should they be?

In fact when he first got into the monastery he felt very much at peace. He firmly believed this structured and orderly life was indeed the perfect life for him, so that when he was expelled it made him feel like he was the worst sort of failure.

Why does entering a monastery bring peace? What is desirable about structure in life? What is the nature of success and failure? Do they depend only on ourselves? What is the difference between blaming others, and finding them to be responsible? What rights and obligations are attached to being a monk? Are there good monks and bad monks?

With the approach of the end of our hour-long session I suggested we might want to discuss his self-esteem in a future conversation.

I often ask my clients what he or she would like to discuss next time, so that I'm not always setting the agenda. Where does self-esteem come from? Can you have too much as well as too little of it? Is self-esteem important? Why or why not? Does everyone require the same amount in order to be "normal"? Is men's self-esteem based on criteria that are different from women's criteria?

When he came to see me the following week he wondered aloud whether his self-esteem might have been damaged by having been expelled after four years in the monastery. He said he believed that he had gotten over it in about five months. Things had gone fairly well at his new part time job as janitor at a Catholic high school until he began to have a sense that people around him at his place of work were insincere, and that they could actually read his mind. This same feeling then began to haunt him in college as well.

How did he get over being expelled? What does being expelled mean? Is there a difference between a Catholic high school and a non-Catholic one? What does sincerity mean? Why is it important? What made him sense that people were insincere, and that they could read his mind? What does this "sense" consist of? What if people could actually read his mind, why does that bother him? What sort of things do we each have in our minds that we would not want others to have access to?

I asked him whether this (mind reading) had ever happened to him in the monastery. He said it hadn't, but that he had gotten some bad feelings from some of the senior instructors.

Is getting bad feelings the same as mind reading? What are bad feelings? Where do they come from? What purposes do they serve? What created the bad feelings he experienced? Are the good or bad feelings we experience always accurately connected to reality? How can you tell when a feeling is justified and correct? What can be done to rid oneself of bad feelings? Is it actually important to get rid of them?

He said they often spoke badly of the monks who had quit, explaining in detail to their classes how these deserters hadn't measured up spiritually.

The issue here is of blame and responsibility. Does quitting always make you a quitter? When is quitting justified? What makes a deserter? What does it mean to measure up spiritually? What does it mean to be spiritual? Who does the measuring? What gives them the right to measure? Can you measure your own spirituality accurately?

Luke remembered worrying that if he should ever leave the monastery he would then also be made into an example of a sinful deserter to be paraded in front of all the classes.

Why is leaving the monastery considered a sin? What is the definition of sin? Who has the authority to say what is a sin and what is not? Is leaving the monastery worse than never having been there in the first place? Is a threat a good way to ensure proper behavior? Who defines proper behavior? How does intimidation affect good reasoning?

Luke told me that some of the senior monks would pretend to be loving and kind and happy in their work when visitors came, but that in reality this was just a cheerful facade they put on and took off at will. They often made fun of visitors behind their backs, and they were openly disrespectful of their young students when there were no visitors about.

This raises the issue of authenticity. Also, how is it possible to judge the true nature of a person, especially one who acts differently from one moment to the next? Is a person's personality the same as their nature? Is there an intrinsic nature that babies are born with? Where does personality come from? What does it mean to be loving and kind to others? Do strangers rightfully deserve to be treated with love and kindness? Why is it wrong to make fun of someone when that person doesn't even know they're being made fun of? What does it mean to be respectful? Does everyone deserve respect? What is the right way to treat young students?

Luke said it was this kind of hypocrisy which led him to question and eventually criticize the senior monks. He said his questions and criticisms were then turned back on him when the monks decided to define him as "a troublemaker" and "a problem in their ranks" that needed to be dealt with. When he was called into the Superior's office Luke was told that he was "prideful and weak" and that he had other shortcomings and failures that were sinful and reprehensible to God.

What is hypocrisy? Is criticism always wrong? Does respect for superiors forbid criticism? What gave him the courage to criticize his superiors? What is courage? What does it mean to be inferior to a superior? Are there some cultures in which superiors are always considered right, regardless of what they do? Is this morally acceptable? What does it mean to be moral? What is the definition of a "troublemaker," a "problem in their ranks"? How does the military term "in their ranks" affect the discussion? And again, what is the definition of sin? What is pride? Is pride a good or bad thing? Who defines what human shortcomings and failures actually are?

But the Superior said he did not have the time to explain any further, and dismissed Luke from his office and the monastery. Luke came to feel that these criticisms were not at all directed at his lack of effort in his religious studies; they were instead aimed directly at himself—at his spirit and his soul.

What are the responsibilities of a superior? Should a superior always explain his actions to others? Is spirituality the same as religious knowledge? Is it possible to judge another person's spirit and soul? Isn't it understood that when you're part of an organization you should either obey its rules or leave? Who gets to interpret an organization's rules?

Luke's telling me about his experience of this cruelty from the Superior and the hypocritical posturing of the other senior monks made him think that perhaps his present feelings—that everyone around him is insincere and inauthentic—might be due to the negative experiences he had had in the monastery.

How is your perception of current reality affected by your past experiences? How accurate is our memory of past experiences? Why is hypocrisy considered wrong? When do negative experiences outweigh the positive? What does it mean to be "authentic" and "inauthentic"? The philosopher Jean-Paul Sartre has a lot to say about this topic.

He also came to see that life in the monastery had been so severely regimented that the senior monks would often know what he was about to do or say as though they could read his mind.

Is a regimented life beneficial or problematic? What is included in a regimented life? When does a regimented life become "severe"? How are predictions made? How can predictions be made based on the observation of routine behavior? Is saying "as though they could read his mind" the same as saying "mind reading"? Why is it worrisome that the others "would often know" what he was about to do or say? Is it better to be predictable or unpredictable? Is it important what others think, believe, or know about you?

He realized that this life in the monastery, and the brutal criticism from the Superior, had made him extremely self-conscious about a sinfulness in himself that God and all the other monks could see but which the Superior monk had refused to explain to him. So Luke asked me to please tell him if he should now take the way of Saint John of the Cross and accept a life of denial, suffering, and constant prayer. I suggested that before he does that he might want to think about what sort of God it is that would require him to endure such a difficult life.

What is self-consciousness all about? Are self-consciousness and self-awareness the same? Is it possible to know what God sees in people? The issue of sin and punishment: what is fair and just, especially given what is believed to be the loving nature of God? What have philosophers said about justice and fair decision-making? What is prayer all about? What is redemption? What is forgive-

ness? Does God demand suffering? There are many other religious issues in th passage that can be explored further.

When he came to see me next, Luke said he had had another parano experience in which he felt as though his thoughts had been broadcast o TV. He said he knew intellectually that this was not very likely, but he felt emotionally that perhaps God was doing this in order to correct his thinking.

What is the definition, and what are the symptoms of, paranoia? What is the difference between some event being possible, and it being likely? What is the difference between knowing, believing, and feeling? How is feeling affected by knowledge? How is knowledge affected by feelings? What constitutes "correct" thinking? How do we know what is a "true" experience and what is only imaginary? What does it mean to "experience" something?

I suggested that perhaps he was seeing meaning where there was none. I gave the example of a flower vase he has received as a gift which has no intrinsic meaning but in which he might see a great deal of meaning because of the personal value with which he had invested it. He agreed that this may have happened with his TV experience.

Again the issue here is the perception of reality. How does an object or person "acquire" meaning? What does it mean to see meaning where there is none? How is it possible to reconcile feeling that something is happening with knowing intellectually that this isn't possible? The issue of intrinsic meaning as opposed to attributed or perceived meaning is also a good discussion topic at this point.

He also said that his having been expelled from the monastery had led him to believe that this meant he was a bad person who had evil things hiding inside. So I suggested he consider for a moment the difference between the institutional rules that maintain the status quo in the monastery and his personal desire to remain true to his own spiritual principles.

Are there "evil things" hiding inside people? Are people either good or bad? What is the relationship between a person and an organization to which he or she belongs? What does "status quo" refer to? Who or what controls the status quo? Can it be altered? How does a person remain true to his own principles? The German philosopher Immanuel Kant had a lot to say about a person's duty to live up to his or her principles. Does living according to your own principles ensure a "good" life? What exactly is a good life? Is it the same for everyone? This can lead into a discussion about the relationship between political philosophy, religious organizations, ethical principles, moral behavior, and personal spirituality.

Yes, he had broken the rules but this didn't mean his personal spirituality was flawed or that he was sinful inside. And furthermore, while he had left his monastic studies did this mean he now had to enter a penitent's life of denial, suffering, and constant prayer as a form of punishment as suggested by the way of Saint John of the Cross? What sort of sadistic guy did he imagine God to be anyway? Would a loving heavenly Father send a misbehaving earthly child to hell to suffer for eternity? An would an all-knowing, super-intelligent being like God be forced to send people into purgatory because he can't make up his mind about them?

When does breaking the rules become sin? How are the rules of an organization related to personal spirituality? Can self-punishment absolve disobedience to rules, or sin? What is the purpose of prayer? What is the nature of God? Who has the authority to define the nature of God? How do they get this authority? How do they know what God's nature actually is? This discussion can lead to a dialogue between logic and religious doctrine.

These questions seemed to brighten Luke up, and we talked for quite some time about how Luke might imagine God to be, and about how, if God is a loving father, He may have meant for us to enjoy life here on earth in the present rather than living a life of denial and suffering in hopes of future rewards in heaven.

Is it possible, or even acceptable, to imagine what God is like? What does the Christian Bible say is the purpose of life? Note: This question is literally answered in the Bible book of Ecclesiastes. This discussion could include the various approaches to answering the question of the meaning or purpose of life. What does God want from us? Does all of life have to have an overall purpose? Is it the same for everyone? How does the promise of a future life in heaven affect how some people live their present lives on earth? Are the promise of heaven and the threat of hell necessary to make people "good"? What does it mean to be good?

I suggested he give this some more thought before our next conversation, but it turned out that this one would be our last. He sent me an e-mail the following week in which he wrote in part,

> I am not going to be calling this evening. The reason being, I figured out who God is for me, and the mind reading symptom has gone away. You were helpful with your advice, especially the advice about the flower vase and me projecting meaning onto that vase, that it may have been my interpretation of things that led to my symptom of mind reading.

Can a person's perception of God be equivalent to what God is "actually" like? Can God be one thing for one person and another thing for someone else? Can God be good for one person and totally bad for another? This part of our discussion also brings to light what in psychotherapy is called the client's internalizing, or accepting as his own, insights and conclusion reached during the discussion. Internalization raises the issue of how much of what happens in counseling and psychotherapy should be the client's own realization, and how much can be direct teaching, persuasion, or indoctrination by the counselor or therapist. In philosophy the client is helped to come to his own conclusions. This is what Socrates meant when he said he was a midwife who helped to bring the thoughts of others into the world. This is true to some extent in philosophical counseling and therapy as well. Of course the counselor or therapist who practices philosophy limits what thoughts she will help bring into this world to what is morally permissible, and—if it's a call to action—to what is reasonably possible. But the philosophical counselor or therapist also goes beyond "midwifery" and acts as a consultant who offers helpful insights and suggestions not previously considered by the client.

He later sent me another e-mail in which he said in part,

> I am at peace. I have no paranoia. . . . I can go places without worrying about what other people are thinking about me. And a lot more. You might be surprised but the thing that helped me the most from our conversations was the idea that I am free to believe what I want. Like the question you asked me, Who is God to you? I never thought I was "allowed" to do that. . . . Growing up in a strict Catholic setting is restricting, and quite frankly, sucked big time.

Issues which can be discussed further are the levels and limits to personal freedom or self-determination, the responsibility which comes with this freedom, and the "angst" or fear that comes with the recognition of that freedom. Are we born with inherent limits to our freedom? How do societal norms and laws—and religion—restrict our freedoms? These are themes central to political philosophy as well as the philosophical theory of existentialism. Who or what determines what we are "allowed" to do, and how is that determined?

And in another e-mail he wrote,

> You said in one of our conversations that me being a monk and facing rejection from the Superior may have been the straw that broke the camel's back. I am here to tell you that our conversations on the phone have not only restored everything broken but have set me on a path to transcendence and have opened me up to a world with infinite possibilities. I have never been happier.

That message arrived in my computer's mailbox in August of 2002. Luke continued to occasionally touch base with me for a few years after that just to let me know he was doing fine.

CASE #2: "KAY": AUTHENTICITY

This second case was conducted entirely by e-mail. A criticism often leveled against case studies presented in the social sciences literature is that the material selected to be presented as a case study by an author who is a therapist or counselor is typically biased and notoriously incomplete. In his essay "Traditional Case Studies and Prescriptions for Improving Them" Donald P. Spence writes,

> The typical case report tells a single story with heavy reliance on anecdote and narrative persuasion, and with a preference for what may be called singular explanation. The anecdotal nature of the typical case report reveals only the highlights of the clinical encounter, with few details; as a result, anyone who wants to assess whether a particular interpretation might have been formed differently or to decide whether

> a particular formulation could have been improved will have to look elsewhere.... The evidence is never so complete that we, as readers, can draw our own conclusions.... The closed texture of the case report effectively cuts off disagreement.... This state of affairs comes about because of the tendency for the case report to highlight the clinical happenings that seem to mesh with received theory and to underplay, or exclude entirely happenings that cannot be explained, that go against theoretical understanding, or that result in bad therapeutic outcomes. (p. 39)

Unlike a face-to-face counseling session in which notes are hand written by the counselor either during the meeting or afterwards from memory, in the case study presented below absolutely every word exchanged between the counselor and client has been included. The following series of dialogical e-mail messages are an attempt to offer a completely "open-textured" case study in philosophical counseling, one which has not been censored or edited. They are collected e-mail communications exchanged between myself and one client over the course of about five months. They are presented with permission.

I offer the following case study for two reasons: first, in order to reveal more than just a few carefully selected highlights of a counseling experience to anyone interested in studying this case; and second, to illustrate what I consider to be a successful instance of philosophical counseling by means of e-mail. The only deletions were a few very brief messages exchanged early on in which we discussed my fee, and in which I asked for time out while I was ill. The evidence is, for all intents and purposes, complete; the text is open, and you, the reader, are free to interpret it for yourself, and to draw your own conclusions. Of course, I have changed the client's name and those few details necessary to maintain confidentiality. The passages presented in *italics* are ones that have been forwarded from a preceding message.

Kay's first message:

> Hello,
> I found out your email address on your web site. I hope you don't mind my asking you a couple of questions.
> I am interested in finding someone to go to for philosophical counseling in my area, but I don't know if there is anyone. Is there a resource I could go to? Or, do you know of anyone in this area?
> I have been to several traditional counselors over the last several years, and none of them have been able to address my fundamental philosophical concerns. My dilemma can be summed up in one question, "How do I live a life of integrity when I am constantly forced to lie to people about who I really am?" (I am gay and very closeted; I live in a conservative rural area.)
> Thank you.

Kay.

My reply:

> Hi Kay,
> I don't know of any philosophical counselors in your area. It's a very new field and there aren't very many of us around yet.
> I appreciate the difficulties you're experiencing, and I agree with you that the issues you're grappling with are well suited to philosophical counseling. Since there aren't any philosophical counselors where you live, and we're too far apart to meet on a regular basis, I'd like to suggest discussion by e-mail. Although e-mail is obviously not as immediate as face-to-face dialogue, I think it's an ideal approach given the circumstances we find ourselves in.
> One negative aspect of e-mail counseling is the level of privacy you are allowed regarding your messages. In other words, please consider carefully whether anyone else will read your e-mails, and whether this matters to you or not.
> The positives of e-mail counseling are (1) it gives us time to read, re-read, and think about each other's messages; (2) we'll both have a permanent record of everything "said," something you don't get from face-to-face counseling, and (3) neither one of us has to worry about meeting at an appointed time since we can write whenever we please.
> If you're interested in going this route let me know and we can come to some sort of agreement and arrangement regarding my fee.
> Best regards,
> Peter

Kay's next message:

> Peter,
> I would like to consider doing the counseling by e-mail. What would your fees be? Thank you for your response.
> Kay.

We discussed a fee Kay could afford and then I wrote:

> Hi Kay,
> I think a good place to start would be for you to tell me more about yourself and the situation you find yourself in. Keep in mind that as you type you'll be able to see in front of you—right there in black and white—what it is you think and feel. This may give you insights that you may not have had before into what it is you believe.
> But don't just read your typing and then delete it before you send it to me. I need to follow your thinking, even when you've typed something and then changed your mind. In other words, don't censor yourself by trying to second-guess what you think might be useful and interesting to me. Let your thoughts flow freely and let them end up in your messages.
> I'm looking forward to receiving your first message
> Regards,

Peter

Kay's first counseling message to me:

> Okay, here goes. I grew up an only child with two loving parents. My parents have their quirks, as do any. My mother is very cold and unemotional. Whenever I did something to displease her as a child, she would give me the silent treatment. . . . which is very much worse than an argument, I think. But I always had everything I needed. They were very supportive of me academically, etc.
> I was a tomboy growing up. (No surprise, huh?) Mom tried to force me to wear pretty dresses and shoes, and I balked and wanted to wear jeans. I am a very sensitive person, and somehow that must have shown. The neighborhood kids used to tease me ruthlessly. I was not your typical tough tomboy. I guess they knew they could take advantage of my naiveté. They often tricked me by telling me one thing, watching me fall for it, and laughing all over themselves. I learned not to trust people very much.
> That was reinforced by my parents. They were and are to this day very reclusive people. They don't make friends easily, and what friends they have had have "betrayed" them in some way and they don't see them any more. I find, unfortunately, that I am very much like that now as well. I knew as a child that I was different—not in the sense of being gay—just different. I liked to read. I was into archaeology. Though I was into different interests, I always tried like crazy to fit in. When I was in junior high, I had my first crushes on girls. I even wrote about them in my journals. I still have those journals. I can go back and look at what I wrote then. But I had no role models. The only gay teacher there was, of course, was the gym coach who was one of those people that everyone whispered about behind her back. Who would want to be like that?
> Throughout high school, I dated boys. When I was eighteen, I met a nice guy with whom I could enjoy doing a lot of things. Our relationship got serious. We got engaged. I remember distinctly a voice in my head questioning this. It said, what about your attraction to women? Oh, that will go away, another part of me thought.
> So, we got married. We were married for quite a few years. He and I were great companions. We enjoyed camping, concerts, reading. . . . but as time went on, we had virtually no sex life. Eventually we began to have some tentative discussions about this. After about a year of struggle, I realized and finally admitted to myself that I was indeed gay.
> It was a wrenching experience for us to separate and eventually divorce. But we knew it was the right thing to do. (We didn't have children.) He went on to remarry. I went on to. . . . well, I've been stripped of the right to marry. . . . (much bitterness about that is what I'm feeling as I type that). . . . but I have a wonderful partner with whom I've been for 3 years now.

At first, it felt liberating to admit who I am and to celebrate it . . . and then reality hit, and I realized that the world does not celebrate who I am with me. Society hates who I am. That is devastating to me. I've always had trouble fitting in anyway, and now. . . . I don't fit in at all. I used to be able to talk about my personal life. "My husband and I went camping last weekend . . . blah, blah, blah. . . . "

Now, I censor myself. Can I say I did something with my partner to this person? Are they gay-friendly? Will they disapprove of me? Fortunately, my parents accepted my coming out to them. They like my partner very much. But they are of the opinion that it's something we don't need to talk about.

I was used to having certain freedoms that I now don't have. I used to hold hands with my husband or put my arm around him in public. I can't do that now. And it makes me angry. It makes me angry to have to hide this part of myself. I have always considered myself a good person. I am kind, sincere, thoughtful. I have a right to live on this planet too. But because I am gay I feel like I am a second class citizen. My integrity is compromised daily because I lie about myself daily. I had to learn how to lie. I have never been good at lying. People could always tell by the expression on my face if I tried to lie about something.

Here are a couple of quotations that sum it up nicely for me: "Character cannot be summoned at the moment of crisis if it has been squandered by many years of compromise and rationalization. The only testing ground for the heroic is the mundane. The only preparation for that one profound decision which can change a life is those hundreds of self-defining seemingly insignificant decisions made in private. Habit is the daily battleground of character." Senator Dan Coats.

"Character is always lost when a high ideal is sacrificed on the alter of conformity and popularity." Anonymous

I feel that by keeping myself closeted and lying about myself, I daily erode away my character and my self respect. But I am afraid to be open. . . .

Kay.

My reply:

Hi Kay,

You wrote:

That was reinforced by my parents. They were and are to this day very reclusive people. They don't make friends easily, and what friends they have had have "betrayed" them in some way and they don't see them any more. I find, unfortunately, that I am very much like that now as well.

There's not much I can do for your parents, unless of course they decide to get counseling from me. So our focus will be on you. Although your parents reinforced certain behaviour in you, it doesn't mean you're destined to either remain the way you are or that you are doomed to become like your parents. I understand that you must realize this to a certain extent already or you wouldn't have approached me for counseling. I'd like to ask you a bunch of questions to make sure I've understood correctly what you wrote in your message. You wrote...

I knew as a child that I was different—not in the sense of being gay—just different. I liked to read. I was in to archaeology. Though I was in to different interests, I always tried like crazy to fit in. When I was in junior high, I had my first crushes on girls. I even wrote about them in my journals. I still have those journals. I can go back and look at what I wrote then. But I had no role models. The only gay teacher there was, of course, was the gym coach who was one of those people that everyone whispered about behind her back. Who would want to be like that?

Why do you think your gym coach was gay?

What was it about your gym coach you wouldn't want to be like?

Throughout high school, I dated boys. When I was eighteen, I met a nice guy with whom I could enjoy doing a lot of things. Our relationship got serious. We got engaged. I remember distinctly a voice in my head questioning this. It said, what about your attraction to women? --Oh, that will go away, another part of me thought.

So, we got married. We were married for a number of years. He and I were great companions. We enjoyed camping, concerts, reading. . . . but as time went on, we had virtually no sex life. Eventually we began to have some tentative discussions about this. After about a year of struggle, I realized and finally admitted to myself that I was indeed gay.

It was a wrenching experience for us to separate and eventually divorce. But we knew it was the right thing to do.

Why did you consider your separation and divorce "the right thing to do?"

(We didn't have children.) He went on to remarry. I went on to . . . well, I've been stripped of the right to marry. . . . (much bitterness about that is what I'm feeling as I type that). . . . but I have a wonderful partner with whom I've been for 3 years now.

When you say you've been "stripped of the right to marry" I assume you mean the right to a legal marriage and ceremony. Is this what you mean? After all, it seems to me you're living in a common law marriage arrangement which is the marriage of choice for many thousands of heterosexual couples. But I assume you're saying you'd like to be able to have a legal marriage if your state allowed it? Why is this important to you?

At first, it felt liberating to admit who I am and to celebrate it. . . . and then reality hit, and I realized that the world does not celebrate who I am with me. Society hates who I am.

I'm not sure all of society hates who you are. I certainly don't. So who do you mean when you say society hates who you are?

That is devastating to me. I've always had trouble fitting in anyway, and now. . . . I don't fit in at all. I used to be able to talk about my personal life. "My husband and I went camping last weekend. . . . blah, blah, blah. . . ." Now, I censor myself. Can I say I did something with my partner to this person? Are they gay-friendly? Will they disapprove of me?

It seems like you're suggesting here that if someone is not "gay-friendly" and they disapprove of you that this is somehow your problem, something you ought to be concerned about, something you ought to censor in yourself. Why?

When you ask, "Will they disapprove of me?" do you mean will they disapprove of you as a total person or just your gayness? Do people disapprove of all of you just because of your gayness?

Do you have friends who know you're gay?

Do you have friends who don't know you're gay?

Fortunately, my parents accepted my coming out to them. They like my partner very much. But they are of the opinion that it's something we don't need to talk about.

When you say your parents accept your coming out but feel it's not something you need to talk about, do you mean they don't need to talk about it or you don't need to talk about it?

Or are you inferring that they don't want to talk about it?

I was used to having certain freedoms that I now don't have. I used to hold hands with my husband or put my arm around him in public. I can't do that now. And it makes me angry. It makes me angry to have to hide this part of myself. I have always considered myself a good person. I am kind, sincere, thoughtful. I have a right to live on this planet too. But because I am gay I feel like I am a second class citizen. My integrity is compromised daily because I lie about myself daily. I had to learn how to lie. I have never been good at lying. People could always tell by the expression on my face if I tried to lie about something.

I don't understand why you say you have to lie about yourself. How do you know your community is that opposed to the idea of a gay couple?

Here are a couple of quotations that sum it up nicely for me:

"Character cannot be summoned at the moment of crisis if it has been squandered by many years of compromise and rationalization. The only testing ground for the heroic is the mundane. The only preparation for that one profound decision which can change a life is those hundreds of self-defining seemingly insignificant decisions made in private. Habit is the daily battleground of character." Senator Dan Coats.

Do you think concealing your gayness from strangers is the same as lying from habit?

"Character is always lost when a high ideal is sacrificed on the alter of conformity and popularity." Anonymous

I assume you would argue that the "high ideal" in your case would be telling the truth about your sexual orientation to everyone. The 17th century German philosopher Immanuel Kant also claimed that in order to be a morally upright person one should always live by the categorical imperative (a principle that cannot be compromised) "never tell a lie." But he forgot to consider the cost of telling the absolute truth on every occasion. I'm sure you can think of situations in which not telling the absolute truth is by far the more kind or sensible thing to do. In other words, I'm sure you can imagine situations in which the price of truth is too high and an avoidance of truth is deemed more morally acceptable. What would be the price you would have to pay if you were to always tell the truth about your sexuality?

I feel that by keeping myself closeted and lying about myself, I daily erode away my character and my self respect.

I can imagine that your situation must be hard on you. But, although I agree that your self-respect is probably suffering, I'm not sure your character is being eroded away. Again, do you think your avoidance of mentioning your sexuality is the same as being a habitual liar?

But I am afraid to be open. . . .

What do you think will happen?

Take care,

Peter

Kay's second message to me:

Thanks for your questions. They have given me good food for thought. You wrote:

Why do you think your gym coach was gay?

What was it about your gym coach you wouldn't want to be like?

I grew up in a small town, and everybody around town seemed to know that she and her lover lived in their own house together. What I don't want to be like is the way these lesbian women seem to have to keep to themselves. They didn't socialize within the community. They may have had lesbian and gay friends outside of the community. They, of course, did not discuss their personal lives. This particular coach never mentioned her significant other, in contrast to the way other teachers might mention their husbands or wives. For five years my then-husband and I worked in a rural, conservative US town. We knew of two lesbians who taught in the public school system. They were extremely reclusive. People laughed and talked about them behind their backs. It's just that I look at my life right now and I think that I personify that same thing. I didn't want to grow up to be a reclusive (outcast) lesbian that people laugh about behind my back. I surmised that one reason these women were so private is that they were probably afraid and aware of the criticism they received, so they tried to stay out of the public's eye as much as possible.

Why did you consider your separation and divorce "the right thing to do?"

I firmly believe that being gay is genetic. My parents were not any different than anyone else's. I did not "become" gay. I just always was. One of my cousins is gay as well. Once I had admitted to myself that I was gay, I could no longer in any way pretend to be straight. To remain married would have been wrong because it would have denied my husband a chance at a normal straight relationship with a woman who likes sex with a man. And it would have denied me the chance to express my sexuality naturally. If we had had children, the situation might have been different. We got along okay, so we might have stayed together for the sake of the children, until they were grown. But, we weren't in that situation. My husband had very low self-esteem sexually and physically while he was with me. He wondered what was wrong with him. After I admitted to being gay, we both realized that there was nothing wrong with him or me, for that matter. His desire for sex was normal; and mine was normal. But we weren't compatible sexually. We had hoped at first that maybe we could remain married, in spite of our incompatibility. But sex is a big part of a marriage. We loved each other very much, but we also both wanted a loving and fulfilling sex life. So, we amicably divorced.

But I assume you're saying you'd like to be able to have a legal marriage if your state allowed it? Why is this important to you?
I feel now that I live in a shadow world—not fully a part of society. When I was to marry my husband, I was able figuratively to "shout it from the rooftops." Now, it is like a dirty little secret. Yes, I would want a legal marriage. I am a traditional person. I value commitment. I value ceremony. My partner and I have considered having a commitment ceremony, but we are afraid to. Her brother and sister-in-law live in the same small town. He is a respected member of the community and would be embarrassed by our doing such a thing. His family would probably not attend. We have no other relatives nearby. It's just not worth the hassle, I guess. If we were a straight couple, we could count on everyone's support and willingness to celebrate our bond. But, it just isn't like that for some gay couples.

I'm not sure all of society hates who you are. I certainly don't. So who do you mean when you say society hates who you are?
The religious conservatives really get under my skin. I am very sensitive to criticism in the first place, and I tend to take their condemnation of gays very personally. I wish I wouldn't. When I go out, I guess I take my bitterness out on straight people (inside my head). I resent them for the freedoms they take for granted. I project my fear of homophobia onto practically every straight person I see. Yes, most of them probably are not homophobic, but I assume that they all are, and I assume a defensive posture, in other words, not revealing anything about my personal life, for fear that they are one of those homophobes that are "out to get me." I don't want you to think that I'm extremely paranoid. But hyper-sensitive, yes.

It seems like you're suggesting here that if someone is not "gay-friendly" and they disapprove of you that this is somehow your problem, something you ought to be concerned about, something you ought to censor in yourself. Why? When you ask, "Will they disapprove of me?" do you mean will they disapprove of you as a total person or just your gayness? Do people disapprove of all of you just because of your gayness?
Do you have friends who know you're gay?
Do you have friends who don't know you're gay?
I have heard people say that often once you are older, you stop caring as much about what other people think of you. I wish I could get to that point right now! I am afraid of not being liked, in general. I always watch what I say to ensure I haven't stepped on anyone's toes. Well, being gay compounds this. I want to be liked. I fear that people who like me now would reject me if I told them I am gay. I have a major area in my life in which I am closeted. I am in a military reserves unit. I love

the organization. We are a civilian arm of the armed forces. We do wear military style uniforms, however. Because of the quasi military nature of this organization, I have not come out to any of my friends in the unit. As you know, our military enforces a "don't ask, don't tell" policy towards gays. Although we are civilians, I have assumed that I simply cannot tell anyone that I am gay. It gets difficult sometimes. We have social events in which we are supposed to invite our spouses.... I always come alone. The irony is, sometimes when it is a potluck, my partner prepares the dish that I bring.... even though she can't come. I hate being in such a situation. I am proud of my partner. I love her. I would love for her to be involved, but what can I do?

When you say your parents accept your coming out but feel it's not something you need to talk about, do you mean they don't need to talk about it or you don't need to talk about it? Or are you inferring that they don't want to talk about it?

Both. I think they feel frustrated with the situation for gays too, but they are helpless to do anything to change it, so why waste time talking about it? They are very closeted as well. They don't discuss my partner with anyone. I would imagine that when they talk about me to friends and colleagues, they omit details that involve my partner.... which effectively negates her existence. And that angers me. But I know that they too are afraid of the homophobes.

I don't understand why you say you have to lie about yourself. How do you know your community is that opposed to the idea of a gay couple?

I have taken what my partner's brother said to us when we were getting ready to move up here to heart. We used to live in a different state. We moved here because her brother had a house we could rent, and we were tired of the southern heat. When he talked to us on the phone, he warned us not to come up here waving our gay pride flags. (He said that in a joking tone, but we knew he was not joking.) After we had lived here for about six months, we also had a little falling out with her sister's family because my partner had talked to one of their teenage daughters about gay issues (the marriage issue, children, etc.). Her sister told us we were not to talk about it any more. So, I've taken her attitude to be reflective of this whole town. My partner's sister and her husband have lived here for over 20 years.

Do you think concealing your gayness from strangers is the same as lying from habit? ... do you think your avoidance of mentioning your sexuality is the same as being a habitual liar?

I see what you mean. No, I don't think it is the same as being a habitual liar. But it still makes me uncomfortable to lie (or omit telling) in situations where straight people are so free. I am always running a compare/contrast program in my head. "This is something I used to be able to freely say.... now I cannot." My partner doesn't have this problem as much as I do because she's never been in a straight relationship and has never experienced those freedoms. She has never talked about her partners in public. She has never held hands in public, etc. She is more used to this hidden way of doing things than I am. But I am stubborn.... I don't think I can ever get used to it.

> *What would be the price you would have to pay if you were to always tell the truth about your sexuality?*
>
> I would have to accept rejection from some people. I also think I would be rewarded with wonderful acceptance from some people as well. But in the case of the military reserves, I feel really stuck because I don't want to be kicked out. I don't think they would blatantly kick me out, but maybe they might use other more subtle ways of ostracizing me to the point where I just stop going. I am afraid to find out.
>
> You have seen the words "fear" and "afraid" a lot in this email. I don't like being afraid. I want to be strong and courageous as I know I am deep down inside. How do I bring that part of me out?
>
> Thanks.
>
> Kay.

At this point I informed Kay that I would need a little time to recover from what seemed to be a cold coming on that was negatively affecting my ability to think clearly.

My eventual reply:

> Hi Kay,
>
> Well, the little head cold I told you about in the short message I sent you a while ago developed into a raging case of the flu that has lasted for the past two weeks. Happily I'm now back to being as "normal" as I ever get. Thanks for your patience. Here are a few observations and questions.
>
> You wrote:
>
> *. . . We knew of two lesbians who taught in the public school system. They were extremely reclusive. People laughed and talked about them behind their backs. It's just that I look at my life right now and I think that I personify that same thing. I didn't want to grow up to be a reclusive (outcast) lesbian that people laugh about behind my back. I surmised that one reason these women were so private is that they were probably afraid and aware of the criticism they received, so they tried to stay out of the public's eye as much as possible.*
>
> What you describe here is very similar to what is encountered by anyone who is being bullied. They find themselves in a vicious circle: bullies criticize them and laugh at their discomfort behind their backs, so they become reclusive, and the bullies are encouraged to make even more fun of them behind their backs. . . and so on. It's a no-win situation for the individuals being bullied (the victim). The concept of "gay pride," which is very strong here in Vancouver, hasn't eliminated the "bullies" who make fun of gays, but it has allowed gays not to back down and hide from criticism. Gay pride is about being proud of who you are and being able to look the bully straight in the eye and say, "What gives you the right to judge me?" (Remember also that those people who condemn gays the loudest are often those who are the most insecure about their own sexual identity.) It allows you to resist accepting the feeling of shame and discomfort the bully wants you to accept. It prevents you from becoming reclusive and thereby inviting the bullies to talk behind your back.

I agree with your assessment of gayness. I'm convinced it's genetic. To argue that gayness is a decision you make is as nonsensical as arguing that heterosexuality is a decision you make. In discussing gayness with students who think gay sexuality is a choice I always enjoy seeing their reactions when I ask them, "So what made you decide to become a heterosexual?"
The religious conservatives really get under my skin.
They get under my skin too, and I'm not gay. But I can't assume your reasons are the same as mine. Let me ask you, Why do they get under your skin?
I want to be liked. I fear that people who like me now would reject me if I told them I am gay.
Are people who reject gays the kind of people you want to like you in the first place?
Because of the quasi military nature of this organization, I have not come out to any of my friends in the auxiliary. As you know, our military enforces a "don't ask, don't tell" policy towards gays. . . . I hate being in such a situation. I am proud of my partner. I love her. I would love for her to be involved, but what can I do?
I'm not sure I understand the "don't ask, don't tell policy" in all its subtleties. Why can't you simply bring your partner to a potluck meal without literally telling anyone you're in fact a gay couple? If they draw their own conclusion that perhaps you're a gay couple, would that constitute having "told"?
I think they (parents) feel frustrated with the situation for gays too, but they are helpless to do anything to change it, so why waste time talking about it? They are very closeted as well.
People in our society simply avoid talking about all sorts of things that make them uncomfortable like aging, death, suicide, physical disfigurement, mental illness, sex, and so on. In your case—if your parents were raised in a conservative household—your parents' discomfort is probably a combination of discomfort with the whole topic of sex in general, and then this strange (to them) kind of sexual orientation you are part of. One way for your parents to become less closeted is for you to initiate conversations with them at home on the topic of sexuality and your own sexual orientation, encouraging them to use what may be "difficult" words for them to say such as "love," "sex," and "homosexual." It won't be until they become comfortable with the language of sexuality in general and gayness in particular in their own home that they'll be able to discuss it openly with others.
I have taken what my partner's brother said to us when we were getting ready to move up here to heart. . . . When he talked to us on the phone, he warned us not to come up here waving our gay pride flags. . . . So, I've taken her attitude to be reflective of this whole town. My partner's sister and her husband have lived here for over 20 years.
What makes you think your partner's brother-in-law's homophobia reflects the attitude of everyone in town?
Do you think having a commitment ceremony or admitting you're a gay couple when asked is "Waving your gay pride flag?" Also, did you

know that statistically speaking two percent of any population is gay? This means that there's a good chance that two percent of the population of your town is gay. Do you know any other gays in your town? It also means that if gayness is kept silent in your town then the "tyranny of the majority" (as Plato called it) has kept two percent of the population from leading self-respecting lives.

I would have to accept rejection from some people. I also think I would be rewarded with wonderful acceptance from some people as well. But in the case of the military reserve, I feel really stuck because I don't want to be kicked out. I don't think they would blatantly kick me out, but maybe they might use other more subtle ways of ostracizing me to the point where I just stop going. I am afraid to find out.

Why are you afraid to find out? What are the possible consequences to you personally?

Also, isn't your fear a bit like wanting to have your cake and eat it too? You seem to want to be open about your gayness within an organization which you say will not allow you to be open about your gayness. There seem to be only two alternatives available to you: (1) quit the reserve and be open about your gayness; or (2) continue to be secretive about your gayness and remain within the reserve. I can't see how you could change the military. Or am I missing some other alternatives?

You have seen the words "fear" and "afraid" a lot in this email. I don't like being afraid. I want to be strong and courageous as I know I am deep down inside. How do I bring that part of me out?

It seems to me you used the word "fear" and "afraid" in connection with the imagined possible outcomes of certain actions. My question to you is, how much do you want to be able to be a couple in public with your partner? What price are you willing to pay—lose a couple of homophobic friends; be rejected by your partner's brother-in-law; move out of town; upset your parents; be dismissed from the military reserve; and so on? At what point does it stop being worth it?

It seems to me that you don't lack strength or courage as such (you say you know you are strong and courageous deep down inside). It seems to me you are simply hesitant to act when you're unsure of exactly what is the best thing to do. In other words, the strength and courage to act comes from knowing what action to take. I think your strength and courage will grow as we continue to examine your situation.

Regards,
Peter

Kay's third message to me:

I am reading a book right now that has given me some new insights into my behavior. It's called "The Highly Sensitive Person" by Elaine N. Aron. I have always been very sensitive, both in the word's positive and negative connotations. I am very observant of things around me — people's moods, subtleties. I have always been a deep thinker. My mother is also that way. We have always felt we were a bit different from a lot of people in the world. We enjoy, for example, discussing philosophy in our conversations. Many people are indifferent to such topics. On the negative side, I am sensitive to people's moods to the extent of taking on their moods or of feeling responsible for their moods. I am more sensitive to noise and crowds than some. I can't "shop 'til I drop." I have to stop and get out of the crowds and have a cup of coffee to regain my calm. (Perhaps caffeine is not the best idea!!!) But, with regard to my coming out problems, I think my sensitivity to other people's feelings gives me more difficulty with this issue than it might for someone else. I am glad to be a sensitive person. I have for many years wanted to change myself into a bold person, but I am learning to accept myself for the way I am and to realize that sensitivity is a gift.

The book talks about sensitive people's difficulties in social situations (being shy, not initiating conversations easily, being uncomfortable in large groups, etc.). The author suggests the "putting on of a persona." Of course, the first thought that went through my head is that that is insincere. But she goes on to explain that having a persona is a very normal thing to the Europeans but is more difficult for Americans to understand. (We want to be always genuine and open.) A German banker, for example, has his or her banking persona, which is taken off when they get home from work.

I thought about applying that idea to my military experience. I could put on a "Kay's military reserve" persona when I am on duty. My persona would be at a different level than the other reserve members' because they are able to be more open about their spouses than I am. I would simply have to accept that my persona chooses not to discuss personal matters. I understand, too, that others in my reserve unit also choose not to discuss their personal lives for whatever reason. Some do; some don't. I think that such an arrangement with myself will assuage my inner "I-desire-to-be-open-to-everyone" self. With this persona, I will be able to set boundaries and be comfortable with it.

I have been to Europe, and now that I think about it, when we Americans claim that Europeans are not very friendly, perhaps that is just because we are seeing them with their "personas" on, so to speak. The banker or the cashier persona is professional and more detached emotionally. Personally, among their friends, these same people are probably very friendly.

You are right, though, about my taking my partner to some military functions and not telling them anything personal. I could simply introduce her as my friend or even my "partner" and let them draw their own conclusions. She and I are also business partners, so they wouldn't be quite sure what I meant. I guess I could live with that. I'm still not completely happy with such mental gymnastics, but I know I have to do something so that I don't suffer as much from this conundrum.

The religious right gets under my skin because I take their insults personally. I feel that I am a good person, and when they say that I am going to go to hell, it makes me angry. In a way, though, I am better now at ignoring them because I don't believe in hell anyway—at least not their version of it—so I am not concerned with their threats.

You have given me some food for thought on initiating or stimulating gay-related conversation topics with my parents. It is true. How could they ever talk about such topics with anyone else outside the home if they're uncomfortable with it within the home? I am taking a trip next week to visit them. I will try to insert the topic into the conversation when there seems to be an opening and also do that in my e-mails to them.

Regarding the homophobia of the small town in which we live: I probably overstate the town's homophobia. One of the elected council members in this town is gay. People know about it, and they don't seem to care. On the other hand, I still feel a need to keep it low key. If we did have a commitment ceremony, I don't think we would put an announcement in the newspaper. In the long term, however, I think my partner and I will eventually move to a more metropolitan area. The city we live closest to is a bit too expensive for us at the moment, but we are considering moving closer to it. Perhaps to live on the outskirts and be able to go in to the city for socializing. There are other gays here in our town but since they are as closeted as we are, we haven't met any of them.

Strength and courage are easier when the decisions are cut and dried, black and white. Being gay in our world is a big gray area. I think that is what is hard for me to come to terms with. What do you think of this "persona" idea? I think it would help me to see my way of being more concretely in the military reserve and would take the ambiguity out of the situation for me. That would put me more at ease.

Kay.

My reply:

Hi Kay,

I'm happy to hear that Elaine Aron's book is giving you an insight into your sensitivity. But I worry a little about a couple of things you say you've found in her book:

1) I'm not sure I agree with her generalization about Europeans being unfriendly in public. My experience is very different. I found Germans to be very friendly in public when I attended a conference in a small town near Cologne there last year, and yet I found New Yorkers rather unfriendly when I was there two years ago. But I'm also generalizing from my own experiences in a small town and the big city of New York. And it's a mistake to generalize from some Germans (or New Yorkers) to all. It's also a mistake to assume that someone else would have the same experiences that I had.

2) I talk very differently on the phone with my son, with a student, with my wife, with a client, and with a stranger. But are these different "personas" that I'm putting on? Some writers have talked about the "masks" we put on and take off. I'm not sure this is what I do. I don't change that much as a person between the time I talk with my wife and I talk with a stranger. What I am doing is adjusting the way I relate to individuals based on my relationships to them. We all do this. We act

differently with people we feel equal to, people we feel inferior and superior to, people we love, and so on. The trouble is, when I feel inferior to a person this can lead me to act in a way I wish I didn't. A temporary solution to this may be to put on a mask or a persona to help me act less inferior. But another, and perhaps better solution, is to determine why I feel inferior to this person (or this type of person) and change my feelings of inferiority by seeing myself differently. By changing my feelings about myself it will change the way I act.

Here's a typical example: a heterosexual young man might find it terribly difficult to talk with a young woman. The reason is because he lacks self-confidence; he feels unworthy of her attention. Putting on a bold persona might help him get through the situation, but it might also be seen by the young woman as a "put-on." Will putting on the persona in this situation help him make friends with the young woman? Will it help him in dealing appropriately with similar situations in future? Will the persona make him feel more worthy? And how long will he be able to sustain the persona?

I have for many years wanted to change myself into a bold person, but I am learning to accept myself for the way I am and to realize that sensitivity is a gift.

In light of what I've said above, can you see that it's not simply a matter of changing yourself into a bold person by force of will? It requires that you change your beliefs of being somehow inferior to others into feelings of equality. The "bold person" you are will emerge on its own accord when you begin to believe that you actually are worthy.

The book talks about sensitive people's difficulties in social situations (being shy, not initiating conversations easily, being uncomfortable in large groups, etc.). The author suggests the "putting on of a persona."

Again, being shy, not initiating conversations easily, being uncomfortable in large groups, and so on are all a function of considering yourself inferior to those around you. It's a matter of lacking self-worth (or self-confidence) not a matter of having the wrong persona on at the time. Putting on a persona is like fooling yourself into thinking you're better than you actually believe. But fooling yourself only works for so long. What you need is to be convinced that living according to who you are is good enough regardless of what others say. This is being true to yourself. This is what the philosophers like Jean-Paul Sartre and Charles Taylor mean by the term "authenticity."

In his book *The Ethics Of Authenticity* (Cambridge, Mass.: Harvard University Press, 1991) Charles Taylor says that each of us has an original way of being human. Each person has his or her own "measure."

... There is a certain way of being human that is *my* way. I am called upon to live my life in this way, and not in imitation of anyone else's. But this gives a new importance to being true to myself. If I am not, I miss the point of my life, I miss what being human is for me. . . . Not only should I not fit my life to the demands of external conformity; I can't even find the model to live by outside myself. I can only find it within. Being true to myself means being true to my own originality. . . . This is the background understanding to the modern ideal of authenticity (28-29).

Being true to yourself is being unashamed of being either black or white, male or female, rich or poor, heterosexual or homosexual. It means feeling worthy of who and what you are regardless of so-called social "norms."

You have given me some food for thought on initiating or stimulating gay-related conversation topics with my parents. It is true. How could they ever talk about such topics with anyone else outside the home if they uncomfortable with it within the home. I am taking a trip to Texas next week to visit them. I will try to insert the topic into the conversation when there seems to be an opening and also do that in my e-mails to them.

May I suggest that you can help make this easier for your parents by letting them know how important it is for you, and how much you need to be able to talk openly with them about yourself. The reason for this is because, as Taylor says,

"an original identity needs and is vulnerable to the recognition given or withheld by significant others. . . . Love relationships (and this includes family) are. . . . crucial because they are the crucibles of inwardly generated identity" (49).

In other words, if you want to become self-confident it can only come by being true to your authentic self. But although this authentic self comes from inside you it can be negatively or positively affected by significant others. It is therefore important that your parents not only put up with or tolerate your gayness, but that they accept you as worthy and good. And this involves allowing you to talk with them about what's important to you in your life

The religious right gets under my skin because I take their insults personally. I feel that I am a good person, and when they say that I am going to go to hell, it makes me angry. In a way, though, I am better now at ignoring them because I don't believe in hell anyway—at least not their version of it—so I am not concerned with their threats.

Ignoring the intellectual bully is one way to deal with "him." Another way is to fight back even if only within your own mind. The religious right contradicts its own beliefs when they attack gays. There are any number of blatant flaws in their anti-gay arguments I could point out to you, and I'd be happy to deal with any specific arguments you care to discuss with me. But here's a couple for starters: The religious right says that God will send gays straight to hell. The problem with this is that a supposedly perfect God is said to be admitting he created an evil or a mistake (the gay person). God is in a sense condemning his own creation—a creation which in Genesis he said was all "good." Also . . . if God created you gay, how could He then blame you for being gay and send you to hell? It makes no sense. If they want to argue that you're going to hell because you "chose" to be gay, then they run into another problem. . . . If God created us with free will (able to choose), and you chose to be gay, why is He condemning the choice you freely made according to the free choice which He allowed you to have? If He meant you to be straight, why allow you a choice? I could go on and on, but you get the idea. By the way, I love discussing the religious right's arguments against gays. They're all so bad—full of fallacies and contradictions!

Another "by the way," despite what the religious right says about Americans hating homosexuals, a recent government survey has shown that in fact 84% of Americans approve of Congress passing laws which guarantee equal rights for gays.

Regarding the homophobia of the small town in which we live: I probably overstate the town's homophobia. One of the elected council members at one of the schools here is gay. People know about it, and they don't seem to care. . . . There are other gays here in our town but since they are as closeted as we are, we haven't met any of them.

I'm glad to hear that you may have overstated the case. What about starting a "support group" (or something similar) for gays in your community?

Strength and courage are easier when the decisions are cut and dried, black and white. Being gay in our world is a big gray area. I think that is what is hard for me to come to terms with. What do you think of this "persona" idea? I think it would help me to see my way of being more concretely in the military reserve and would take the ambiguity out of the situation for me. That would put me more at ease.

If you think using the idea of "persona" will help you, then by all means go ahead and try it. But I think your strength and courage to be yourself will grow as you become more sure of the fact that you're a decent person just the way you are. The more you believe this, the less shy you will be, and the more you'll be able to be more comfortable and even outgoing in public. I hope this message gets to you before you begin your travels. Have a great trip.

Best regards,
Peter

Kay's fourth message to me:

Peter,
Sorry it has taken me so long to reply to you. I returned from my trip a couple of weeks ago and then dove right back into the business. I saw that you visited our web site and signed the guest book. Thank you! We had some problems while our computer was down, but now it is fixed, and we are going full steam ahead. We sell most of our items via an Internet auction site, and we are doing well with that. Recently, we placed an item up for auction. I think we started the bidding at $50.00. The auction ended at $575.50!!! We were astounded. . . . and very pleased.

I had a nice visit with my parents. Talking about gay issues went well with them. I think they have sort of reached a new level with the gay stuff. They seem to keep up with gay issues in the news, and they are angered by things they see. . . . like the murder of Matthew Shepard in Montana. My dad asked me for some advice on how he should talk to a young man he works with (16 years old or so) about how he handles his sexual orientation. The boy is gay and is very open about it, but he lives in a small town, and he "catches a lot of hell" about it, as my dad put it. I told him that the boy is probably feeling very defiant. . . . like, "I'll be who I want to be. . . . regardless of what others do to me or think." I told my dad that I understand that defiance and even admire it. I wish I could be more open like that regardless of the consequences, but I am too afraid to be.

My mom revealed to me that she had known all along that I was gay. I asked her if that was why she didn't want me to get married, and she said yes. (I wanted to ask her, "Why didn't you tell me?" but she probably felt it wasn't her place to say anything at the time.) She said she knew when I was growing up, but she wouldn't tell me how she knew. I was surprised.

A lot of times the people all around you know something about you even before you yourself know it! I reached sort of a comfortable position about being out, as well, while my mom and I were talking. She suggested that most people probably know that I am gay anyway. . . . though I have not told them. So, I should just talk about Emmy as my partner, etc. and let them draw their own conclusions. They probably know anyway, was what she thinks.

That brings me to the military reserve. As I have said, though we participate in helping the regular military, we are a civilian organization. Recently, I was promoted to a higher position in our unit. I am very proud of that.

For the last two days, I went out on patrol with our unit in support of security measures for a very important event being held in the city nearby. I spent two days in close quarters with other members of my unit. The others often ask me about my business. . . . how's your business going. . . . how's Emmy? I suspect that they are on to me as well. . . . especially my superior officer. I think she knows I am gay. I think the others suspect it. Nothing has been said to me outright, but I am picking up clues. Right now, though, I am still scared to death to tell them. I think they would probably still accept me okay. My commanding officer has on several occasions asked me about getting Emmy to join the reserve. I imagine it would probably be a relief to all of us if I would make it clear. It makes it awkward for everyone. . . . my being in this unclear relationship with this woman. . . . Who is she, really? I'm sure is what they're thinking. But, still, I can't bring myself to make it any clearer. . . . If I felt I could confide in one of the members of the unit first to gauge what their reaction would be, I would do that. But I don't have anyone I feel I could confide in. I know they all like me as a person. I am just afraid that if I told them, it would suddenly put a strain on our relations.

Something's got to give eventually, though. I can feel that. I can tell that after being in this organization for all this time, people are wanting to know a little more about me, and I won't tell them much.

I do think, that the straight people in a gay person's life go through a coming out process as well. They go through similar stages that the gay person goes through. . . . denial (no, she can't be gay), to wondering (you think she is?), to wanting certain knowledge (I wish she would just say something!). You think I'm right about that?

I hope things are going well for you. Overall, things are going well here. I'm still in my usual quandary, but progress is being made.

Take care.

Kay.

My reply:

Hi Kay,

Wow, I had no idea your products sell for so much. But I guess there is a lot of time and effort invested in the items. Congratulations on the outcome of the bidding!

My dad works with young people, and he asked me for some advice on how he should talk to a young man (16 years old or so) about how he handles his sexual orientation. The boy is gay and is very open about it, but he lives in a small town, and he "catches a lot of hell" about it, as my dad put it. I told him that the boy is probably feeling very defiant. . . like, "I'll be who I want to be. . . . regardless of what others do to me or think." I told my dad that I understand that defiance and even admire it. I wish I could be more open like that regardless of the consequences, but I am too afraid to be.

I'm glad your visit with your parents went so well. I think it's wonderful that your dad asked for your advice in this matter. It's not often that parents ask their kids for advice. You're lucky to have a dad like that.

You probably know the old adage that our biological makeup gives us basically two options when threatened: fight or flight. Both these work well, and neither is better than the other in every situation. It sounds to me that the boy at your dad's school has chosen to fight. It may have been because of how others react to his gayness. He may have been pushed into a corner from which the only escape is to fight. In other words, he may have been forced into fighting. This is not an unusual experience for boys who are considered "different" by their peers.

When I was in grade 11 in high school one of my classmates was known to be gay. I don't know how the other kids treated him, but our gym teacher treated him as though he were ill. He was not required to take gym with us and he was made to sit in a balcony which is where I ended up when my leg was put in a cast from a football injury. In other words, the gay boy was made to go where sick or injured (non-normal) boys went. At the time I thought it was benevolent treatment from our gym teacher, but now I'm not so sure any more. I guess the gym teacher thought he was doing what was best for the boy.

My mom revealed to me that she had known all along that I was gay. I asked her if that was why she didn't want me to get married, and she said yes. (I wanted to ask her, "Why didn't you tell me?" but she probably felt it wasn't her place to say anything at the time.) She said she knew when I was growing up, but she wouldn't tell me how she knew. I was surprised.

Please remember that parents feel responsible (and are held responsible by their community) for the way their children's character develops. And in many communities gayness was at one time considered a weakness or defect in character. It must have been very hard for your mother to accept your gayness when you were young if the community around her saw gayness as some sort of character defect. Admitting that you were gay would have meant your mother (and the community) would have considered her responsible for the "defective" character you were developing. Many parents don't talk about their children's gayness because they hope that it's "just a phase" that their children will eventually grow out of. It's not surprising that your mother didn't talk about it at that time.

A lot of times the people all around you know something about you even before you yourself know it! I reached sort of a comfortable position about being out, as well, while my mom and I were talking. She suggested that most people probably know that I am gay anyway. . . .though I have not told them. So, I should just talk about Emmy as my partner, etc. and let them draw their own conclusions. They probably know anyway, was what she thinks.

I believe that there are a lot of people who don't really mind gays "so long as they keep to themselves." What seems to really irritate people is what some call "in your face" gayness, like when you see men and women in outrageous makeup parading around half naked in the streets during Gay Pride day, and so on. Students in my classes have said as much. They'll say something like, "I have nothing against gays. I just don't like it when they flaunt it. We don't flaunt our heterosexuality, do we?" It's a difficult issue, because most people understand that "Gay Pride" is an attempt to have gayness become more acceptable. But many people see it as gays going overboard. And, of course, because of what they see on TV they think that all gays like to parade around half naked in the streets.

That brings me to the military reserve. . . . If I felt I could confide in one of the members of the reserve first to gauge what their reaction would be, I would do that. But I don't have anyone I feel I could confide in. I know they all like me as a person. I am just afraid that if I told them, it would suddenly put a strain on our relations.

I'm sure you know that telling someone something they're not ready to hear can create unwanted problems. If I were you I would wait until I was asked. Why push it on anybody?

Here are some thoughts about straight reaction to gays. . . . The worry many straight men have about a gay man in their midst is that this gay man may "come on" to one of them. Of course being the target of a come-on, or as Simone de Beauvoir put it "being an object and prey" defines that person as female in our society. That's why straight men in our society often react so viciously against gay men: because the gay man (who may come on to them) is perceived as seeing them as prey, which is an insult to their own masculinity.

But women are used to being openly admired and pursued as objects of desire. Therefore I imagine that a group of women would not feel their female identity threatened if there was a lesbian in their midst who "might" come on to them. Being desired is not part of being male in our society, but it is part of being female. So I suspect a group of straight women would not act with the same hostility toward a gay woman in their midst as straight men would to a similar situation. By the way, it is a common mistake among my students that they believe a gay man identifies himself as a woman, and a lesbian identifies herself as a man. I think this fits in with what I have said above.

I do think, that the straight people in a gay person's life go through a coming out process as well. They go through similar stages that the gay person goes through. . . .denial (no, she can't be gay), to wondering (you think she is?), to wanting certain knowledge (I wish she would just say something!). You think I'm right about that?

This is a very profound insight that I've never heard or read anywhere before! I agree with you, and I think it makes a lot of sense.

Besides some recent computer trouble, things are going well for me. I'm looking forward to the Christmas holidays. Stay well and write again anytime.

Best regards,
Peter

This was our last counseling session by e-mail. There followed a few brief friendly exchanges and then Kay got on with her busy life. I found this case very rewarding because of the articulate nature of the exchange and, of course, because of the positive outcome. But I also found the exchange somewhat inhibiting due to the natural limitations on messages exchanged in this medium. While it would not take very long to speak 1500 words aloud, not many people would want to struggle through a 1500 word essay sent by e-mail.

Due to the lack of technical jargon and philosophical terms in these e-mail messages, it may seem to some readers that there wasn't much philosophy going on in them. But look again. The philosophical issues discussed included personal identity, the concept of "self" creation, the concept of authenticity, social "norms," the morality of lying, the nature (philosophy) of bullying, the origins of sexual orientation, the problem inherent in religious conservatism, the importance of ritual and ceremony (in this case marriage ceremony), family relationships, the risks inherent in questioning the rules of an organization to which you belong, the accurate imagining of future possibilities and their consequences, the definition of "man" and "woman," fallacious and contradictory reasoning, the difference between possible and probable events, the definition of courage, the scope of freedom, marriage, trust, self-respect, bullying, the use of self-help books, the problem with generalizing from some to all, an inquiry into what is meant by the claim that we all "wear masks," an inquiry into the concept of a "persona," the philosophy of religion, military organizational protocol, and of course the nature of sexuality.

I have purposely avoided doing any sort of after-the-fact analysis of this case in order to give readers the opportunity to come to their own insights and conclusion.

CASE #3: "HARDING": A MAN OF WAR

This third case is presented in narrative form without supplementary comments. Since it is not a verbatim account of the session it serves only to illustrate, in broad brushstrokes, how counseling or therapy with philosophy is accomplished. The unusual and interesting feature about this case is that the sessions were all conducted entirely by telephone. "Harding" and I have never met.

"Harding" called me on the telephone late one evening. He was calling from a city in the United States some two thousand miles away from the Canadian city where I live and teach. He spoke very politely, but I found it odd that he called me "sir" a number of times. He told me that he had coincidentally come across my website on the Internet and wanted to know what philosophical counseling is all about. I explained to him that I'm a professor of philosophy at a university, but that I also use philosophy to help people from the community who are not my students to deal with real-life issues. Harding told me that he had a degree in psychotherapy, that he had a practice of his own, and that he wanted to know why philosophical counseling is different from psychotherapy. I told him that what I do is similar to the cognitive kinds of therapies such as Rational Emotive Behavior Therapy (REBT), Logo Therapy, and Existential Therapy. But I reminded him that these "talk therapies" were devised by psychotherapists, and that the philosophy used in them is generally very rudimentary because psychotherapists typically aren't educated in philosophy.

"I understand, sir. So would philosophical counseling help me with, for example, some issues I'm having with my father?" he asked.

"Yes, it's very likely that philosophical counseling would be helpful to you," I said. But I could tell by the way he had asked the question that he had something else on his mind.

"Well, that's not the main reason I'm calling you," he said. "The truth is, sir, I'm not just another therapist. I'm in the US military. I'm going to be dealing with soldiers who have been killing people in Iraq. They're going to be coming to me with some very serious problems."

He went on to tell me that he is in his thirties; many of the men in his family had been in the military. Harding had been on active duty in Afghanistan and been part of a company of men who had killed a number of Afghanis, both military men and civilians. When he finished his tour of duty, and they asked him to re-enlist to fight in Iraq, he declined. He told me he did not want to fight in Iraq because he could see that the reasons the US administration was giving for the military invasion of Iraq were even less compelling than the ones they had given for being in Afghanistan. Instead he decided to go back to university to finish his degree in psychotherapy and establish a small counseling practice in his home town. But he eventually decided to reenlist to serve as a military psychotherapist.

"I saw what the men were like who came back from Afghanistan," he told me. "I was one of them. We were confused, ashamed, feeling guilty for what we had done to those people. I mean, my God, what do you do when you can't tell the difference between an enemy soldier and a local shopkeeper? You ask yourself, Is it OK to shoot the shopkeeper just in case he's the enemy? But what if he's not? These are the same problems my father's generation faced in Vietnam. Now there's a whole new bunch of men coming back from an even worse war in Iraq. I want to help these men, but I don't see psychotherapy being able to give them enough of the kind of things they need. Sir, do you think your philosophical counseling could help?"

I told him I thought philosophy could be very helpful But privately I wondered whether helping Harding understand philosophy, especially areas such as morality, would create in me feelings of conflict and regret. I wondered, will I be asked to help him justify killing innocent people in an illegal war? Should I try to talk him out of being a patriotic soldier who is willing to obey commands even when he knows he must act contrary to his own moral values? What does morality mean on the battle field, when that battle field is some humble market place or village square or someone's home? Is it OK to put personal morality on hold when a man goes to war? I thought of the atrocities that have been committed by the US in the very recent past, the bombing of civilian shelters, the illegal prison camps in Iraq and Cuba, the withholding of legal help for prisoners, the disregard for due process of law, the administration's use of Syrian torturers as its proxy, the imprisonment of hundreds of US citizens in the name of national security on nothing more than vague suspicions and anonymous tips. I'm sure Harding could sense my hesitation.

"Of course I've got some issues with my father too, I suppose like most sons, but I'm not really asking for personal philosophical counseling from you," he continued. "I'm more interested in understanding how you would suggest I use philosophy to help the men who have been fighting in this war to make sense of it all. You have to understand, these men are not psychopaths; they're not born killers. They're trained to do as they're told. Have you heard the saying that to a man with a hammer everything looks like a nail? Well, to a military man every person looks like a potential enemy. And once your government starts a war, military men are trained to believe it's justified, otherwise they'd have no motivation to kill a fellow human being. Is there a philosophical way of helping these men look at both their training and war in general?"

I told him that philosophers have for centuries been discussing this very question: What makes a war morally justified? Their suggestions are considered part of what's called "just war theory." I told him a war is

considered morally justified only when all of the following conditions apply:
1. the leadership are actually representing the wishes of the majority of their people;
2. the reason for war is honorable—such as in self-defense;
3. the goal of the war is peace, that is, if the intention is to defend against an aggressor and not to invade out of greed or envy;
4. all other means have been unsuccessful in reducing or eliminating the threat;
5. there is no doubt that the other nation's actions are a hostile attack
6. going to war is not simply going to be a sacrifice of human lives without the chance of resolving the hostile situation;
7. the unequivocal intention behind the war is the establishment of peace;
8. the amount of force used against the other nation is just enough to end hostilities and no more;
9. the target of hostilities is the armed opposing military force and no other. A war is *unjust* if any of these conditions are not met, and especially so if they are intentionally ignored.

"So, going by that list," he said, "it seems pretty clear to me now that our invasion of Iraq was an unjustified invasion. We tried to justify it by saying it was a war against terrorism. But most of the terrorists who attacked the World Trade Center in New York were from Saudi Arabia, not Iraq. So if our hostilities in Iraq can be considered a war at all it is clearly an unjust war."

I said nothing, allowing him to consider what he had just said. There was a long silence on the phone. Finally Harding spoke. "It's going to be hard for me to convince our soldiers that they were fighting an unjust war."

"But it's not the job of a philosophical counselor to convince anyone of anything," I said.

"What do you mean?" he asked.

"Being a philosopher is not like being in command of the person you're counseling," I said. "You can't just order someone to believe what you say to them. Philosophical counseling is about careful reasoning and gentle suggestion, not telling people what to think or do ."

"So you're saying I need to reason with them and only suggest things to them?"

"Exactly," I said. "Philosophical counseling involves helping others to examine the reasons they have for the values they hold as good, and the beliefs they hold as true, so that they can free themselves from blindly following tradition, slavishly obeying the dictates of authority figures, or acting only on feelings that come up."

"So in my case, I'd be helping my soldiers to examine their reasons for the values they have and the beliefs they have, even about what they did behind a gun in Iraq?"

"Yes," I said. "You'll be helping them to improve their thinking about those things for themselves. You'll be helping them to examine their reasoning. . . . One book I read puts it this way, 'Our authority over our reasons depends on our being able to say what they are; this requires attention, rather than searching for a hypothesis or making an observation.' Philosophical counseling is not about searching for a hypothesis in order to make a diagnoses. It's about helping people to reason better."

"Sir, can you teach me to do this before I'm shipped out to Iraq in six weeks?" he asked.

Beginning that evening, and twice a week for the next six weeks, over the telephone, I taught Harding as much as I could about reasoning, or what some philosophers call critical and creative thinking. I began by explaining how to simplify what a soldier might tell him, by reducing it down to a short three-sentence statement, called either a categorical or conditional deductive syllogism. We all do this to a certain extent, but knowing how to do it intentionally can be extremely helpful when trying to understand someone's complex reasoning. I told Harding that all of critical thinking is concerned with putting into practice a systematic way of looking at what's being said in order to make better sense of it.

I told him that one of the most important things he will need to be able to do as a counselor is to understand whether his soldier client is simply offering him an opinion about something or making an argument to explain his position. If the soldier offers him an opinion then it's merely a conclusion, a statement of his belief. In this case Harding can't really work with what the soldier has said. But a discussion is possible if the soldier offers him an argument, that is if the soldier offers both his opinion in the form of a conclusion and the reasons he has for holding this opinion. So I made it clear to him that one of the most important reasoning "tools" a philosophical counselor has is asking the question "Why?" This request for the soldier client's own assistance in discovering and examining the reasons he has for his beliefs, values, and assumptions is very different from the many approaches in psychotherapy where the therapist is the "archaeologist" of the patient's mind searching for buried psychological causes that are believed to create pathological thinking and behaviors.

I told Harding he also needs to listen carefully to his soldier clients in order to hear what their unspoken assumptions are, both about reality and about values. In other words he will have to find out what these soldiers assume is really true about the war, about the enemy, about their commanders, about the country, and about themselves; and he'll have to discover what these soldiers assume has value. These discoveries will go a long way in helping his soldier clients come to terms with what they have done to the people of Iraq.

I suggested he should also help his soldier clients to understand what morality is, and where their morality has come from. He needs to help them see that morality is ultimately about trying to avoid harming others, and that their moral values originally came from their parents, their church, their peers at school, and their comrades in arms. He needs to discuss with them how to balance their belief that being moral is simply doing their duty as Immanuel Kant argued, with the moral theory that advocates doing the best for the most people which John Stuart Mill called "utility," with Carol Gilligan's claim that being moral is about caring for others. But he must then also help them to see that as adults we can decide among our moral values, we can choose which to keep, and which to discard or alter.

His soldiers will need to learn some of the many approaches to moral decision-making they can use that will allow them to think beyond simple obedience to their commanders. This is absolutely necessary if they are to return to living in a civilian society where they will need to be able to decide for themselves, and by themselves, what is the good and right thing to do in non-combat situations.

I suggested that he also help his soldier clients understand the very significant difference between possible and probable. Soldiers returning from an illegal war may have disturbing thoughts and nightmares that will lead them to believe impossible events are possible. It's important that they recognize that everything is possible, no matter how absurd, but that the *probability* of these events actually occurring is remote or non-existent. This comprehension of the difference between possible and probable will help them to reconnect with the everyday realities of life.

I mentioned that when his soldier clients are reintegrated back into civilian society they will also need to understand the power of language, especially in the way politicians and the media portray what has gone on and what is still going on in Iraq. These soldiers will need to be taught to challenge ambiguity, vagueness, contradictory clichés, euphemisms used to sanitize killing and death, the denotation of words in contrast to their connotation or meanings, and the reification and naming that occurs both on the battlefield and in many forms of psychotherapy. When they learn these things they will be able to defend themselves against the power of the very language that was used to justify sending them overseas to kill the Iraqi people in the first place. And I told him that soldiers, especially those who have been traumatized, need to be helped to become aware of their own ethnocentrism which leads them to think their country, their culture, and their religion is the best or the only right one; they need to be helped to overcome their egocentrism which leads them to believe that a man in uniform can do no wrong; they need to learn that by rationalizing their role in Iraq, as being beyond their own control, they are lessening their own humanity; they need to avoid denying what they did and accept it as a decision made in the past that can't be changed, but that was originally without good enough reasons; and finally they need to learn that, contrary to military training, conformity to military behavior does not make the world a better place, nor does it make their own life easier to live.

Harding said he could see how all of these reasoning strategies will be very useful in his work with these men. I told him it will take practice and patience, both with his soldier clients and with himself, to become good at it. Then for the remaining weeks I discussed with him some of the many reasoning errors or fallacies that will, no doubt, be used both intentionally and unintentionally by his men in their discussions with him.

We talked at length about the fallacy of faulty analogy, like when a soldier says the "war" in Iraq is like the second World War (this is a faulty analogy because while the US helped defend against an illegal invading force in World War II, the US is instead itself the illegal invading force in Iraq); the fallacy of false cause in claims such as that Iraq is to blame for terrorism all over the world; the fallacy of slippery slope which is always a prediction of disaster such as saying if we don't kill terrorists in Iraq then they'll spread terror all over the world and the world will be taken over by lawless hordes; the fallacy of making a hasty conclusion such as that because one Muslim extremist made himself into a human bomb therefore all Muslims are extremists who will make themselves into human bombs; the bandwagon fallacy which was used to persuade nations to help the US invade Iraq by claiming that most nations were going to join the US invasion; the appeal to tradition which was used to convince young American men to fight in Iraq just like their fathers and grandfathers had fought in the two World Wars; the either/or fallacy which US president Bush used when he told the world, "You're either with us, or against us" which left no other alternative; the fallacy of begging the question which claims Iraq is a threat to the world without any clear evidence that this is true; the fallacy of improper appeal to authority with which a soldier might excuse a terrible war crime simply by claiming he was ordered to do so by a superior officer; the fallacy of two wrongs which says it's acceptable to kill people in Iraq because terrorists from Iraq (supposedly) killed people in the US; the straw person fallacy which a soldier might use to argue that Iraq was invaded to make the world safe from terrorists, when in fact there are other reasons for the invasion, such as to secure the source of oil; the fallacy of irrelevant reason when a soldier says that Iraq was invaded because it was producing weapons of mass destruction; the often-used fallacy called freeloading term in which the word "terrorist" or "insurgent" is used to describe people fighting to protect their villages from an invading foreign army;

and the fallacy of guilt by association which causes soldiers on the battle field to see all Iraqi people as enemy combatants.

"These are just some of the many possible fallacies your soldier clients may bring up in discussion with you. Not only will they use these reasoning errors when they tell you about what they believe and value, but they'll also be encountering them when they go back to civilian life. So you need to help them to be able to recognize them and respond to them in civilian life."

"Wow," Harding said the day we finished discussing what I considered to be the most important fallacies. "I can really see where knowing this stuff will make a real difference both to me in my practice and to the men who will be coming to me for therapy."

"I'm glad to hear you say that," I said, "because this information just useless theory if you don't put it into practice."

"Oh, I'm going to put it into practice alright," he assured me. "But the critical thinking stuff isn't all there is to philosophical counseling, is it?"

"No, there's lots more for you to learn,"

But we both knew we couldn't go on because the six weeks were up and Harding was about to be assigned to a unit in Iraq.

"Sir, I have one more question for you," he said.

"That's all?" I joked. "Just one more?"

"Remember I told you at the beginning that I was having some issues with my father?"

"Yes."

"Well, if you don't mind I'd like to clear them up before I leave the country. My father is not only a military man; he's a fighting military man. And he thinks that my doing therapy and counseling work in Iraq cowardly. What do you think of that?"

I took a moment to consider how to respond.

"I think that's a terrible thing for your father to say to you," I said. "But that's not important. What really matters is how you're going to deal with what your father said."

"I don't know where to begin," he replied. I could tell that Harding wanted me to take the lead and make some suggestions.

"I'm not sure about this," I said, "but it seems to me that you're leaving one war at home to go to some other war overseas."

"What do you mean?" he asked.

"It sounds to me like you're fighting some sort of war with your father. He seems to want you to be something you don't want to be."

"That's exactly right," Harding said. I could hear a tone of relief in his voice. "My dad wants me to come back a decorated war hero. Whenever he tells his war stories to anyone he always tells them loud enough for me to hear. It's like if I don't measure up to his standards I'm not worthy to be his son. It's like he's constantly attacking me, and I'm constantly having to defend myself and what I want to do. He makes me doubt myself a lot."

This gave me an idea.

"If your dad is at war with you, maybe we can apply the just war theory to what your dad is doing," I suggested.

"OK, but I'm not sure I know what you mean."

"Remember that just war theory says there are nine conditions that have to be met in order for a war to be just?"

"Yes sir."

"Well, let's go through those one at a time, and see if your dad's war against you is just. If we discover his war against you is unjust it may help you get your self-confidence back."

"Alright. I'm willing to give it a try."

I began by asking him if his dad was a legitimate authority.

"Yes sir. I would say so. He's the head of the household, and I accept him to be the leader of the family."

"OK, then does he have just cause in attacking your courage?"

"No, because my enlisting to serve as a therapist and counselor is not because I lack the courage to fight. It's not like I've never fired a weapon. I was in active combat in Afghanistan. But I don't want to kill people in Iraq in a war I know is illegal. I want to help the men coming back from combat who realize what we're doing in Iraq is wrong."

"Does your dad have right intention when he calls you a coward?"

"No, I don't think so. He isn't stating a fact; he's just trying to intimidate me into doing what he wants me to do: kill women and children in an illegal war."

"So is you dad's war of insults on you his last resort?"

"I guess he thinks it is, because he hasn't been able to change my mind otherwise."

"Alright, are you a real and certain danger to your dad?"

"You know I think he believes I'm a real and certain danger to the honor of our military family."

"And are you?" I asked bluntly.

"No, I'm not. In fact I'm going to be upholding the highest military honor by helping my comrades in arms."

"Does you dad believe he has a reasonable probability of success in trying to convince you to take a weapon to Iraq rather than philosophy?"

"I think his insults show that he knows he's not going to change my mind."

"What about proportional end? Is what your dad doing to you justified in the name of family honor?"

"No, not at all. He's willing to make an enemy of his son. He has been making an enemy of me just because he'd rather see me shooting so-called insurgents than counseling suffering soldiers."

"Is your dad using proportional means to oppose what he sees as your threat to the family honor?"

"I don't think you can call driving a son away from the family with insults, and breaking up our family, proportional means. It's contradictory."

"And what about non-combatant immunity?" I asked finally.

"Now that's a good one," Harding said. "What my dad is doing to me is hurting both my mother and my sister. They shouldn't have to go through all this family conflict when they know that I'm about to be sent off to a dangerous combat zone."

"Well then," I said, "because your dad's war on you doesn't meet all the criteria of a just war, it looks to me like your dad's war against you unjust."

There was a long pause. I could hear Harding's breathing at the other end of the telephone line some two thousand miles away. I was worried that perhaps our philosophical examination had gone too deep.

"Thank you, sir," I finally heard him say. "That helps a lot."

"You're welcome," I said. "And Harding, one more thing…"

"Yes sir?"

"You don't need to call me sir," I said. "Just call me Peter. After all we're comrades… in counseling."

"OK. . . . Peter," he said with a chuckle.

And then he said his final good bye.

This ended my philosophical counseling sessions by long distance telephone calls with Harding, the man of war.

CONCLUSION

These three cases were meant to offer an insight into what using philosophy in counseling or psychotherapy looks like. It may at first seem like there's not much "real" philosophy present because of the lack of formal academic language, and the absence of references to famous philosophers like Plato or Hegel or Sartre. But the philosophy is ever-present in the mind of the counselor, and it informs every question and every issue raised by the counselor. Philosophy does not have to be wrapped in scholarly robes and the esoteric paraphernalia of academic jargon to be a substantive and effective element of the conversation.

I have no hesitation in pronouncing all three of these former clients of mine as recovered from the distress brought on by their predicaments. I feel justified in using the word "recovered" for several reasons. First, each of these clients said they felt so much better after our sessions that they no longer required my assistance in exploring their problems or resolving them. And second, they all continued their contact with me for a time after their formal sessions ended, showing that the reason for the termination was not dissatisfaction with what had transpired during our sessions. Although I used no empirical tests to determine their state of mind—since the results of such tests require subjective interpretation by the counselor or therapist, and are therefore unreliable—I accepted their sincere reports of recovery. Counselors and psychotherapists who employ philosophy have no hesitation in proclaiming their clients as "recovered" or "cured" from their distress. But, until recently, the words "recovery" and "cure" were rarely discussed as achievements in the psychotherapeutic literature. Recovery and cure are still almost completely absent as goals in the practices of psychoanalysts and biological psychiatrists.

ELEVEN
Recovery, Cure, and Philosophy

Some thirty years ago while Wes was in his mid-teens, he attempted suicide. The psychiatrist who was subsequently assigned to his case labeled him with the ambiguous diagnosis of "schizophrenia." He was prescribed a smorgasbord of potent psychotropic drugs, some to be taken orally and some to be regularly administered by injections. When I first got to know him he was very shy, somewhat clumsy, and could barely put three words together into a coherent sentence. After ten years, in which our discussions transformed our informal counseling relationship into a friendship, he got a part-time job, he has a girlfriend, he's playing chess with me at least once a week (and winning at times), and carrying on very ordinary conversations to the point where his medical doctor decided to reduce his oral medications. But although he has improved noticeably over the past decade, I noticed that the two or three days immediately following his regular bi-weekly psychotropic drug injections his speech, and his ability to concentrate and focus his attention on our conversations always deteriorated for several days. So I suggested he ask his psychiatrist if it would be possible to have his injection schedule tapered off to once every two weeks, or perhaps even terminated altogether.

The first time Wes asked the psychiatrist if it would be possible to reduce his psychotropic injections, not only because of the many side effects that were making his life miserable but also because the injections were disrupting the clarity of his mind, and because he was generally feeling much better, the psychiatrist's response was, "So you've got a medical degree now?" When Wes respectfully repeated the question the psychiatrist replied, "Why should we fix what isn't broken?" The injected drugs continued unaltered because this clinician held the nomothetic or scientific perspective in regard to his patient. He viewed Wes as a quant tative statistic belonging to the set of patients that are labeled "schizophrenics," and whose standard treatment protocol is the continuous administering of high doses of potent pharmaceuticals. This protocol is based on the erroneous assumption that schizophrenics rarely improve, and never recover. More will be said about the recovery rates from schizophrenia below.

Several months later, when Wes asked for a second time if the frequency of the injections could be reduced, the psychiatrist's response was to have him removed from his subsidized apartment and placed in a halfway house for a month. There he was not allowed independent access to the outside world, and his use of a telephone was restricted to five minutes per call. I had no way of finding out where he was or what was going on because Wes was not answering his home phone. His month-long absence from his part-time job resulted in his being laid off. The psychiatrist also *increased* his medications telling Wes that he seemed to be "going off the deep end." In other words, his psychiatrist "diagnosed" Wes's subjective feelings of improvement, and his questioning the frequency of his injections, as negative symptoms of his so-called mental illness. Wes's desire for an improved circumstance—a place on the road to recovery—led to a number of detrimental consequences for him brought on by the very mental health service provider whose mandate is to improve his condition.

In discussing the common problem of clinicians who disregard their patients' autonomy, Abraham Rudnick, Associate Professor in the Department of Psychiatry and Philosophy at the University of Western Ontario, reports that empirical research has shown that many individuals who are forced to receive treatment as patients

> are severely traumatized by this and consequently develop post-traumatic stress disorder, which may cause severe psychological harm. Furthermore, paternalism stigmatizes individuals (e.g., by infantilizing them), and may therefore cause them considerable social harm as well as psychological harm. (2012a, p. 306)

Several weeks later, after having dealt with the shock and humiliation of what had happened to him, Wes gathered the courage to phone me and tell me about it. He wondered aloud why asking the psychiatrist—one of his supposed "carers"—a simple question about the meds he was receiving had gotten him into so much trouble. It was a question I wasn't sure how to answer. It would have involved a lengthy and complex explanation about a number of inter-connected factors such as the faulty assumptions held by clinicians about the origins of so-called mental illnesses, their diagnoses and their treatment, the false assumption that medications are required to treat the distress and suffering that is labeled "schizophrenia," the problematic assumptions by mental healthcare services providers that the subjective insights of their patents into their own conditions are worthless because they are "unprofessional" and "unscientific," and the devastating assumption that their so-called mentally ill patients will never recover.

I asked Wes if he would like me to speak with the psychiatrist but he declined, worried that there might be more negative repercussions from an authority figure who obviously doesn't like his "mentally ill" patient questioning his psychopharmacodynamics decisions. As philosopher John Davis so aptly put it, when the individual is seen only as a part of the system "he has no significance except as he fits into the system. His self-respect is undermined... and the healthy person who rebels is regarded as sick" (p. 19). Although Wes was certainly not rebelling, it seemed to me that he was being taught a very clear lesson: Don't ask questions of a member of the medical establishment who sees all cases of diagnosed schizophrenia equally: as life-long chronic illnesses requiring medication.

Wilma Boevink, Professor of Recovery at Hanze University, and former mental patient herself, says that it is very difficult for a psychiatric patient to retain his or her own values, opinions, and self-esteem when in therapy. Psychiatrists do not regard their patients as serious discussion partners. The attending psychiatrist hears "only what is significant to the diagnostic examination. . . . We are examined but not really seen, and we are listened to but not heard." Everything the patient says and does is regarded "as a logical manifestation of the diagnosed disorder" (p. 1, 21). In his essay title "Recovery and Advocacy: Contextualizing Justice in Relation to Recovery from Mental Illness," Marcus Yu-Lung Chiu, Associate Professor at the Department of Social Work, National University of Singapore points out that in scientific positivism, which is modern medicine's dominant approach to mental illness,

> the individual's (patient's) description of how they feel is regarded as less important than the mental health professional's task of confirming or refuting the existence of psychopathology such as delusional thoughts, mood fluctuations, and hallucinations. (p. 287)

Expert assessment—the observation of signs pointing to a diagnosis—is considered to be the most important activity in the examination room. Even the client's own symptomatic reports are considered superfluous because reports from "the mentally ill" are held to be unreliable. Clinical psychologists Paul and John Lysaker put it this way: "Institutionally sanctioned knowledge claims about people are habitually taken to trump claims from those very individuals" (Rudnick p. 172). In other words, the psychiatrist's opinion on all aspects of so-called mental illnesses is "conclusive and exclusive" (Chiu p. 287). The psychiatric patient's subjective experience of feeling better is simply discounted if the nomothetic knowledge of the attending clinician cannot confirm the patient's experience. But Mike Slade, Professor of Health Services at the Institute of Psychiatry in King's College, London warns that blind spots are created for the clinician when the client's idiographic or subjective experiences are downgraded. Since a diagnosis of "mental illness" is never based on the results of a biometric test, a diagnosis is always only a hypothesis based on the attending clinician's observations. Devaluing the client's personal insights "can lead to a belief that a diagnosis is true rather than just a hypothesis" (Slade p. 85).

Today's mental healthcare services users find themselves in the same paradoxical no-win situations as Freud's patients almost a century ago. If Freud told his patient she was suffering from hysteria and the patient disagreed with him Freud simply diagnosed her as being in denial, or suffering from repression, or of being resistant. Today's patients who believe they're feeling better, or are actually getting better, are told they're either mistaken or delusional. When absolute diagnostic authority lies in the "objective" evaluation carried out by the clinician, the patient's subjective perspective is simply dismissed as either irrelevant, or as mistaken, or worse, as symptomatic. This is not a simple matter of a debate about what is true, whether the "objective" appraisal of the patient's condition by the clinician is more accurate than the patient's subjective sensations. When the clinician simply disregards or dismisses the reality of the patient's lived experiences it causes a significant negative impact on the patient's self-esteem and self-identity. This adds to the patient's already extant mental suffering, which is in turn added to the already existing impact on the patient's physical health, and ultimately his quality of life, by the mandatory ingestion of powerful psychotropic drugs.

The assumption that there is no cure for, nor recovery from, mental illness is pervasive in the field of mental healthcare. While there has been a gradual shift in the stance on recovery and cure in the counseling and psychotherapeutic literature, there is no evidence of its general acceptance by clinicians nor of its awareness in the general population. Even among mental health services users the possibility of recovery or cure is seldom recognized. Perhaps one of the reasons for this is because treatment has been predominantly driven by the pharmaceutical industry which has neither produced, nor actively sought to find, methods for recovery nor cures. Joel Paris, Professor of Psychiatry at McGill University in Montreal, points out that the so-called "triumph of psychopharmacology" is just in its ability to bring symptomatic improvement. Psychiatrists have not been able to cure most of the conditions they treat with medications because that is not the goal of the medications (p. 10). The drug industry's most profitable approach is to promote the so-called "management" of symptoms, "stabilization" of brain chemistry, and "control" of the patient, which all require long-term drug consumption, often over a lifetime. This creates what I call the medication trap.

THE MEDICATION TRAP

If a patient's improvement is attributed to the medications he's taking, then logic says he should continue taking the medication. In somatic medicine generally, when the patient feels better he can stop taking the medication only if the body is not reliant on it for proper functioning. For example, a medication like insulin must be taken regularly because it is the insulin itself that is maintaining the body's homeostasis. A medication like an antibiotic that is taken for an infection can be stopped after the infection is overcome. But there is a problem with psychotropic medications: it has not been determined which type of drug they are, and how they function. Research has shown that psychotropics don't cure conditions the way that, say, an antibiotic does (Paris 10). But they have also not been shown to work like insulin does. This has only been assumed. While medical science understands that these agents can control symptoms, "we do not know how they work. Psychiatric drugs were discovered by serendipity, and their mechanism of action is still largely a mystery" (Paris p. 11). The assumption is that if these drugs don't cure any conditions, but they do reduce symptoms, then they must act something like insulin does, as a replacement for a substance that is missing from the brain. But after three decades of research, there is no evidence for the belief that any of the various psychoactive drugs correct organic problems, such as a monoamine deficiency, by replacing elements missing from the brains of the so-called mentally ill (Valenstein 1998). The widespread belief that so-called mental illnesses are the result of "chemical imbalances" in the brain (which psychoactive drugs supposedly correct) "is an over-simplified and misleading view of a complex problem" (Paris p. xiii). Medical science has no tests to determine whether the brain of a "mentally ill" person has either a chronic deficiency that must be replenished or a problem analogous to an infection which can be cured. This means that when a patient tells his psychiatrist he is improving, the psychiatrist has no way of determining how this improvement has come about. Is the symptomatic reduction the result of the medication's actions, or has the medication begun to eradicate the organic cause of the "mental illness"? Psychiatrists concerned about the welfare of their patients take the safe route and continue prescribing the medications, no doubt reasoning that if the medications have "cured" the "illness" then more of it will do no harm, but if the medication is replacing a missing element then their continued consumption is clearly indicated. This is the "medication trap" into which the patient is gently led for his own good. With the logic of "the mind is just the brain," and the "medical model" of treatment for so-called mental illnesses, the patient cannot escape a lifetime of drug consumption. The so-called mental healthcare consumer will indeed remain a consumer for life.

A different, but equally serious, concern that has been expressed by several of my clients is that if they recover, or even just improve, they will find themselves cut off from the support they have been receiving from government Social Services agencies (in the form of money, accommodation, medications, etc.). These are individuals who are dependent on the government for their very basic needs. They are, for the most part, unskilled and untrained, short on education, lacking in work experience, without any employment contacts, and therefore unable to find any but the very lowest paying, and probably most demeaning, jobs. This situation puts them into the difficult position of trying to "get well" but only to a point. If the government agencies on which they depend find their recovery to be too dramatic they risk losing their financial support. They are then faced with the question of whether they should attempt to improve, or simply remain in a state of helplessness which will continue to be diagnosed as some sort of "mental illness" deserving of social assistance. I misunderstood one of my clients when he said he didn't want to reduce the medications he was taking, despite being offered this option by his mental health team. He said he wanted to continue with the same dosages because, as he put it, they have provided him with an apartment, telephone, clothes, and money for food. I understood him to mean that he felt indebted to them, that he felt hesitant to "get better" because, in some strange way, he felt obligated to keep playing the role of the dependent "mentally ill" person for their benefit. But I came to see this was a misunderstanding on my part. What he was trying to tell me is that his mental health services team literally supports him financially. What he's worried about is that his agreeing to reduce his medications will give them the signal that he is improving, which may prompt them to reduce or even terminate his financial support. So to keep his apartment and food on his table he's willing to continue taking the medications at the same dosages, despite knowing that he really doesn't need them to feel better, and despite the fact that the terrible side effects they cause actually make him feel worse. He says this is just living according to his philosophy: "Don't bite the hand that feeds you."

There is still another side to the dependency on Social Assistance programs for mental health services users. This is the fact that, when individuals are at a level of difficulties that requires them to request financial assistance, they are then required by the government to give up almost all of their personal rights, such as the right to privacy, their favorite diet, personal grooming decisions, decision-making concerning financial matters, and decisions about the medications they're required to consume. They give up the right to autonomously manage virtually all aspects of their lives. A more recent client of mine lives with the constant fear of being sent back to the mental hospital because one of her acquaintances, also in social assisted housing, was found to have "too big a mess" in her apartment. Because of this, she was returned to the mental hospital against her will. My client worries that "messiness" is now being treated as a diagnosable "mental illness." She wonders how it will be possible to ever come out from under such oppressive circumstances.

If an individual accepts money from a government agency then the agency requires them to accept their terms and conditions, which amounts to giving the agency paternalistic control over their private lives. It's no wonder that so many people prefer to live in poverty and on the streets rather than accept government funding. The mental healthcare patient has to live with the absolutely contradictory message that he may refuse the prescribed medications but it will cost him the assistance on which he is totally dependent. The mental healthcare services user's life style is completely contingent on his "medication compliance." Another of my clients made this point in a dramatic fashion by saying, "If you take their money, they take your life." Clinicians and mental health services providers seem to be completely oblivious to this irrational "Catch 22" situation—the inadvisability and impossibility of recovery—in which they lock their patients.

THE DENIAL OF POSSIBILITY

Studies have found that, surprisingly and unfortunately, psychiatrists generally have negative prognostic views about their patients. Clinicians on the whole don't see cure, recovery, or even mere improvement as likely in most patients diagnosed with so-called serious mental illnesses. One study found that most psychiatrists were simply ambivalent as to whether their patients would recover. Another found that 40% of mental health professionals believed that it was completely or partly true that "there is little to be done for these patients apart from helping them live in a peaceful environment." Only 2 percent believed that people with schizophrenia could make a complete recovery. This is despite that fact that research has shown from 50–67 percent of people with schizophrenia exhibit considerable improvement, or even complete recovery, from the diagnosed "condition" (Flanagan p. 267). The fourth edition of the American Psychiatric Association's *Diagnostic and Statistical Manual of Mental Disorders* (*DSM–IV*) asserted that there is a low probability that mental health services users with schizophrenia will make a full return to normal functioning. But both first-person accounts and evidence from medical outcomes of global longitudinal studies indicate that, in fact, many individuals do recover and return to living a "normal" life (see, for example Amering and Schmolke).

The term "schizophrenia" is often accompanied by the general public's fear of unpredictability, embarrassment, and violence, and the mistaken clinical assumption of inevitable deterioration in the future (Kingdon and Turkington p. 89). But the incurability of schizophrenia is a myth.

that has evolved from its original pronouncement by Emil Kraeplin (1856–1926) a century ago. He first labeled the mental confusion and hallucinations of his patients as *dementia praecox* and pronounced it as chronic and always involving a steadily progressing deterioration. It was his opinion that anyone who is said to have recovered from schizophrenia could not have been properly diagnosed in the first place. A meta-analysis of longitudinal data on the course of schizophrenia throughout the twentieth century found many people with schizophrenia can recover substantially, if not completely over time (Lysaker and Lysaker p. 166). This study showed that 36–77 percent of schizophrenics can be classified as "recovered" or "improved" at the time of final assessment. Another study, a meta-analysis of 320 clinical trials, estimated that 40 percent of people with schizophrenia showed signs of improvement within a few years of starting treatment. Michaela Amering, with the Department of Psychiatry at the Medical University of Vienna, and Margit Schmolke, at the German Academy for Psychoanalysis in Munich write that the myth of schizophrenia's chronicity "still lives on" and that its persistence "is hard to understand, given that it has little to do with reality." They point out that schizophrenia can follow "rather divergent courses over time" and that symptomatic remission is common. They point to research by Davidson et al. (2007) which shows that recovery can occur in almost 70 percent of cases. They emphasize this point for their readers: "You can recover in spite of schizophrenia; you can recover and be healed of schizophrenia" (Amering and Schmolke p. 104).

The reason for the variation in percentages of recovery is due to the fact that the official diagnostic criteria for "schizophrenia" is still contested, and therefore it is ambiguous and equivocal in both the clinical literature and the diagnostic manuals (Chiu p. 280). Although recovery from mental illnesses like schizophrenia has been written about and discussed for over 30 years (Ciompi), a paradigm shift with respect to the erroneous assumption of a poor prognosis for so-called mental illnesses has still not taken place (Amering and Schmolke p. 115). In their discussion of psychiatric authority, psychiatrist Douglas Porter and Professor of Psychology Peter Zachar explain that

> The entrenched belief that schizophrenia is an incurable disease . . . is rooted not in a factual understanding of the prognosis of schizophrenia, but in a prejudicial "myth" of incurability. (Porter and Zachar p. 204)

Clinicians in North America today seem to be either unaware of the recovery statistics in their own literature or simply deny their validity. They continue to approach their patients diagnosed with schizophrenia as though they were in fact incurable. It has been argued that practicing clinicians tend to make pessimistic predictions about the prognosis of all types of "mental illnesses" because they work most often with severe and chronic cases (Hunsley and Lee p. 657). But over thirty years of research has provided strong evidence that psychological interventions are efficacious. This is according to John Hunsley, Director and Professor of Clinical Psychology at the University or Ottawa, and Catherine M. Lee, Professor of Psychology at the same university, and authors of the essay "Prognosis and Psychological Treatment." They go on to say that, using meta-analysis, "numerous researchers have found that interventions for children, adolescents, and adults can have substantial positive effects" (p. 657). And just like in the area of physical medicine, the terms "positive effects" and "efficacious interventions" mean that people are helped to recover. Psychiatrist and university professor Norman Sartorius, former director of the World Health Organization's Division of Mental Health, and former president of the World Psychiatric Association notes that "iatrogenic stigma" of mental illness—stigma that is created by the mental health services providers—begins with the behavior and attitudes of medical professionals, especially psychiatrists (p. 1470). The belief in the incurability of so-called mental illnesses and the non-recovery of mental health services users originated in the helping professions. It has a long history and continues to be sustained by those who stand to gain, either professionally or financially, from this belief.

Recall that one of the differences in treatment goals between the physician and the psychotherapist is the fact that the physician typically treats symptoms with the goal of a cure in mind while, in general, the psychotherapist sees no such possibility. Many psychotherapists continue to erroneously believe that recovery from serious mental illness is exceedingly rare, if not impossible (L. Davidson p. 252). When recovery does occur it is often attributed to a less than perfect initial diagnosis, or dismissed as "temporary" with a confident expectation of the patient's relapse. Like the adage in alcohol recovery programs which asserts that "once an alcoholic, always an alcoholic" psychotherapy seems to disseminate, or at least subscribe to, the same mistaken mantra. Despite contrary empirical evidence from outcome studies in both addiction recovery and recovery from so-called mental illnesses there is relatively little clinical literature on the recovery from, or cure of, so-called mental illnesses.

The conventional approach in psychotherapy at this time in history is aimed at the "stabilization" of the illness, the "management" of the diagnosed symptoms, and the "control" of the patient. The primary method is medications because this is what is considered to be the most cost-effective. The number of prescriptions for anti-depressants and anti-psychotic medications have skyrocketed in the last decade, due, in part, to the resistance of health insurers to pay for cognitive psychotherapies and the many treatment hours that are assumed to always be required (Graham p. 47). But the claim of the greater cost-effectiveness of medications over counseling or psychotherapy is arguable, and raises a number of issues. For example, the assumption held by clinicians, that the majority of mental health services users will not improve (Flanagan p. 267), and therefore can only be managed but not cured with the medications, often results in a lifetime of money spent on costly medications for their patients. On the other hand, philosophical "talk therapy" can bring improvement and even a cure in far less time, most certainly less than a lifetime, sometimes in as little as half a dozen one-hour visits. This makes talk therapy a much less costly, much more cost-effective, treatment approach. In fact research has shown that talk therapy is often simply more effective, period.

Jonathan Davidson, a medical doctor with the Anxiety and Traumatic Stress program at Duke University, cites research which found that patients who were treated with Cognitive-Behavior Therapy (CBT) fared better after six months than did those who were treated with both CBT and sertraline, an antidepressant of the selective serotonin reuptake inhibitor (SSRI) class. It was found that sertraline lowered symptoms too rapidly, thereby undermining the effects of the talk therapy. Davidson theorizes that when a treatment that consists exclusively of medication is terminated relapse is much more likely to occur, "perhaps because appropriate learning of new behaviors, social skills sets, and interpretation biases has not taken place." He goes on to say that SSRI drugs and talk therapy "may in fact be working in opposition (i.e., antagonistic) ways" in several diagnosable "mental illnesses" such as depression, social phobia, and other forms of anxiety (J. Davidson p. 122).

Medications are often mistakenly assumed to be the reason for a patient's improvement, while other life factors which may have contributed are simply ignored. For example, Ademola Adeponle, a resident in psychiatry at the University of Manitoba, Canada, recounts the experiences of a twenty-eight-year-old single woman whose third fiancé unexpectedly, once again, called off their wedding. This made her, understandably, very emotionally upset. She was diagnosed by her psychiatrist as being "mentally ill" and admitted to a psychiatric hospital where she was given antipsychotic medications. Adeponle writes that, after three weeks on the drugs, her "condition" finally "stabilized" (Adeponle et al. p. 120–21). With this simple statement Adeponle implies that it was the medications which "stabilized" the patient's emotions. But this raises the question, What else happened during those three weeks which may have contributed to her "stabilization'? Whom did she come in contact with during that time? There seems to be an enormous explanatory gap in which the reader is left to infer that three weeks' worth of medications while lying in a hospital bed was all that was required to lead to the patient's improvement. This kind of "as-if-by-magic-potion" explanation of "stabilization" and "symptom management" by medications, in which it seems as though nothing else had transpired in the patient's life, is not uncommon in the psychiatric literature. This is a huge, completely unjustified, but common assumption about the assumed remedial potency of medications. It is analogous to the mistaken cliché that "time heals all wounds."

It discounts all the discussions with hospital staff, and the emotional assistance from parents, siblings, friends, and colleagues that may have been significant factors in her improvement. Despite the supposed "triumph" of psychotropic drugs, some clinicians in the mental healthcare field have felt compelled to point out that, while drugs can control or manage symptoms and "stabilize" patients, these drugs have not been able to help patients recover, nor have they cured any of the most common "conditions" they are meant to treat, such as depression, anxiety, and schizophrenia (Paris p. 10).

Early nineteenth century folklore, prejudice, and social expediency all conspired to suggest that insanity involved "permanent, irreversible, global obliteration of the rational faculties" (Charland p. 65). But there have been dissenting voices. William Battie may have been the first asylum doctor to have officially declared (in his *Treatise on Madness* published in 1758) that insanity is in fact sometimes curable. Conclusive corroboration of Battie's controversial observation only became possible later in the nineteenth century when scientific principles were applied to the study of patients in therapeutic asylums. But the idea of recovery, and a "recovery model," has not gained the popularity of the so-called "medical model." According to Tim Thornton, Professor of Philosophy and Mental Health, the recovery model has been widely debated, "but no model has yet been articulated that really does contest or rival a medical model" (p. 237). Juan Mezzich, President of the World Psychiatric Association from 2005–2008 emphasizes that pathology has occupied a monopoly in the discussion of health and clinical care. This means that positive aspects of health, such as the possibility of recovery and even cure, have been largely ignored in the research, publications, and practice of clinical psychiatry (Amering and Schmolke p. 47). While today's dominant treatment model in psychiatry and psychotherapy is on patient management, stabilization, and control, social scientist and Professor of Recovery, Wilma Boevink, former user of psychiatric services herself, argues that the primary aim of psychiatric care should be "to enable us to lead our lives in the manner that we wish. Care is a means to an end, not an end in itself" (p. 16). Recovery and cure ought to always be the goals.

THE "NEW" CONCEPT OF RECOVERY

The so-called new "recovery movement" had its beginnings only about twenty years ago, in the 1990's. Bradley Lewis is an Associate Professor of Medical Humanities and Cultural Studies in New York. He observes that a major force driving the recovery movement is "an increasing chorus of criticism of what are seen as one-dimensional medical model approaches" (p. 146). As recently as 1998 the New Zealand Mental Health Commission noted that the recovery movement in the US that grew out of psychiatric rehabilitation, was still "circumscribed by the medical model, and was driven more by the needs of professionals than by those of service users" (Adeponle p. 113). Michaela Amering and Margit Schmolke explain in their book *Recovery of People with Mental Illness* that in order to experience recovery the individual must "stop blaming the illness for all the problems you have in life, and you have to stop using some kind of chemical instability in the brain as an excuse." They say that it is more accurate to say, "You are experiencing severe emotional distress due to a combination of losses, traumas, and lack of support which interferes with your life in the community" than it is to believe that you are "mentally ill, or that your mental illness is caused by a genetically or biochemically based brain disorder" (p. 68–69). This change in perspective is the first step toward the adoption of a new personal paradigm of recovery which includes a switch from "stabilizing" medications to curative philosophical counseling and psychotherapy.

The words "recovery" and "cure" are difficult, if not impossible, to find in the indexes of most books on counseling and psychotherapy. Much of current literature on the psychiatric and psychotherapeutic practices emphasizes symptom-based diagnosis and treatment of so-called mental disorders. One consequences of this emphasis is that "notions of recovery are often framed in terms of clinical outcomes" such as symptom reduction, risk management, and crisis containment (Adeponle p. 109). The US organization called "Recovery International" is said to aim for "psychotherapeutic management" meaning that the patient is brought to a state in which "the sensation can be endured, the impulse controlled, the obsession checked" (Frank p. 251). Professor Emeritus of Psychiatry Jerome D. Frank and psychiatrist Julia B. Frank write of "psychotherapeutic management" which leads to "increases in well-being and a diminution of psychological symptoms" (1993 p. 251). But is this enough? Does "increasing well-being," "psychotherapeutic management," helping suffering individuals to "endure," and "controlling" and "checking symptoms" amount to anything resembling actual recovery?

The traditional psychiatric perspective of the so-called mentally ill patient associates the illness with loss of free will and a significant curtailment of personal responsibility which the psychiatrist feels justified in taking over. The recovery perspective, on the other hand, "attributes to people experiencing mental illness the capacity to change their attitudes, values, feelings, goals, skills, and/or roles" (Kravetz and Hasson-Ohayon p. 192). The terms "recovery" or "cure" mean that a "mental illness" is understood to be emotional suffering and/or cognitive distress brought on by difficult exogenous life circumstances which can be humanistically ameliorated, as opposed to being endogenous malfunctions of the biological brain requiring medical intervention.

The experience of suffering and healing or recovery, varies significantly according to place, culture, and social configuration. Recovery in

North America and Europe tends to be built on "individualism, and a ego-centric concept of the person as self-sufficient, self-determining, and independent." But indigenous cultures tend to have a more sociocentric (integration with family and community environments), ecocentric (connected to the land and the natural environment), or cosmocentric (relationship with a larger world of departed ancestors or spirits) conception of personhood. A recovery program in non-Euro-American societies requires careful consideration of often unfamiliar social contexts and cultural systems of value and meaning (Adeponle p. 118). This is done in the philosophical approach to counseling and psychotherapy. But social context and cultural considerations have no place in the so-called "medical model" approach.

The editor of the book *Recovery of People with Mental Illness*, Abraham Rudnick introduces the volume with the observation that the notion of recovery from "mental illness" "has emerged as a leading notion in the mental health field in the last couple of decades or so" (p. 3). This may seem a surprising revelation, even startling to those who have held the belief that recovery was the leading impetus and the ultimate goal of treatment for any sort of illness. Health care, whether physical or mental, is typically understood to be a means to an end—recovery—not an end in itself (Boevink p. 17). But while only a limited number of physical ailments are considerred chronic by medical practitioners, so-called mental illnesses have been the subject of sweeping "chronification" by mental healthcare providers. The assumption of persistent invalidity in all types of so-called mental illnesses has, until very recently in the history of medicine, eclipsed any discussion of recovery (Amering and Schmolke).

Psychaitrist Beate Schrank and her associates point to psychiatric research which has demonstrated that the course of a "mental illness" does not necessarily involve chronic suffering or an inexorable decline. They point to a meta-analysis of longitudinal data on the course of schizophrenia in the twentieth century which found that approximately 20 percent recover with a loss of psychotic symptoms and a return to the pre-illness level of functioning, and about 40 percent recover socially by regaining their economic and residential independence and exhibiting low levels of social disruption. Because this kind of recovery focuses on quantifiable levels of symptomatology, social functioning, relpase prevention, and risk management, it is refered to as "clinical recovery." But mental health care services users also advance an understanding of recovery they have called "personal recovery." It emphasizes "the centrality of hope, identity, meaning, and personal responsibility" in the client's approach to life (Schrank et al. p. 133).

When the psychotherapeutic literature discusses recovery, it mentions both clinical and personal recovery. Clinical recovery is said to involve symptom remission or alleviation, and the patient's relatively independent functioning, while personal recovery includes the patient changing his attitudes, values, feelings, goals, skills, and/or roles (Slade p. 78). It might be argued that different approaches are called for in the attainment of these goals. But if symptom remission refers to the reduction or alleviation of suffering and distress, and if changing one's attitudes, values, feelings, goals, skills and/or roles can in fact alleviate suffering and distress, then there seems to be a distinction without a difference between the clinical and the personal in terms of what leads to recovery.

In an essay on the interrelationship between mental and physical health in a report for the World Health Organization (WHO), authors Raphael, Schmolke, and Wooding discuss six stages of recovery: anguish (feeling at the lowest point of your life); awakening (turning point); insight (finding out more); action plan (finding ways to get better); determined commitment to become well (working hard toward getting well); well-being/empowerment/recovery (accomplishing wellness and other achievements) (Amering and Schmolke p. 164). Furthermore, Eliahu Shamir, chairperson of the NGO "Ozma," the Israeli association of families of people coping with mental illness, writes that the notion of recovery from chronic or persistent illness is said to appear in two forms:

1. *objective*—termination of symptoms of illness and recovery of normal functions, such as self-care, employment, and social relationships
2. *subjective*—termination of despair and of the desolate situation, and the revival of hope and purpose in life.

Shamir maintains that in reality both of these forms merge into one, namely in the control of one's life as a responsible adult (p. 53). Interestingly, Shamir also mentions that extensive studies have shown that a sizeable proportion (around 40 percent) of seriously mentally ill persons achieve recovery after only short-term treatment, or without any treatment whatsoever (Ibid).

In the Freudian analytical approach recovery involves "abreacting" psychic trauma within a transference relationship that is said to free the energies that keep troubling memories suppressed and sustain neurotic symptoms. The essence of the psychoanalytic cure is "a conscious awareness of the truth of one's own experience." Achieving an ability to know, comprehend, and live within the truth permits one "to more satisfactorily discharge the demands of biological (sexual and aggressive) drives" (Bankart p. 162). Of course it is very much an open question as to whether a "cure" can actually be achieved in the psychoanalytic approach. Freud did not have a laudable success rate in curing his patients. In Adlerian psychotherapy, recovery consists of discovering the truth about oneself, including correcting one's selfish, infantile, and neurotic lifestyle. Adler's system sees becoming more ethical as the focus in the attempt to achieve a "cure" (Ibid). So, according to Bankart's characterization of two of the foremost methods in therapy for the mind, recovery and cure are touted as goals within their theoretical orientations. But as mentioned above, in reality psychiatrists and psychotherapists who practice these methods typically don't actually hold the belief that what they're doing has any real potential of producing either recovery or a cure; practice does not follow theory.

In the late eighteenth century there existed one overarching feature of the concept of insanity at two legendary asylums: the York Retreat in England and the Salpêtrière Hospital in Paris, France. Both institutions held that insanity represents a derangement of ideas; a malfunction of the understanding or the imagination. This meant that the "recovery" of the mind was mainly a cognitive or intellectual endeavor which involved reestablishment in the patient of ordered thinking and ideation, and restoration of accurate perception and sound judgment. But attention was also given to the passions, emotions, and feelings due to the understanding that they can both overthrow or undermine reason. It was accepted that what psychology calls "affects" play an important role in recovery (Charland p. 69). The directors of those institutions, William Tuke at York and Philippe Pinel in Paris, recognized that factors within the home and family environment were often the initial trigger of "insanity." It was therefore taken that the insane often had to be removed from those environments if they were to recover (Ibid p. 71). For both Tuke and Pinel "a healthy mind and a sound mind is also necessarily an ethical mind—that is, a mind that follows the dictates not only of reason, but also of morality" (Ibid p. 65). It therefore seems reasonable to conclude that their concept of "recovery" must have included teaching their patients reasoning skills and an understanding of what it means to be a moral person. But this approach was slowly eroded and then completely overshadowed with the advent of drugs as a replacement for therapeutic discussions.

It has been found that psychotherapy or "talk therapy" in its many forms is generally effective. It is estimated that approximately 80 percent of those undergoing psychotherapy improve as a result of it (Erwin 1997, p. 144). Beyond improvement, the *idea* of recovery from so-called mental illness is gaining more attention. But while this idea has emerged as a leading notion in the mental health field in the last few decades or so, and while it is now *claimed* as the ultimate aim of mental health care services in many countries, and a leading priority for people with "mental illness" (Rudnick 2012a, p. vii, 3), it is still largely missing from contemporary practice. Recovery is still perceived as a non-issue, a distraction from the important work of providing ongoing mental healthcare services.

Recovery is highly subjective as both the experience of a process and an end state. While clinicians doubt the possibility of recovery, former patients point out that an essential part of recovery is to "look back at what has happened to you and to create your own story about it. . . . What is important is that *you*, and no one else, give meaning to what has happened" (Boevink p. 21). An idiographic viewpoint—one that focuses on the specifics of individual lives rather than general groups statistics—is necessary if recovery from serious mental illnesses is to be understood as an individual's personal journey, as varying from one individual to another, and as a change in self-image along a non-linear, unpredictable course (K. Gill p. 97). A study of available personal accounts of recovery identified four essential recovery processes—finding hope, re-establishing personal identity, finding meaning in life, and taking responsibility for recovery, i.e., personal autonomy (K. Gill p. 100). In their book *Cognitive Therapy of Schizophrenia* psychiatrists David Kingdon and Douglas Turkington write that in the "normalization" of psychosis for example, "much of what we aim to do has its roots in the philosophy of care" (p. 87). Care includes empathetic listening, careful discussion, and helpful suggestion. The claim that so-called psychotic patients can't benefit from philosophical psychotherapy (see Brown 2012) is based on the mistaken assumption that psychosis is a permanent state. In fact psychotic states are episodic, and individuals who suffer from them also experience times of "normal" lucidity where empathetic discussions can be very helpful in reducing the frequency of those episodes. (see Kingdon and Turkington). A psychotic episode can be likened to a nightmare. Medications are administered to sedate the patient as a convenience for the caregivers, but this does not end the patient's internal struggle with the nightmare. What that person needs is someone with the patience and willingness to help him slowly "wake up" back into the world of "normal" experiences. Philosophical psychotherapy, even in the case of so-called psychotic patients, helps to reduce suffering and return the person to a form of "normalcy" that is acceptable to him.

Normalization is the process by which thoughts, behaviors, moods, and experiences are compared and understood in terms of similar thoughts, behaviors, moods, and experiences attributed to other individuals in society who are *not* diagnosed as "mentally ill." Negative experiences often precipitate some form of stress. But often the only difference between distress and so-called mental illness is that the stress is often not understood by diagnosticians as being the result of life circumstances, nor treated by clinicians as being such (Kingdon & Turkington p. 87–88). Some of the aims of "normalization" are to reduce the client's or patient's fear of going mad, facilitate reattribution of hallucinations, find alternative explanations for delusions, improve self-esteem, reduce feelings of isolation, and reduce stigma (Ibid). None of these aims is achievable by means of the "medical model" of treatment, nor the exploration of the so-called hidden unconscious carried out in psychoanalysis.

Research has shown that mental healthcare is most useful to patients and clients when it attends to both "controlling" the so-called illness and enabling them to rebuild their lives (K. Gill p. 104). What does "controlling" an "illness" imply? And is mere "control" a reasonable goal? Rather than being merely another object of professional examination and control, in the active state of recovery the client becomes a contributing agent in decisions made within and about the therapeutic process. In this way the person retains her identity as an effectual agent with personhood, rather than being just another statistic in the "set" of the "mentally ill" needing to be handled in the manner prescribed by psychological treatment manuals. If clinicians treat the person as a "case" of "mental illness," and as being beyond recovery or cure, this invariably has an inexorably negative influence on that person's self-image. This means that "the *way* that mental health staff work with people in the 'patient' role may be as important as *what* they do" (Slade p. 89). What is required is a shift in both social convention which currently stigmatizes those who are troubled, and in clinical practices in which counselors and therapists approach an individual's suffering, distress, and confusion as though they were organic "mental illnesses."

A PARADIGM SHIFT

Many of my students, especially those majoring in psychology, tend to be very incredulous during their first few weeks in my "Philosophy for Counselors" course. The same is true for individuals who have been previously diagnosed by psychotherapists as being mentally ill and have subsequently become my clients, or who have attended one of my public seminars. There is astonishment that I would say medication is rarely necessary in the alleviation of mental distress and suffering. They find it extremely difficult to grasp the difference between the biological brain and the propositional mind. In defense of the medical model status quo, they cite textbook examples of mental illnesses described as endogenous brain diseases. They cite their psychology class notes which claim that there is always a genetic weakness, a chemical imbalance, a brain malfunction, and so on at the root of all so-called mental illnesses. They give examples of a friend of a friend who would not be able to live normally within society without taking psychotropic medications. They recall movies and novels in which madness was said to have sprung up, for no reason, from the criminal's dark unconscious, or because the criminal's brain simply and unexplainably malfunctioned one day. Students simply can't accept that the enormous amount of published "empirical" data they have studied which claim that so-called mental illnesses are caused by chemical imbalances in the biological brain are unreliable, ambiguous, vague, contradictory, and misleading, and that some of that information has a hidden economic agenda. They don't believe at first that I could possibly have "empirical data" as well as philosophical logic that contradicts the reductionist biomedical mind/brain equivalency hypotheses. It takes time, usually three to four three-hour classes, before they start to actually hear the arguments I offer, read the scientific materials I hand out, visit the websites I recommend, and grasp the reasoning behind the conclusion that "mental illness" is not what we have been led to believe it is. This is the sort of time not taken by those who simply dismiss the idea of philosophy in the service of counseling and psychotherapy because it is, in their opinion, nonsense since it is not scientific, not medical, and not "real" philosophy.

In his essay titled "Philosophy and Therapy: Professional Training and Certification" Sam Brown points out that some commentators believe that when philosophy is used in counseling "to soothe a client's distress" the philosopher/counselor is no longer practicing pure philosophy because the aim is "emotional tranquility and psychological balance." In counseling the attainment of philosophical wisdom is no longer the primary aim. He goes on to say that while the practice of philosophy in counseling and psychotherapy is a deviation from academic philosophy, "it is entirely legitimate as a form of counseling" because this is just "psychological counseling using philosophical methods" (p. 159). But while Brown's attempt to defend philosophical counseling and therapy is commendable, it is a mistake to claim that the practice of philosophy is just "psychological counseling using philosophical methods." In fact in chapter 8 of this book there is a list of twenty significant differences between the two. The practice of philosophy is certainly not psychological counseling. The exact opposite is true: the therapeutic part of psychology has largely been turned into philosophical discussions. The many schools of psychological counseling or psychotherapy have extensively borrowed from the content and practice of philosophy to help suffering people in their communities in a way that academic philosophers themselves have not been doing since the days of Socrates and Plato. To state it more boldly, psychotherapy has become a watered-down version of philosophy and not vice-versa (Deurzen-Smith p. 158). Psychotherapy has attempted to adopt philosophy for good reason: because so-called "talk therapy" has been found to be the most effective form of psychotherapy. It has proved to be better and less expensive than medications at long-term relief of symptoms. The symptomatic relief it brings is not accompanied by any side effects; and it goes beyond symptomatic relief to address the causal factors which initiated the onset of the individual's suffering. True philosophical talk therapy improves the person's quality of life; it reduces the risk of relapse; it often results in a cure; and it can be "administered" prior to onset of any symptoms as a prophylactic to prevent mental illness (Bolton 2008, p. 258).

The public's perception of so-called mental illness is that it is complicated, difficult to understand, deep, and mysterious. The reason for this is because this is how the mental health care field has portrayed itself since the time of Freud. To begin with, the psychoanalyst's physical position in the consultation room—hidden from the patient's field of vision—first established the mystique of the omniscient therapist. Then the pseudo medical language invented within the field has guaranteed that understanding both the diagnosis and treatment remains beyond the comprehension of both the layperson and the patient. This maintenance of mystery has forced the patient to perceive himself helpless in any attempt at recovery in the absence of the omniscient expert clinician. It has ensured the dependency of the patient on the professional for a specific pharmaceutical treatment protocol that is said to be demanded by the formal diagnosis. In a sense, mental healthcare, as epitomized by psychoanalysis, ensures the omission of the patient from participation in his or her own treatment. This is exactly opposite to the methodology employed in any method of counseling or psychotherapy that emulates the practice of philosophy. Here an explicit partnership always exists between the suffering person and the practitioner.

As mentioned earlier, it's important that the counselor or therapist presumes at least the possibility of the client's recovery. If the clinician convinced that mental illnesses are incurable, life-long conditions then the client's belief (and hope) in recovery could result in his being diagnosed as suffering from the comorbid condition of delusional ideation. If the clinician "knows" stabilization is all that is achievable then recovery or cure are not treatment motivating. The idea of recovery from, or cure of so-called mental illnesses requires the counselor or therapist to experience yet another paradigm shift, this time in epistemology. Recovery or cure requires a knowledge of its probability, and not simply a grudging toleration of its distant possibility.

This is not to say that there ought to be a shift of the epistemologic center from clinician to client. A partnership of objective knowledge and subjective perceptions is essential if the goal of satisfactory recovery or cure is to be reached. The point is that the clinician's initial epistemological stance on the ontology, etiology, and prognosis of so-called mental illnesses, before any treatment begins, ought to include an awareness of the ever-increasing positive statistics on recovery and cure. In other words, treatment ought to always commence with an understanding of the very strong likelihood of the client's recovery or cure.

Professional practitioners have only relatively recently begun to use the word "recovery" and "cure" in relation to the goals of counseling and psychotherapy. But the media and the general public continue to cling to the long-standing belief popularized by the originator of Alcoholics Anonymous (AA): "Once an alcoholic, always an alcoholic." Of course this belief would be justified if it were true that an addiction is precipitated by the addictive nature of the ingested or injected substance. But this is false. For example, in his essay "Marriage and the Prevention of Psychiatric Disorder" W. Kim Halford, Professor of Psychology at the University of Queensland in Australia, writes that research has shown that many drinkers report that stressful interactions with their spouses increase their urge to drink. Severe marital conflict is the most commonly reported reason for alcoholics to relapse back to uncontrolled drinking (p. 121). More succinctly, stressful interactions with a spouse, not the chemical structure of alcohol, "causes" the consumption of alcohol. While the term "recovery" has been used by Alcoholics Anonymous and the "12-step programs" since the mind-twentieth century, it refers only to a fragile, often temporary, remission of symptoms. These type of programs view individuals with alcohol or other addictions as having to perpetually endure a lifelong vulnerability to relapse. As a result, total remission or full cure is not considered a real possibility (Adeponle p. 115). Even books written by psychiatrists mention a "vulnerability and proneness to addiction" to alcohol (Amering and Schmolke p. 11) as though it is the alcohol which is what the suffering individual craves. But an addiction is not a craving for a substance; it is an attempt to reduce personal mental and emotional suffering. Alcohol "appears to have a direct effect of reducing awareness of self (as well as thinking about events in relation to the self)" (Lynn and McConkey p. 293). When they are not an attempt to dissociate from negative conceptions of one's self, addictions are often a craving for love, self-respect, the respect of others, a functional family life, and a meaningful place in society. The "addictive" substance is merely the means chosen for either slow self-destruction or for coping with, and reducing, painful existential torment. The use of alcohol is a "default" approach to ending suffering when the individual has exhausted his or her own mental and emotional resources, and has been unable to locate any other, more effective coping strategy.

For a more comprehensive discussion about the significant influence of life factors in the onset of addictive behaviors and relapse see Louis Berger's book *Substance Abuse as Symptom*. He argues that drugs and alcohol are clearly not the problem. He cites Bell and Battjes who explain that correlational studies have found that drug abuse "is associated with attitudes, beliefs, and values, as well as other personality factors such as feelings of self-esteem, self-reliance, and alienation" (p. 49). He quotes B. K. Alexander who argues that the treatment system that has emerged from the logic of the disease model of addiction is "expensive, coercive and ineffective" (p. 45). What the sufferer needs is to find different, less self-destructive ways, of dealing with difficult life circumstances and low self-esteem, and ways of acquiring or re-gaining love, self-respect, and so on. Why is the craving for love, respect, a functional family life, and a meaningful place in society perceived and diagnosed as an addiction, or a chronic illness? This is in effect what happens when the consumption of alcohol is erroneously labeled as the problem caused by a "vulnerability and proneness" to the substance itself.

The Alcoholics Anonymous model of ending the consumption of a substance is flawed. The accepted adage "Once an alcoholic, always an alcoholic" is simply not factual. A suffering individual can become dependent on a substance if that individual is given no alternative way of dealing with his or her emotional suffering and cognitive distress. The problem with the AA approach is that the only alternative to a dependence on alcohol that is offered in the 12-Step program is a dependence on "God." But for many people abstinence with a dependence on God is not a viable replacement for the mental and emotional relief gained from the consumption of large quantities of mind-dulling alcohol. Given that the "God solution" of abstinence is the only alternative offered, it is no wonder that the AA protocol sees alcohol addiction lasting a lifetime. Treatment for any type of addiction will always be ineffective if it only involves attempting to prevent the individual from accessing their substance of choice, without offering ways of dealing with the life problems which bring on the desire for the pain relief in mind-dulling substances. The same argument applies to so-called obsessive–compulsive disorders (OCD), which are simply addictive behaviors. If an addiction is not about the nature of the substance, but is instead the compulsive use of a substance (or repetitive action) to diminish emotional distress and mental suffering, then logic dictates that the removal of the substance will ultimately not be helpful to the individual because the causal life problems remain. Once that individual regains access to the substance the addiction behavior will reoccur. Clearly what is required for actual recovery is treatment that includes dealing with the emotional, familial, social, and political factors that precipitated the addictive behavior in the first place. What is required is the assistance that is available from philosophical discussions.

Alcoholism and other substance addictions are not illnesses like cancer which, once they are in remission, may recur at any time, or like diabetes which is a chronic, non-curable but manageable condition. An addiction is more like an attempt to deal with a wound from an injury that, once it is healed, does not recur unless there is a second injury. Once healed, the site of the injury may even be stronger than it was prior to the injury. Prevention of relapse in the case of addictions means, not a wariness about a possible future attack from a disease, but a fortification of the self-protective ability of the individual to defend herself against the life circumstances that were the cause of her mental injury. This can be accomplished with philosophy. Of course some physical injuries are so severe that they don't allow a return to the previous state of health after they are healed. In such cases the individual must adapt by finding ways of coping with their altered condition. The same applies to mental distress and suffering: some mental "injuries" can be so severe that they continue to have an effect on the individual's life indefinitely. Philosophy can help such individuals adapt and cope by teaching strategies that will restore self-esteem and improve life despite the injury's lingering aftermath. The lasting after-effects of a physical injury do not need to define the individual. The same thing applies to mental "injury."

Just like recovery from addiction is not about avoiding the substance, mental illness is not about altering the chemicals in the brain. Anita Everett, Community psychiatrist and former senior medical adviser for the US Substance Abuse and Mental Health Services Administration, has stated that recovery is "a critical paradigm shift for all individuals involved in the lives of persons with serious mental illnesses" (B. Lewis p. 146). The so-called recovery movement makes a further paradigm shift from more mainstream psychiatric approaches "by emphasizing the importance of social and political factors in mental health" (Ibid p. 147). Furthermore, recovery includes the exact opposite to a dependency on diagnosticians, clinicians, and government social services. Recovery calls for the empowerment of clients and patients—the assertion of the agency of the patient—in order that they may be able to defend themselves, and fend for themselves. For community psychiatrist Kenneth Thompson empowerment is so important to the recovery paradigm "that the whole movement could arguably be called the 'empowerment movement'" (K. Lewis p. 147).

In the second chapter of this book I mentioned that there is a relatively small group of philosophers who believe that a revolution in mental healthcare is necessary. But in today's political climate the word "revolution" has rather negative connotations. A better term is Thomas Kuhn's "paradigm shift." What is required in the field of mental healthcare is a paradigm shift in both theory and practice. This raises two questions: Why is there only a small group of philosophers with this frame of mind, and Why is such a shift necessary?

The paradigm shift that is called for consists of a number of permutations: from "the mind is the same as the brain" to "the mind is the nonmaterial content within the material brain"; from "suffering from a mental illness" to "suffering from painful emotions and distressing thoughts"; from "biomedical treatments with drugs" to "talk therapy"; from "psychologically oriented psychotherapy" to "counseling and psychotherapy based on the practice of philosophy"; from "philosophy only as after-the-fact therapy" to "philosophy as preventive medicine"; and from "stabilization" to "recovery" and "cure."

A sweeping paradigm shift in thinking about the causes and appropriate treatments for so-called mental illness can't be far away. The current biomedical platform is creaking and swaying under the heavy load of counter-evidence refuting that paradigm.

In his influential book *The Structure of Scientific Revolutions* Thomas S. Kuhn argues that

> in any scientific discipline that deals with the unknown, difficult-to-perceive, or inexact phenomena, there exists a certain *status quo* that is accepted by most authorities. This *status quo* is a theory or set of theories that attempts to explain observed phenomena and tries to predict

future occurrences.... As this theory begins to fail, various reasons are given by its adherents to explain the exceptions.... The exceptions pile up until they become unwieldy.... Each [newly formulated] paradigm attempts to better explain the phenomena and more accurately predict future results. Slowly the old theory collapses.... The experts devise experiments and tests to help them determine which new theory, if any, is acceptable. Finally, sometimes dramatically, the experts gravitate toward one theory, which becomes the new *status quo* (from a précis by Heisman p. 7-8. Italics in the original).

Kuhn's theory applied to the current state of mental healthcare would point to biopsychiatry as the current status quo that is accepted by most authorities. It attempts to explain observed phenomena and tries to predict future occurrences. Since an increasing number of biomedical explanations, such as the genetic theory, are failing various reasons are being given by its adherents to explain the burgeoning exceptions. New paradigms have been constructed to maintain the mind/brain equivalence and the so-called medical model of mental healthcare. Attempts at predicting the future of psychopharmacology and the "medical model" treatment of "mental illnesses" have been notoriously unreliable. The new paradigm which is emerging from the collapse of biomedical psychotherapy is that of "talk therapy," also called the practice of philosophy.

The explicit use of philosophy in counseling and psychotherapy avoids some of the most common pitfalls inherent in a non-philosophical approach. Psychologist C. Peter Bankart explains these pitfalls as being the following: considering the patient to be "cured" only after he or she has accepted the insights of the therapist; persuading the victims of emotional or sexual abuse that they must "work through" their "own" conflicted feelings toward their abusers "and thereby assume emotional responsibility for their own victimization"; trying to "fix problems" such as homosexuality or fear of failure "without questioning the assumptions underlying the client's wishes to be 'normal' and 'well-adjusted'; applying psychological explanations and psychiatric diagnostic labels to distress and suffering from existential difficulties; sending the client back into the world without having shared a critical evaluation of the economic assumptions, political attitudes, and social norms that lead to personal suffering; "solving" the client's problems without teaching him the reasoning skills, or helping him develop the emotional resources, necessary for personal empowerment; and refusing to discuss significant topics such as the meaning of life and death (p. 325, 368). There continue to be many misconceptions about therapy for the mind that are commonly held by both members of the general public and trained clinicians, that require a paradigm shift in order to be corrected. These are some examples:

- that so-called "mental illnesses" can't be prevented
- that individuals diagnosed with "mental illnesses" can't recover or be cured
- that hidden unconscious forces drive a person to be who he or she is
- that schizophrenia, anxiety, and depression (and other diagnoses) are biological diseases
- that because a medication is used to "treat" or at least counteract symptoms the medication points at a biological cause of these symptoms
- that diagnoses are based on scientific reasoning and evidence
- that "mental illnesses" are cross-culturally identical
- that when a "mental illness" runs in a family it therefore must be genetically transmitted
- that a mental illness can only be treated by a professional
- that the diagnosis of one client will be consistent among several therapists
- that phenomenological diagnosis and treatment of symptoms takes priority over dealing with life problems
- that the source of "mental illness" is always within the individual sufferer
- that a therapist will diagnose one symptom the same way—as the same "condition"—in two different clients
- that similar symptoms will be diagnosed the same in men and women
- that therapists work with the most up to date research data on illnesses such as schizophrenia, anxiety, depression, and addictions
- that there are medical tests which will indicate the presence of a "mental illness"
- that a patient's answers to questions on a psychological "test instrument" are interpreted identically by all therapists who evaluate them
- that all mental illnesses are ultimately organic in origin
- that there is no politics in diagnostic criteria and treatment methodology
- that the bottom line of pharmaceutical companies is focused on the mental health and well-being of individuals in their community
- that the best way to "heal" mental illness is to treat the individual symptoms
- that there is no self-healing in mental healthcare
- that only the doctor knows what the patient needs
- that a person's subjective perceptions of their own suffering is irrelevant in treatment decision-making
- that there is a different drug uniquely tailored to each of the diagnosable mental illnesses

- that biological markers have been found for many mental illnesses
- that mental illnesses are an escape from reality
- that when a person is in mental anguish or distress there is something wrong *with that person*
- that research in psychotherapy is medical science
- that the medical establishment considers psychotherapy to be based on empirical data
- that psychotherapy respects diversity in ways of thinking and being human
- that the unconscious needs to be purged of bad memories with therapy.

In light of the suffering that has been caused by the medical model of mental healthcare, and the treatment of emotional suffering and distress with psycho-pharmaceuticals, it's high time for a new paradigm in mental healthcare. What is required is a renaissance of the ancient practice of philosophy as therapy, in which individuals are helped to overcome mental distress and suffering without the use of brain-altering drugs. A new model of "mental illness" and mental healthcare must involve a paradigm shift that gives up the erroneous beliefs and claims listed above and replaces them with factual information. Here are a few examples:

1. The standard clinical treatment for "mental illness" does not conform to a medical model.
2. Medications for "mental illnesses" are not illness specific, targeting distinct conditions.
3. "Mental illnesses" are not separate, clearly defined entities.
4. "Mental illnesses" are not discovered through scientific investigations. They are symptom-based inventions agreed upon by a committee of clinicians and theorists.
5. "Mental illness" does not cause misery. But misery can lead to a diagnosis of any number of "mental illnesses."
6. "Mental illnesses" are neither genetically caused nor inherited.
7. There are no laboratory tests, no biometrics, that can reveal the existence of "mental illnesses."
8. A so-called mental illness is not an organic pathology; it is a label applied to a collection of symptoms.
9. The claims that "mental illnesses" are caused by chemical imbalances in the brain is a theory that has not, and cannot, be proved because of the distinctly different ontologies of the proposition mind and the biological brain.
10. The diagnosis of a "mental illness" is a subjective theory, not medical fact.
11. The ascendance of biological psychiatry since the 1980's has not improved the recovery rate of psychiatric patients, although it has

substantially improved the profit margin of multi-national pharmaceutical corporations.
12. The very term "mental illness" is a misnomer that conjures up a model of the cause of human misery which does not reflect the actual existential origins of cognitive confusion and emotional suffering.

Philosophical counseling and philosophical psychotherapy begin with a presupposition of shared rationality between client and practitioner. David Kingdon and Douglas Turkington discuss in their book *Cognitive Therapy of Schizophrenia* the possibility of returning the client to a state of "normalcy" if the psychotherapist starts with the presumption that the so-called mental illness is the result of severe stress rather than caused by some biological malfunction. As mentioned previously, even in the case of an individual diagnosed with psychosis the client will still experience periods of "normal" rationality. The presupposition of rationality within the client sees each individual who has been diagnosed with having a "mental illness" as being erroneously defined as paradoxically "determined" by chemicals in the biological brain that are said to be the cause of an illness in the non-biological mind. What is called "mental illness" by the psychotherapist is seen instead by the philosophical counselor or therapist as a coping mechanism, a last-resort strategy that the distressed individual has employed in order to survive in a life full of difficult problems. The philosophical practitioner understands that, because life is not determined solely by material causation, even severely distressed individuals can be helped to use their rationality to examine and change those areas of their own life experiences that are emotionally upsetting and mentally confusing, such as conflicting values, irrational thoughts, problematic peer or family relationships, past experiences of abuse or neglect, and the suffering brought on by socio-political factors such as poverty, unemployment, or discrimination. A review of 30 recovery narratives revealed that one very important theme in recovery is the individual's own view of the origin of their so-called "illness" (K. Gill p. 98). The suffering individual is often very well aware of what brought on the suffering, but the clinician's biased biologically oriented mind-set can dismiss the client's narrative of troubling life situations in favor of the standard "medical model" diagnostic approach. The term "cause" is often applied to problematic life circumstances, but an existential "cause" — more correctly termed an influence or reason — is not the same as a material or biological cause. The discovery within the philosophical setting of the client's or patient's reasons for their misery will suggest options for dealing with them, and frees the client from being labeled the helpless victim of a mental illness — the effect of a cause.

As mentioned above, a large percentage of people who have been diagnosed as "suffering *from* schizophrenia" recover without any clinical intervention. It would be naive to assume that the recovery from schizophrenia and other so-called mental illnesses are all simply "spontaneous remissions or religious miracles. No one lives in a vacuum devoid of the activities of life. Recovery is usually the result of the diagnosed individual having escaped from a toxic family or societal environment, and having gained the support of a friend, a pastor, a teacher, a counselor/therapist, or a formerly absent family member. Mental suffering and cognitive distress that is diagnosed as a "mental illness" is a "closed system" which locks the individual into both a self-identity and a social identity based on their problematic beliefs, values, fears, and assumptions. This damaging "knowledge set" does not dissipate on its own volition; the person who is locked in by what it contains must access external, more objective points of view, either through personal effort or with the assistance of empathetic others. It's only after the "mental illness" knowledge set is confronted, challenged, and abandoned that a new identity as a recovered, cured, "normal" individual can be shaped into taking its place.

There is the possibility of an ironic result when counselors and psychotherapists trained in philosophy must contend with clients who are also under the parallel care of a medical doctor or psychiatrist. When the client begins to improve due to the benefits of greater insights into self, others, and their social circumstances it is possible that, while the client regards these improvements are due to the ongoing philosophical discussion, the physician may attribute the client's improvement to the medications that have been prescribed. I have had clients who were in on-going counseling with me, whose doctors actually increased the psychotropic medications due to the erroneous belief that it was the effect of the medication that was creating the improvement in their condition. It might be argued that the physician's perspective is in fact the correct one: the medications are working. But when the medications that have been the client's staple for many years have produced only "stabilization without improvement, and yet a half dozen philosophical counseling discussions do result in noticeable improvement, it is clearly a mistake to attribute these recent positive changes to their long-standing regimen of medications.

Clinical psychologists Paul and John Lysaker maintain that recovery includes the patient's ability of "metacognition," which they describe as a set of capacities for self-reflection as well as reflection about the thoughts and feelings of others. This metacognition can contribute to the resolution of a number of challenging diagnoses, including "schizophrenia." They hold that in metacognition people "gain a sense of themselves through the activity of *thinking* about themselves and *generating* subjective interpretations of themselves" (p. 170; italics in the original). Metacognitive acts, according to the Lysakers, "are not incorrigible, but open to contestation—that is, it is in principle possible that they could be false" (Ibid). Metacognition includes thinking plus an evaluation of those thoughts, with the understanding and acceptance that they could be either right or wrong. But authentically objective metacognition does not come automatically; it must be learned as part of the counseling or therapeutic process. The Lysakers maintain that "there are probably few pathways to recovery that exclude the cultivation of metacognitive abilities" (Ibid). The goal of metacognition is "not to find the correct solution to a specific dilemma, but to help people to think about themselves as concrete individuals facing a dilemma, and to examine how they respond to that dilemma and similar situations" (p. 172–3). Interestingly, their description of "metacognition" in narrative therapy is precisely the way philosophical inquiry, philosophical self-scrutiny, and the teaching of philosophical skills can also be described. In fact the metacognitive element of narrative therapy is very similar in many respects to what is often referred to as the practice of Philosophical Counseling. It seems fair to assume that, rather than an exclusive education in psychology, additional training in philosophy would make the practitioner of narrative therapy much more proficient and helpful to clients.

PHILOSOPHY

Much of the recovery literature includes words of caution to both patients and practitioners not to expect the services user to regain the "premorbid" state of "normalcy" (see Amering and Schmolke; also Rudnick 2012a). But, unlike standard psychotherapy, the use of philosophy has the potential to bring the client to a cognitive and emotional state, and an ability level, that is actually superior to that which led them into their emotional suffering and cognitive distress in the first place. If "normal" refers to a state relatively devoid of suffering, but there was an onset of a so-called mental illness, then the "pre-morbid" state of that individual must have been below "normal," that is, he or she must have been in a situation that precipitated suffering which she was unable to resolve. If that individual is then helped with philosophy to not only resolve the current problem, but also accepts the offer to learn the wisdom and skills necessary for living a philosophical life, then he or she will reach a state that is better than simply being back to "normal" where he or she was lacking the ability to defend herself from the onset of suffering. To put in another way, learning philosophy will increase the client's set of protective and preventive capabilities past the level with which he or she came to the initial counseling or therapy session. This is very different from the approach in those psychotherapeutic methods where the goal is merely to "turn the clock back" with a reduction of symptoms, where the client is returned to the same, previously vulnerable, state. The term "recovery" is misplaced when it refers to a person's continued defenselessness and dependence on a clinician for future problem resolution. Perhaps this is why the word "recovery" appears so infrequently in the field of standard psychotherapy. Philosophy, unlike psychotherapy, does not simply return the client to an earlier vulnerable state. The philosopher, unlike the average counselor or psychotherapist, is willing to teach the client the very wisdom and methods she employed to help him overcome his original difficulties, as well as achieve a state that is beyond his previous defenseless condition of "normalcy." Philosophy does not merely facilitate a return to "normal"; it is an enhancement or enrichment of the client's abilities to resolve future life difficulties.

Larry Davidson, Professor of Psychiatry and Director of the Yale Program for Recovery and Community Health at the Yale School of Medicine, maintains that "it is very uncommon for a person to go from being 'normal' to being 'mentally ill' and then back to being 'normal' again" (2012 p. 254). This is true in the standard psychological sense of the term "mental illness." But it is not quite true in the sense in which "mental illness" is used in this book—as emotional suffering and cognitive distress caused by life circumstances. When a client in this non-biological sense of "mental illness" is helped to resolve their difficulties with philosophical discourse that client will indeed return to their "normal" state of life. But, as explained above, they will not be the same as they were previous to their "philosophical encounter" because the philosophy will not only have helped him to overcome their misery, but will have taught him how to deal with similar issues in the future. He will not simply be returned to his previous "normal." The philosophical counselor will have been willing to teach the client as much as he likes about the content and practice of philosophy in order to enhance the client's own knowledge and reasoning abilities. Philosophical counseling is thereby not only therapeutic, it is educational. The client learns ways to improve his ability to deal with many similar, and diverse, future circumstances.

Philosophers Gilles Deleuze, Jacques Lacan, Félix Guatteri, and Michel Foucault can be considered to have re-introduced the idea of recovery into the discussion of treatments for so-called mental illness in the late 1970s—if not to mainstream psychiatry, then at least to philosophy. Deleuze and Guatteri do so specifically by reference to the ontology of, and therapy for, schizophrenia; Lacan argues that the patients' participation in any diagnostic and therapeutic process should be substantially increased—in contrast to Freud, for example, who maintained that it is only the therapist who can interpret symptoms and assign a diagnosis. These philosophers argued that patients should actively participate in decisions about their own treatment, and help the therapist learn from their experiences. This anticipates an attitude that has gained a small momentum only very recently in the literature of mainstream psychiatry, in the form of the so-called recovery movement (Schrank p. 138). But it also harks back to the ancient practice of philosophy as therapy, where philosophcal discussion involved the perspectives of both the philosopher and the individual requesting his counsel.

The nature of mental health and treatment for so-called mental illnesses can be characterized in terms of several antinomies: Values and facts: the values held by society, individuals, and therapists, and the facts about what actually constitutes a so-called mental illness; free will and determinism: the human ability to make choices, even in the case of emotional responses to situations, in contrast to the belief that it is the brain or genetics which unavoidably causes mental illness in some; mind and brain: the difference between the propositional content and the biological container; and idiographic and nomothetic methodology: the relationship between personal, subjective experience of mental states, and biomedical generalizations about so-called conditions and the arranging of patients into diagnostic and treatment categories. Psychotherapy and the "medical approach" is shaped by values based on a strictly deterministic view of the individual, couched in terms of genetic inheritance. It focuses on the brain as the cause of mental activity and distress, and generalizes diagnoses from specific theories to many differing individuals (adapted from Kravetz and Hasson-Ohayon p. 190–91). On the other hand, philosophy as therapy is based on an examination of the "non-hard facts" of the individual's life circumstances and experiences which shape the person's beliefs, values, assumptions, and fears; on the freedom of the individual to reason, to decide, and to make choices. It is thereby based on the idea of the person's ability to change his or her mind; on a non-material mind; and on the belief that the decisions made by the person can potentially be changed with reasoning and argument. Philosophy sees the categorization of symptoms into "illness" or "disorder" labels as not only a mere reductionist materialist convenience for clinicians, but also as both dehumanizing and dismissive of the uniquely individual life of the suffering person. Philosophy as therapy is an idiographic methodology which sees each person, and each person's life circumstances, as unique and deserving of individual attention.

Tim Thornton, Professor of Philosophy and Mental Health at the University of Central Lancashire, UK, argues that if the aim of mental healthcare is a goal that is selected by the client according to what he or she hopes to achieve, according to what he or she values as right in living the kind of life they see as good, then it is the counselor or therapist's job to help the client weigh and evaluate the reasons for that goal. This will ensure that the goal is both reasonable and morally permissible, in the sense that it will cause no harm. The characterization of the goal, and its value to the client, is not independent of why it is wished for. It is tied to the client's reasons, and it is thereby tied to philosophy rather than biological pathology or material causality (Thornton 2012, p. 249). Biopsychiatry, and any other methods in psychotherapy that aspire to treat the mind as though it were the brain, cannot accommodate reasons nor reasoning. Because of this, the biological model of mental healthcare falls far short of offering human beings the kind of assistance to living a good life that is possible with a therapeutic approach based on philosophy. In order to be truly helpful to individuals, mental healthcare services must be capable of not only supporting the goals of their clients, they must also be capable of first helping them to define their goals and then devise the means to achieve them. Neither of these tasks are, or can be, carried out with the employment of biomedical methods.

Psychiatrists Amering and Schmolke argue that treatment must aim at teaching service users to make autonomous decisions, and then to trust them (p. 54). This is clearly contrary to the top-down decision-making strategy on which the so-called medical model of mental healthcare is firmly based. In philosophical counseling and therapy the emphasis on the lived experiences of the individual shifts authority away from clinicians and their institutional affiliations toward the afflicted individual's own self-understanding and agency (Adeponle p. 111). It is a re-establishment of that individual into the life they have chosen for themselves rather than one that has been medically prescribed. This is not a radical or even new model in mental healthcare. It is a method that harks back to ancient times. It has proven itself to be very effective despite the fact that the operative elements of philosophy have been concealed for more than a century under layers of both the academy's abstract theorizing and appropriation by both psychoanalysis and the various methods in psychotherapy.

What frequently appears to those around the suffering individual, and to clinicians, as signs of "mental illness" are not in fact chemical imbalance in the brain, but instead failed attempts at coping with existential problems (Amering and Schmolke p. 169). The biomedical approach which labels suffering and distress as depression, anxiety, schizophrenia, and so on defines the individual as a problem to be solved—a case of abnormality—and treats the symptoms as though the causes of suffering were internally generated by that person's faulty biological structures. To a certain extent this is true: much suffering originates internally. People suffer because others have led them to believe they are worthless; they suffer because they fear others; and they suffer because they have been confused by others about their rightful place within the family and society. But while the suffering comes from the person's own thoughts, these thoughts have their origins in what others have done to them, and not in their biology. The so-called mental illness of clinical depression is sometimes actually a broken heart. The circumstances of a person's life, and the people involved in those circumstances, can have an enormously negative impact on a person's beliefs, values, fears, and assumptions. This may have a long-lasting harmful effect. But this doesn't mean that people must necessarily be defenseless in the face of external influences. The British philosopher John Stuart Mill brought this fact to the attention of the readers of his *Autobiography* in which he discusses his recovery from a feeling of profound melancholy, or what would today be diagnosed as the "mental illness" of depression. After much reflection he came to the conclusion that

> I perceived that the word Necessity, as a name for the doctrine of Cause and Effect applied to human action, carried with it a misleading association; and that this association was the operative force in the depression and paralyzing influence which I had experienced: I saw that though our character is formed by circumstances, our own desires can do much to shape those circumstances; and that what is really inspiring and ennobling in the doctrine of free-will, is the conviction that we have real power over the formation of our own character; that our will, by influencing some of our circumstances, can modify our future habits or capabilities of willing. (Timko and Hoff p. 25)

While other people, as well as contingent life circumstances, can have a negative impact on an individual's life, that person has the potential to defend him- or herself against the constraints, biases, and hindrances raised by others. But having only the potential or desire to defend oneself is not enough. Each person must develop the capacity and skills to do so. The capacity to exert insight and judgment on life's vicissitudes requires being capable of "assimilating certain information, evaluating its relevance, considering it judiciously and, based on all this, making a choice or an informed decision" (Amering and Schmolke p. 122). The ability to carry out these steps can be developed with the help of instructors in the formal study of philosophy, or informally with the help of a philosophically trained counselor or therapist. Informal education is a process that should always accompany any therapeutic relationship because the people who suffer from psychiatric symptoms, so-called mental illnesses, are seeking information that can help them discover what is good for them and which steps they have to take to not only recover from but avoid future suffering (Mead and Copeland p. 71f).

Interestingly, studies have shown that "a sizeable proportion" of non-psychiatric inpatients also frequently lack good reasoning capacities (Ibid). This means that not only would philosophy be useful in therapeutic settings with individuals who are asking for specific help, but also that the general population could benefit from studying philosophy as well, probably from the very first grade of elementary school onward. By teaching young people and others, even before they are challenged with difficult life situations, to think about and discuss problems philosophically it is possible to significantly reduce the current human addiction to psychotropic medications and other harmful substances in the attempted alleviation of the pain and misery that result from life's difficult problems. Albert Einstein is said to have defined irrationality as doing the same thing over and over again and expecting different results. Learning philosophical reasoning as an alternative to the repeated filling of prescriptions for psychoactive medications seems the rational thing to do.

Thornton explains that rationality is not merely a statistically normal pattern of reasoning. "It involves, essentially, a notion of what one ought to think in the face of various reasons, evidence, and values" (2012, 243). Philosophy helps struggling or suffering individuals to decide what ought to be done, and to regain their rightful place as "normal among normals." Developing "a new sense and meaning of life" is essential growing beyond the catastrophic outcomes of a diagnosed psychiatric "condition" (Amering and Schmolke p. 16). Learning to rationally think about, and discuss with others one's conceptions of oneself, one's place in society, and the contingencies of the often unpredictable events in life is vital part of a philosophical process which reaches beyond recovery cure. The aim of philosophy is human flourishing—Martha Nussbaum says this many times in her book. Human flourishing is the cure because it is the opposite of suffering. Psychiatrists Amering and Schmolke remind us that life is meant to be lived and enjoyed within human society, not simply endured as a medical problem within the mental healthcare system (Amering and Schmolke p. 140). While the biomedical methods in psychotherapy tend to aim merely at symptom management, medication stabilization, and patient control, philosophy helps suffering individuals to not only regain a place in "normal" human society, but to "flourish."

When counselors and psychotherapists are educated in the content and practice of philosophy they will be better able to assist their clients and patients to overcome the emotional suffering and cognitive distress that is currently being improperly diagnosed as "mental illness."

Appendix

Oppositional Defiant Disorder (ODD)

"Oppositional Defiant Disorder (ODD)" is one of the most recent "mental illnesses" invented by the psychiatrists and other professional members of the Advisory Board for the latest edition of the American *Diagnostic and Statistical Manual of Mental Disorders (DSM)*. The description below was posted on the Internet by The U.S. National Library of Medicine, which promotes itself as "The World's Largest Medical Library."

It can be found at the following link:
http://www.ncbi.nlm.nih.gov/pubmedhealth/PMH0002504/

Below that is a brief critical discussion of this new so-called childhood mental disorder.

OPPOSITIONAL DEFIANT DISORDER

Causes, incidence, and risk factors

This disorder is more common in boys than in girls. Some studies have shown that it affects 20 percent of school-age children. However, most experts believe this figure is high due to changing definitions of normal childhood behavior, and possible racial, cultural, and gender biases. This behavior typically starts by age eight, but it may start as early as the preschool years. This disorder is thought to be caused by a combination of biological, psychological, and social factors.

Symptoms

- Actively does not follow adults' requests
- Angry and resentful of others
- Argues with adults
- Blames others for own mistakes
- Has few or no friends or has lost friends
- Is in constant trouble in school
- Loses temper
- Spiteful or seeks revenge
- Touchy or easily annoyed

To fit this diagnosis, the pattern must last for at least 6 months and must be more than normal childhood misbehavior. The pattern of behaviors must be different from those of other children around the same age and developmental level. The behavior must lead to significant problems in school or social activities.

Treatment

The best treatment for the child is to talk with a mental health professional in individual and possibly family therapy. The parents should also learn how to manage the child's behavior. Medications may also be helpful, especially if the behaviors occur as part of another condition (such as depression, childhood psychosis, or ADHD).

Prevention

Be consistent about rules and consequences at home. Don't make punishments too harsh or inconsistent. Model the right behaviors for your child. Abuse and neglect increase the chances that this condition will occur.

Critical Discussion

A critical examination of the above information about this so-called new mental illness raises some very troubling questions. For example, who determines when a child's behaviors are "different from those of other children around the same age and developmental level"? Should differences always raise concerns? Should differences lead to a diagnosis of "mental illness"? Also, when they say that "the behavior must lead to significant problems in school or social activities" who is experiencing those problems: the child or others in the child's life?

Under "Causes, incidence, and risk factors" they say "most experts believe this figure is high due to changing definitions of normal childhood behavior, and possible racial, cultural, and gender biases." But didn't the "experts" come up with this number? Are they disagreeing with their own numbers? Also, why are there "changing definitions of normal childhood behavior, and possible racial, cultural, and gender biases"? Do the experts keep changing their definitions of normal childhood behaviors? Are the experts racist, and do they hold cultural and gender biases?

Under "Treatment" when they say "The best treatment for the child is to talk with a mental health professional in individual and possibly family therapy," what should they talk about? Will the talk be about the child as the problem, or about the family environment as the problem? Will the talk be about the changing definitions of "normal childhood behavior"?

Or will it be about the racism, or biases of the experts? And when the say "medications may also be helpful" what sort of medications should they be, and what do they mean by "helpful"? Helpful in doing what? Helpful to whom: the child or others?

The passage under the heading "Causes..." actually gives no causal explanations at all. The "Prevention" section further down points to the presumed causes: "punishments too harsh or inconsistent; abuse, and neglect." Given these terrible causes, the so-called disorder seems to be a completely appropriate behavioral response by a child trying to survive in a hostile environment. What treatments do they recommend for parents who administer punishments that are too harsh or inconsistent, or abuse or neglect their kids?

Bibliography

Achenbach, Gerd. (1998). "On Wisdom in Philosophical Practice." In *Inquiry: Critical Thinking Across the Disciplines*. Vol. xvii, No. 3. Upper Montclair, NJ.: Institute for Critical Thinking. pp. 5–20.
Adeponle, Ademola, Robert Whitley, and Laurence J. Kirmayer. (2012). "Cultural contexts and constructions of recovery." In Rudnick pp. 109–132.
Al-Shawi, Hakam. (2006). "Psychotherapy's Philosophical Values: Insight or Absorption?" In *Human Studies*. 29: 159–179. New York: Springer.
Alexander, Franz. "The Dynamics of Psychotherapy in the Light of Learning Theory" In Goldfried pp. 64–77.
Allen, Laura B., and David H. Barlow. (2006). Treatment of Panic Disorder: Outcomes and Basic Processes." In Rothbaum pp.166–180.
Amering, Michaela, and Margit Schmolke. (2009). *Recovery in Mental Health: Reshaping Scientific and Clinical Responsibilities*. Hoboken, N.J.: Wiley-Blackwell.
Anthony, W. (1993). "Recovery from mental illness." *Psychosocial Rehabilitation Journal* 16. pp. 11–23.
APA (American Psychiatric Association) (2000). *Diagnostic and Statistical Manual of Mental Disorders*, 4th edn, text rev. Washington, DC: APA.
Applebaum, Stephen A. "Pathways to Change in Psychoanalytic Therapy." In Goldfried. pp. 143–154.
Aristotle. *Eudemanian Ethics*. In Barnes. pp. 1922–1981.
Arpaly, Nomy. (2005). "How it is not 'just like diabetes': mental disorders and the moral psychologist." In *Philosophical Issues 15*. 282–298.
Athanasopoulos, Constantinos. (2012). "Towards a Conceptual and Methodological Renaissance in Philosophical Practice." In Humanities Institute. Vol. 1. pp. 217–230.
Atkinson, Anthony P. (2012). "Emotion." In Symons and Calvo eds. pp. 543–555.
Averill James R. and Thomas A. More (2000). "Happiness." In Michael Lewis and Jeannette Haviland-Jones (eds.), *Handbook of Emotions*. New York: Guilford Press.
Bakan, David. (1991). *Maimonides on Prophecy: A Commentary on Selected Chapters of the Guide for the Perplexed*. Northvale, N.J.: Jason Aronson.
Bakan, Joel. (2011). *Childhood Under Siege*. Toronto: Allen Lane Canada.
Ballou, Mary and Laura Brown, eds. (2002). *Rethinking Mental Health and Disorder*. New York: Guilford.
Ballou, Mary. "Toward a Feminist Ecological Theory of Human Nature" in Ballou and Brown eds. pp. 99–144.
Bankart, C. Peter. (2007). *Talking Cures*. Mason, OH: Thomson.
Barham, Peter (1993). *Schizophrenia and Human Value*. London: Free Association.
Barnes, Jonathan, ed. (1995). *The Complete Works of Aristotle*. Princeton N.J.: Princeton University Press.
Bartol, Curt R. and Anne M. Bartol. (2011 ed.). *Criminal Behavior: A Psychological Approach*. Upper Saddle River, N.J.: Prentice Hall.
Bateson, Gregory. (2000). *Steps to an Ecology of Mind: Collected Essays in Anthropology Psychiatry, Evolution, and Epistemology*. Chicago: University of Chicago Press.
Bayer, Ronald. (1987). *Homosexuality and American Psychiatry: The Politics of Diagnosis*. Princeton, N.J.: Princeton University Press.
Bechtel, William and Cory D. Wright. "What is Psychological Explanation?" In Symons and Calvo. pp. 113–130.

Bennett, M. R., and P. M. S. Hacker. (2003). *Philosophical Foundations of Neuroscience.* Oxford: Blackwell Publishing.
Ben-Ze'ev, Aaron (1996). "Typical Emotions." In William O'Donohue and Richard Kitchener, (eds.), *Philosophy of Psychology.* London: Sage Publications.
Berger, Louis S. (1991). *Substance Abuse as Symptom.* Hillsdale, N.J.: The Analytic Press.
Bergo, Bettina. "Psychoanalytic Models: Freud's Debt to Philosophy and His Copernican Revolution." In Radden (ed.). pp. 338–350.
Bernstein, Douglas A. et al. (2003). *Psychology* 6th ed. Boston: Houghton Mifflin.
Blanch, Andrea et al. (1997). "Consumer-Practitioners and Psychiatrists Share Insights About Recovery and Coping." *Psychological and Social Aspects of Psychiatric Disability.* Roy Spaniol et al. eds. Boston: Boston University.
Boehlich, Walter (ed.) (1990). *The Letters of Sigmund Freud to Eduard Silberstein, 1871–1881.* Cambridge, Mass.: Harvard University Press.
Boevink, Wilma. (2012). "Life Beyond Psychiatry." In Rudnick. pp. 15–29.
Bolton, Derek. (2008). *What is Mental Disorder?* Oxford: Oxford University Press.
———. (2003) "Meaning and Causal Explanations in the Behavioural Science." In Fulford et al. (2003). pp. 113–125.
———. and J. Hill. (1996). *Mind, Meaning, and Mental Disorder: The Nature of Causal Explanation in Psychology and Psychiatry.* Oxford: Oxford University Press.
Borowicz, Jon. (1996). "How is Philosophical Practice Practical?" In Vlist. pp. 91–105.
Brady, John Paul, et al. "Some Views on Effective Principles of Psychotherapy." In Goldfried pp. 155–190.
Brooks-Harris, Jeff E., J. Judd Harbin, Laura W. Doto, Paulette M. Stronczek, and Bert H. Epstein. (2000). *Outreach Coordinator's Handbook.* http://ccvillage.buffalo.edu/Village/WC/wsc/coordinators_corner/outreach_coordinators_handbook/02.html
Brown, George. (2000). "Emotion and Clinical Depression: An Environmental View." In *Handbook of Emotions.* Michael Lewis and Jeannette M. Haviland-Jones eds. (pp. 75–90).
Brown, Sam. (2012). "Philosophy and Therapy: Professional Training and Certification." In *Humanities Institute.* Vol. 2. pp. 147–170.
Bugental, James. (1987). *The Art of the Psychotherapist.* New York: Norton.
Burnston, R. and R. Frie (2006). *Psychotherapy as a Human Science.* Pittsburgh: Duquesne University Press.
Byrne, Peter. (2000). "Stigma of mental illness and ways of diminishing it." *Advances in Psychiatric Treatment.* In the *Bulletin of The Royal College of Psychiatrists.* 6: pp.65-72.
Cahill J., M. Barkham, G. Hardy, A. Rees, D. A. Shapiro, W. B. Stiles, and N. Macaskill. (2003). "Outcomes of patients completing and not completing cognitive therapy for depression." *British Journal of Clinical Psychology,* 42. 133–143.
Campbell, Neil (2005). *A Brief Introduction to the Philosophy of Mind.* Orchard Park: Broadview Press.
Caplan, Paula J. "Gender Issues in the Diagnosis of Mental Disorder." In Edwards pp. 156–165.
Chaffee, John. (2013). *The Philosopher's Way.* Upper Saddle River, N.J.: Pearson Education.
Charland, Loui C. (2012). "Benevolence and discipline: the concept of recovery in early nineteenth-century moral treatment." In Rudnick pp. 65–77.
Chiu, Marcu Yu-Lung. "Recovery and advocacy: contextualizing justice in relation to recovery from mental illness in East Asia." In Rudnick pp. 279–303.
Choi, Heebong. (2012). "The Case of Hume's Self-Cure through a True Philosophy." In *Humanities Institute.* Vol. 1. pp. 317–324.
Ciompi, Luc. (1980). "Catamnestic long-term study on the course of life and aging of schizophrenics." *Schizophrenia Bulletin.* Vol. 6 no. 4. pp. 606–18.
Cohen, Elliot D. (2003). *What Would Aristotle Do?* New York: Prometheus.
Cohn, Hans W. (1997). *Existential Thought and Therapeutic Practice.* London: Sage.
Cooper, Rachel. (2013). "What's So Special About Mental Health and Disorder?" In Downes (2013). pp. 487–499.

———. (2012). "Being ill and getting better: recovery and accounts of disorder." Rudnick pp. 217–235.
———. (2007). *Psychiatry and Philosophy of Science.* Montreal: McGill-Queen's University Press.
Corey, Gerald (1996). *Theory and Practice of Counseling and Psychotherapy.* 5th edn. Pacific Grove: Brooks/Cole Publishing.
Cottingham, John, Robert Stoothoff, and Dugald Murdoch, eds. (1993). *Descartes: Selected Philosophical Writings.* New York: Cambridge University Press.
Cushman, Robert E. (2001) *Therapeia: Plato's Conception of Philosophy.* New York: Transaction Publishers.
Davidson, Jonathan R. T. (2006). "Social Phobia: Then, Now, the Future." In Rothbaum. pp. 115–131.
Davidson, Larry. (2012). "Considering recovery as a process: or, life is not an outcome." In Rudnick pp. 252–263.
Davidson, L., Harding, C., and Spaniol, L. Eds. (2007). *Recovery from Serious Mental Illness: Research Evidence and Implications for Practice.* Boston: Boston University Press.
Davis, John W. (1963). "Is Philosophy a Sickness or a Therapy?" *The Antioch Review.* Vol. 23, No. 1. pp. 5-23.
Day, Susan X. (1999). *Theory and Design in Counseling and Psychotherapy.* Boston: Houghton Mifflin.
Deurzen-Smith, Emmy van. (2000). *Everyday Mysteries: Existential Dimensions of Psychotherapy.* New York: Brunner-Routledge.
Diestler, Sherry *Becoming a Critical Thinker: A User Friendly Manual.* (2012). Upper Saddle River, N.J.: Pearson.
Doidge, Norman. (2007). *The Brain That Changes Itself.* New York: Penguin.
Dollard, John and Neal E. Miller. "Techniques of Therapeutic Intervention." In Golfried. pp. 58–63.
Dominowski, Roger L. and Pamela Dallob. (1995). "Insight and Problem Solving." In Sternberg and Davidson. pp. 33–62.
Downes, Stephen M. and Edouard Machery. (2013). *Arguing About Human Nature.* New York: Routledge.
Dryden, Windy. (1991). *Reasons and Therapeutic Change.* London: Whurr.
Edwards, Rem B. (1997). *Ethics of Psychiatry.* Amherst, N.Y.: Prometheus Books.
———. (1997). "Mental Health as Rational Autonomy." In Edwards. pp. 50–62.
Ellenbogen, Sara. "Against the Diagnosis of Evil: A Response to M. Scott Peck." *Philosophical Practice: Journal of the American Philosophical Practitioners Association.* Vol. 8 No. 1. March, 2013. pp. 1142–1148.
Elliott, Carl. "Mental Health and Its Limits." In Radden. pp.426-37.
Ellis, Albert. (1976). "Philosophy and Rational-Emotive Therapy." *Counseling and Values.* Donald Biggs et al, eds. Washington: American Personnel and Guidance Association.
———. (1977) *Handbook of Rational Emotive Therapy.* Albert Ellis and R. Grier eds. New York: Springer.
———. and R. J. Yeager (1989). *Why Some Therapies Don't Work.* Buffalo, NY: Prometheus Books.
Enright, S. J. (1997). "Cognitive Behavioural Therapy: Clinical Applications." *British Medical Journal.* 314. pp. 1811–1816.
Epictetus. (1995). *The Discourses, The Handbook, Fragments.* London: Everyman.
Erskine, Richard G. (1995). "A Gestalt Therapy Approach to Shame and Self-Righteousness: Theory and Methods." In *British Gestalt Journal.* Vol. 4, No. 2. pp 108-117.
Erwin, Edward. (2012) "Freud and the Unconscious." In Symons and Clavo. pp. 59–7.
———. (1997). *Philosophy & Psychotherapy.* London: Sage.
Falikowski, Anthony. (2004). *Experiencing Philosophy.* Upper Saddle River, N.J.: Pearson Education.

Faraone, Stephen, Ming Tsuang, and Debby Tsuang. (1999). *Genetics of Mental Disorders*. New York: Guilford Press.

Faust, David. (2012) *Coping With Psychiatric and Psychological Testimony*. 6th ed. New York: Oxford University Press.

Fay, A. and A. Lazarus. (1993). "On necessity and sufficiency in psychotherapy." *Psychotherapy in Private Practice*. 12.

Flanagan, Elizabeth. (2012). "Recovery and stigma: issues of social justice." In Rudnick pp. 264–279.

Flew, Antony, ed. (1991). *David Hume: An Enquiry Concerning Human Understanding*. La Salle, Ill.: Open Court.

Foucault, Michel. (1965). *Madness and Civilization*. New York: Vintage Books.

Foucault, Michel. (1984) *The Foucault Reader*. Paul Rabinow, ed. New York: Random House.

Frances, Allen. Interviewed in Kingston. pp. 52-56.

Frank, Jerome D. (1999). "Psychotherapies: A Different Perspective." In Schill (1999). pp. 130–145.

———. and Julia B. Frank (1993) *Persuasion and Healing* 3rd ed. Baltimore: Johns Hopkins University Press.

Frankl, Viktor E. (1988). *The Will to Meaning*. New York: Meridian.

Freud, Sigmund. (1995 ed). *The Basic Writings of Sigmund Freud*. New York: Modern Library.

———. (1987 ed) *The Pelican Freud Library Volume 12*. Albert Dickson ed. New York: Penguin Books.

———. (1957). *General Introduction to Psychoanalysis*. New York: Simon & Schuster.

Fromm, Erich. (1962). *Beyond the Chains of Illusion*. New York: Simon and Schuster.

———. (1976). *To Have or to Be*. New York: Harper and Row.

Fulford, K. W. M. (Bill) (1994). "Mind and Madness: New Directions in Philosophy of Psychiatry." In *Philosophy, Psychology, and Psychiatry*. Griffiths. pp. 16–23.

Fulford, Bill, Katherine Morris, John Sadler, and Giovanni Stanghellini eds. (2003). *Nature and Narrative: An Introduction to the New Philosophy of Psychiatry*. New York: Oxford UP.

———. (2004) "Facts/Values: Ten Principles of Values-Based Medicine." In Radden. pp. 203–234.

Fulford, K.W.M., Tim Thornton, and George Graham (2006). *Oxford Textbook of Philosophy and Psychiatry*. New York: Oxford University Press.

Gambrill, Eileen. (2005). *Critical Thinking in Clinical Practice* 2nd ed. Hoboken, N.J.: John Wiley & Sons.

Gaylin, Willard. (2000). *Talk Is Not Enough*. New York: Little Brown.

Gert, Bernard and Charles M. Culver. (2004). "Defining Mental Disorder." In Radden ed. pp. 415-425.

Gick, Mary L. and Robert S. Lockhart. (1995). "Cognitive and Affective Components of Insight." In Sternberg & Davidson. pp. 197–228.

Gill, Christopher. (1985)"Ancient Psychotherapy." *Journal of the History of Ideas*. Vol. 46, No.3. July-Sept. 1985. pp. 307–325.

Gill, Kenneth. (2012) "Contrasting conceptualizations of recovery imply a distinct research methodology." In Rudnick. pp. 95–108.

Gillett, Grant (2009). *The Mind and Its Discontent*. New York: Oxford University Press.

Glasser, William. (1992). "Reality Therapy." *New York Journal for Counseling and Development*. 7 (1).

Godlfried, Marvin R. (1982). *Converging Themes in Psychotherapy*. New York: Springer Publishing.

Gordon, Paul and Rosalind Mayo. (2004). *Between Psychotherapy and Philosophy*. London: Whurr Publishing.

Graham, George. (2010). *The Disordered Mind*. New York: Routledge.

Griffiths, A. Phillips ed. (1994). *Philosophy, Psychology and Psychiatry*. Cambridge: Cambridge UP.

Grill, Robin and Beth Macgregor. "'Good Children—at What Price?: The Secret Cost of Shame." http://www.naturalchild.org/robin_grille/good_children.html
Gruengard, Ora. (2012). "Philosophical Counseling: A Dialogue in the Critical Philosophical Tradition." In *Humanities Institute*. Vol. 2. pp. 371–391.
Haas, Leon de. (2012). "Philosophical Questioning in Narrative Counseling." In *Humanities Institute*. Vol. 2. pp. 187–193.
Hadot, Pierre. (1995). *Philosophy as a Way of Life*. Cambridge, Mass.: Blackwell Publishing.
Hales, Dianne and Robert E. Hales. (1995). *Caring for the Mind*. New York: Bantam.
Halford, W. Kim. (1995). "Marriage and the prevention of psychiatric disorder." In Raphael and Burrows. pp. 121–137.
Hankin, Benjamin and John Abela, eds. (2005). *Development of Psychopathology: A Vulnerability-Stress Perspective*. London: Sage.
Hansen, Jennifer. (2004). "Affectivity: Depression and Mania." In Radden (ed.). pp. 36–53.
Harteloh, Peter, Tetsuya Kono, and Taro Mochizuki. (2012). "Philosophical Practice for Asia: a Textbook." In *Humanities Institute*. Vol. 1. (pp. 81–84).
Harteloh, P. P. M. "The Socratic Attitude in Philosophical Counseling." In *Humanities Institute*. Vol. 1. (pp. 325–33).
Heidegger, Martin. (1996). *The Principle of Reason*. Bloomington, Ind: Indiana University Press.
Heisman, Dan. (2010). *Elements of Positional Evaluation*. Milford, Conn. Russell Enterprises.
Held, Barbara. (1995). *Back to Reality*. New York: W.W. Norton.
Hembree, Elizabeth A., and Norah C. Feeny. (2006). "Cognitive-Behavioral Perspectives on Theory and Treatment of Posttraumatic Stress Disorder." In Rothbaum pp. 197–211.
Herman, Judith H. (2007). "Shattered Shame States and Their Repair." The John Bowlby Memorial Lecture. http://www.cha.harvard.edu/vov/publication/Shattered%20Shame-JHerman.pdf
Hersch, Edwin L. (2003). *From Philosophy to Psychotherapy*. Toronto: University of Toronto Press.
Homma, Naoki. (2012). "Community Approach to the Philosophical Practice." In *Humanities Institute*. Vol. 1. pp. 139–147.
Honderich, Ted. (1995) *The Oxford Companion to Philosophy*. New York: Oxford University Press.
Hopton, J. (2006). The future of critical psychiatry. *Critical Social Policy*. 26 (1). pp. 57–73.
Horwitz, Allan V. (2002). *Creating Mental Illness*. Chicago: University of Chicago Press.
Horstman, Judith. (2010). *Brave New Brain*. San Francisco: Wiley.
Horton, R. (1998). "The new public health of risk and radical engagement" *Lancet*, 352.
Howard, Alex. (2000). *Philosophy for Counselling and Psychotherapy*. London: Macmillan Press.
Howard, D. H. (1968). *The Dynamics of Feminist Therapy*. New York: Hawthorn Press.
Hughes, John R. and Robert A. Pierattini. (1997). "An Introduction to Pharmacotherapy for Mental Disorders." In Edwards pp. 336–358.
Humanities Institute. (2012). The 11th International Conference on Philosophical Practice and the 4th International Conference on Humanities Therapy. Vol. 1 & 2. Kangwon National University.
Hunsley, John and Catherine M. Lee. (2012). "Prognosis and Psychological Treatment." In Faust pp. 653–667.
Ingram, Rick, Jeanne Miranda, and Zindel Segal. (1998). *Cognitive Vulnerability to Depression*. New York: Guilford Press.
Inwood, Brad and L.P. Gerson eds. (1994). *The Epicurus Reader*. Indianapolis: Hackett Publishing.

Inwood, Brian (1985). *Ethics and Human Action in Early Stoicism*. Oxford: Clarendon Press.
Ivey, Allen E., Michael D'Andrea, Mary Bradford Ivey, Lynn Simek-Morgan. (2002). *Theories of Counseling and Psychotherapy: A Multicultural Perspective*. (5th ed.) Boston: Allyn & Bacon.
Jablensky, Assen and Robert E. Kendell. (2002). "Criteria for Assessing a Classification in Psychiatry." In Maj et al eds. pp. 1-24.
James, William. (1987). Review of *Grundzuge der Physiologischen Psychologie*, by Wilhelm Wundt (1975). In *Essays, Comments and Reviews*. Cambridge, Mass.: Harvard University Press.
Jamison, Kay Redfield. (1999). *Night Falls Fast: Understanding Suicide*. New York: Vintage.
Jaynes, Julian. (2000). *The Origin of Consciousness in the Breakdown of the Bicameral Mind*. Boston: Mariner Books.
Jesus–Zayas, Selma R. De, Rudolfo Buigas, and Robert L. Denny. (2012). "Evaluation of Culturally Diverse Populations." In Faust. pp. 248–265.
Johnson, Jeffrey G., Pamela G. McGeoch, Vanessa P. Caskey, Sotoodeh G. Abhary, Joel R. Sneed, and Robert F. Bornstein. (2005). In Hankin and Abela. pp. 417–464.
Jopling, David A. (2008). *Talking Cures and Placebo Effects*. New York: Oxford UP.
Jung, Carl G. (1957) "Psychotherapy and a Philosophy of Life." In *Essays on Contemporary Events*. R. F. C. Hull, trans. Princeton, N.J.: Princeton University Press. 1989 edition.
———. (1990). *The Archetypes and the Collective Unconscious*. Princeton, N.J.: Princeton University Press.
Kandel, E. R. (1998). "A new intellectual framework for psychiatry." *American Journal of Psychiatry*. 155 (4): 457-69.
Kantrowitz, Barbara and Pat Wingert. (2009). *The Menopause Book*. New York: Workman Publishing Company.
Kaufman, Walter. (1975). *Existentialism from Dostoevsky to Sartre*. New York: Meridian.
Kemker, Susan S. "Residency and Psychiatry: Assumptions We Learn." In Ross pp. 242–248.
Kendell, R. (2001). "The Distinction Between Mental and Physical Illness." *British Journal of Psychiatry*. 178. pp. 490–493.
Kendler, Kenneth S., Joself Parnas. (2008). *Philosophical Issues in Psychiatry*. Baltimore: Johns Hopkins University Press.
Kiekegaard, Søren. (1983) *The Sickness Unto Death*. Princeton, N.J.: Princeton University Press.
Kingdon, David G. and Douglas Turkington. (2005). *Cognitive Therapy of Schizophrenia*. New York: Guilford.
Kingston, Anne. "Is She a Brat, or is She Sick?" Maclean's Magazine. Markham, Ont. March 25, 3013.
Kiselica, Mark S., Christine T. Look. (1992). "Mental health counseling and prevention: Disparity between philosophy and practice?" *Journal of Mental Health Counseling*. 12/ 1992.
Kirsch, Irving, et al. (2008) *Initial Severity and Antidepressant Benefits: A Meta-Analysis of Data Submitted to the Food and Drug Administration*. http://www.plosmedicine.org/article/info:doi/10.1371/journal.pmed.0050045
Kleiner, Kurt. (2011). *University of Toronto Magazine*. Toronto: University of Toronto.
Kloster, Moira, and Anastasia Anderson. (2005). *Think it Through: Reasoning in Everyday Life*. Scarborough, ON: Nelson College Indigenous.
Koestenbaum, Peter. (1978). *The New Image of the Person: The Theory and Practice of Clinical Philosophy*. Westport, Conn.: Greenwood.
Kornstein, Susan and Anita Clayton eds. (2002). *Women's Mental Health*. New York: Guilford.
Kosky, Robert John, and Robert Donald Goldney. (1995). "Youth suicide: risk and prevention." In Raphael and Burros. pp. 443–457.

Kravetz, Shlomo and Ilanit Hasson-Ohayon. (2012). "Some social science antinomi and their implications for the recovery-oriented approach to mental illness ar psychiatric rehabilitation." In Rudnick pp. 185–202.

Kuhn, Thomas S. (1970). *The Structure of Scientific Revolutions.* Chicago: University Chicago Press.

Lahav, Ran. (2012). "Voices of Philosophical Self-Transformation" In *Humanities Ins tute.* Vol. 1. pp.455–458.

Lageman, August G. (1989). "Socrates and Psychotherapy." *Journal of Religion a Health.* Vol. 28, No. 3. pp. 219-223.

Laing, R.D. (1990a). *Self and Others.* New York: Viking Penguin.

———. (1990b). *The Divided Self.* New York: Viking Penguin.

Laing, Ronal David. (1986). *Wisdom, Madness, and Folly: The Making of a Psychiatri* New York: Mcgraw-Hill.

Laing, R.D., D.G. Cooper, and Jean-Paul Sartre. (1983). *Reason and Violence: A Decade Sartre's Philosophy, 1950-1960.* New York: Pantheon Books.

Lareau, Craig R. (2012). "The *DSM–IV* System of Psychiatric Classification." In Faus pp. 209–228.

Larochelle, Marie, Nadine Bednarz, and Jim Garrison, eds. (1998). *Constructivism a Education.* Cambridge: Cambridge University Press.

Lazarus, Arnold. (1989). *The Practice of Multimodal Therapy.* Baltimore: Johns Hopki University Press.

Lemery, Kathryn S. and Lisa Doelger. "Genetic Vulnerability to the Development Psychopathology." In Hankin. pp. 161-198.

Lewis, Bradley (2012). "Recovery, narrative theory, and generative madness." In Ru nick pp. 143–165.

Lewis, H. B. (1990). "Shame, repression, field dependence, and psychopathology. *Repression and Dissociation: Implications for Personality Theory, Psychopathology, a Health.* J. L. Singer, ed. Chicago: University of Chicago Press. pp. 233-57.

Lindseth, Anders. (2012). "Possibilities of Philosophical Practice in Health Care ar Psychotherapy." In *Humanities Institute.* Vol. 1. pp. 189–201.

Lipman, Matthew. (2003). *Thinking in Education.* (2nd ed.). Cambridge: Cambrid University Press.

———. (1988). *Philosophy Goes to School.* Philadelphia: Temple University Press.

Lunau, Kate. "The Mental Health Crisis on Campus." *McLean's Magazine On Campi* September 5th, 2012. http://oncampus.macleans.ca/education/2012/09/05/th mental-health-crisis-on-campus/

Lynn, Steven Jay and Kevin M. McConkey, eds. (1998). *Truth in Memory.* New Yo Guilford Press.

Lysaker, Paul and John Lysaker. (2012). In Rudnick (2012). pp. 166–177.

Madison, Gary Brent. (2010). *On Suffering.* Hamilton, Ont.: Les Érables Publishing.

Mahoney, Michael J. (1991). *Human change and processes: The scientific foundation psychotherapy.* New York: Basic Books.

Maj, Mario et al. (eds.) (2002). *Psychiatric Diagnosis and Classification.* West Sussex: Jol Wiley & Sons.

May, Rollo. (1953). *Man's Search for Himself.* New York: Dell Publishing.

McLoughlin, Brendan, Tomas Blanes, and Simon Darnley. (1995). "Anxiety disorde risk and possibilities for prevention." In Raphael and Burrows. pp. 547–567.

Mead, S. and Copeland M. (2005). "What recovery means to us: consumers' perspe tives. In Davidson et al. (2005) pp. 69-81.

Meissner, William W. (1999). "The Future Role of Psychoanalysis and Psychoanalyti Oriented Therapy." In Schill (1999). pp. 97–108.

Merrill, K. A., V. E. Tolbert, and W. A. Wade. (2003). "Effectiveness of cognitive ther py for depression in a community mental health center: A benchmarking stud *Journal of Consulting and Clinical Psychology,* 71. 404–409.

Mezzich, Juan. (2005). "Positive health: conceptual place, dimensions and implic tions." *Psychopathology.* Vol. 38 No. 4. pp. 177–79.

Miller, Nancy E. et al, eds. (1993). *Psychodynamic Treatment Research*. New York: Basic Books.
Millon, Isabelle. (2012). "Training Philosophy as Practice." In *Humanities Institute*. Vol. 2. pp. 409–423.
Moore, Brooke and Richard Parker. (2004). *Critical Thinking*. New York: McGraw Hill.
Morris, Charles. (1959). "Philosophy, psychiatry, mental illness and health." *Philosophy and Phenomenological Research*. Vol. 20, No. 1, pp. 47–55.
Nagel, Thomas. (2012). *Mind & Cosmos: Why the Materialist Neo-Darwinian Conception of Nature is Almost Certainly False*. New York: Oxford University Press.
Nathanson, D. L. (1996). "About Emotion." In *Knowing Feeling: Affect, Script and Psychotherapy*. D. L. Nathanson ed. New York: Norton. pp. 1-21.
Nestler, E. J., M. Barrot, R. J. Dileone, A. J. Eisch, S. J. Gold, and L. M. Monteggia. (2002). "Neurobiology of depression." *Neuron, 34*. 13-25.
Nietzsche, Friedrich. (1968). *Beyond Good and Evil*. Walter Kaumann trans. Toronto: Random House.
Norman, Trevor R. and Graham D. Burrows. (1995). "Psychoactive medication and prevention." In Raphael and Burrows. pp. 637–652.
Nussbaum, Martha C. (1994). *The Therapy of Desire*. Princeton, N.J.: Princeton University Press.
Oden, Thomas. (1974). *After Therapy What?* Springfield, Ill., Charles C Thomas Publishers.
Orange, Donna M. (2010). *Thinking for Clinicians*. New York: Routledge.
Orbach, Susie. (200). *The Impossibility of Sex*. New York: Scribner.
Paris, Joel. (2010). *The Use and Misuse of Psychiatric Drugs*. Hoboken, N.J.: Wiley-Blackwell.
Parnas, Josef and Dan Zahavi. (2002). "The Role of Phenomenology in Psychiatric Diagnosis and Classification." In Maj et al, eds. 138–162.
Parsons, Talcott and Edward Shils. (2001). *Toward a General Theory of Action*. New York: Transaction Publishers.
Perls, Frederick. *Gestalt Therapy Verbatim*. (revised ed.) (1992). San Francisco: Gestalt Journal Press.
Persons, J. B., A. Bostrom, and A. Bertagnolli. (1999). "Results of randomized controlled trials of cognitive therapy for depression generalized to private practice." *Cognitive Therapy Research, 23*. 535–548.
Peterman, James F. (1992). *Philosophy as Therapy*. Albany, N.Y.: State University of New York Press.
Pihl, Robert O. and Amélie Nantel-Vivier. "Biological Vulnerabilities to the Development of Psychopathology." In Hankin and Abela. pp.75-103
Plato. *Collected Dialogues*. Edith Hamilton and Huntington Cairns eds. (1961). Princeton, N.J.: Princeton University Press.
Pojman, Lois P. (2002). *Introduction to Philosophy: Classical and Contemporary Readings*. New York: Oxford University Press.
Porter, Douglas and Peter Zachar. (2012). "Recovery and the partitioning of scientific authority in psychiatry." In Rudnick pp. 203–216.
Prochaska, J. O. & Norcross, J.C. (2010) *Systems of Psychotherapy: a Transtheoretical Analysis* 7th ed. Belmont, CA: Brooks/Cole.
Prozan, Charlotte Krause. (1992). *Feminist Psychoanalytic Psychotherapy*. Northvale, N.J.: Jason Aronson.
Raabe, Peter B. (2006). *Philosophical Counselling and the Unconscious*. Amherst, N.Y.: Trivium Press.
———. (2002) *Issues in Philosophical Counseling*. Westport, Conn.: Praeger.
———. (2001) *Philosophical Counseling: Theory and Practice*. Westport CT. Praeger.
Radden, Jennifer ed. (2004). *The Philosophy of Psychiatry*. New York: Oxford UP.
Raphael, Beverly and Graham D. Burrows eds. (1995). *Studies on Preventive Psychiatry*. Amsterdam: Elsevier Sciences B. V.

Rhee, Young E. "A teleological approach to philosophical practice." In Humaniti s Institute. Vol. 2. pp. 57–65.
Rigby-Weinberg, D. N. (1986). "A future direction for radical feminist therapy" In H. Howard. pp. 191-205.
Rikard-Bell, Christopher J. (1995). "Depression risk and prevention." In Raphael ar Burrows. pp. 423–442.
Risch, Neil et al. (2009). "Interaction between the Serotonin Transporter Gene (HTTLPR), Stressful Life Events, and Risk of Depression." *Journal of the America Medical Association.* Vol. 301 No. 23, June.
Robertson, Donald. (2010). *The Philosophy of Cognitive-Behavioural Therapy (CBT).* Lo don: Katnac.
———. (2005). "Stoicism as Philosophical Psychotherapy." *British Association for Cou selling and Psychotherapy (BACP) Magazine.*
Robinson, Daniel N. (1985). *Philosophy of Psychology.* New York: Columbia UP.
Rogers, Carl. (1961). *On Becoming a Person.* Boston: Houghton Mifflin.
Ross, Colin and Alvin Pam. (1995). Pseudoscience in Biological Psychiatry. New Yor John Wiley & Sons.
Rosenhan, D. (1973). "On Being Sane in Insane Place." *Science.* 179: 250-58.
Rothbaum, Barbara Olasov ed. (2006). *Pathological Anxiety: Emotional Processing in E ology and Treatment.* New York: Guilford Press.
Rudnick, Abraham. ed. (2012a). *Recovery of People with Mental Illness.* Oxford: Oxfo University Press.
———. (2012b). "Ethical and related practical issues faced by recovery-oriented me tal healthcare providers: a risk analysis." In Rudnick pp. 304–314.
Russell, Bertrand. (1986). *The Will to Doubt.* New York: Philosophical Library.
———. (1993). *Our Knowledge of the External World.* New York: Routledge.
———. (1912) *The Problems of Philosophy.* Oxford: Oxford University Press.
Rutter, M. (1995). "Psychosocial adversity: risk, resilience, and recovery." *Southe African Journal of Child and Adolescent Mental Health.* Vol. 7 No. 2. pp. 75–88.
Ryle, Gilbert. (1949). *The Concept of Mind.* New York: Barnes and Noble.
Sanders, Matthew R., Mark P. Dadds, and Paula M. Barrett. (1995). "The prevention anxiety and stress related disorders in children." In Raphael and Burrows. p 399–421.
Sartorius, Norman. (2002). "Iatrogenic stigma of mental illness." *British Medical Jou nal.* Vol. 324. pp. 1470-1.
Sartre, J-P. (1948). *The Emotions: Outline of a Theory.* New York: Philosophical Library.
———. (1997). *Essay in Existentialism.* Secqucus, N.J.: Carol Publishing Group.
———. (2003). *Being and Nothingness: An Essay on Phenomenological Ontology,* trans. l E. Barnes, Abingdon: Routledge.
Schill, Stefan de. (2000). *Crucial Choices, Crucial Changes.* Amherst, N.Y.: Promethe Books.
Schill, Stefan de and Serge Lebovici eds. (1999). *The Challenge to Psychoanalysis a Psychotherapy.* London: Jessica Kingsley Publishers.
———. (1999). "The Convenience of Convenient Assumptions." In Schill and Lebovi 1999. pp. 179–210.
Schopenhauer, Arthur. (1966). *The World as Will and Representation.* E. Payne tran New York: Dover.
Schrank, Beate, Johannes Wally, and Burghart Schmidt. "Recovery and Hope in Rel tion to Schizophrenia." In Rudnick pp. 133–144.
Schuster, Shlomit C. (1999). *Philosophy Practice.* Westport, Conn.: Praeger.
Scott, Jan and Eugene Paykel. (1995). "Depression: risk and possibilities for preve tion." In Raphael and Burrows. pp. 513–529.
Searle, John R. (1998). *The Rediscovery of the Mind.* Cambridge: Bradford.
Shamir, Eliahu. (2012). "Families and Patients With Mental Illness: on the Recove Road." In Rudnick. (pp. 39–57).

Sharma, Sohan Lal. (1986). *The Therapeutic Dialogue*. Albuquerque, N.M.: University of New Mexico Press.
Shipka, Thomas A. and Arthur J. Minton. (2004). *Philosophy: Paradox and Discovery*. New York: McGraw-Hill.
Shorter, Edward. "Mind Games."http://www.magazine.utoronto.ca/feature/psychiatry-diagnosis-dsm-diagnostic-and-statistical-manual-of-mental-disorders-edward-shorter/
Siegel, Daniel J. (2012). *The Developing Mind*. New York: Guilford Press.
Simon, Laurence. (2003) *Psychology, Psychotherapy, Psychoanalysis, and the Politics of Human Relationships*. Westport, Conn.: Praeger.
Simpson, Helen Blair, and Michael R. Liebowitz. (2006). "Best Practice in Treating Obsessive-Compulsive Disorder: What the Evidence Says." In Rothbaum pp. 132–146.
Singh, Ilina. (2004) Doing their jobs: mothering with Ritalin in a culture of mother-blame." *Science in Context*. 15, 557–603.
Skinner, B. F. (1972). *Beyond Freedom and Dignity*. New York: Bantam Books.
Slade, Mike. (2012). "The Epistemological Basis of Personal Recovery." In Rudnick pp. 78–94.
Smith, Steven. (1995). "Getting Into and Out of Mental Ruts." In Sternberg and Davidson. pp. 227–251.
Snyder, C. R. and Shane Lopez (2007). "Increasing Happiness in Your Life." In Snyder pp. 141–162.
Snyder, Charles R. and Jennifer T. Pedrotti. (2011). *Positive Psychology*. Thousand Oaks: Sage Publications.
Spaniol, Roy et al. eds. (1997). *Psychological and Social Aspects of Psychiatric Disability*. Boston: Boston University.
Spence, Donald P. "Case Studies and Prescriptions for Improving Them." In Miller et al. pp. 38–40.
Stein, Dan J. (2008). *Philosophy of Psychopharmacology*. New York: Cambridge University Press.
Stein, Dan J. and Eric Hollander. (2002). *Textbook of Anxiety Disorders*. Washington: American Psychiatric Publishing.
Sternberg, Robert J. and Janet E. Davidson eds. (1995). *The Nature of Insight*. Cambridge, Mass: MIT Press.
Stone, Michael H. "Personality disorders: are there opportunities for prevention?" In Raphael and Burrows. pp. 569–582.
Stumpf, Samuel Enoch and Donald C. Abel. (2002). *Elements of Philosophy*. Boston: McGraw-Hill.
Strunk, Otto Jr. (1979). "The World View Factor in Psychotherapy." In *Journal of Religion and Health*. Vol. 18, No. 3. pp. 192-197.
Strupp, H. R., R. Fox, and K. Lessler. (1969). *Patients View Their Psychotherapy*. Baltimore: Johns Hopkins Press.
Swarbrick, Margaret. (2012). "A Wellness Approach to Mental Health Recovery." In Rudnick. pp. 30–38.
Symons, John and Paco Calvo. (2012). *The Routledge Companion to Philosophy of Psychology*. New York: Routledge.
Szasz, T. S. (1961). *The Myth of Mental Illness*. New York: Hoeber-Harper.
———. (1978). *The Myth of Psychotherapy*. Garden City: Doubleday-Anchor Press.
Tannen, Deborah. (1990). *You Just Don't Understand*. New York: Ballantine.
Tanner, Adrienne. (2003). "Narcissism Led Him to Kill: Doctor." *National Post*. Sept. 26.
Thornton, Tim. (2012) "Is recovery a model?" In Rudnick pp. 236–251.
———. (2007). *Essential Philosophy of Psychiatry*. New York: Oxford UP.
———. (2004). "Reductionism/Antireductionism" In Radden (ed.). pp. 191–204.
Timko, Robert M. and Joan Whitman Hoff. (2001). *Philosophies for Living*. Upper Saddler River: Prentice Hall.

Ustun, T. Bedrihan "International Classifications and the Diagnosis of Mental Disorders: Strengths, Limitations and Future Perspectives." (2002). In Maj et al. eds. p 25–46.

Valenstein, E. S. (1998). *Blaming the Brain: The Real Truth About Drugs and Mental Health*. New York: Free Press.

Van Deurzen-Smith, Emmy. (1997). *Everyday Mysteries: Existential Dimensions f Psychotherapy*. New York: Routledge.

Vaughan, S. C. (1997). *The Talking Cure: The Science Behind Psychotherapy*. New Yor Grosset/Putnam.

Velasquez, Manuel (2011). *Philosophy: A Text With Readings*. 11th ed. New York: Wadworth.

Vlist, Wim van der. ed. (1996). *Perspectives in Philosophical Practice*. Leiden: Verenigii voor Filosofische Praktijk.

Vygotsky, L.S. (1962). *Thought and Language*. ed. and trans. E. Hanfmann and F. Vaka Cambridge, Mass.: MIT Press.

Wampold, Bruce E. (2001). *The Great Psychotherapy Debate: Models, Methods, and Fin ings*. New York: Routledge.

Watts, Richard E. (2003). "Adlerian Therapy as a Relational Constructivist Approach *The Family Journal: Counseling and Therapy for Couples and Families*. Vol. 11, No. 139–147.

Weiner, Harry. "The Genetics of Preposterous Conditions." In Ross pp. 193–210.

Wingert, Pat and Barbara Kantrowitz. (2009). *The Menopause Book*. New York: Worman Publishing.

Winston, David. (1981). *Philo of Alexandria*. New York: Paulist.

Wittgenstein, Ludwig. (1967). *Remarks on the Foundations of Mathematics*. Edited by H. von Wright et al. Trans. G. E. M. Anscombe. Cambridge, Mass.: MIT Press.

Wolff, Robert Paul. (1992). *About Philosophy*. Upper Saddle River, NJ: Pearson Education.

Yi, Jin-Nam. (2012). "Resettism: A Philosophical Disease?" In *Humanities Institute*. V 2. pp. 195–203.

Young, Elizabeth, Ania Korsun, and Margaret Altemus. (2002). "Sex Differences Neuroendocrine and Neurotransmitter Systems." In Kornstein and Clayton eds. p 3–30.

Ziskin, Jay. (1995a). "Challenging principles and systems of classification." In J. Zisk ed. pp. 128–194.

———. (1995b). ed. *Coping With Psychiatric and Psychological Testimony*. Los Angele CA: Law and Psychology Press.

Index

abreaction, 161, 188, 352
academic philosophers, 5, 17; poor reputation, 184
Achenbach, Gerd, 17, 243, 252
addiction, 33, 358; and God, 359; as symptom, 40; is not craving for substance, 358; need for alternative to, 162, 359; problems with disease model of, 358
Adeponle, Ademola, 348
ADHD (Attention Deficit Hyperactivity Disorder), 64, 176; as endogenous disease, 73; disease or illness model, 202; linked to diet and sleep, 293
Adlerian Therapy, 107–109, 154; influenced by philosopher Hans Vaihinger, 154; collaborative effort, 109; primarily cognitive approach, 124; recovery in, 352
advice, 51
affect. *See* emotions/passions
After Therapy What?, 236
Age of Reason, 8
agoraphobia, 57
Alexander, B. K., 358
Alexander, Franz, 161
alternative perspectives, 205–208
Alzheimer's, 39, 87
Alcoholics Anonymous (AA) 8.41 11.52 11.54
Amering, Michaela, 13, 36, 76, 216, 346, 350
Anderson, Anastasia, 268
anorexia, 86
Anselm, St., 6
anti-depressants, 75; no more effective than placebos, 64, 213
Antiphon, 136

anxiety, 57, 58, 215, 271; fearfulness diagnosed and labeled as, 83; genetics and, 93; in existentialism, 114; life events precipitate, 80; medication and, 199; neurotic; normal; existential, 111
Applebaum, Stephen A., 163
applied ethics, counseling specific, 27
Aquinas, St. Thomas, 6
argue, learning to, 264
argument, trying to win, 264, 265
Aristotle, 6, 63, 137; influence on Freu 5.16; on emotions, 180; study of, 14
Aron, Elaine N, 319
Arpalay, Nomy, 61
Attention Deficit Hyperactivity Disorder (ADHD), 40
Athanasopoulos, Constantinos, 158, 241–242
Augustine, St., 8
Aurelianus, Caelius, 141
Aurelius, Marcus, 138
authenticity, 304, 307–328, 322
authority, 55, 206; in psychodynamic tradition, 162
Autobiography, 369
autopoiesis, 294

bad faith, 200
Ballou, Mary, 149
Bankart, C. Peter, 119–120, 163, 234, 291, 292; pitfalls in psychotherapy, 361
Bartol, Curt and Anne, 52, 86
Bateson, Gregory, 83
Battie, William, 349
Beauvoir, Simone de, 327
Behavior therapy, 116–117, 125, 158
behaviorism, 10, 150; as infinite regress, 88; as technology of

behavior, 88; empty of meaning and significance, 88
Beck, Aaron, 119, 158
Bennett, M. R., 28, 243
Berger, Louis, 358
Berkeley, Bishop, 275
"beyond method method", 243, 252
bibliotherapy, 119
bicameral mind, 29
Bible, The, 269; and meaning/purpose of life, 306
Binswanger, Ludwig, 155
bio-medical approach, 6, 360
biopsychiatry, 24, 25, 60, 69; and subjective mental states, 60; critical errors in, 39
bipolar disorder, 36, 73, 213; life circumstances and, 78
birth order, 108
blame/responsibility, difference, 192
blaming the victim, 55, 241
blind spots, 188
bobsledding, change in thinking, 283
body-mind dualism, 8, 27, 147
Boevink, Wilma, 208–209, 341; cure/recovery as goal, 349
Bolton, Derek, 35, 209
Boss, Medard, collaboration with Jung and Heidegger, 156
Brady, John Paul, 161, 163
brain, 27, 28; as container, 33; and addictions, 33; biochemical malfunctioning/imbalances, 151, 343; chemistry changed by psychosocial influences, 83; structures, abnormal, 84, 91
brain scans, flaws in, 32
Brain That Changes Itself, The, 98
Brave New Brain, 32
Brentano, Franz, 30
British Journal of Psychiatry, 62
broken heart. *See* depression
Brown, George, 80
Brown, Laura, 149
Brown, Sam, 181, 235, 356
Buber, Martin, 165, 247
Buddha, 206
Buigas, Rudolfo, 57

Caplan, Paula J., 24
Caring for the Mind: A Comprehensive Guide to Mental Health, 221
cases, short examples, 257–258, 271–272; three detailed studies, 295–337
categorical imperative, 276, 313
category mistake, 28, 39, 72, 281
Catholic, 296
cause (and-effect), 29, 30, 45, 370; and meaning, 89; anorexia as, 86; causal factors, 39, 60, 79, 82, 122, 353; causal claims, naturalistic, 85; definition in psychology, 86; diagrams, 78–79; excited delirium causing death, 86; etiology 2.64; exogenous/endogenous, difference, 193; exogenous cause of depression, 65; free will and, 86–92, 241, 370; genetics as, 92; iatrogenesis, 77, 79; knowing the cause of, 85; of bad chess move analogy, 72; material vs. non-material, 87, 90; naturalistic claims, 85; reasons for suicides, 92; theories of, 87; two meanings in psychology, 86–88; vs. influences, 90, 91
Celsus, 141
cephalalgia syndrome, 25
Chaffee, John, 178
change, motivation for, 116
Charmides, 137
chemical imbalances, 4, 343
chess, 4, 72, 238
Challenge to Psychoanalysis and Psychotherapy, The, 33, 66
Chicago Institute for Psychoanalysis Report, The, 23
Chodorow, Nancy, 121
Choi, Heebong, 183
Christ, Jesus, 206
Christian fundamentalism, 53
Chiu, Marcus Yu-Lung, 341
Chryssippus, 137
Cicero, 138, 140
classical and operant conditioning, 117
classification and diagnosis, 34, 35, 35–36, 40; ambiguity in, 241; reasons for, 41–42

clients, attitudes and competencies, 265
Clinical and counseling psychology, 107, 124
clinical philosophy, 209–210
clinical psychologists, 3
Cloninger, C. Robert, 36
Coats, Senator Dan, 56
cognitive dissonance, 194
cognitive errors and delusional beliefs, 153
cognitive shock, 205
Cognitive Therapy /Cognitive-Behavior Therapy, 118–119, 158–159; as most cost-effective, 159; as philosophical, 125; effectiveness of, 348; for suicide, 214
Cognitive Therapy of Schizophrenia, 52, 354, 364
Cohen, Elliot, 195; twenty-two common fallacies, 264
Cohn, Hans W., 199
community of inquiry, 32, 189, 220–221, 247; distinguishes psychotherapy from philosophy, 248; in philosophy café, 226
comorbidity, 73, 242
compulsive hand washing, 199
compulsive hoarding syndrome, 41
Concept of Mind, The, 27
consciousness, 31, 88, 108
constructivism, 224
Cooper, David, 156
Cooper, Rachel, 62, 64, 67, 93
Copernicus, Nicolaus, 8
Corey, Gerald, 120, 155
counseling: as archeology, 253; as philosophical therapy, 186; collaborative effort, 289; enhanced by philosophy, 236; finding issues, 249–256; narrative in, 237; necessary and sufficient ingredients, 233–237; neutrality in, 244; power structure in, 244; theory, 237–238
counselors, 3, 233–237; familiarity with philosophical themes, 189; lack education in philosophy, 232; attitudes and competencies, 265
Creating Mental Illness, 54
creationist, 269

criminals as poor decision-makers, 262–263
criminology, 18
crisis thinking mode, 263
critical thinking/reasoning, 267–269, 332–335
Critical Thinking in Clinical Practice, 16
Critique of Pure Reason, 8
cross-dressing, 58
Cultural specificity, 13
cure, 42, 163, 187; first claims of, 349; largely ignored in research, publications, practice, 349, 350; litt clinical literature on 11.23
Cushman, Robert E., 132

dark ages, 7
Daseinanalysis, 155
Davidson, Jonathan, 348
Davidson, Larry, 367
Davis, John, 29, 186, 209, 341
Day, Susan: good reasoning vs. mental mistakes, 167
defining oneself, 174, 279–281
dementia praecox. *See* schizophrenia
Democritus, 136
demon possession, 7, 51, 102
denial, 46, 50–51
Denny, Robert L., 57
dependent personality disorder, 13
depression, 36, 57, 73, 79–80, 199, 261, 272; as broken heart, 369; as descriptive/definitional, 83; as the cause of suffering, 82; and sexual abuse in childhood, 60; causes, 77, 81; "depression hurts", 79; environmental stressors, 65, 76, 81; exogenous causes of, 65; family trauma and, 81; genetics and, 92; heart disease statistics and, 104; in antiquity, 131; in youth, 80; life circumstances, 78, 81, 215; ontological status of, 40; reactive n endogenous, 80; Royal Ottawa Healthcare Group on, 77; serotonin transporter genotype and, 93
Descartes, René, 8, 141; on passions/emotions, 194–195; thinking with, 288

Deurzen-Smith, Emmy van, 90, 155, 237; meaning, 208; on failed British experiment, 162; problems in living as mental illness, 216–217
Developing Mind, The, 99
devil, 7, 73
Dewey, John, 142, 180, 247
diagnostic manuals comparison, 85
diagnosis, 6, 66, 241; as labeling, 42; as external evaluation, 47; contingent, 57; informal, 44, 45; judgment in, 66; not consistent, 36; not objective or value-free, 36, 55; not empirical science, 55; parental demands, 58; phenomenological perspective, 47; pragmatic criteria for, 43; scientific instruments used in, 66; social/cultural influences, 56; subjectivity in, 66
Diagnostic and Statistical Manuals of Mental Disorders (DSM), 33, 35, 41, 63, 174, 345; as profoundly unscientific, 37; changes in nosology, 38, 59; labels as common language, 37; numerous problems with, 36; on religious beliefs, 56; recovery, 345; voting, 38, 40, 57
disgraced monk case, 296–299; annotated, 299–307
Dissociative Identity Disorder (DID), 38. *See also* Multiple Personality Disorder (MPD)
Divided Self, 153
doctrinal compliance, 58
Doelger, Lisa, 97
dopamine, 30
Doidge, Norman, 98
Dollard and Miller, 161
domino effect, 73
dreams, 113, 273; interpretation of, 244
drugs, side effects, 71; dependency and shame, 202
Dryden, Windy, 164
dysthymia, 58

Eastern philosophy, 288–289
eating disorders, 57
Eclecticism or Multi-Modal Therapy, 121–122, 125, 160

Edwards, Rem B., 266
Eight Chapters on Ethics, 141
Einstein, Albert, 224; on irrationality, 370
Elliot, Carl, 55
Ellis, Albert, 11, 118, 152, 159; interactionism, 187; on emotions, 187
e-mail counseling case, 307–328, 309
emotions/passions, 116, 118, 135, 137, 142, 163, 183, 191–195, 197; and philosophical discussion, 264; appropriate, 173, 174, 205; as motivating, 183; distorts logic, 262; Ellis on, 187; male, 193; Nussbaum on, 143; philosophy as inadequate for, 180; psycho-pharmaceuticals and, 363; rational or irrational, true or false, 194; relief, 200; recovery and, 353; suffering as mental illness, 216, 240, 241, 350; Sartre on, 142–143; understanding, 232
empathy, 235
Empiricism, 8
ennui and nihilism, 109
Entwicklungsdrang (the urge to develop), 224, 253
environmental stressors and depression, 65, 76, 81
Epictetus, 118, 138, 159, 160
Epicureans, 135, 196–197
Epicurus, 6, 133, 139–140
epigenetics, 98
epiphenomenalism, 27
epistemology 6.81 9.37 9.55-9.58: paradigm shift in, 357
Erikson, Erik, 120
eros/libido, 146
Erskine, Richard, 157, 203
Erwin, Edward, 146
ethical theories and applied ethics, 276–277
ethics, 164, 167, 172; applied–counseling specific, 277; healthy mind and, 353
Ethics Of Authenticity, The, 322
Eudemian Ethics, 137
Everett, Anita, 360
evil, 206

evolution, 179
excited delirium, 86
existentialism 9.53 9.63: alternative to psychoanalysis, 155; diluted by clinicians, 157; effects on Winnicott, Minkowsky, Horney, Kohut, Langs, and Freud, 153; environmental, 277; Frankl, 156; Heidegger, 155; Jaspers, 156; on human nature, 110; Sartre, 155; Yalom, 157
Existential psychotherapy, 12, 109–111, 124, 152, 155–157; as philosophical approach, 155
exorcism, 144

Falikowski, Anthony, 132, 135, 167
fallacies/reasoning errors, 25, 123, 167–168, 264, 333–334; Beck, common distortions, 167; appeal to tradition, 144; circular reasoning, 231; illogicalities, 164; Kingdon, David and Douglas Turkington on, 167; list of some of 200, 168; mental mistakes, 167; mereological, 28; slippery slope, 172; twenty-two most common, 264; true by definition, 231
family trauma and depression, 81
Faraone, Stephen, 94
Farnsworth, Dan L., 208
faulty cognitions or cognitive errors. *See* fallacies
fear, shame and guilt, 191
feelings, 115. *See also* emotions/passions
feminism, types of, 120, 121; and reality, 277; biological determinism, 120; marriage, 120; philosophy, 277
Feminist Psychotherapy, 119–121, 160
fetal alcohol syndrome, 39
financial aid/social services, 344
Flanagan, Elizabeth, 219
Foucault, Michel, 97, 142, 193
Frances, Allen, 33
Frank, Jerome D. and Julia, 196, 234, 236, 350
Frankl, Viktor, 11, 110, 152, 156
free association, 49
free will, 323, 370

Freud, Sigmund, 3, 9, 10, 11, 34–35, 20 ; abreaction, 161, 352; authority of therapist, 367; borrowed concepts from philosophy, 146; denies philosophy, 151, 169; diagnostic terminology, 45; did not work alone, 105; misinterpretation of, 44 negativism, 51; reductionist, mechanistic view, 150; repression, 48; resistance, 50; therapy as medical science, 148; recognized as philosophical thinker, 151; references Plato, 153
friends, 188–189
Fromm, Erich, uses Marx, Hegel, Aquinas, and Spinoza, 153
From Philosophy to Psychotherapy, 233
Fulford. William (Bill), 38, 151, 153; philosophy needed in clinic, 169
functional Magnetic Resonance Imaging (fMRI), 32

Gadamer, Hans-George, 166
Galileo, 8, 290
Gambrill, Eileen, 123, 164
gay pride, 317, 327
Gaylin, Willard, 244
Gemeinschaftsgefühl (social interest), 1(;
General Psychopathology, 156
genetics, 92–98; and depression, 92; as blaming the victim, 96; as cause, 92 constitutional weakness, 96; ignore sociocultural stressors, 96; mutations unlikely cause of menta disorders, 93; not responsible for mental illness, 97; runs in families, 95; tendency, 84; vicious circle of explanation, 95; vulnerability/predisposition/weakness, 93, 94, 9(99, 202, 293
Genetics of Mental Disorders, 94
germ phobia, 196
Gestalt Therapy, 111–113, 124; philosophy in 5.42-5.44
Gill, Christopher, 141, 163–164
Gill, Kenneth, 225
Gillett, Grant, 25
Gilligan, Carol, 120, 121, 333
Glasser, William, 115, 158

God, 275, 298–299, 323
Goldbloom, David S., 37
good life defined, 134–135
good wife syndrome, 24
Graham, George, 153
Great Philosophers, 156
Great Psychotherapy Debate: Models, Methods, and Findings The, 234
Grill, Robin, 203
Group Psychology and the Analysis of the Ego, 146
Gruengard, Ora, 247, 248
guilt, antidote for, 200–205

Halford, Kim W., 357
happiness defined, 74; pills, 74
Hacker, P. M.S., 28, 243
Hadot, Pierre, 134
Harteloh, P. P. M., 247
heart, 148
Held, Barbara, 87
Hegel, George Wilhelm Friedrich, 149
Heidegger, Martin, 200
Hembree, Elizabeth, 181
Herman, Judith, 204, 205
hermeneutics, 281
Hersch, Edwin L., 14, 25, 34, 182, 233; and phenomenology, 154; philosophical terms in psychology, 168; philosophy unavoidable in, 232
heuristics. *See* teaching
Highly Sensitive Person, The, 319
homophobia, fear of, 315
homosexuality, 56, 171; as social deviance, 57; as sociopathic personality disturbance, 57; case 10.78-10.289
hormones, 25, 30
Horney, Karen, 121
Horowitz, Alan, 43, 54, 92; psychotherapists use symbolic systems, 169
Horstman. Judith, 32
Howard, Alex, 166
Hughes, John, 71
human beings as mechanistic organisms, 150
humanistic methodology, 117; psychology, 114

human rights, 197, 198
Hume, David, 8, 141; on emotions, 183
Hunsley, John, 181, 235, 347
hyper-diagnosia, 40, 43, 226
hypomania, 36
hysteria, 51, 56

iatrogenic origin of illness, 16, 79
iatrology (healing with words), 161
ICD (World Health Organization's International Classifications of Diseases), 63
id, ego, and super ego, 11, 146, 150
ideas, behavioral potency of, 89, 92
idiographic accounts/viewpoint, 295, 353
illogicalities, 164
independent personality disorder, 13
informal diagnoses, 44
infallibility, 51
Ingram, Rick, 76
insanity, sometimes curable, 349; family environment and, 353
insight 6.78-6.92
institutional rules, 298
intellectual assaults, 193
intentionality 1.17 1.19 8.28
intentions, 4, 29
interconnectedness, 108
interdependence, 108, 206
internalization, 192, 306
International Classification of Diseases (ICD), 44
intrapsychic conflict, 278; phenomena, 35
introspection, 193
Involuntary treatment/institutional confinement, 246, 340
issues, definition, 251; discussed, 266; finding, 249–256; in e-mail case, 328; related to areas of philosophy, 256
issues tree 8.54 8.65-8.70: diagram, 254; morality, 255; phenomenology and, 255; six questions, 255–256; of knowledge, 254
Issues in Philosophical Counseling, 244, 266, 284, 287

James, William, 142, 177; on reality, 273

Jamison, Kay Redfield, 25
Jaynes, Julian, 29
Jaspers, Karl: influenced by Spinoza, Kant, Kierkegaard, and Nietzsche, 156
Jesus-Zayas, Selma R. De, 57
Jewish philosophers, 140
Journal of the American Medical Association, The, 61
Judaeus, Philo of Alexandria, 140
Jung, Carl, 9, 147, 148; Nietzsche's *Zarathrustra*, 5.25; problematic analysis of a dream, 286; psychotherapists practicing philosophy, 147
just war theory, 330–331; applied to father, 336–337

Kandel, Eric, 98
Kant, Immanuel, 8; categorical imperative, 276, 313; duty, 305; influence on Freud, 150–151; influence on Adler, 154; practical philosophy, 177
Kantrowitz, Barbara, 43
katharsis, 151
Kemker, Susan, 31
Kendell, Robert, 62
Kendler, Kenneth, 38
Kemker, Susan, 73
Kingdon, David, 94, 354; cognitive errors and delusional beliefs, 153; return to normalcy, 341
Kierkegaard, Søren, 142, 274; losing oneself, 280
Kirsch, Irving, 75
Kloster, Moira, 268
Koestenbaum, Peter, 209
Kohlberg, Lawrence, 120
Kraeplin, Emil, 346
Kuhn, Thomas S. 11.57-11.62

labeling, 183; creates biased perception, 42; dehumanizing and dismissive, 368
Lacan, Jacques: indebted to Heidegger and Sartre, 157
Lageman, August G., 168
Lahav, Ran, 246

Laing, R. D. (Ronald David) 6.30: anti psychiatry, 156; read Skeptics, Epictetus, Montaigne, Voltaire, Marx, Nietzsche, Sartre, Merleau-Ponty, Husserl, and Wittgenstein (156; précis of Sartre's books, 156; references Sartre, Heidegger, and Kierkegaard, 153
Lareau, Craig R., 35
late luteal phase dysphoric disorder (LLPDD). *See* premenstrual syndrome (PMS)
Lazarus, Arnold, 117, 121, 158
learning vs. memorizing, 289
Lebovici, Serge, 33
Lee, Catherine M., 181, 235, 347
Leibniz, Gottfried Wilhelm, 8; influence on Freud, 151
Lemery, Kathryn S., 97
lesbian, 314
Letters to Lucilius, 140
Letter to Menoeceus, 139
Levinas, Emmanuel, 166
Lewis, Bradley, 237, 349
life circumstances and depression, 78, 81, 215
life, value and meaning of, 110; as text 253; examination of 6.57; path of, 274; worth living, 207
Lipman, Matthew, 32, 220, 226, 247; Philosophy for Children, 189, 247
Locke, John, 8
locus, of self-evaluation/power/contro 193
logical errors. *See* fallacies
logical positivism, 10, 12, 149, 152
logos, 131
Logotherapy, 12, 110, 124, 152
luck, 89
Lysaker, Paul and John, 341, 365

Macgregor, Beth, 203
Madison, Gary, 31
Magnetic Resonance Imaging (fMRI). *See* functional
Mahoney, Michael, 294
Maimonides, Moses, 141
manic-depressive. *See* bi-polar
Manual, 159

Marx, Karl, 142; influence on Adler, 154
masturbation, 56, 282
May, Rollo: appeals to Descartes, Mill, Kafka, Nietzsche, Heidegger, and Sartre, 153
meaning, 205, 208–209, 237; analytic philosophy and, 243; semiotic being, 194
meaning of life, 281, 371; *Ecclesiastes*, 306
medical insurance, 12
medical model, 59, 158, 242; completely theoretical, 84; definition of, 66; deterministic, 368; contradictions/problems in, 65, 100; medication trap, 343; nine factors sustaining it, 67; one-dimensional, 349; predictions poor, 361
medical philosophy, 182, 198
medical student syndrome, 40
medications (psychotropic), 16, 68, 71, 243–244; anti-depressants no more effective than placebos, 64, 213; as essential for clinical depression, 216; assumed remedial potency of, 348, 365; based on paradox, 243; can cause flat affect, 73; can interfere with recovery, 73; case example, 257–258, 296; compliance, 345; cost-effectiveness claims, 347; don't cure, 343; dulling of brain functions, 74; justification for use of, 96; like a bandage, 226; not illness specific, 70, 76; on quitting cold turkey, 72; over-prescription of, 290; philosophy as substitute for, 162; question ontology and etiology of 9.111; side effects, 71; SSRI drugs, 348; symptomatic relief, 199; trap, 342–345; unclear mechanisms of, 70, 343; vicious circle of dependency and poverty, 77, 290; work like alcohol, 70. *See also* side effects; psychopharmaceuticals
Menopause Book, The, 43
men/women difference, 293
mental healthcare, paradigm shift, 360

mental illness (disorders), 1, 2, 6, 7, 11, 12, 13, 62; absence of a valid definition of, 43; alter individual's conceptions of self, 280; antinomies, 368; are not medical, 99; as demon possession, 203; as effects not causes, 81; as existential problems, 369; as metaphor, 45; as mysterious, 356–357; assumptions about, 25; as social deviance, 233; as transition, 190; based on consensus, 37; believed to be permanent, 354; biases are knowledge structure, 291; biological explanations of, 81–82; biological model of, 32; causes of, 54; characteristics of the mentally ill, 203; chemical imbalances in brain and, 82, 355; chronification of, 351; clinical, 82; cognitive capture of, 76; constituents of, 34; control of, 354; created or invented, 56; critical errors in defining, 39; damaging knowledge set, 342; definition of in *DSM*, 40; disorder, disordered room, 204; does not cause misery, 363; equivocation in, 32; etiology (origins) of, 217, 240, 364; evaluation (measurement) of, 38; facts about, 363–364; family environment and, 353; first claims of curability, 349; genes not responsible for, 97; identical to physical illness, 61–62; life events as cause of, 81; include, 175; marital quality as cause of, 79, 357–358; media portrayal of, 41, 61, 77, 85, 86, 291; medicalization of, 26; messiness as, 344–345; misery causes, 83; murder as, 41, 231; no disease-specific markers for, 65, 73; normalization in, 354; no tests for, 343; ontological status of, 40, 56, 217; parental role in, 80; plague, 41; prevention, 213–222; reification of symptom clusters, 33, 37, 39, 40, 96, 202; relapse, deterrence of, 214; relativism of, 81; statistics on, 41; suffering as, 86, 369; treatment misconceptions, 362–363; voted into/out of *DSM*, 38, 40, 54. *See also*

classification and diagnosis mental, content, 32; morbidity, 217; ruts, 199; supervenes on the physical, 175
mereological fallacy, 28
Merleau-Ponty, Maurice, 166
messiness as mental illness, 344–345
metacognition, 180–181, 262, 365
meta-ethics, 276
metaphysics, 149, 269–274
Metaphysics, 141
Mezzich, Juan, 349
Michaud, Shawn, 14
midwifery, 161
Mill, John Stuart, 333, 369–370
Millon, Isabelle, 265
mind, 27, 28, 32; as contents of brain, 88; as epiphenomena of the brain, 69; as natural object (Freud), 35; healthy, 261–262; mind/brain, 25, 26; reading, 297; reductionist/realist model of, 39
Mind and its Discontents, The, 25
mind/body problem, 25
Minton, Arthur, 178
Miranda, Jeanne, 76
mirroring, 234
misdiagnosis, intentional, 261
misery causes mental illness, 363
Mobley, Jerry A., 4
moral/morality, 141, 172, 173, 206, 245, 333; definition of, 164; instruction in, 215; not telling the truth, 176; slave ownership, 289; supersedes religion, 289; why be, 276
motivation, 116
Multiple Personality Disorder (MPD), 38, 56, 279. *See also* Dissociative Identity Disorder (DID)
murder, as mental illness, 41, 231
Myth of Mental Illness The, 55
mythology in psychoanalysis, 45

Nantel-Vivier, Amélie, 82
National Library of Medicine, US, 373
need for approval, 173
negativism, 51–52
New Image of the Person, The, 209

Night Falls Fast: Understanding Suicide 25
Nagel, Thomas, 31
natural laws, 29
New Introductory Lectures, 35
neuroplasticity, 98
neurotransmitter imbalance, 84
Nicomachean Ethics, 194
Nietzsche, Friedrich, 142, 206; influence on Adler, 154; self-overcoming, 247; waiting for philosopher physician, 180
nightmares, 191
normalization, 354
Notebooks, 142
Nussbaum, Martha, 133, 134, 135, 139, 143, 181, 193, 211; human flourishing, 210, 371; medical philosophy, 182, 198, 294; psychotherapy as client education, 223

obedience, 288
obsession, 272
Obsessive-Compulsive Disorder (OCD), 37, 196, 359
Oden, Thomas, 236
open-textured case study, 308
Oppositional Defiant Disorder (ODD), 373–375; presumed causes of, 375
Orange, Donna M., 165
Othello syndrome, 261
Oxford Textbook of Philosophy and Psychiatry, The, 153, 175

Pavlov, Ivan, 11, 150
Pam, Alvin, 24, 31, 97
panic attacks, 84
paradigm shift, 350, 355–365; Kuhn, Thomas S., 360–361; in mental healthcare, 360
paradox of health, 291
paranoia, 296
parental alienation syndrome, 58
parenting skills, 73
parents behavior causing mental illnesses in offspring, 80
Paris, Joel, 63, 70, 75, 83, 98, 103, 342
Parnas, Josef, 38

past life regression, 131
passions. *See* emotions
Passions of the Soul, The, 194
paternalism, 47, 204, 340
Pediatric Bipolar Disorder (PBD), 40
perception of reality, 174
Perls, Frederick, 111, 157
person, 4; corporation as, 283; ecocentric/egocentric/cosmocentric/sociocentric, 350–351; understanding of, 65
persona, putting on, 320, 321–322, 335
personality disorders, 57
Person-Centered Therapy, 114–115, 124, 157–158
Persuasion and Healing, 234
Peterman, James, 142
pharmaceutical industry, 342
phenomenology, 108, 281; as self-scrutiny, 111; in Gestalt therapy 5.42
philosophers, 9, 12; as philosophic doctors, 147; authenticity, 247; doctors of psychic diseases, 136; not everyone is a, 177; philosophical attitudes, 247; list of eight, 265; competencies, 265
Philosophical Counseling, 17, 49, 186, 295, 366; as educational, 367; "beyond method method", 243; patient participation in, 367; leads to better than normal state, 366
Philosophical Counseling and the Unconscious, 50
Philosophical Counseling Theory and Practice, 263
philosophical disposition, 191–192; investigation, 188
Philosophical Investigations, 142
Philosophical Issues in Psychiatry, 38
philosophical maturity, 294
Philosophical Practice, 186
philosophical therapy/therapeutic philosophy,6.44 6.136: in antiquity, 133–140; in more recent history,4.39-4.49; requires practice, 292; takes courage, 238
philosophy, 123; and argument, 250; application of, 238; as a kind of medicine, 136; as art of life/living, 133, 136; as enhancement or enrichment, 367; as inoculation/immunization, 15, 212, 216, 219, 226; as liberating, 211; as life-saving, 279; as preventive/proactive, 213–222, 218, 356; as substitute for, 162; as substitute for medications, 162; as treatment for serious mental disorders, 181; as useless and frustratingly abstract, 147; can improve the clinical work, 165; clinical, 209–210; creation of wisdom, 205; defined, 5, 9, 126, 176–185; difficult for clinicians, 154; eclectic and multi-modal, 126; enhances effectiveness of treatment, 236; feminist, 277; for counselors course, 250, 266, 283–287, 355; function of in ancient times, 131; healing through clarification, 142; heuristic, 218–219; in antiquity, 132, 134; in psychoanalysis, 153–154; for children (P4C) 6.58 7.29; Freud's contempt for, 35; goal/aims, 135, 139, 143; method in, 243; moral, 149; more helpful than counseling and psychotherapy, 186; non-Western, 288–289; not acknowledge by therapists, 167; of human identity, 279; of human nature, 278; of human relationships, 278–279; of religion, 282; of self-development, 279; open, 177; original intent, 132–133; practical, 137; preventive, 213–222; philosophy/psychotherapy, differences, 240–249; purification of the intellect, 136; real/pure, 186, 356; respect for authority, 288; schools of, 132, 135; self-conscious self-scrutiny, 136; social and political, 283; substitute for medications, 162; taught at Royal College of Psychiatrists, London, 238; therapeutic benefits of, 161–169; therapeutic content in, 153; therapeutic role of, 132; training in, 246; William James definition, 177
philosophy café, 226

Philosophy for Children (P4C), 189, 220
Philosophy for Counseling and Psychotherapy: Pythagoras to Postmodernism, 166
Philosophy of Cognitive-Behavioral Therapy (CBT),The, 159, 166
Philosophy of Psychopharmacology, 27
Philosophy of Psychiatry, The, 154
Problems of Philosophy, The , 126
Physics, 141
Piaget, Jean, 120
Pierattini, Robert, 71
Pierce, C. S., 247
Pihl, Robert O., 82
Pinel, Philippe, 353
placebos, 75–76, 105
Plato, 6, 132, 136–137, 146; tyranny of the majority, 319; cave of ignorance, 246; meditation on death,5.34; as philosophical therapist, 132
pluralism in philosophy, 242
Porter, Douglas, 346
postmodernism, 282
postpartum depression (PPD), 1, 25
pragmatism, American: Adolf Meyer, Norman Cameron, and Harry Stack and, 153
preconscious, 47
premenstrual syndrome (PMS), 24, 25
prevention, philosophy as, 213–222, 240; avoids physical ills, 215–216; builds resilience, 215; costs of, 218; evidence for, 219–220; involves entire population, 221; less costly than treatment, 218; Precautionary Principle, 220; teaching (heuristics), 222–226; three types of, 220–221
Premenstrual Dysphoric Disorder (PMDD), 43
projection, 52–53
prophylactic philosophy. *See* philosophy, preventive
Prozan, Charlotte, 36, 66, 120, 121, 245
psuchē, 134
Pseudoscience in Biological Psychiatry , 31
psychiatric syndromes, arbitrariness of, 35

psychiatrists, 63, 213; create iatrogenic stigma, 347; superiority of, 190
Psychiatry and Philosophy of Science, 67
psychiatry/psychiatric theory, 24, 106 and the language of science 2.3; as value laden, 151; Dilthey, Wilhelm Edmund Husserl, and Martin Heidegger and, 153; largely ignore life stressors, 84; phenomenologica 153
psychoanalysis, 3, 4, 9, 106, 296; as learning theory, 161; foundation, 148; mythology disguised as reporting, 45; patient omitted from treatment, 357; philosophy in, 153–154; pseudo-medical language in, 356; recovery in Freudian, 352
Psychodynamic therapy, 105–106, 123
psychological freedom, 91
psychologists, clinical, counseling, forensic, health, neuro, sport, 107; doing philosophy, 147
psychology, B03.25: abnormal, 293; affects/emotions, 353; behaviorism 150; cause, two meanings in, 86–88 clinical, 63, 120, 124; cognitive dissonance, 194; cognitive theories in, 183; counseling, 356; definition of cause in, 86; feminists on clinical 120; focus of courses, 233; giving it away, 224; humanistic, 114; informal diagnostic terms, 44; internalization, 192; language of, 2 male and female, 277; misinformative texts, 84; naturalistic causal claims, 85; "… o Dream-Processes", 48; philosophical influences on, 149, 285; philosophical issues in, 233; pop maxims, 193; problematic, 108 research on unconscious, 244; science of, 104, 107, 146, 169, 246; self, 29
psychopharmaceuticals/psychotropic 11, 63, 70; cost-effectiveness claims 347; compared to alcohol/scotch, 7 compared to morphine, 71; little change in 30 years, 72; side effects of, 71; symptomatic improvement

from, 342; See also medications
psychosis, mistaken as permanent, 354
psychotherapists, 3, 233–237; as teachers, 223; believe cure is rare/impossible, 347; indebted to ancient philosophy, 168; lack education in philosophy, 232
psychotherapy, 12, 186; abandonment of Freudian unconscious, 160; and biopsychiatry, 63; as iatrology (healing with words), 161; as reaction to philosophy, 149; most common pitfalls, 361; critical and creative thinking in, 165; enhanced by philosophy, 236; issues, finding, 249–256; management, 350; morally neutral free space, 164; narrative in, 237, 251; necessary and sufficient ingredients, 233–237; neutrality in, 244; power structure in, 244; psychotherapy/philosophy, differences, 240–249; schools of, 186–187, 242; theory in, 237–238; training in, 246; watered-down version of philosophy, 356
Psychotherapy as a Human Science, 232
psychotic symptoms, 271
psychotropics. *See* psychopharmaceuticals.. *See also* medications
Post-Traumatic Stress Syndrome (PTSD), 181

quality-of-life score, 64
questioning, 161; some questions better than others, 233

Radden, Jennifer, 154
rape, blame for, 51
Rational Emotive Behavior, 12, 152, 159; Immanuel Kant, Baruch Spinoza, Arthur Schopenhauer, Karl Popper, and Bertrand Russell influences on, 159; See also Cognitive-Behavior Therapy
rationality, seven main features, 266; return to, 364
reality, 5, 8, 269; and dreaming, 293; assumptions, 272; definition, 271;

feminism, 277; nine kinds of, 270; perception of, 174
Reality Therapy, 115–116, 124, 158
Reason and Therapeutic Change, 164
recognition, 188
recovery and/or cure, 19, 216, 245, 290, 291, 292, 294, 337, 340; as subjective, 353; as continued defenselessness/dependence, 366; chapter on 11.0-11.125; clinical, 351; Deleuze, Gilles and 11.116; denial of possibility, 345–349; empowerment, 360; Foucault, Michel and, 367; from schizophrenia, 364; Guatteri, Félix and, 367; Lacan, Jacques and, 367; largely ignored in research, publications, practice, 349, 350; little clinical literature on, 347; new concept of, 349–354; perspective, 350; personal, 351; presuming possibility/likelihood of, 357; professor of, 341; psychiatrists ambivalent about, 345; six stages of, 352; two forms of, 352; without treatment, 352
Recovery of People With Mental Illness, 350, 351
Rediscovery of the Mind, The, 33
reeducation, 108
reification of symptom clusters, 33, 37, 39, 40, 96, 202, 242
religion, 174, 286; beliefs, 301; fears, 193. *See also* Bible; God
Renaissance scholasticism, 141
repression, 48–50
resistance, 50
respect for authority, 288; for self, 289; for tradition, 289
Rethinking Mental Health and Disorder, 149
Rhee, Young E., 241
Rikard-Bell, Christopher J., 219–220
Robertson, Donald, 138, 168, 177; connects modern psychotherapy with Ancient philosophers, 166
Rogers, Carl, 114, 157; successful therapy, 196
Ross, Colin, 24, 31, 97
Rousseau, Jean-Jacques, 246

Royal College of Psychiatrists, London, 238
Rudnick, Abraham, 340, 351
Russell, Bertrand, 126, 137, 142; philosophy not for most men, 184
Ryle, Gilbert, 27

safe place, intellectual, 190
sane for insane mistake, 67
sanity, 262
Sartorius, Norman, 347
Sartre, Jean-Paul, 200, 274; authenticity, 304, 322; critique of unconscious,3.25 6.49; mental illness as existential crises, 155
Schill, Stefan de, 33, 45, 60, 63, 66
schizoaffective disorder, 296
schizophrenia, 42, 272, 339, 345; ancient diagnosis of, 68–69; and shame, 202; argued as endogenous, 73; as identity, 204; as scientific delusion, 74; Bergson, Henri-Louis theories on, 153; childhood sexual abuse and, 73–74; cure/recovery, 345, 346; dementia praecox, 346; family dynamics, 293; genetics and, 97; life circumstances and, 78, 215; medications and, 340; no clear definition of, 82; negativism in, 52; paranoid, 201; parents and, 80; philosophical approach to, 181; poorly understood, 52; proper, 204; pseudo-patients, 67; recovery from, 364; suffering from, 83; twin studies and, 93–94; unacceptable impulses, 53; unchanged pharmacotherapy for, 72
Schmolke, Margit, 36, 76, 216, 346, 350
scholasticism, 141
schools of psychotherapy, 186–187, 242, 295
Schopenhauer, Arthur, 142; Philosophy is "fencing in front of a mirror", 184
Schrank, Beate, 353
Schuster, Shlomit, 240
science, five characteristics of rigorous, 62–63

scientific positivism 11.7: reductionism, 28
Searle, John, 33
Segal, Zindel, 76
semiotic being and meaning, 194
skepticism, 275
Selective Serotonin Re-uptake Inhibitors (SSRIs), 75
Self and Others, 153
self, aspect of, 278, 280; losing oneself, 280
self-awareness and alcohol, 358
self, conceptions of and mental illness 280
Self-defeating personality disorder (SDPD), 24
self-defense, 263
self-derogatory ideation, 214
self-esteem/confidence, 71, 297, 322, 336; undercut by mental healthcare system, 341, 342
self-help groups, 225–226
self-identity, 342
self-management, 224–225
self-transformative aim, 246
Seneca, 138, 140, 184
serotonin transporter genotype and depression, 93
session notes, problems with, 251
sexual addiction, 57; advances by therapist, 52
sex bias and sex-role stereotyping, four areas, 120
shame, 59, 201; antidote for, 200–205; as learned, 202–203; Gestalt therap approach to, 203
Shamir, Eliahu, 217, 352
Sharma, Sohan, 62, 65, 151
Shipka, Thomas, 178
Shorter, Edward, 37
side effects, 71; dismissed, 190
Siegel, Daniel J., 98
Simon, Laurence, 29, 76, 91
Singh, Ilina, 64
Skeptics, 135
Skinner, B. F., 88
Slade, Mike, 223, 341–342
Smith, Steven, 199

social and political activism, 18, 290–292
social deviance, 233
social services/financial aid, 344
society as sick, 210
Socrates, 6, 132, 136, 137, 168, 206; gadfly, 163; last days of, 155
Socratic attitude, 247; method, 113; midwifery, 161, 174, 185
solipsism, 275
soul, 132, 148; as mind, 134; illness of, 133; cure of, 134
Spence, Donald P., 307
Spinoza, Benedictus (also Baruch), 8, 141
Spitzer, Robert, 59
SSRI drugs, 348
Stein, Dan J., 27, 58, 60, 70, 97
stigma, antidote for, 200–205, 245; iatrogenic, 347; self-stigmatization, 200; stereotypes, 291
Stoics/Stoicism, 6, 118, 134, 135, 137–138, 177, 183; awakening, 246; Aurelius, Marcus, 138; Chryssippus, 137; Cicero, 138; emotions 4.47-4.48; Epictetus, 138; in Cognitive therapy, 159; in Gestalt therapy, 157; love of wisdom, 177; psychic sickness/mental illness, 138; Seneca, 138
Stone, Michael H., 80
stress, relief from, 191
Structure of Scientific Revolutions, The, 360
students, 4, 5
subjective feeling, devalued, 341, 342
substance abuse, 33; as symptom, 358
suffering, emotional, 350; as mental illness, 216, 240, 241, 350
suicide, 23, 25, 50, 80, 92, 102, 171, 188–189, 201, 272, 277; attempt in distant past, 272–273; case example, 257–258; cognitive therapy of, 214; higher order explanation, 214; morality of, 286; reasons for, 92; soap box derby car racer, 213
suppression, 53
Swarbrick, Margaret, 77
symptomatic relief, mere, 105

syndromes not diagnosed in North America, 57
Szasz, Thomas, 39

talk therapy(ies), 3, 5, 103, 127, 181; and philosophy @ 6.47 8.24 10.292 11.48; as edification, 223; cost effectiveness of, 348; effective, 353
Taylor, Charles, 322, 323
teaching, 222; as prevention, 222–226; clients, 117; reasoning skills, 258; sanity, 261
teacher's job, 46
teleology, 108
telephone counseling case, 329–337
the good, 210
therapeia, 132
Therapeia: Plato's Conception of Philosophy, 132
therapeia tēs psuchē, 134, 136
Therapeutae, 140
therapeutic alliance, 190
Therapeutic Book, The, 137
therapeutic circle, internal and external, 191
Therapeutic Dialogue, The, 151
therapeutic philosophy. *See* philosophical therapy
therapy, 4; autonomy and, 369; as partnership, 200; collaborative effort, 289; goal of, 368; just listening is not enough, 166; misconceptions about, 361–363; narrative in, 237; necessary and sufficient ingredients, 233–237; neutrality in, 244; power structure in, 244; theory in, 237–238
Therapy of Desire, 134
therapy of the soul, 6, 7
Thinking for Clinicians: Philosophical Resources for Contemporary Psychoanalysis and the Humanistic Psychotherapies, 165
Think it Through: Reasoning in Everyday Life, 268
thinking, change in, 283
Thompson, Kenneth, 360
Thornton, Tim, 153, 349, 368
"time heals all wounds", 199

Tourette syndrome, 39, 87
Tractacus, 142
transference, 46, 47–48, 158, 188
treatment, 13, 15, 66; autonomy and, 369; biopsychiatric or neuropsychiatric, 31; driven by pharmaceutical industry, 342; enhanced by philosophy, 236; forced, 340; goal of, 368; modality, 12, 76; options, 60; patient and, 357, 367; psychopharmaceutical, 31, 35, 63; recovery without, 352; request only focus, 219; talk therapy 1.41 2.22 2.133; two errors in, 217; volunteering as, 208
trust, 189–191
trusting the counselor, 264
"Truth", 8, 10, 49, 51, 179–180; paradox of pursuit of, 177; postmodernism's abandonment of, 282; truth, 149, 198, 313
Tuke, William, 353
Turkington, Douglas, 94, 353; return to normalcy, 364; cognitive errors in delusional beliefs, 153
Tusulanae Disputationes, 140
twin studies, 93–94
tyranny of the majority, 319

UFV (University of the Fraser Valley), 61
unacceptable impulses, etc, 53
unconscious, 4, 9, 187, 241; and preconscious, 47; ancients held no theory of 5.66; defended by Schopenhauer, Nietzsche, Hartman, and Herbert, 146; diagnosis of resistance relies on, 50; dreams and free association, 49; existence of long been disproved, 33; foundation of psychoanalysis, 148; projection of unknown hostility and, 52; repression and,1.90; Sartre's critique of,3.25
Use and Misuse of Psychiatric Drugs, The 103
utilitarianism, 102

values, 268, 315; in combat 10.317
Vaughan, Susan, 99
Velasquez, Manuel, 178, 284
victim, blaming the, 55, 241
Voltaire (François-Marie Arouet), 138
Vygotsky, Lev, 32

Wampold, Bruce E., 234
wants and needs, 172–176
war, 329–337; with father, 336–337; just war theory, 330–331
Watts, Richard, 154
What Would Aristotle Do?, 195, 264
Wingert, Pat, 43
wisdom, love of, 177
Wisdom, Madness, and Folly: The Making of a Psychiatrist, 156
Wittgenstein, Ludwig, 142, 180
Wolff, Paul, 178
Woodward, James F., 214
worldview, 173–174, 199, 210; in Gestalt psychology and Freudian psychoanalysis, 165

Zachar, Peter, 346
Ziskin, Jay, 66

About the Author

Peter B. Raabe received his PhD from the University of British Columbia in 1999. He is the first person in Canada to receive a doctorate for his writing and work in philosophical counseling. He teaches a variety of philosophy courses at the University of the Fraser Valley including reasoning, metaphysics and epistemology, philosophy of mind, philosophy of psychiatry, and a specialized upper-level course of philosophy specifically designed for students of counseling and psychotherapy. He facilitated a public philosophy café for eight years, and established three mental health discussion groups. He is the author of many journal articles, international conference presentations and workshops, and is on the editorial board of several international peer-reviewed journals. He is also the author of two books: *Philosophical Counseling: Theory and Practice* and *Issues in Philosophical Counseling*. He is a contributing author and editor of *Philosophical Counseling and the Unconscious*. He has a private philosophical counseling practice in North Vancouver.